"*Preparing Leaders of Nonprofit Organizations* is a welcome and worthy successor to the line of pathbreaking books, begun in 1986 with *Educating Managers of Nonprofit Organizations*, that helped define and establish the field of university education for nonprofit managers and leaders. The distinguished authors in this volume break new ground on multiple fronts including theoretical foundations, teaching methodology, contemporary nonprofit leadership challenges, and the academic context with which nonprofit studies programs contend. A must read for current and future nonprofit scholars and educators and contemporary nonprofit leaders"

Dennis R. Young, *Professor Emeritus, Georgia State University and Case Western Reserve University, USA*

"Nonprofit studies as a field of study has witnessed a 50 year growth. This edited work provides an excellent overview of the history and current approaches to preparing individuals for contributing and leading in civil society. Brown and Hale have assembled some of the best voices in our field today to guide faculty and administrators to meet contemporary challenges and opportunities in nonprofit/philanthropic education. A must read for the newcomer as well as the experienced educator."

Dwight Burlingame, *Indiana University, USA*

"As nonprofit education continues to grow around the world, faculty, staff, and administrators are increasingly leading dedicated nonprofit and philanthropy programs in higher ed. *Preparing leaders of nonprofit organizations: Contemporary perspectives* provides valuable insight into how nonprofit education is changing in response to developments like program accreditation, social trends like public service reform and political polarization, and demands to incorporate critical perspectives and applied learning. It's an important and timely contribution to the state of nonprofit education today."

Elizabeth Dale, *Seattle University, USA*

"Many books about nonprofit organizations have a management perspective and focus on the day-to-day operation of the organization. *Preparing Leaders of Nonprofit Organizations: Contemporary Perspectives* takes a different approach. It focuses on taking nonprofit educational programs and hence nonprofit leaders beyond where they currently operate. It presents discussions on topics such as the challenges of international differences, moving beyond two rounds of NACC accreditation, and how to prepare the next generation of nonprofit community leaders. This book will make the serious nonprofit educator or leader reflect critically on what they do."

Norman A. Dolch, *Editor-in-Chief, Journal of Nonprofit Education and Leadership*

"This seminal book excellently positions itself as a critical overview and practical guidebook on nonprofit management and nonprofit education. Remarkably embracing comparative, global, and interdisciplinary lenses! I strongly recommend this book for instructors' graduate-level course teaching as well as scholars' bricks for theoretical overview. The mosaic pieces of thorough historical reviews and current trend analyses of this book leave the most crucial task to envision and design the future of the field to readers. This book is a must-read for anyone willing to assume this critical role as a transformative leader amid this field's professional management and social movement impulses."

Bok Gyo Jeong, *Kean University, USA*

"The field of philanthropic and nonprofit studies has evolved over the last few decades to establish a foothold in the academic world informing research agendas and contributing to an array of academic programs. This volume documents that progress and lays the foundation for further development as the field becomes contested, blurred, and transformed reflecting the dynamics across the sectors. For those who are new to the field, it provides an important context and perspective. And, for those who have been part of the journey, it provides an opportunity to reflect on accomplishments and chart new directions."

Jim Ferris, *University of Southern California, USA*

PREPARING LEADERS OF NONPROFIT ORGANIZATIONS

There are more than 1.8 million nonprofits in the United States and at least 3 times that many internationally. Workers in these nonprofits and civil society organizations increasingly look to academic programs to provide leadership and management training. This edited volume is designed to provide new and experienced faculty and program administrators with a broader conception of how the nonprofit leaders of the future are and could be educated. The chapters are written by experienced nonprofit program leaders who provide guidance on all aspects of building and more importantly maintaining a successful nonprofit program. Many of the chapters are written by former leaders of the Nonprofit Academic Centers Council (NACC), a recognized international leader in nonprofit management curricular development, while others are written by successful founders and administrators of nonprofit programs both in the US and internationally. All chapters are however grounded in the experience of the authors, supplemented with research on best practices and focusing on future trends in the field.

Preparing Leaders of Nonprofit Organizations examines key issues and challenges in the field from multiple perspectives, some of which are curricular and intellectual while others are related to program administration and oversight. The text explores core concepts, distils distinctive features of new or emerging academic programs, and identifies ways program leadership might ensure those features are reflected in their programs regardless of where these are housed within a university. The book is an essential resource for faculty and administrators who work with or are seeking to develop a nonprofit education program. It is also a useful guide for graduate students seeking a career in the nonprofit academy.

William A. Brown is Professor in the Bush School of Government and Public Service at Texas A&M University and holds the Mary Julia and George Jordan Professorship. He also serves as the Director of the Center for Nonprofits & Philanthropy. His research focuses on nonprofit governance, strategy, and organizational effectiveness. He teaches Nonprofit Management, Social Innovation and Entrepreneurship, Human Resource Management and Capstone courses. His books include an edited volume *Nonprofit Governance: Innovative Perspectives and Approaches* (Routledge 2013) with Chris Cornforth and a textbook entitled *Strategic Management in Nonprofit Organizations*, published in March 2014.

Matthew L. Hale is Associate Professor in the Department of Political Science and Public Affairs at Seton Hall University. His research focuses on the intersection of media and technology and the public and nonprofit sectors. His articles have appeared in *Journal of Nonprofit Education and Leadership, The International Journal of Press Politics, Nonprofit and Voluntary Sector Quarterly, Mass Communication Society and the Stanford Law Policy Review.* Hale recently served as president of the Nonprofit Academic Centers Council (NACC). In that capacity, he successfully led an effort to develop an international accreditation process for programs in Nonprofit Management. Hale is an elected official in his hometown of Highland Park, New Jersey and frequent media commentator on New Jersey politics and has appeared on *NPR, CNN, Fox News, CNBC, the New York Times and Washington Post.*

ROUTLEDGE PUBLIC AFFAIRS EDUCATION

EDITORS
BRUCE D. MCDONALD III
Associate Professor of Public Budgeting and Finance
North Carolina State University, Raleigh NC

WILLIAM HATCHER
Associate Professor of Public Administration
Augusta University, Augusta GA

The Routledge Public Affairs Education series, edited by William Hatcher and Bruce D. McDonald III, publishes books designed to assist faculty in the classroom and in the management of public administration, public affairs, and public policy programs. To accomplish this, the book series explores evidence-based practices, commentary about the state of public administration education, and pedagogical perspectives. The Routledge Public Affairs Education series examines the future of public administration education, teaching practices, international public administration education, undergraduate public administration programming, and other relevant topics to advance the field's knowledge. For more information about the series, or to submit a book proposal, please contact series editors William Hatcher at wihatcher@augusta.edu and Bruce D. McDonald, III at bmcdona@ncsu.edu.

Recently Published Books

Preparing Leaders of Nonprofit Organizations: Contemporary Perspectives
William Brown and Matthew Hale

The Public Affairs Faculty Manual
Bruce D. McDonald III and William Hatcher

Undergraduate Public Affairs Education
Madinah F. Hamidullah

Teaching Public Budgeting and Finance
Meagan M. Jordan and Bruce D. McDonald III

PREPARING LEADERS OF NONPROFIT ORGANIZATIONS

Contemporary Perspectives

Edited by William A. Brown and Matthew Hale

Routledge
Taylor & Francis Group
NEW YORK AND LONDON

Cover image: Getty Images

First published 2023
by Routledge
605 Third Avenue, New York, NY 10158

and by Routledge
4 Park Square, Milton Park, Abingdon, Oxon, OX14 4RN

Routledge is an imprint of the Taylor & Francis Group, an informa business

Library of Congress Cataloging-in-Publication Data
Names: Brown, William A., 1964- editor. | Hale, Matthew L., editor.
Title: Preparing leaders of nonprofit organizations : contemporary perspectives / edited by William A. Brown and Matthew Hale.
Identifiers: LCCN 2021059628 (print) | LCCN 2021059629 (ebook) | ISBN 9781032277813 (hardback) | ISBN 9781032277806 (paperback) | ISBN 9781003294061 (ebook)
Subjects: LCSH: Nonprofit organizations–Management. | Leadership.
Classification: LCC HD62.6 .P74 2022 (print) | LCC HD62.6 (ebook) | DDC 658/.048–dc23/eng/20220314
LC record available at https://lccn.loc.gov/2021059628
LC ebook record available at https://lccn.loc.gov/2021059629

ISBN: 978-1-03-227781-3 (hbk)
ISBN: 978-1-03-227780-6 (pbk)
ISBN: 978-1-00-329406-1 (ebk)

DOI: 10.4324/9781003294061

Typeset in Bembo
by Newgen Publishing UK

CONTENTS

CONTRIBUTORS

Robert F. Ashcraft is Executive Director of Arizona State University's Lodestar Center for Philanthropy and Nonprofit Innovation and Saguaro Professor of Civic Enterprise in the Watts College of Public Service & Community Solutions, School of Community Resources & Development. He led efforts at ASU resulting in the nation's first B.S. Degree in the field and one of the few named master's degrees in Nonprofit Leadership and Management. His research interests have resulted in numerous publications on topics such as nonprofit education models, collaboration strategies and volunteer management. Under his leadership, ASU's Lodestar Center is considered a leading nonprofit academic center, renowned for its research, education, leadership programs, technical assistance and conference activities. As a past member of the Nonprofit Times "Power and Influence Top 50" list, he is recognized for helping to shape education in the field through transdisciplinary approaches to achieve enduring results.

Katherine Badertscher is Director of Graduate Programs at the IU Lilly Family School of Philanthropy. She teaches a variety of BA, MA, and doctoral courses and The Fund Raising School's Ethical Fundraising course. Dr. Badertscher has published articles in *Pharmacy in History* and *Indiana Magazine of History*. She is the Nonprofits and Philanthropy Consulting Editor for *The Digital Encyclopedia of Indianapolis.* Dr. Badertscher received the IUPUI Office for Women, Women's Leadership Award (2019), the Lilly Family School of Philanthropy Graduate Teaching Award (2019 and 2020) and the Indiana University Trustees' Teaching Award (2021).

Heather Carpenter is Associate Professor and Director of the 100% online nationally accredited M.S. in Nonprofit Administration program at Louisiana State

University Shreveport. She has published articles and books on talent management, nonprofit technology, service-learning, nonprofit management education, and nonprofit leadership. Her most recent book projects include co-editor of the Sagamore Nonprofit book series, co-editor of Teaching Nonprofit Management, and co-author of Nonprofit Crisis Management: Response to COVID-19. She also serves as Associate Editor of Case Studies for the Journal of Nonprofit Education and Leadership and Board Treasurer of the Nonprofit Academic Centers Council.

John Casey is a Professor in the Marxe School of Public and International Affairs at Baruch College, City University of New York. From 1999 to 2007, he was a Senior Lecturer in management, leadership and governance at the Australian Graduate School of Policing, Charles Sturt University. Prior to his academic career, he held executive positions in public and nonprofit organizations in Australia, Spain and the USA. He is the author of numerous articles and books on the nonprofit sector, immigration and policing. He is the author of *The Nonprofit World: Civil Society and the Rise of the Nonprofit Sector*, published in 2016. For more information and access to his publications see: http://baruch.cuny.edu/mspia/faculty-and-staff/full-time-faculty/john-casey.html

Nathan Dietz is a senior researcher with the Do Good Institute (DGI) in the School of Public Policy at the University of Maryland College Park. His research focuses on social capital, volunteering and giving to charity, civic engagement and social entrepreneurship; he also teaches a graduate course on nonprofit and public-sector financial management. He is the coauthor of several Do Good Institute publications, including a recent report on trends in civic health in the state of Maryland. His recent publications include articles in peer-reviewed journals including *Nonprofit and Voluntary Sector Quarterly*, *American Journal of Community Psychology* and *Nonprofit Policy Forum*; he is also the principal investigator for a new project funded by the Generosity Commission on trends in civic engagement.

Maureen Emerson Feit is Director and Assistant Professor of Nonprofit Leadership at Seattle University. Her primary research focuses on the role of community organizations in racial formation, citizenship and representative democracy. In her most recent project, she and her colleagues completed a critical qualitative study of staff as they interpreted shifting policy and navigated the complexities of race, trust and representation in the United States census count. She has also published on the application of critical race theory in nonprofit management education. She serves on the leadership of the Critical Perspectives Interest Group and the Undergraduate Diversity Scholars Committee with ARNOVA and is a former board member of the Nonprofit Academic Centers Council. She received her MA and PhD in Cultural Anthropology from the University of Michigan.

Robert L. Fischer is an associate professor at the Jack, Joseph and Morton Mandel School of Applied Social Sciences of Case Western Reserve University. Dr. Fischer is faculty chair of the Master of Nonprofit Organizations (MNO) degree program and teaches courses in evaluation methods, data use and program design. He also serves as Co-Director of the Center on Urban Poverty and Community Development at the Mandel School where he leads a range of evaluation and community-engaged research studies. His research focuses on the evaluation of social/behavioral interventions in regard to delivery and effectiveness and non-profit program research and outcome measurement. His research has appeared in Nonprofit Management & Leadership, Children & Youth Services Review, Evaluation and Program Planning, and Public Administration Review.

Charlee Garden is the Chief Culture and Innovation Officer for Haven Technologies, a purpose-driven SaaS insurtech company. Prior to joining Haven Tech, Charlee worked in leadership development at The University of Texas at Austin where she launched the CoachUT program and served as a clinical professor for the LBJ School of Public Affairs. After starting as an electrical engineer at Bell Labs, Charlee found her calling in enabling technically minded folks to be effective leaders.

Katlin Gray is a program manager for the Do Good Institute at the University of Maryland and an adjunct faculty member in the School of Public Policy. As program manager, she oversees the strategic development of the Do Good Campus, a campus-wide initiative that seeks to provide education, opportunities and resources to develop the next generation of nonprofit leaders, social innovators and civic-minded students. Using hands-on and experiential learning approaches, Katlin develops and delivers curriculum focused on social impact and civic engagement. She also provides support and consultation to living-learning programs, academic programs and faculty seeking to bolster or incorporate these concepts into their courses and programs. Her research interests are focused on the intersections between pedagogy, social impact and civic education, and project-based and experiential learning. Katlin has worked in the higher education sector for more than eight years and has taught courses in social innovation, student leadership and public speaking.

Robert T. Grimm Jr. is the Levenson Family Chair in Philanthropy & Nonprofit Leadership and the founding director of the Do Good Institute in the School of Public Policy at the University of Maryland. The Network of Schools of Public Policy, Public Affairs and Public Administration (NASPAA) recognized the Institute's campus-wide educational initiatives (the Do Good Campus) with its inaugural Voinovich Public Innovation Prize. Started with two courses and a Do Good Challenge prize competition, thousands of students (from the sciences to the humanities) enroll annually in programs today that prepare them as nonprofit leaders, social innovators and civic-minded individuals. His research publications include recent reports on the decline of American charitable behaviors, a book on American philanthropists and articles in *Nonprofit & Voluntary Sector Quarterly*, the *Journal of Policy Analysis & Management* and *Stanford Social Innovation Review*. He previously served as senior counselor to the CEO and the director of research & policy development at AmeriCorps.

Monika Hudson is an associate professor at the University of San Francisco and teaches entrepreneurship, family business, organizational behavior and public administration on both the graduate and undergraduate levels. She directs USF's Gellert Family Business Center, which promotes and supports family firms in the Bay Area. She is also the Area Coordinator for USF's undergraduate international business program. Dr. Hudson's research interests include entrepreneurship, identity and behavior and the strategic implementation of the same within the private, public and nonprofit sectors. Dr. Hudson received her undergraduate degrees from Northwestern University, Illinois; her Master of Business Administration from the University of San Francisco; her doctor of business administration from Case Western Reserve University, Ohio; and her doctor of education from University of San Francisco. A 2017–2018 Fulbright Scholar, she is currently conducting entrepreneurship research in Cali, Colombia; Montevideo, Uruguay and Jinan, China.

Renée Irvin serves as Associate Head of the School of Planning, Public Policy & Management and directs the Nonprofit Management program at the University of Oregon. Her doctorate is in Economics from the University of Washington (Seattle). Her current research focuses on family foundations; policies affecting asset-building and wealth; nonprofit financial stabilization and dark money advocacy organizations. Recent publications include an article examining optimal nonprofit reserves (forthcoming, Nonprofit & Voluntary Sector Quarterly) and an article in Nonprofit & Voluntary Sector Quarterly on how family foundations shift their missions over generations of trusteeship. Irvin is a University of Oregon Faculty Excellence Award winner, a Public Administration Review 75th Anniversary Most Influential Article award winner, and was a Fulbright Scholar in Guangzhou, China. She is the immediate past president of the Nonprofit Academic Centers Council.

Jaclyn Le is the Director of Corporate Engagement for the Texas Higher Education Coordinating Board. She develops and executes strategy for engaging corporate and other partners in strategic initiatives that strengthens Texas' talent pipeline. Earlier in her career, Jaclyn designed large-scale philanthropic initiatives and improved policy alignment across the K-12, postsecondary and workforce systems. Jaclyn holds a bachelor's degree with distinction in political science from Stanford University and received a master's degree in public affairs from the LBJ

School of Public Affairs and an MBA from the McCombs School of Business at The University of Texas at Austin.

Duncan Mayer is a PhD candidate in social welfare at the Jack, Joseph and Morton Mandel School of Applied Social Sciences, Case Western Reserve University. His research interests span nonprofit management including finance and data use, and community-organization dynamics, investigating issues of equity, stability and the benefits of nonprofit organizations.

Stuart C. Mendel is author of over 100 funded research reports, scholarly articles, book chapters and conference readers, including most recently Partnerships the Nonprofit Way: What Matters, What Doesn't with Jeffrey L. Brudney. Dr. Mendel specialty areas are academic and practical involving community organizations, fund raising, public private and nonprofit-first partnerships. Dr. Mendel regularly advises community leaders, nonprofit executives and board members and has served on numerous boards and committees. A leader and skilled operations professional, is actively engaged in social enterprise and innovation by developing projects, raising funds and creating the conditions for successful nonprofit organizations.

Roseanne Mirabella is a Professor in the Department of Political Science and Public Affairs, Director of the MPA program and Executive Director of the Center for Community Research and Engagement at Seton Hall University. She conducts research on philanthropy and nonprofit management education, international education for managers of NGOs, and critical perspectives on nonprofit organization management. Mirabella recently co-edited "Reframing Nonprofit Organizations: Democracy, Inclusion and Social Change," which provides students of nonprofit organizations with perspectives not typically included in the curriculum and is working on a co-edited volume, "The Handbook of Critical Perspectives on Nonprofit Organizing and Voluntary Action." Her research has been published in Public Administration Review, Administrative Theory and Praxis, Nonprofit and Voluntary Sector Quarterly, PS: Political Science & Politics, and Nonprofit Policy Forum.

Khánh Nguyễn is a nonprofit practitioner with over 15 years of program development, management and evaluation experience. His research interests include race, critical perspectives and praxis, immigration, anti-racist curriculum and critical nonprofit management education. His research has appeared in the Journal of Nonprofit Education and Leadership and Administrative Theory & Praxis.

Robert M. Pallitto is a political science professor at Seton Hall University and a former public interest lawyer. He received his B.A. *cum laude* from Rutgers University, his law degree from the University of Michigan Law School, and his Ph.D. from the New School for Social Research. As a lawyer, he was lead counsel or co-counsel in several precedent-setting New Jersey cases involving public entitlements and housing rights. Pallitto researches and writes on civil liberties, executive power, constitutional law, critical theory and contemporary political thought. His latest book, *Bargaining with the Machine*, was published in August of 2020 by the University Press of Kansas. His previous publications include 3 books: *In the Shadow of the Great Charter* (Kansas 2015), *Presidential Secrecy and the Law* (2007 – co-authored with William Weaver) and *Torture and State Violence in the US* (2011). He has also authored and co-authored numerous articles for the scholarly and popular presses.

Paul Palmer is a professor and management educationalist with extensive knowledge and experience in charity, philanthropy and financial planning. He is a Principal Fellow of the Higher Education Academy, trained as a Chartered Company Secretary and completed his doctorate in Internal Auditing. Within Bayes Business School (formerly Cass), he is the Director of the Centre for Charity Effectiveness and an Associate Dean. His work encompasses both Private and Voluntary Sectors. Paul is the Principal Investigator of an action research project funded by the Portal Trust, where since 2015 undergraduates of Bayes study a course in coaching and mentoring. A number then go on to near peer mentor in local schools on STEM subjects. He acts as an independent consultant on Charities and Philanthropy to UBS Wealth Management, and is a NED for Jarrovian Wealth. Internationally, he is a Vice President of the Nonprofit Academic Centres Council. He was appointed a Deputy Lieutenant for Greater London in 2018 and serves on the Heritage Committee.

Pier C. Rogers is Director of the Axelson Center for Nonprofit Management at North Park University, where she also teaches graduate and undergraduate courses in nonprofit management in the School of Business and Nonprofit Management. She considers herself a "pracademic" and has pursued research interests in philanthropy in communities of color, and in managing faith-based organizations. Dr. Rogers currently serves as President of ARNOVA (Association for Research on Nonprofit Organizations and Voluntary Action), where in 2009 she co-founded the "Diversity Scholars and Leaders Professional Development Workshop," which serves doctoral students of color from all over the world whose studies focus on the nonprofit sector.

Patrick M. Rooney is the Glenn Family Chair in Philanthropy, and a Professor of Economics and Philanthropic Studies, as well as the Executive Associate Dean for Academic Programs at the IU Lilly Family School of Philanthropy. Previously, while he served as the Executive Director of the Center on Philanthropy, he worked closely with the Center's Faculty, Board of Visitors, and the IU administration for the Center to become the IU Lilly Family School of Philanthropy – the world's first school of philanthropy. Before that, Rooney also served as the

Center's first full-time Director of Research, building the Center into one of the nation's premier philanthropy research organizations, leading research projects for organizations such as Giving USA, Bank of America, American Express, Gates Foundation, Google, and the United Way Worldwide. He has served on the boards and advisory committees of many nonprofits. A nationally recognized expert on philanthropy and charitable giving, Dr. Rooney has published many academic and practitioner-focused papers. He speaks frequently across the country on issues related to philanthropy and nonprofit management and has been quoted by national news media outlets such as PBS's *Nightly Business Report*, *The New York Times*, *The Wall Street Journal*, *The Washington Post*, *The Chronicle of Philanthropy* and *USA Today*. He earned his BA, MA and PhD in Economics at Notre Dame.

Steven Rathgeb Smith is the executive director of the American Political Science Association and adjunct professor at the McCourt School of Public Policy at Georgetown University. Previously, he taught at several universities including the University of Washington where he was the Nancy Bell Evans Professor at the Evans School of Public Policy and Governance and director of the Nancy Bell Evans Center for Nonprofits & Philanthropy. He is a past president of the Association for Research on Nonprofit Organizations and Voluntary Action and formerly editor of the association's journal, *Nonprofit and Voluntary Sector Quarterly*. He is also a past president of the International Society for Third Sector Research (ISTR). He is the author of several books including most recently, *The Changing Dynamic of Government–Nonprofit Relationships: Advancing the Field(s)*, co-author Kirsten A. Gronbjerg (2021).

David W. Springer is the Director of the RGK Center for Philanthropy and Community Service and a University Distinguished Teaching Professor at The University of Texas at Austin, LBJ School of Public Affairs. Bridging direct practice and public policy, his research and teaching coalesce around effective leadership, nonprofits and systems to strengthen communities. He leads the RGK Center team in preparing the next generation of nonprofit and philanthropic leaders, where he teaches graduate courses on nonprofit and community leadership.

Peter C. Weber is an assistant professor in philanthropy and nonprofit studies at Auburn University. His research interests include the institutionalization of nonprofit education, civil society in contemporary and historical perspective, and philanthropic innovations through the lenses of program-related investments (PRIs). As a multidisciplinary scholar, he has published extensively in edited volumes and peer reviewed journals, including diverse disciplinary outlets such as *Voluntas*, *Nonprofit and Voluntary Sector Quarterly*, *Journal of Civil Society*, *Global Society*, *Central European History*, *Journal of Public Affairs Education* and *Journal of Nonprofit Education and Leadership*.

Michelle Wooddell is associate professor and director of the Masters of Philanthropy and Nonprofit Leadership program at Grand Valley State University. Her research interests include the intersection of the government and nonprofit sectors, nonprofit fundraising and nonprofit management education. She is also the founder of The Nonprofit Spot, an organization which is dedicated to supporting the nonprofit sector and the individuals who serve it.

INTRODUCTION

Matthew Hale and William A. Brown

This book draws on a long history in the field of nonprofit studies, as noted in Chapter 1 (Peter C. Weber) and Chapter 15 (Robert F. Ashcraft) to consider how to educate managers and leaders in nonprofit organizations. In particular, we took inspiration from seminal work by Michael O'Neill and Dennis Young (1988) entitled *Educating Mangers of Nonprofit Organizations* and the updated version *Nonprofit Management Education*, edited by Michael O'Neill and Kathleen Fletcher (1998). These initial publications contributed to the formation of the Nonprofit Academic Centers Council (NACC) curricular guidelines (2001) that have been used by educators to structure and guide program development. This edited volume compiles material from program leaders to distill some key perspectives in preparing leaders for the nonprofit and philanthropic sector. For many of us stepping into the role as a program director and manager is a daunting task. The experience was akin to our parents deciding to go away for the weekend and all of sudden we had keys to the house. It was kind of exciting, a little scary and we really had no idea what we were doing or what we were supposed to do. This seems to be a common experience for people leading nonprofit programs, and for new faculty members who join departments where "nonprofit people" are often a small minority. We are often just thrown in the pool and asked to swim with the sharks.

And yet as a field we survive and even thrive. Nonprofit management is now the largest concentration within schools of public administration, it is fast growing as a subfield within business schools and returning to schools of social work. The growth of stand-alone nonprofit/philanthropy programs and even entire schools coupled with the development of accreditation programs for those programs and schools shows that somehow, despite being thrown in the deep end, our field is making it work. We are swimming with the sharks and doing quite well. Thank you very much.

The primary goal of this book is to make the process of leading and teaching the next generation of nonprofit and philanthropy leaders a little bit easier. The

DOI: 10.4324/9781003294061-1

book is loosely divided into three parts. Like everything in the nonprofit world "divided" might be a bit strong. There is a fair amount of blurring between some of the sections and within many of the papers. But as a general rule the book is divided into three parts: They are (1) emerging trends in nonprofits and society, (2) emerging trends in nonprofit curriculum, and (3) emerging trends in nonprofits studies and academia.

The first five chapters (Weber; Brown; Hale; Rooney and Badertscher; and Smith) all seek to situate nonprofit and philanthropy education within emerging trends not only at our own institutions but also within larger societal trends. These chapters help leaders in nonprofit education gain a sense of where their programs fit in the broader landscape and how their programs may need to adapt to the changing landscape of nonprofits as a field, nonprofits with the university, and nonprofits within larger society.

In Chapters 6–13, the focus turns toward curriculum and how we teach the about nonprofits and philanthropy. We believe that these chapters will be most useful to faculty members who teach or who are being asked to teach for the first-time specific topics in the nonprofit/philanthropy field. Some of these chapters stick to the specifics of topics of management (Fischer and Mayer), finance (Palmer), law (Pallitto), and leadership (Mendel). Others move beyond a specific course to discuss ways of implementing perspectives on critical theory (Mirabella, Nguyễn, and Feit), community leadership development (Le, Springer, and Garden), and applied approaches (Rogers and Hudson) through the entire curriculum. As such this section, will also be useful to leaders new and old of nonprofit/philanthropy programs.

The final five chapters (Wooddell; Ashcraft; Dietz, Gray, and Grimm; Carpenter; and Irvin) return to the administrator side of the equation by focusing on ways to help programs survive and thrive in the shark infested pool that is higher education today.

Taken together this book gives those just getting the house keys to their nonprofit/philanthropy home several places and several ways to start figuring out what to do next. We hope that the emerging trends identified through this book will spark debates and conversations on how we help make the next generation of nonprofit/philanthropy leaders even better. We want to thank all of the contributors to this book as well as series editors William Hatcher (Augusta University) and Bruce McDonald (North Carolina State University) for prompting this collection of materials about the field.

References

O'Neill, M., & Fletcher, K. (Eds.). (1998) *Nonprofit management education: US and world perspectives*. Westport CT: Praeger Publisher.

O'Neill, M., & Young, D. R. (Eds.). (1988). *Educating managers of nonprofit organizations*. New York, NY: Praeger Publisher.

1

INSTITUTIONALIZATION INTERRUPTED

The Evolution of the Field of Nonprofit Studies

Peter C. Weber

Introduction

Since the early 1980s, the field of nonprofit studies has grown rapidly. It evolved from individual scholars and a few pioneering academic research centers to a growing network of academic departments, centers, and programs devoted to philanthropy, nonprofit sector, and civil society. A cohesive knowledge base developed around a range of theoretical frameworks and thematic areas, which Ma and Konrath (2018) recently quantitatively reviewed. Likewise, graduate and undergraduate academic programs are offered at institutions of higher learning of different size, location, and programmatic orientation (Mirabella, Hoffman, Teo, & McDonald, 2019; Weber & Brunt, 2020). In this context, academic centers continue to serve as connectors between academic degree programs and nonprofit professionals (Prentice & Brudney, 2018).

The field emerged in part as a response to the demands of practice. Policy challenges as well as increasing need for professionalization originated in the 1969 Tax Reform Act and were accelerated by the Reagan Administration's policies (Abramson & McCarthy, 2012; O'Neill, 2005). External funders explicitly supported nonprofit management education within the broader framework of initiatives building the capacity of the US nonprofit sector (Heidrich & Long, n.d.; Poscio, 2003). Demand for professionalization of nonprofit management and access to external funding created the context for academic entrepreneurs to develop the academic centers that are credited with starting the field (Larson & Barnes, 2001).

The development of nonprofit studies aligns with the more general process underlying the growth of scientific/intellectual movements (SIMs), as discussed in Frickel and Gross (2005) and Hambrick and Chen (2008). SIMs are "collective

DOI: 10.4324/9781003294061-2

efforts to pursue research programs or projects for thought in the face of resistance from others in the scientific or intellectual community" (Frickel & Gross, 2005, p. 206) and the interplay of differentiation, mobilization, and legitimacy building typically characterizes their development (Hambrick & Chen, 2008). Drawing on these models, this chapter argues that nonprofit studies as an area of scholarly inquiry morphed from a broad, polycentric interest in philanthropy, voluntary action, and associational life to a narrower focus on the nonprofit sector. Studies in adjacent disciplines continue but are not fully integrated in the official "field." The chapter describes the field's evolution and identifies forces that both supported and hindered this institutionalization process.

The chapter is organized as follows. The next section lays out the conceptual framework guiding the analysis. It defines emerging academic fields, setting an ideal trajectory that serves to analyze the development of nonprofit studies. The following section contextualizes the emergence of a loose network of scholars interested in philanthropy and nonprofit sector and the emergence of increasingly interconnected support structures as part of the nonprofit sector's reaction to policy challenges. The chapter then identifies key forces contributing to the field's establishment in the academy. The analysis of these forces, however, also highlights major challenges facing the field, which may prevent its full institutionalization as an independent academic discipline. As a result, the case of nonprofit studies may be one of an institutionalization interrupted, as nonprofit studies gained academic credibility as a legitimate field of scientific inquiry in various established disciplines without fully establishing its own autonomy as an academic discipline.

The Institutionalization of Academic Disciplines

Academic fields are difficult to define, not least because of differences between disciplines. Biglan (1973) argues that paradigm clarity, degree of application, and concern with life systems influence boundaries with adjacent fields of knowledge, indicating the challenge of establishing clear boundaries for fields with an amorphous subject of inquiry. The emergence of new academic fields involves a combination of cognitive and structural drivers in an ideal transition from paradigm development and talent cultivation to academic institutionalization (Clark, 1973). The institutionalization of a discipline ensures its reproduction and survival (Krishnan, 2009, pp. 9–10), as it creates the spaces within which faculty members socialize and perform their teaching, research, and service responsibilities.

The institutionalization question is a crucial one for an emerging discipline, as it speaks to its long-term sustainability within the ever-shifting context of higher education and its scientific autonomy. At the core, SIMs advance a coherent scientific program, share intellectual practices, and are intrinsically political because of their inherent contentiousness (Frickel & Gross, 2005, pp. 206–207). New fields need to differentiate themselves from existing fields while avoiding being perceived as a threat, mobilize resources by taking advantage of political opportunities, shared interests, and social infrastructures, and legitimize themselves in the eyes of members, allies, and resource providers (Hambrick & Chen, 2008, pp. 35–38). This interplay of differentiation, mobilization, and legitimacy drives the institutionalization process.

Drawing on Frickel and Gross (2005) and Hambrick and Chen (2008), four broad "theoretical propositions" for the development of SIMs are particularly relevant in the development of nonprofit studies. These four propositions characterize the differentiation, mobilization, and legitimacy of nonprofit studies, highlighting the emergence of six forces driving the field's institutionalization (drivers).

1. SIMs emerge when they can claim **external relevance** with a focus that is both socially important and corrects practices in existing scientific fields or areas of practice. The *context* section shows how nonprofit studies reacted to the need for a professionalized nonprofit sector in the context of government devolution of social programming responsibilities.
2. SIMs are successful when **structural conditions** not only provide access to key resources but also sustain the field's reproduction. *External funders* (third driver) and the first *nonprofit academic centers* (second driver) provided the emerging field with opportunities for employment, intellectual prestige, and organizational resources in the 1980s and 1990s.
3. The emergence of SIMs depends on access to **micro-mobilization contexts**. Against the background of a growing *internationalization* (sixth driver), *scholarly associations and conferences* (first driver), as well as *academic programs* (fifth driver) provide opportunities for socializing, creating shared interests and values, and developing alternative forums to those of related disciplines such as public administration, business, and social work.
4. The legitimization of SIMs depends on their ability to develop a clear **intellectual identity**, which underlies "a collective identity, its historical origins, and its relationship to various competitor movements" (Frickel & Gross, 2005, p. 222). The development of a *knowledge base and research paradigms, the growth in number and prestige of academic journals and publication venues* (fourth driver), and the emergence of accreditation programs testify to efforts to legitimize the new field within, and in relation to more established academic disciplines.

This evolutionary perspective distinguishes between full institutionalization and academic credibility. Scholarly communities may aspire to fully institutionalize into separate fields of knowledge with their own identity and disciplinary boundaries, thus independent of adjacent academic fields. Conversely, **academic credibility** views the recognition of a set of ideas and body of work as a legitimate subject of scientific inquiry as the outcome of this evolutionary process, fully integrating into traditional disciplines (Larson & Long, 2000). The tension between full institutionalization and an arguable more limited focus on academic credibility underlies the evolution of nonprofit studies, raising normative questions around the ideal outcome of this evolutionary process.

The following section contextualizes the emergence of nonprofit studies. It highlights the slow progression from a loosely connected network of individual scholars to a field with an established presence in academia. It shows how the field emerged in reactions to policy changes and practical needs and integrates macro trends with human agency by recognizing the role of academic entrepreneurs in founding scholarly associations, academic centers and programs, and journals. The remaining of the chapter discusses six key drivers of the field of nonprofit studies.

Context

Two commentaries published in the *Nonprofit and Voluntary Sector Quarterly* (*NVSQ*) in 1999 exemplify conflicting conceptualizations of the field. In open debate, Stanley Katz and Peter Dobkin Hall present two contrasting views on the origins of the "serious study" of philanthropy. Hall (1999) identifies the field's multipolarity, pointing to various research foci dating back to the early 20th century and contributing to the vibrancy of the study of philanthropy, voluntary action, and associational life. While a source of innovation, this porosity complicates the establishment of clear disciplinary boundaries. By contrast, Katz (1999) anchors the field's origins to the structural conditions of the 1960s and 1970s. The "invention of the nonprofit sector" provides the context for a more linear history, substantiating claims for disciplinary autonomy. As a coherent sector with clear sectorial boundaries, the nonprofit sector provides scholars with a clearly delimitated subject of inquiry and, by emphasizing the nonprofit sector's distinctiveness, legitimizes a distinct "nonprofit" management next to the established academic areas of management of public and private entities.

The study of philanthropy and nonprofit organizations originates in the broad interest, shared across multiple scholarly communities for forms of social and human action that would later be captured by concepts such as philanthropy, charity, and nonprofit organizations. Before the 1960s, research in the field lacked the unifying power of a research paradigm, which could connect a dispersed set of scholarly inquiries (Ma & Konrath, 2018). In this period, dissertations across a variety of disciplines focused on philanthropy and charity, which also captured the attention of policy scholars (Hall, 1999). This early scholarly interest in philanthropy also emerges from the 1956 Princeton Conference on the History of Philanthropy sponsored by the Russell Sage Foundation and organized by historian Merle Curti, which led to the publication of some seminal monographs between 1956 and 1970 (Hall, 1999).

The broadness of the field is also reflected in educational efforts preparing students for future careers in human service and youth development organizations. In the early 20th century, the Young Men's Christian Association (YMCA) developed training programs at the Springfield College and the Chicago College, granting bachelor degrees in humanics and associational studies for students entering careers in human service organizations (Lee, 2010). These proto-nonprofit management degrees influenced the founding of American Humanics in 1948 (Ashcraft, 2001). The American Humanics integrated management education in a broader liberal arts framework emphasizing service to the humanity (Ashcraft, 2001). The concept of "Humanics," broadly indicating a cultivation of the full spirit of a person, connected the YMCA trainings and the American Humanics, signaling a broader framing of management training in the decades before the origins of formalized nonprofit management education in the 1980s.

Rooting the field in the economic, political, and cultural context of the 1970s and 1980s links nonprofit studies to intentional efforts to define the nonprofit sector in reaction to the policy challenges that resulted in the 1969 Tax Reform Act. This approach supports an institutionalization perspective because the Filer Commission on Private Philanthropy and Public Needs (1973–1975) created an abstract, coherent sector that helped establishing clearer boundaries around the subject of the scholarly inquiry. From this perspective, the field of study is inextricably linked to the transformations of the newly invented nonprofit sector (Weber & Witkowski, 2016), supported by parallel developments in higher education favoring professional and management education (O'Neill, 2005).

The "invention of the nonprofit sector" resulted from growing concerns over organized philanthropy's role in American society. Political and ideological attacks from across the political spectrum as well as scrutiny from the Treasury Department for alleged fiscal and fiduciary abuses resulted in the 1969 Tax Reform Act (Simon, 1995). While imposing some regulations, the 1969 Act primarily exposed organized philanthropy's vulnerability (Hall, 1992, p. 406). Against this background, organized philanthropy sought to address what it perceived as a lack of understanding of philanthropy's role in American society (Frumkin, 1998). In this context, the Filer Commission substantiated the notion that tax-exempt organizations formed a cohesive sector and gave it concrete expression by establishing Independent Sector (1980), which became the voice and served as a common meeting ground for all entities in the nonprofit sector (Hall, 1992, pp. 407–417).

In a parallel development, changes in the relationship between the nonprofit sector and government agencies in the 1960s–1980s increased the demand for better managed nonprofit organizations. The Johnson Administration's War on Poverty and Great Society programs increased public welfare spending, and by 1980 over 40% of all the funds spent by federal, state, and local governments in human services supported delivery by nonprofit organizations (Grønbjerg, 2001; Salamon, 1993). This interconnectedness between nonprofit sector and government – in what Salamon (1987) defined third-party government – while expanding the sector's size and scope came with significant challenges in the areas of governance, accountability, financial management, and performance measurement (e.g., S. Smith & Lipsky, 1993).

The Reagan Administration policies of the 1980s further increased the need for professional management in the nonprofit sector. Changes in federal government spending challenged the nonprofit sector to seek alternative revenue sources, professionalize management, and compete with for-profit entities (Salamon, 1993). Reagan policies stimulated scholarly research investigating the relationships between nonprofit sector and government (see the pivotal Salamon & Abramson, 1982). Independent Sector, particularly its Research Program led by Virginia Hodgkinson, supported these research efforts aiming to define the role of philanthropy and nonprofit sector in American society and polity. At the same time, government devolution stimulated the development of nonprofit management education (Young, 2002).

The 1999 debate between Hall and Katz has implications for how we define nonprofit studies and view its institutionalization as a stand-alone discipline. At a conceptual level, subject porosity challenges efforts to categorize knowledge around a set of agreed methodologies, lines of inquiry, and theoretical frameworks. The somehow artificial "invention of the nonprofit sector" in the 1970s created a subject of analysis with clearer boundaries and with organizational characteristics that set the nonprofit sector apart, thus worth of its own discipline and training programs. The distinction between these two perspectives is, however, not purely analytical, as the field's narrowing characterizes its differentiation, mobilization, and legitimization.

The Drivers of Institutionalization

Since the 1970s, six interrelated forces shaped nonprofit studies. First, scholarly associations and conferences provide scholars with independent spaces for microsocialization. Second, academic centers are flexible institutional structures that escape the narrow boundaries of disciplinary-focused academic departments and support the differentiation of an emerging field of research. Third, outside funders provide the new field with financial resources and outside legitimacy. Fourth, publication opportunities increased in number and quality, both supporting the development of research paradigms and providing scholars with respected outlets to publish research. Fifth, the exponential growth of academic courses in nonprofit management signals both the field's penetration into traditional academic structures and the existence of both an internal and external demand for academic degrees. Sixth, underlying the other five drivers is the field's increasing internationalization.

First Driver: Scholarly Associations and Conferences

In the United States, the organizational resources supporting the emergence of the field developed around the Association of Voluntary Action Scholars (AVAS) and Independent Sector, spearheaded by David Horton Smith and Virginia Hodgkinson. Smith, a professor at Boston College, founded AVAS in 1971 to support interdisciplinary research efforts in a field crossing disciplinary boundaries (D. H. Smith, 2003, p. 459). Starting in 1982, under Hodgkinson's leadership (Vice President for Research at Independent Sector), Independent Sector's Spring Research Forums complemented these networking efforts, stimulating research in the field and the interdisciplinary exchange of ideas (Hodgkinson, 2018). These organizations, symposia, and forums provided otherwise isolated scholars with a communication system to discuss ideas (for innovation studies, see Fagerberg & Verspagen, 2009), and conferences more broadly serve the purpose of socializing younger scholars (Egri, 1992).

A broad network of scholarly associations and conferences provide academics with opportunities of interactions. The Association for Research on Nonprofit Organizations and Voluntary Action (ARNOVA) is the premier organization in the United States and supported formal and informal networks of scholars, facilitating the socialization of young scholars through, e.g., the Emerging Scholars Section. As the field grew and nonprofit courses integrated in public administration and business programs, special sections and interest groups were established in the scholarly organizations of related disciplines (e.g., Berlan, Shen, & Klay, 2019). Noteworthy are the Section on Nonprofit Policy, Practice and Partnerships within the American Society for Public Administration and the Academy of Management's Public and Nonprofit Division. The special interest groups within the scholarly associations of adjacent disciplines signal the academic credibility of scholarly investigations of nonprofit and philanthropic entities.

The networking effort of the last two decades of the 20th century had a field-building component. Dennis Young and Michael O'Neill convened the nonprofit management education conferences in the Bay Area in 1986 and 1996 that created a first body of knowledge on the administration of nonprofit programs and curricular development (O'Neill & Fletcher, 1998; O'Neill & Young, 1988). These benchmark conferences evolved into the Nonprofit Academic Centers Council's (NACC) biennial conferences (Ashcraft, 2007). The Benchmark Conferences were opportunities for networking and field development. During the 1986 conference in San Francisco, for example, Peter Ellis, a program officer at the W. K. Kellogg Foundation, conceptualized a strategy to support nonprofit management education, planting the seeds for a series of Kellogg Foundation funding initiatives that had a lasting impact on the field's development (Long, 1996, November 20–21).

The development of these organizational resources was, however, not without challenges. The efforts of Independent Sector's Research Program to support research through academic centers and research forums faced resistance both within and outside academia as nonprofit management was not considered a distinctive field (Hall, 1992). Nonprofit management's distinctiveness was openly discussed at the 1986 conference on nonprofit management education, with some arguing against overemphasizing industry specificity in management education. While acknowledging the distinctiveness of nonprofit organizations, Cyert (1988), for instance, advocated for generic management education programs, with some attention to institutional peculiarities, preparing students to manage any type of nonprofit organizations.

Nevertheless, however contested, the management frame provided a powerful reference for the emerging field. The broader emphasis on management education in US higher education favored the emergence of nonprofit studies (O'Neill, 2005). The renaming of AVAS into ARNOVA in 1990 reflected both the centrality of management and professional education of the 1980s and a reconceptualization of the subject of analysis, shifting – or broadening, depending on interpretation – the focus from voluntary action to a sectorial perspective. In 2003, also American Humanics morphed into the more nonprofit-centric Nonprofit Leadership Alliance, after developing over the course of the 1990s a competency-based educational model funded by the W.K. Kellogg Foundation.

Second Driver: Academic Centers

Academic centers devoted to the study of philanthropy, nonprofit sector, and voluntary action emerged in the 1980s. Located outside traditional academic structures, academic centers are better suited than academic departments for producing applicable knowledge and fostering interdisciplinary research (Clausen, Fagerberg, & Gulbrandsen, 2012; Geiger, 1990; Sá, 2008). In most cases, faculty entrepreneurs established centers, pioneering the new field and recognizing community needs (Larson & Barnes, 2001), although at times external funders and philanthropists were the original driving force, as in the cases of the Mandel Center for Nonprofit Organizations at Case Western Reserve University and the Dorothy Jonson Center of Philanthropy at Grand Valley State University.

Dennis Young and Michael O'Neill recognized the need to create an informal support group and foster inter-center collaborations. They convened the first meeting of the Vista Group at the 1986 International Sector's Research Forum, which became NACC in Atlanta at the 1991 Independent Sector Conference (Rooney & Burlingame, 2020). With a small, club-like atmosphere, NACC supported academic center directors who often were isolated at their home institutions (Ashcraft, 2015). Over the years, NACC started organizing biennial conferences, continuing the education-focused conference tradition initiated by O'Neill and Young in 1986, developing indicators of quality, curriculum guidelines, and an accreditation process for nonprofit programs.

Since the 1980s, academic centers significantly grew in number. Weber and Brunt (2022) find 53 academic centers active in 2019, up from 19 in 1988 (Hodgkinson, 1988). These academic centers are quite diverse in terms of scientific profile (institutional home, educational background of staff, and substantive focus), size (based on staff and budgets), funding sources (primarily, university's operating budget, foundation grants, and fees for services), and activities (Weber & Brunt, 2022). Academic centers provide a broad range of services, assisting the nonprofit sector as a whole, individual nonprofits, and local communities (Prentice & Brudney, 2018), bridging the gap between academia and practice that earlier scholarship had noted (R. Smith, 1997).

The evolution of nonprofit academic centers is, however, a history of mixed successes. Many of the leading centers of the 1980s and 1990s faltered, including the Mandel Center on Nonprofit Organizations and the Institute for Nonprofit Organization Management at the University of San Francisco. In line with early trends noted by Hall (1992), Weber and Brunt (2022) argue that both structural (funding, institutional support, and academic credibility) and environmental factors (the ability to build a clear niche identity and placing its development in a field-building context) explain the success of some centers and demise of others. In other instances, as Young (1998) predicted, academic centers reintegrated into traditional university structures losing their autonomy. While the integration of nonprofit content into academic units may represent a loss to some, it signals the increased legitimacy of nonprofit studies as a field of scientific enquiry, even though this legitimacy may come with an integration into traditional structure and a possible loss of autonomy.

Third Driver: External Funders

Organized philanthropy supported the field's development since its beginnings. Increasing the understanding of philanthropy's role in society was at the center of foundation funding in the 1970s and 1980s (Hall, 1992), an objective that the academic entrepreneurs establishing centers and programs in the 1980s shared (Tempel, 2001). While the intertwining of philanthropy, industry, and higher education is a characterizing feature of the United States (Zunz, 1998), it raises concerns about the commercialization of science and power structures (Fisher, 1983; Weinryb, Blomgren, & Wedlin, 2018). For emerging fields, access to financial resources is, however, critical (Frickel & Gross, 2005), as they provide external validation and leverage additional resources, both internally and externally (Larson & Long, 2000, pp. 40–41).

Between the 1980s and the early 2000s, foundations funded academic programs and centers as part of broader funding initiatives aiming to increase the capacity of the nonprofit sector. The most notable were the W.K. Kellogg Foundation, Atlantic Philanthropies (known, at the time, as the "anonymous donor"), Ford Foundation, William and Flora Hewlett Foundation, and David and Lucile Packard Foundation. These investments aimed to create a more professional, effective, and diverse social sector. The strategy assumed that better prepared leadership, stronger organizations, and effective support systems would improve the sector's impact on local and national communities (Harder+Company Community Research, 2013; Heidrich & Long, n.d.; Poscio, 2003).

Most initiatives ended in the early 2000s in the belief that academic programs successfully integrated in academia and were financially sustainable. Both funders

(Larson & Long, 2000, pp. 40–41) and leading academic entrepreneurs (O'Neill, 2007, p. 174S) noted the necessity to balance internal and external funding to ensure these programs' integration in traditional academic structures. With few exceptions, however, external funding did not successfully leverage internal support, leaving centers exposed to the shifting priorities of both funders and academic administrators (Weber & Brunt, 2022). Noteworthy, these external funders were "inside funders" as they specifically funded nonprofit studies. The competition for funding was therefore primarily internal within the field rather than external with programs in disciplines, potentially limiting the legitimacy building effect and paradoxically undermining financial sustainability, as university administrators may have seen these centers as "cash cows" able to attract specifically earmarked funds, losing their usefulness once these external funders changed funding priorities.

External funders' leading role in developing nonprofit studies is, however, at the center of one of the field's key tensions. At least initially, many scholars in the field aimed to correct existing narratives that underappreciated the role of philanthropy and voluntarism in US society, a misunderstanding that had major policies implications under the Reagan Administration. The role of foundations in funding academic research complicated this tension, as organized philanthropy became at once both the subject and the funder of academic inquiry. This tension was recognized early by commentators (Bailey, 1988) and at the center of tensions between scholars and academic entrepreneurs (Katz, 2019).

Fourth Driver: The Cognitive Infrastructure

Ma and Konrath (2018) suggest that we are currently in a mature phase of the field, after the paradigm building decades of the 1970s and 1980s. The number of dissertations on nonprofit organizations and philanthropy written in the past three decades substantiates this assessment (Shier & Handy, 2014, pp. 817–818). Throughout these years, scholars developed the theoretical frameworks explaining the distinctive roles and behaviors of nonprofit organizations (Anheier, 1995; DiMaggio & Anheier, 1990), the frameworks that draw sectorial boundaries and support theoretically the nonprofit sector's distinctiveness. The emergence of a research paradigm with methodologies, concepts, and propositions both intellectually guides and integrates scholars in the field (Clark, 1973), establishing a common ground between academics and the "domains of actions" that they propose to study (Hall, 1993, p. 6).

The transition from paradigm building to full maturity paralleled the development of the field's three premier journals. *NVSQ*, *Voluntas*, and *Nonprofit Management and Leadership* are widely considered top-ranking academic journals (Walk & Andersson, 2020). These journals are complemented by teaching-oriented journals, such as the *Journal of Nonprofit Education and Leadership*, and thematic journals, such as the *Journal of Philanthropy and Marketing* (previously, *International*

Journal of Nonprofit and Voluntary Sector Marketing), *Nonprofit Policy Forum*, and the *Journal of Civil Society*. Additionally, several international academic journals testify to the growing global interest in nonprofit studies, with for instance the British *Voluntary Sector Review*, the *Canadian Journal of Nonprofit and Social Economy Research*, and *The China Nonprofit Review*. Yet, both dissertations and articles still predominantly originate in the United States (Ma & Konrath, 2018, p. 1146; Shier & Handy, 2014, p. 820).

Nonprofit studies' institutional location traditionally emphasized the article format over books. Some edited volumes, such as *The Nonprofit Sector: A Research Handbook* (Powell, 1987; Powell & Bromley, 2020; Powell & Steinberg, 2006), developed the field's cognitive infrastructure.[1] After publishing notable monographs with a strong footing in the liberal arts, Indiana University Press's specialized *Philanthropic and Nonprofit Studies* series is shifting toward more practice-oriented publications with the retirement of its two longtime editors, Dwight Burlingame and David Hammack. Comparable, specialized series like Springer's *Nonprofit and Civil Society Series* and Berghahn's *Studies on Civil Society* have published almost exclusively edited volumes. Georgetown University Press's new *Philanthropy, Nonprofit and Nongovernmental Organizations* book series is too new to assess but its editorial board indicates a diversity of perspectives and promise to attract scholars from both nonprofit studies and adjacent disciplines. While ARNOVA awards annual book prizes to valuable contributions to the field, including the new historical prize in honor of the late historian Peter Dobkin Hall, most books are discipline-specific and fall into the field primarily because of topic rather than disciplinary focus.

As scholars developed a foundational knowledge base, knowledge production increased while narrowing. *NVSQ*'s antecedent, the *Journal of Voluntary Action Research*, was more broadly conceptualized encompassing all research in voluntary action (Hall, 1993, p. 9; Van Til, 2019). Some evidence suggests that the focus of dissertations and main academic journals progressively narrowed with an increase of academic recognition and prestige. Articles in the field's premier journals mirror this narrowing, with a shift from a focus on the positive impact of nonprofit and philanthropic organizations and their role in society to an increasing emphasis on management, performance, and outputs (Marberg, Korzilius, & van Kranenburg, 2019). Likewise, in their analysis of dissertations, Shier and Handy (2014) find a growing concentration on subject areas such as the intra-organizational context and management practices (p. 826). The adoption of this managerial terminology suggests the attempt to legitimize a field by adopting the managerial frame dominant in academia (Marberg et al., 2019, pp. 126–127).

The field's practical relevance was a strong force in the development of the field with a legitimizing effect. Scholars noted the scholar-practice divide (Brudney & Kluesner, 1992), emphasizing the sense superiority of academics over practitioners (Feeney, 2000, p. 7) and the need to adopt research methodologies facilitating applicable knowledge (Taylor, Torugsa, & Arundel, 2018). Discussing the lack of applicability of most research published in *NVSQ*, Bushouse and Sowa (2012) conclude that practical relevance is the precondition for the field on nonprofit studies to remain relevant. At the same time, however, the search for academic legitimacy emphasized academic rigor, traditional academic research and publishing standards, and traditional academic reward system (Hambrick & Chen, 2008, pp. 37–38), paradoxically contributing to the widening gap between academic knowledge production and practical applicability.

Fifth Driver: Academic Programs

Courses and programs on nonprofits, social entrepreneurship, and philanthropy increased significantly over the past three decades. Roseanne Mirabella tracked courses and programs in the Nonprofit Management Education Database at Seton Hall University, noting an increase from 17 graduate programs in 1990 to 82 in 1996 and 218 in 2016 (Mirabella et al., 2019; Rooney & Burlingame, 2020). The growth at the undergraduate level is more moderate with only 26 academic majors existing in 2019 (Weber & Brunt, 2020). The growth is more striking at the course level, with a 95% increase at the graduate level and a 127% increase at the undergraduate level between 1996 and 2016 (Mirabella et al., 2019, p. 66). This data is important because academic degrees signal the breakthrough of emerging disciplines in the scientific community (Larson & Long, 2000).

The best-place debate focused on institutional location's influence on course content but also highlighted the independence of programs from adjacent disciplines. Half of graduate programs (defined as having three or more specialized courses) are located in a College of Arts and Sciences or a School of Public Affairs and Administration (Mirabella et al., 2019, pp. 66–67). The decline of programs housed in interdisciplinary schools and the marginal role of business schools (Mirabella et al., 2019) highlights tensions over an independent "nonprofit" management (Cyert, 1988; Young, 2002). Institutional location of undergraduate programs mirrors graduate trends, although a greater percentage of programs is located in small colleges with a religious affiliation, testifying to the Nonprofit Leadership Alliance's influence at the undergraduate level (Weber & Brunt, 2020).

The centrality of graduate education relates to the strong emphasis on practical training at the field's origins. Studies document how advanced academic degrees are gatekeepers for promotion and entrance among nonprofit leaders (e.g., Suarez, 2010). Kuenzi, Stewart, and Walk (2020) found that the nonprofit-specific degree attracted students pursuing graduate nonprofit programs, in line with the professionalizing trend of the nonprofit sector. The emphasis on nonprofit organizations' internal operations and interactions with external stakeholders rather than on the broader context and societal roles confirms the practical orientation of most programs (Baggetta & Brass, 2014; Mirabella & Wish, 2001).

The increased presence of nonprofit programs in higher education shows that traditional academic disciplines increasingly recognize the field. NACC and the

Nonprofit Leadership Alliance developed curricular guidelines and competencies to both identify the knowledge needed by future nonprofit leaders and support the development of academic programs in the field. Unsurprisingly, curricular content across academic programs is increasingly similar, particularly among institutions members of the same professional associations (Mirabella et al., 2019).

The recent efforts to develop accreditation systems further support these isomorphic tendencies. The field-building aspiration of proponents of accreditation is clear as accreditation becomes a strategy to legitimize nonprofit studies as an independent and fully institutionalized field (Hale & Irvin, 2017; Mendel, 2017). These efforts, however, risk undermining the field's interdisciplinary and multidisciplinary nature, which many describe as its main strength (Hall, 1999; O'Neill, 2007). Accreditation, therefore, risks strengthening isomorphic tendencies in its efforts to set standards and codify curriculum content and scope, curtailing the field's heterogeneity and innovativeness (Mirabella & Eikenberry, 2017; Mirabella et al., 2019).

While the parallel development of accreditation systems by NACC and NASPAA points to the challenge of differentiation, it more fundamentally raises questions about the need for stand-alone nonprofit studies programs. At the 1996 Benchmark Conference, Salamon (1998) argued that the key question should not be how to best manage nonprofit organizations – the justification of nonprofit management programs – but rather how to manage the complex intersectoral collaborations and networks that address society's most pressing problems. Salamon (1998) suggests that the best educational response is less in independent nonprofit management programs but rather blended programs preparing students for the managerial challenges of these intersectoral networks. Nonprofit management education was in this view to be welcomed as a first step, as a counterweight to business management and public administration, toward the development of fully intersectoral management programs. To a degree, the incorporation of nonprofit content in programs of public administration, affairs, and policy represents a response to Salamon's call (Saidel & Smith, 2015).

Sixth Driver: Internationalization

While the focus here is on US developments, the driving forces reflect the field's increasing global interconnectedness and its awareness of the international dimension of voluntary action, philanthropy, and associational life. Yet, Ma and Konrath (2018) note the dominance of scholarship produced in the Anglo-American world in the most mature phase of the field's knowledge production. Academic programs, organizational resources, and scholarly endeavors have a growing international scope, but the field's Western centrism is undeniable.

Educational and support infrastructures rapidly developed outside the United States. Throughout the 1980s, various conferences aimed to support scholarly exchanges in the new field and resulted in the establishment of the International

Society for Third Sector Research (ISTR) in 1992, which would play a central role in supporting comparative and international research on the third sector (Gidron, 2019; Katz, 1999). Various associations and networks, both regional and national, have been established, often using ARNOVA's interdisciplinary approach as a model (D. H. Smith, 2013). The growth of civil society organizations stimulated academic and training programs developing leadership and human resources for these organizations. Comparative studies of educational programs highlight regional and national variations in emphasis, influenced by administrative traditions and cultural factors (Mirabella, Gemelli, Malcolm, & Berger, 2007), making the identification of a common terminology able to capture these phenomena in different geographical and academic settings a challenge (Mirabella, Hvenmark, & Larsson, 2015).

Intentional efforts of US institutions to internationalize parallel the field's growing international scope. Initially, these efforts were part of the field-building aspirations of both funders and the first pioneering academic centers. The Center on Philanthropy at Indiana University–Purdue University Indianapolis (IUPUI) was arguably the institution with the most explicit field-building strategy beyond US borders, developing partnerships and supporting the development of centers and programs internationally, including the University of Bremen (Germany) and the University of Bologna (Italy) (Tempel, 2001). Also, Kellogg Foundation's Building Bridges Initiative (1997–2002), which strategically sought to build a network of academic institutions, included multiple programs based in Latin America.

More recently this trend became part of a growing awareness of internationalization. ARNOVA consciously developed an international identity and under the leadership of Shariq Siddiqui (executive director from 2013 to 2019) established regional forums and conferences, such as the ARNOVA-Asia conferences and the ARNOVA-Africa conferences. ARNOVA also supported The Association for Research on Civil Society in Africa (AROCSA), which co-organizes the annual ARNOVA-Africa conferences. Likewise, over the years, NACC emphasized the international dimension in its curricular guidelines, pointing not only to the comparative dimension but also to the multiple cultural, historical, and political factors, influences voluntary, philanthropic, and nonprofit actions internationally (see Appendix A).

This increasing international orientation is rooted in a growing awareness of philanthropy's and voluntary action's global dimension. A growing body of knowledge supported the internationalization of the field's organizational infrastructure. The John Hopkins Comparative Nonprofit Project started in 1991 and, relying on local experts, collects data on volunteering, philanthropy, and civil society organizations. Researchers analyze the size and scope of the nonprofit sector, voluntary sector, charitable sector, and social economy, discussing what entities were to be included in different national contexts and how political, cultural, and economic developments influence varying relationships between state, market, and social sector (Anheier, Lang, & Toepler, 2020).

The attention to associational practices benefited from the attention to civil society in the 1970s and 1980s. Resistance to the communist regimes in East Europe and the military dictatorships in Latin America renewed the interest in associational practices as democracy's preconditions. Particularly in the post-Cold War world with the democratic transition of former communist countries, the interest in nonprofit sector, particularly in its political-democratic rather than service providing function, became relevant (Salamon, 1994). At the same time, against the background of post-colonial studies, the field's underlying Western-centric assumptions were increasingly scrutinized. If on the one hand scholars criticized comparative projects searching common definitions across national boundaries for imposing US centric concepts (e.g., Einolf, 2015; Kabalo, 2009), on the other hand the criticism leveled against the civil society concept points to the underlying Western exceptionalism at the center of these conceptualizations (e.g., Lewis, 2002). There is a tension then between the institutionalization of an academic field largely driven by forces originating in the Anglo-American world and the heterogeneity of meanings, roles, and functions of forms of social actions that the concepts of philanthropy, charity, and nonprofit organizations only partially capture.

Conclusion

The chapter describes the evolution of the field since the 1980s leading to a rapid institutionalization in the late 1990s and 2000s. The field established a strong presence in academia with academic programs, reputable academic journals, micro-socialization structures, and responsiveness to both internal and external demands. Macro trends created the precondition for the emergence of nonprofit studies, and micro events and human agencies acted upon these opportunities as academic entrepreneurs and scholars created micro-socializing structures, academic centers, and programs. I applied the framework of Hambrick and Chen (2008) to describe how the six driving forces emerging from external relevance, structural conditions, micro-mobilization contexts, and intellectual identity intertwined in the process of differentiation, mobilization, and legitimization. This evolution, however, raises questions concerning some of the crucial tensions, which have been highlighted in reviewing the six institutionalizing forces shaping the emergence of nonprofit studies.

The creation of knowledge that informs practice was one of the drivers contributing to the field's emergence, which is deeply rooted in societal relevance. There seems to be a tension between the interest of faculty and long-term efforts of the discipline and the interests of two other, overlapping constituents, students and nonprofit community. Developments in higher education might shift the emphasis on practice, as decreasing state appropriations and emphasis on vocational training and outside funders go in that direction. The key question then is whether efforts to increase the field's academic credibility contribute to the widening of the gap between academic and practical knowledge.

Scholars in the field have long served as both advocates and researchers. The field is rooted in the efforts to show the relevance of philanthropy and nonprofit sector in society. The scholar-advocate is therefore a characterizing feature of the field. In addition, organized philanthropy's long-term influence as both funder and subject of analysis complicates the picture as the hope for foundation funding may inhibit overly critical accounts of foundation activities ("Editor's Introduction The Hidden Hand: How Foundations Shape the Course of History," 2015; Roelofs, 2007). Unsurprisingly critical analyses of philanthropy, while not completely lacking, are a minority and at least initially originated outside the field. Also, the practical orientation of most students, who aim to pursue careers in the nonprofit sector, encourages practical and managerial approaches over big questions concerning the potentials and limits of voluntary action. The key question here centers on the objectivity requirement at the center of social sciences and to what degree the subjectivity at the center of voluntary and philanthropic action reflected also in the approaches to research and teaching can and must survive. The objectivity challenge is not unique to the field, as historians have long dealt with similar questions (Novick, 1988). The challenge then is less avoiding these tensions but rather recognizing and acknowledging them.

A third key question relates to institutionalization's isomorphic tendencies. The creation of a coherent body of knowledge, accreditation standards, rewards systems, etc., narrows the field in terms of both curricular developments and research. The legitimization process requires or at least encourages the adoption of languages, institutional structures, and methodological tools that adjacent disciplines recognize as legitimate. The emphasis on a professionalizing terminology in the leading journals, the incorporation of centers into traditional academic structures, the development of accreditation programs, etc., point to these legitimizing efforts. Academic credibility then is coming with a loss of innovation, which arguably was one of the driving forces of the field.

The evolution of the field and its underlying tensions suggest a parallel development of institutionalization and integration. Echoing O'Neill (2007), the challenge for nonprofit studies in the future years may be the danger of success as the integration of nonprofit studies into university structure comes with a subtle reshaping of programs to fit institutional interests and programmatic needs. The integration of nonprofit studies in adjacent disciplines signals its academic credibility, while potentially "interrupting" its evolution as a stand-alone field. This development then raises a broader normative question of whether academic credibility is a point of arrival or a step toward establishing nonprofit studies as a stand-alone field, as envisioned by some of its advocates (e.g., Mendel, 2015). Perhaps the long-term sustainability of nonprofit studies and its partner programs lies in shared intellectual foundation and value-based relationship within academia, cutting across disciplinary silos at the cost of its own disciplinary independence.

Note

1 An attentive reviewer noted the evolution in contributors between the first and third editions of *The Nonprofit Sector: A Research Handbook*. The reviewer points out that first edition contributors shared connections with Independent Sector and the Program on Non-Profit Organizations (PONPO) at Yale University, marking the beginning of systematic research on the nonprofit sector, whereas third edition contributors authored few chapters in the earlier editions, appear less connected to the field's infrastructure organizations, and are firmly rooted in traditional disciplinary departments. To the reviewer, this evolution suggests an integration of nonprofit studies into adjacent disciplines, thus cautioning against broader institutionalization narratives. While partially agreeing, I would argue that the handbook's third edition reflects the approach of the institutional home of its editors. The Stanford Center on Philanthropy and Civil Society (PACS) is an interdisciplinary research center that does not house a degree-awarding nonprofit studies program. Rather, it leverages the expertise of an interdisciplinary group of affiliated faculty members from various disciplines. To a degree, Stanford's PACS is a return to the past when nonprofit academic centers were positioned across disciplines providing opportunities of interdisciplinary research to affiliated faculty with different disciplinary homes.

References

Abramson, A. J., & McCarthy, R. (2012). Infrastructure Organizations. In L. Salamon (Ed.), *The State of Nonprofit America* (2nd ed., pp. 423–458). Washington, DC: Brookings Institution Press.

Anheier, H. (1995). Theories of the Nonprofit Sector: Three Issues. *Nonprofit and Voluntary Sector Quarterly, 24*(1), 15–23.

Anheier, H., Lang, M., & Toepler, S. (2020). Comparative Nonprofit Sector Research: A Critical Assessment. In W. Powell & P. Bromley (Eds.), *The Nonprofit Sector* (3rd ed., pp. 648–676). Stanford: Stanford University Press.

Ashcraft, R. (2001). Where Nonprofit Management Education Meets the Undergraduate Experience: American Humanics after 50 Years. *Public Performance & Management Review, 25*(1), 42–56.

Ashcraft, R. (2007). BenchMark 3: The Third Decennial Conference on Nonprofit and Philanthropic Studies: Editor's Introduction to This Special Issue. *Nonprofit and Voluntary Sector Quarterly, 36*(4_suppl), 5S–10S.

Ashcraft, R. (2015). The Nonprofit Academic Centers Council: Its Past and Future Promises. *The Journal of Nonprofit Education and Leadership, 5*(1), 2–5.

Baggetta, M., & Brass, J. N. (2014). Context-Based Instruction: What Traditional Social Science Disciplines Offer to Nonprofit Management Education. *Journal of Public Affairs Education, 20*(4), 579–596.

Bailey, A. (1988, September 21). Philanthropy Research's Built-in Conflict. *Chronicle of Higher Education, 34*, A36.

Berlan, D., Shen, R., & Klay, W. E. (2019). The History and Evolution of the Southeastern Conference for Public Administration. *Journal of Public and Nonprofit Affairs, 5*(1), 6–20.

Biglan, A. (1973). The Characteristics of Subject Matter in Different Academic Areas. *Journal of Applied Psychology, 57*(3), 195–203.

Brudney, J., & Kluesner, T. (1992). Researchers and Practitioners in Nonprofit Organization and Voluntary Action: Applying Research to Practice? *Nonprofit and Voluntary Sector Quarterly, 21*(3), 293–308.

Bushouse, B., & Sowa, J. (2012). Producing Knowledge For Practice: Assessing NVSQ 2000–2010. *Nonprofit and Voluntary Sector Quarterly, 41*(3), 497–513.

Clark, T. (1973). The Stages of Scientific Institutionalization. *International Social Science Journal, 23*(4), 658–671.

Clausen, T., Fagerberg, J., & Gulbrandsen, M. (2012). Mobilizing for Change: A Study of Research Units in Emerging Scientific Fields. *Research Policy, 41*(7), 1249–1261.

Cyert, R. (1988). The Place of Nonprofit Management Programs in Higher Education. In M. O'Neill & D. Young (Eds.), *Educating Managers of Nonprofit Organizations* (pp. 33–50). New York: Praeger.

DiMaggio, P., & Anheier, H. (1990). The Sociology of Nonprofit Organizations and Sectors. *Annual Review of Sociology, 16*(1), 137–159.

Editor's Introduction The Hidden Hand: How Foundations Shape the Course of History. (2015). *American Journal of Economics and Sociology, 74*(4), 631–653.

Egri, C. (1992). Academic Conferences as Ceremonials: Opportunities for Organizational Integration and Socialization. *Journal of Management Education, 16*(1), 90–115.

Einolf, C. (2015). The Social Origins of the Nonprofit Sector and Charitable Giving. In P. Wiepking & F. Handy (Eds.), *The Palgrave Handbook of Global Philanthropy* (pp. 509–529). London: Palgrave Macmillan UK.

Fagerberg, J., & Verspagen, B. (2009). Innovation Studies – The Emerging Structure of a New Scientific Field. *Research Policy, 38*(2), 218–233.

Feeney, S. (2000). Introduction. *Nonprofit and Voluntary Sector Quarterly, 29*(1), 5–10.

Fisher, D. (1983). The Role of Philanthropic Foundations in the Reproduction and Production of Hegemony: Rockefeller Foundations and the Social Sciences. *Sociology, 17*(2), 206–233.

Frickel, S., & Gross, N. (2005). A General Theory of Scientific/Intellectual Movements. *American Sociological Review, 70*(2), 204–232.

Frumkin, P. (1998). The Long Recoil from Regulation: Private Philanthropic Foundations and the Tax Reform Act of 1969. *The American Review of Public Administration, 28*(3), 266–286.

Geiger, R. (1990). Organized Research Units: Their Role in the Development of University Research. *The Journal of Higher Education, 61*(1), 1–19.

Gidron, B. (2019). The Early History of ISTR. *NACC Newsletter.* Retrieved from: https://mailchi.mp/23d40fbfcafd/nacc-news-april-1977093

Grønbjerg, K. (2001). The U.S. Nonprofit Human Service Sector: A Creeping Revolution. *Nonprofit and Voluntary Sector Quarterly, 30*(2), 276–297.

Hale, M., & Irvin, R. (2017). A Position Paper on Accreditation on Nonprofit/Philanthropy University Curricula. *Journal of Nonprofit Education & Leadership,* 7(Special Issue I), 126–137.

Hall, P. D. (1992). Teaching and Research on Philanthropy, Voluntarism, and Nonprofit Organizations: A Case Study of Academic Innovation. *Teachers College Record, 93*(3), 403–435.

Hall, P. D. (1993). Of Books and the Scholarly Infrastructure. Nonprofit and Voluntary Sector *Quarterly, 22*(1), 5–12.

Hall, P. D. (1999). The Work of Many Hands: A Response to Stanley N. Katz on the Origins of the "Serious Study" of Philanthropy. *Nonprofit and Voluntary Sector Quarterly, 28*(4), 522–534.

Hambrick, D., & Chen, M.-J. (2008). New Academic Fields as Admittance-Seeking Social Movements: The Case of Strategic Management. *The Academy of Management Review, 33*(1), 32–54.

Harder+Company Community Research. (2013). *Improving the Practice of Philanthropy: An Evaluation of the Hewlett Foundation's Knowledge Creation and Dissemination Strategy*. Menlo Park, CA: The William and Flora Hewlett Foundation.

Heidrich, K., & Long, R. (n.d.). *The Story of the Building Bridges Initiative*. Battle Creek, MI: W. K. Kellogg Foundation.

Hodgkinson, V. (1988). Academic Centers and Programs Focusing on the Study of Philanthropy, Voluntarism, and Not-for-Profit Activity: A Progress Report. Independent Sector Records, 1971–1996. (Box 34, Folder 12). Ruth Lilly Special Collections and Archives, IUPUI University Library, Indiana University Purdue University Indianapolis.

Hodgkinson, V. (2018). In the Beginning. … The Launch of the Independent Sector Research Program 1982–1987. *NACC Newsletter*. Retrieved from: https://mailchi.mp/94c49aad479f/nacc-news-august-1771321

Kabalo, P. (2009). A Fifth Nonprofit Regime?: Revisiting Social Origins Theory Using Jewish Associational Life as a New State Model. *Nonprofit and Voluntary Sector Quarterly, 38*(4), 627–642.

Katz, S. (1999). Where Did the Serious Study of Philanthropy Come from, Anyway? *Nonprofit and Voluntary Sector Quarterly, 28*(1), 74–82.

Katz, S. (2019). The Philanthropy Critic As Pain In The Ass: Robert Payton On Peter Dobkin Hall. Retrieved from https://histphil.org/2019/12/30/the-philanthropy-critic-as-pain-in-the-ass-robert-payton-on-peter-dobkin-hall/

Krishnan, A. (2009). *What Are Academic Disciplines? Some Observations on the Disciplinarity vs. Interdisciplinarity Debate*. NCRM Working Paper Series.

Kuenzi, K., Stewart, A., & Walk, M. (2020). Nonprofit Graduate Education: Who Gets the Degree and Why? *Journal of Public Affairs Education, 26*(1), 11–30.

Larson, S., & Long, R. (2000). Academic Centers: Moving Beyond the Periphery. *Journal of Public Service and Outreach, 5*(2), 39–47.

Larson, S., & Barnes, S. (2001). *Building Philanthropy and Nonprofit Academic Centers: A View from Ten Builders* (W. K. Kellogg Foundation Ed.). Battle Creek, MI: W. K. Kellogg Foundation.

Lee, M. (2010). The Role of the YMCA in the Origins of U.S. Nonprofit Management Education. *Nonprofit Management and Leadership, 20*(3), 277–293.

Lewis, D. (2002). Civil Society in African Contexts: Reflections on the Usefulness of a Concept. *Development and Change, 33*(4), 569–586.

Long, R. (1996, November 20–21). *Philanthropy and Volunteerism in Higher Education: Building Bridges between Practice and Knowledge. [A Program Initiative Progress Report to the Board]*. Robert Long Papers. Personal Collection, Murray, KY.

Ma, J., & Konrath, S. (2018). A Century of Nonprofit Studies: Scaling the Knowledge of the Field. *Voluntas, 29*(6), 1139–1158.

Marberg, A., Korzilius, H., & van Kranenburg, H. (2019). What Is in a Theme? Professionalization in Nonprofit and Nongovernmental Organizations Research. *Nonprofit Management and Leadership, 30*(1), 113–131.

Mendel, S. (2015). Nonprofit First: The Promise and Potential of the Nonprofit Academic Centers Council. *Journal of Nonprofit Education and Leadership, 5*(1), 30–37.

Mendel, S. (2017). Nonprofit First as Grounding for Nonprofit Studies Pedagogy, Research, Service to the Community Accreditation and National Rankings. *Journal of Nonprofit Education and Leadership,* 7(Special Issue I), 5–13.

Mirabella, R., & Wish, N. (2001). University-Based Educational Programs in the Management of Nonprofit Organizations: An Updated Census of U.S. Programs. *Public Performance & Management Review, 25*(1), 30–41.

Mirabella, R., Gemelli, G., Malcolm, M.-J., & Berger, G. (2007). Nonprofit and Philanthropic Studies: International Overview of the Field in Africa, Canada, Latin America, Asia, the Pacific, and Europe. *Nonprofit and Voluntary Sector Quarterly, 36*(4_suppl), 110S–135S.

Mirabella, R., Hvenmark, J., & Larsson, O. S. (2015). Civil Society Education: International Perspectives. *The Journal of Nonprofit Education and Leadership, 5*(4), 213–218.

Mirabella, R., & Eikenberry, A. (2017). A Critical Perspective on Nonprofit Accreditation. *Journal of Nonprofit Education & Leadership,* 7(Special Issue I), 24–31.

Mirabella, R., Hoffman, T., Teo, T., & McDonald, M. (2019). The Evolution of Nonprofit Management and Philanthropic Studies in the United States: Are We Now a Disciplinary Field? *Journal of Nonprofit Education and Leadership, 9*(1), 63–84.

Novick, P. (1988). *That Noble Dream: The "Objectivity Question" and the American Historical Profession.* Cambridge: Cambridge University Press.

O'Neill, M., & Young, D. (1988). *Educating Managers of Nonprofit Organizations.* Westport, CT: Praeger.

O'Neill, M., & Fletcher, K. (1998). *Nonprofit Management Education: US and World Perspectives.* Westport, CT: Praeger.

O'Neill, M. (2005). Developmental Contexts of Nonprofit Management Education. *Nonprofit Management and Leadership, 16*(1), 5–17.

O'Neill, M. (2007). The Future of Nonprofit Management Education. *Nonprofit and Voluntary Sector Quarterly, 36*(4_suppl), 169S–176S.

Poscio, T. (2003). *The Foundations of Civil Society: A Review of Investments by the Atlantic Philanthropies in the Fundamentals of the U.S. Philanthropic Sector, 1984–2001.* New York, NY: The Atlantic Philanthropies (USA) Inc.

Powell, W. (Ed.) (1987). *The Nonprofit Sector. A Research Handbook* (1st ed.). New Haven, CT: Yale University Press.

Powell, W., & Steinberg, R. (Eds.). (2006). *The Nonprofit Sector. A Research Handbook* (2nd ed.). New Haven, CT: Yale University Press.

Powell, W., & Bromley, P. (2020). *The Nonprofit Sector: A Research Handbook* (3rd ed.). Stanford: Stanford University Press.

Prentice, C., & Brudney, J. (2018). Are You Being Served? Toward a Typology of Nonprofit Infrastructure Organizations and a Framework for Their Assessment. *Journal of Public and Nonprofit Affairs, 4*(1), 41–58.

Roelofs, J. (2007). Foundations and Collaboration. *Critical Sociology, 33,* 479–504.

Rooney, P., & Burlingame, D. (2020). Build It and They will Come! Or, Built to Last?: Nonprofit and Philanthropic Studies Programs and Centers. *Journal of Nonprofit Education & Leadership, 10*(4), 414–428.

Sá, C. (2008). University-Based Research Centers: Characteristics, Organization, and Administrative Implications. *The Journal of Research Administration, 39*(1), 32–40.

Saidel, J., & Smith, S. R. (2015). Nonprofit Management Education in Schools with Public Affairs Curricula: An Analysis of the Trend Toward Curriculum Integration. *Journal of Public Affairs Education, 21*(3), 337–348.

Salamon, L., & Abramson, A. (1982). *The Federal Budget and the Nonprofit Sector.* Washington, DC: Urban Institute Press.

Salamon, L. (1987). Partners in Public Service: The Scope and Theory of Government-Nonprofit Relations. In W. Powell (Ed.), *The Nonprofit Sector. A Research Handbook* (pp. 99–117). New Haven, CT: Yale University Press.

Salamon, L. (1993). The Marketization of Welfare: Changing Nonprofit and For-Profit Roles in the American Welfare State. *Social Service Review, 67*(1), 16–39.

Salamon, L. (1994). The Rise of the Nonprofit Sector. *Foreign Affairs, 73*(4), 109–122.

Salamon, L. (1998). Nonprofit Management Education: A Field Whose Time Has Passed? In M. O'Neill & K. Fletcher (Eds.), *Nonprofit Management Education: U.S. and world perspectives* (pp. 137–154). Westport, CT: Praeger.

Shier, M., & Handy, F. (2014). Research Trends in Nonprofit Graduate Studies: A Growing Interdisciplinary Field. *Nonprofit and Voluntary Sector Quarterly, 43*(5), 812–831.

Simon, J. (1995). The Regulation of American Foundations: Looking Backward at the Tax Reform Act of 1969. *Voluntas, 6*(3), 243–254.

Smith, D. H. (2003). A History of ARNOVA. *Nonprofit and Voluntary Sector Quarterly, 32*(3), 458–472.

Smith, D. H. (2013). Growth of Research Associations and Journals in the Emerging Discipline of Altruistics. *Nonprofit and Voluntary Sector Quarterly, 42*(4), 638–656.

Smith, R. (1997). Building the Nonprofit Sector Knowledge Base: Can Academic Centers and Management Support Organizations Come Together? *Nonprofit Management and Leadership, 8*(1), 89–97.

Smith, S., & Lipsky, M. (1993). *Nonprofits for Hire: The Welfare State in the Age of Contracting.* Cambridge: Harvard University Press.

Suarez, D. (2010). Street Credentials and Management Backgrounds: Careers of Nonprofit Executives in an Evolving Sector. *Nonprofit and Voluntary Sector Quarterly, 39*(4), 696–716.

Taylor, R., Torugsa, N., & Arundel, A. (2018). Leaping Into Real-World Relevance: An "Abduction" Process for Nonprofit Research. *Nonprofit and Voluntary Sector Quarterly, 47*(1), 206–227.

Tempel, E. (2001). Increasing the Knowledge and Understanding of Philanthropy: The Center on Philanthropy at Indiana University. *Fund Raising Management, 32*(9), 27–32.

Van Til, J. (2019). As I Recall: The Origins of JVAR/NVSQ. *NACC Newsletter.* Retrieved from: https://mailchi.mp/ae3172542ace/nacc-news-august

Walk, M., & Andersson, F. (2020). Where Do Nonprofit and Civil Society Researchers Publish? Perceptions of Nonprofit Journal Quality. *Journal of Public and Nonprofit Affairs, 6*(1), 79–95.

Weber, P., & Witkowski, G. (2016). Philanthropic Disruptions: Changing Nonprofit Education for an Engaged Society. *Journal of Public Affairs Education, 22*(1), 91–106.

Weber, P., & Brunt, C. (2020). Continuing to Build Knowledge: Undergraduate Nonprofit Programs in Institutions of Higher Learning. *Journal of Public Affairs Education, 26*(3), 336–357.

Weber, P. C., & Brunt, C. (2022). Building Nonprofit Studies in the US: The Role of Centers and Institutes in New Academic disciplines. *Journal of Public and Nonprofit Affairs, 8*(1), 1–26. https://doi.org/10.20899/jpna.8.1.1-26.

Weinryb, N., Blomgren, M., & Wedlin, L. (2018). Rationalizing Science: A Comparative Study of Public, Industry, and Nonprofit Research Funders. *Minerva, 56*(4), 405–429.

Young, D. (1998). Games Universities Play: An Analysis of the Institutional Contexts of Centers for Nonprofit Studies. In M. O'Neil & K. Fletcher (Eds.), *Nonprofit Management Education: US and World Perspectives* (pp. 119–136). Westport, CT: Greenwood Publishing Group, Inc.

Young, D. (2002). The Evolution of University-Based Nonprofit Management Education in the US. *The Nonprofit Review, 2*(1), 1–10.

Zunz, O. (1998). *Why the American century?* Chicago: University of Chicago Press.

2

CONSIDERING THE CHARACTER OF ORGANIZATIONS IN THE THIRD SECTOR

William A. Brown

The general principle of third sector organizations as operating distinct from public entities and for-profit businesses is generally accepted and widely prevalent around the world (Billis, 2010; Salamon, 1994). These organizations take many different forms and typically enact public benefit objectives, but can also prioritize private or member interests (Anheier, 2014). It is important to recognize that the chapter relies on idealized archetypes and that there is inherent variability within and between organizational types (see also Chapter 9 by Casey for a discussion of these complexities in a global context). There is significant research and literature that recognizes the hybrid nature of many organizations that blend and incorporate the characteristics from across idealized organizational forms (Skelcher & Smith, 2015).

Comparing and contrasting for-profit businesses, government entities, and nonprofits or social sector organizations can be informative. The three sectors of society are legal categories and the entities within those categories can take different forms, for example, there are local governments, state governments, and federal governments. Similarly, for-profit entities take various forms such as sole-proprietor, partnerships, or corporations. Social sector organizations can be loose collaborations of individuals (i.e., voluntary groups) or organized as nonprofit corporations. Furthermore, there are a number of hybrid type organizations that convolute clear and definitive boundaries between the sectors (Gümüsay, Smets, & Morris, 2020; Mikołajczak, 2020). For instance, for-profit corporations with dual profit incentives and public benefit objectives.

DOI: 10.4324/9781003294061-3

Differences between Organizational Types

In recognition of the inherent challenges to define universal features of third sector organizations, Frumkin (2009) suggests that nonprofits exhibit three distinctive features: nonprofits do not coerce participation, they operate without distributing profit, and they exist without simple clear lines of ownership (see also Nonprofit Academic Centers Council [NACC]) curricular guidelines for graduate programs #1 and #2; see Appendix). These ideas are useful to distinguish between the different sectors of society. Public entities inherently benefit from the ability to coerce engagement and as a result can exert significant and often universal impact on citizens and those under their authority. This is particularly relevant concerning revenue and the capacity to tax and mandate revenue mechanisms. The recognition that nonprofits cannot exert such influence is a fundamental aspect of the "voluntary" nature of organizations operating as nonprofits. They inherently must address the interests of multiple stakeholders in ways that garner support and engagement. While this might be comparable to for-profit entities, in that for-profits cannot require engagement, nonprofits are distinct in that ownership rights, which tend to be fairly straightforward in for-profit business is convoluted in the nonprofit context. This implies that accountability expectations in nonprofits are often ambiguous and difficult to quantify (Candler & Dumont, 2010; Tacon, Walters, & Cornforth, 2017). Billis (2010) summarizes research to suggest that ownership and funding are significant factors that can distinguish organizational forms. In addition, Billis (2010) suggests that consideration of operational practices are informative in relation to organizational form and hybridity. The next section extends these ideas and explores the implications for programs that prepare individuals to manage and lead third sector organizations. Summarizing prior research, Table 2.1 lists key differences between the sectors

TABLE 2.1 Fundamental Differences between Organizational Types

Characteristics	*For-Profit*	*Government*	*Nonprofit*
Ownership	Individuals, partners, stockholders, etc.	Citizens/Public	Non-specific "community"
Revenue	Sales	Tax revenue, fees	Donated, Contracted, or sales
Capital	Investors, public offering, or debt	Bonds (debt), tax revenue	Donated, limited debt
Customer or Service Beneficiary	Individual choice	Public or objective criteria	Some choice, but also nonprofit decides
Rationale for being/ Institutional Logics	Market/Economic	Public Management or State Bureaucracy	Values-based, or faith-based

related to ownership, financial concerns (i.e., revenue and capital), customers and/or beneficiaries interactions, and the logic or rationale for being. This last concept, "institutional logic" (Thornton & Ocasio, 2008), reflects the culture, identity, or ethos that guides decision-making and operations in the organization.

Ownership

Ownership is a central proposition for decision-making in organizations (Fama & Jenson, 1983). Substantial research reflects how different ownership regimens influence decision-making practices, program and services, and employee engagement (Crossland & Hambrick, 2011; Mak & Li, 2001; Rosko, Jon, Zinn, & Aaronson, 1995). In a for-profit organization, there are principles (owners) with particular rights (Billis, 2010). Decision making is driven by the underlying presumption that for-profit entities generate a financial surplus that will at some point be returned to the owners (Fama & Jenson, 1983). For government entities, ownership is more convoluted, but it is reasonable to consider that "the public" own the government. It is more problematic for decision-making as the "interests" are much more complex than the financial "bottom-line" in business. Nonprofits face similar ownership problems (Hansmann, 2000). Does the community own the nonprofit? Yes, to a degree nonprofits are quasi-public organizations that have public purposes and receive preferences that further recognize the public aspects of their work. In most instances, nonprofits are not anywhere near the size to suggest that they meet the needs of an entire community. The board or founder serve as stewards of the mission and often are instrumental in the success of the organization, but they do not own the assets of the nonprofit. Those assets exist for public purposes and cannot be transferred to individuals for personal benefit. Consequently, nonprofits often struggle to figure out to whom they are accountable (Candler & Dumont, 2010). This principle underlies many nonprofit management challenges (see Chapter 6 by Fischer and Mayer as well as Chapter 12 by Mirabella, Nguyen, and Feit for additional perspectives) because nonprofits are accountable to broad array of stakeholders and financial considerations (Young, Peng, Ahlstrom, Bruton, & Jiang, 2008). Nonprofit leaders can prioritize different stakeholders but the clarity of "return on investment" is not easily determined. The ambiguity of ownership has significant implications for decision-making and the systems of accountability that are created to guide operations (Connelly, Tihanyi, Certo, & Hitt, 2010).

Capital Structure

Access to capital is another fundamental difference between the sectors (see also NACC curricular guidelines for graduate programs #9 and #11). Capital structure is defined as the combination of financing methods, such as debt or equity, and plays a crucial role in their sustainability and development (Bowman, 2002; Yan, Denison, & Butler, 2009). Because nonprofit organizations do not have owners, and the source of external equity to nonprofits is philanthropy (Sloan, 2000), they will not generate dividends in real dollars. Three components of capital structure: internal revenues, debt, and equity are confronted in different ways by for-profit, public, and nonprofit entities. Access to capital is a barrier to growth for all organizational entities. Businesses access capital through investors or a public offering. Investors engage in the process with the expectation that they will benefit from profits that are generated through the expanded ability to provide services or develop products. Businesses can also access capital through debt and bonds. The funds are loaned with the expectation that additional capital provides the capacity to increase revenue and profits, which form the basis of the arrangement. Businesses can also retain profits overtime to build capital assets that can be used to expand. Governments can access capital through the bond markets because of the reliable tax revenue. They are constrained by the necessity to place large bond measures on the ballot and as a result must demonstrate the political as well as social benefit. Government expenditures on large capital expenses are often justified through the expectation that improved infrastructure facilitates business and residential development which generates more revenue. Although, this is not always the case as governments can seek capital funds to rehabilitate existing infrastructures, which might or might not add to tax revenue. There are similarities between public debt and nonprofit debt in that they are both used to finance capital infrastructures, which usually require significant resources and raise concerns for solvency. Nonprofit managers have to rely on the good will of donors to "invest" in their activities, but those "investments" do not generate financial returns to the investor (see also Chapter 7 by Palmer for a discussion of these issues). Rather nonprofits must demonstrate a purpose or value that justifies the contributions. It is a significant constraint for nonprofit managers as they try to expand services. Increased capital expands the ability to provide services but does not guarantee increased revenue. There is increased pressure from donors to consider how investments in nonprofit infrastructures can generate quantifiable returns, but in most instances, these returns are difficult to quantify beyond an increased number of individuals served. Fundamentally, increased capacity relates to the ability to fulfill mission objectives and as noted early does not result in a financial return to investors. These capital concerns are amplified by revenue concerns that tend to also challenge nonprofit organizations.

Revenue

Revenue sources are another obvious difference among the three sectors (see also NACC curricular guidelines for graduate programs #10 and #11). Nonprofits depend on three general types of revenue to support their mission-related work: private contributions, including individual and corporate donations and foundation grants; funding from government; and fees which might include selling goods and services related or unrelated to the nonprofit's mission (Froelich,

1999). The single largest determinant of nonprofit organization success is financial sustainability (Schatteman & Waymire, 2017). Businesses generate revenue primarily through commercial activity and the provision of products or service. They make products or provide services and consumers pay a premium that exceeds cost of production. Government can mandate its source of revenue through taxes or they can charge a fee. Most nonprofits can do neither, consistently charge a premium for services or require support from the community. Nonprofits often provide services below cost and as a result, nonprofits seek funds based on the philanthropic interests of donors. Nonprofits rely on the support of those in the community and/or they are contracted to fulfill a purpose predetermined by the government (see also Chapter 5 by Smith for additional discussion on state nonprofit relations). Revenue is generated indirectly through services that meet needs in the community. Nonprofits can charge for services but revenue generated through the direct provision of services may not cover all the costs. If the organization is merely engaged in the provision of services for a fee then the tax-exempt purposes are potentially in question. Why should an organization that generates all its revenue through payment from customers receive preferential treatment by the government unless the entity can clearly demonstrate charitable purposes? Excess revenue from services is not the only test because some industries do rely on fees for a significant portion of their revenue (i.e., education and healthcare) and a case is made that these entities provide public benefits in excess of the services fees charged. In summary, businesses primarily rely on revenue through sales, governments rely on revenue through taxation and nonprofits rely on a mix of revenue streams that include fees for services, contracts with government entities, private foundation grants and donations, and educational programs.

Citizen, Service Beneficiary, or Customer

Another difference has traditionally been the way individuals interact with the entities. A consideration is the distinction between exchange and communal relationships (Clark & Mills, 1979). Exchange relationships are primarily transactional whereby participants exchange components of equal or comparable value. This reflects the tendency to pay fees for goods or services and in many ways guides interaction in a for-profit context. Whether that be investors or consumers. Communal relationships are guided by goodwill and not intended to follow exclusively a quid pro quo expectation (see also Chapter 12 by Mirabella, Nguyen, and Feit). This does not explain all interactions in the nonprofit sector, but there is a recognition or expectation that the interaction between nonprofits and the beneficiary is complex and not based on solely private quid pro quo interests. Another distinction in regards to public entities is the ability to compel engagement, with the government all citizens are required to comply with various rules and regulations such as the need to register a vehicle to drive on public roads. The concept of customer choice is pervasive through capitalistic economies and we have often grown to expect competition and choice. As citizens we have responsibilities toward the government and we are accountable for our actions through the legal system. As citizens our engagement with government is complicated by the multiple roles governments play in our lives. For nonprofits, service recipients sometimes have a choice, but often there may be no other option. Consider for instance a program that delivers meals to homebound individuals. The meals are often delivered at very low or no cost to the recipient. There are typically more individuals who need the meals than the agency can accommodate and there is very rarely an alternative service. Nonprofits often coordinate services and try to cover as many families as they can (Hasenfeld, 2009). This is related to the next section that considers how these factors come together to form a logic that guides organizational behavior.

Rationale for Being: The Influence of Institutional Logics

Institutional logics are cognitive frames that operate in organizations and shared by constituencies. These frames influence structures, guide behavior, and constrain options (Thornton & Ocasio, 2008). Institutional logic reflects the accepted way to do "business" in the organization. While it is not possible to detail all the institutional logics that operate in organizations, this discussion recognizes some dominate logics that seem to compete for manager's attention. Broad meta-philosophies are often, although not exclusively, aligned with legal classifications. It is recognized that competing logics often operate in organizations and that is one of the challenges managers must address. This is exhibited in nonprofits that may align with business oriented logics, public oriented logics, or community-based logics just to identify a few that may operate in nonprofits. Identifying idealized institutional logics and the influence on managing organizations is potentially useful (see Table 2.2).

TABLE 2.2 Idealized Institutional Logics across Sectors

Characteristics	*Market/Economic*	*Government/State System*	*Values*
Purpose	Profit accumulation	Creating and maintaining social systems	Philosophical and social
Strategy Frame	Market share and dominance	Public benefit	Impact
Power and Authority	Financial	Political	Social
Capital Investment	Increased production and operations	Social infrastructure	Stability
Structural Frame	Innovation and opportunity	Hierarchy and control	Inclusive and decentralized

Idealized institutional logics are rarely "pure" and the variations are complex as they are enacted in different organizations (Thornton & Ocasio, 2008). This is true in all types of organizations but it seems particularly true in nonprofits that exist to enact a wide range of philosophical purposes (Mullins, 2006) and confront complex resource challenges. A *market or economic logic* suggests that the primary purpose is financial, which is enacted through profit and wealth accumulation. *Government and state systems* are primarily about creating and maintaining social systems that provide stability to society. A *values orientation* presupposes that the organization exists to promote a philosophical ideal that is often articulated in the mission of the organization. These idealized institutional logics capture the rationale and purpose for organizational actions. The purpose is going to guide all kinds of organizational activities, for example, how funds are invested. Organizations with a market and economic orientation are going to invest in capital to improve production and achieve efficiencies. Government and state systems invest in public infrastructure. Values focused organizations often invest to increase or obtain stability. For example, nonprofits build endowments (funds held and invested) to ensure that the organization can exist in perpetuity. These are idealized types and there is significant variety and rarely a pure system in an organization.

For-profit entities exist with a market or economic logic. They exist because they are able to provide a service or develop a product and then extract a profit from the exchange relationship. There are for-profit businesses that exist with high ideals and principles. For instance, Tom's Shoes (TOMS Company Overview) has "The Buy-One, Give-One" principle. For every shoe sold Tom's Shoes provides a pair of shoes to an underprivileged child in a developing country. They sell one pair of shoes for a premium and part of the surplus capital is used to provide a second pair of shoes to someone else. They are selling shoes *and* the philanthropic value of the product. It is a fascinating model and holds significant promise. Nevertheless, they have a superordinate proposition that requires the organization to generate sufficient profit to afford their charitable activities. Consumers have to be willing to purchase the shoes for a price that covers production costs and provides sufficient surplus to fulfill charitable and investor concerns. This is recognized as the logic of the market and includes wealth accumulation, ownership, competition, and efficiency as part of the system (Bryson, Crosby, & Stone, 2006).

Government entities are different because they exist for a broad range of public purposes. Some have described this as the state bureaucratic system or new public management. Bozeman (2007) discusses a spectrum that encapsulates economic influences on one axis and political influences and authority on another. This model illustrates that governments tend to be less economically based and are more responsive to political authority. Governments are about regulating markets and providing infrastructure (e.g., roads and bridges) in ways that are not addressed by either sector. Government entities are most directly influenced by the political context to achieve public value. This is characterized by elections that instill different leadership with different priorities. These priorities are translated into the other sectors, through regulations or laws but government entities enact those priorities and are constrained by political priorities in a way that is distinctive to that sector. Governments exist for broad public purposes and choices are informed by political influences that are institutionalized into bureaucracies and legislation.

Nonprofits are heterogeneous entities operating in multiple industries, with a myriad of purposes. In some ways this summary distills the stereotypical nature constrained by the legal requirements. It is difficult to define succinctly the logic of nonprofits. Several of the chapters in this book highlight these ideas and distill key features of the sector that require careful consideration in regards to preparing leaders. One option is to consider what nonprofits are not. There is an identifiable logic toward the market and a second that reflects state bureaucracies. Scholars have described the remaining logics as "professional," "religious," "family," "voluntary," or "democratic." Any of which might reflect some of how nonprofits frame their work. The logic of a nonprofit has to reflect a charitable or public benefit purposes, which is often articulated in the organization's mission. These charitable purposes are expressed through the mission and articulated in values that form the core of why the organization exists. The nature and character of those values reflect why the nonprofit exists. The translation of values into management practices is difficult and influenced by both economic and political forces.

Competing institutional logics are the reality for most managers (Mitchell, 2016). DiMaggio (1991) explored the different logics that exist in art museums; one related to artistic concerns of creativity and freedom of expression and the other to administrative concerns related to institutional sustainability. Stone (1996) also provides a case study to explore how different institutional logics developed in a social service agency that grew from a small grassroots entity into a multi-million-dollar enterprise that was contracting with the state to provide social services. These conflicting logics ultimately lead to a split in the organization. There is growing research on hybrid organizations that recognize the need to understand and coordinate different logics. For example, microfinance organizations often have to balance the development (nonprofit) logic with the banking or capitalistic logic (Battilana & Dorado, 2010). There must be some system in place to protect the tendency to exploit a profit when markets are unable to control this behavior. One of the fundamental challenges for nonprofit managers is creating and reinforcing organizational systems that support a values perspective (Bushouse, 2011). Ideally nonprofit leaders create structures and institutional logics that promote impact and social value over financial returns (Bernardin, 1999; Place, 2007).

Summary

These organizations operate in between economically oriented enterprises and state bureaucracies. They exist to fulfill public purposes but are private entities created by individuals and groups to achieve objectives defined by those individuals. Nonprofits are ownerless, rely on multiple revenue sources, and operate in a "failed" market to achieve public benefits. Mission becomes a defining rationale for these organizations because it is one way to solidify what they are doing. Therefore, the mission is fundamental to distinguishing the nonprofit. The mission is more than a marketing tool; it is central to who the organization is. The mission can distill the primary institutional logic and purpose of the organization. Without a hard and fast financial "bottom-line," which reflects an economic logic; nonprofits seek performance indicators that are more elusive. Academic theory has not resolved all the dilemmas associated with nonprofits. The standard economic model does not apply well to the distinctive nonmarket situation of nonprofit organizations (Helmig, Jegers, & Lapsley, 2004). Public models as well fall short of fully informing nonprofit practice. Market and consumer-oriented logics provide some insight and consequently the need to refine and build systems as well as professionals remains pressing. This edited volume is another contribution to understanding how to prepare leaders for these complex, multifaceted organizations.

References

Anheier, H. K. (2014). *Nonprofit Organizations: Theory, Management, Policy*. London: Routledge.

Battilana, J., & Dorado, S. (2010). Building Sustainable Hybrid Organizations: The Case of Commercial Microfinance Organizations. *Academy of Management Journal, 53*(6), 1419–1440.

Bernardin, J. C. (1999). Making the Case for Not-for-Profit Health Care. In *Celebrating the Ministry of Healing* (pp. 83–93). St. Louis: Catholic Health Association of the United States.

Billis, D. (2010). Towards a Theory of Hybrid Organizations. In D. Billis (ed.) *Hybrid Organizations and the Third Sector: Challenges for Practice, Theory and Policy* (pp. 46–69). New York: Palgrave Macmillan.

Bowman, W. (2002). The Uniqueness of Nonprofit Finance and the Decision to Borrow. *Nonprofit Management and Leadership, 12*(3), 293–311. doi: https://doi.org/10.1002/nml.12306

Bowman, W. (2011). *Finance Fundamentals for Nonprofits*. Hoboken, NJ: Wiley.

Bozeman, B. (2007). *Public Values and Public Interest: Counterbalancing Economic Individualism*. Washington, DC: Georgetown University Press.

Bryson, J. M., Crosby, B. C., & Stone, M. M. (2006). The Design and Implementation of Cross-Sector Collaborations: Propositions from the Literature. *Public Administration Review, 66*, 44–55. doi:10.1111/j.1540-6210.2006.00665.x

Bushouse, B. K. (2011). Governance Structures: Using IAD to Understand Variation in Service Delivery for Club Goods with Information Asymmetry. *Policy Studies Journal, 39*(1), 105–119. doi:10.1111/j.1541-0072.2010.00398.x

Candler, G., & Dumont, G. (2010). A Non-Profit Accountability Framework. *Canadian Public Administration, 53*(2), 259–279. doi:10.1111/j.1754-7121.2010.00126.x

Clark, M. S., & Mills, J. (1979). Interpersonal Attraction in Exchange and Communal Relationships. *Journal of Personality and Social Psychology, 37*(1), 12–24. doi:10.1037/0022-3514.37.1.12

Connelly, B., Tihanyi, L., Certo, S.T., & Hitt, M.A. (2010). Marching to the Beat of Different Drummers: Their Influence of Institutional Owners on Competitive Actions. *Academy of Management Journal, 53*(4), 723–742.

Crossland, C., & Hambrick, D. C. (2011). Differences in Managerial Discretion across Countries: How Nation-Level Institutions Affect the Degree to Which CEOs matter. *Strategic Management Journal, 32*(8), 797–819. doi:10.1002/smj.913

DiMaggio, P. J. (1991). Constructing an Organizational Field as a Professional Project: US Art Museums, 1920–1940. In W. W. Powell & P. J. DiMaggio (Eds.), *The New Institutionalism in Organizational Analysis* (pp. 267–292). Chicago: University of Chicago.

Fama, E. F., & Jenson, M. C. (1983). Separation of Ownership and Control. *Journal of Law & Economics, 26*(June), 301–326. Retrieved from www.jstor.org/stable/725104

Froelich, K. A. (1999). Diversification of Revenue Strategies: Evolving Resource Dependence in Nonprofit Organizations. *Nonprofit and Voluntary Sector Quarterly, 28*(3), 246–268. doi:10.1177/0899764099283002

Frumkin, P. (2009). *On Being Nonprofit: A Conceptual and Policy Primer*. Cambridge, MA: Harvard University Press.

Gümüsay, A. A., Smets, M., & Morris, T. (2020). "God at Work": Engaging Central and Incompatible Institutional Logics through Elastic Hybridity. *Academy of Management Journal, 63*(1), 124–154. doi:10.5465/amj.2016.0481

Hansmann, H. (2000). *The Ownership of Enterprise*. Cambridge: Harvard University Press.

Hasenfeld, Y. (2009). *Human Service Organizations* (2nd Ed.): Los Angeles, CA: Sage Publications.

Helmig, B., Jegers, M., & Lapsley, I. (2004). Challenges in Managing Nonprofit Organizations: A Research Overview. *Voluntas: International Journal of Voluntary and Nonprofit Organizations, 15*(2), 101–116.

Mak, Y. T., & Li, Y. (2001). Determinants of Corporate Ownership and Board Structure: Evidence from Singapore. *Journal of Corporate Finance, 7*(3), 235–256. doi: https://doi.org/10.1016/S0929-1199(01)00021-9

Mikołajczak, P. (2020). Social Enterprises' Hybridity in the Concept of Institutional Logics: Evidence from Polish NGOs. *Voluntas: International Journal of Voluntary and Nonprofit Organizations, 31*(3), 472–483. doi:10.1007/s11266-020-00195-9

Mitchell, G. E. (2016). Modalities of Managerialism: The "Double Bind" of Normative and Instrumental Nonprofit Management Imperatives. *Administration & Society, 50*(7), 1037–1068. doi:10.1177/0095399716664832

Mullins, D. (2006). Competing Institutional Logics? Local Accountability and Scale and Efficiency in an Expanding Non-Profit Housing Sector. *Public Policy and Administration, 21*(3), 6–24. Retrieved from http://ppa.sagepub.com.lib-ezproxy.tamu.edu:2048/content/21/3/6.full.pdf

Place, M., D. (2007). *The Importance of Not for Profit Health Care*. 13th Annual Conference on Catholic Sponsorship. Speech. Center for Catholic Health Care and Sponsorship, Loyola University, Chicago.

Rosko, M. D., Jon, A. C., Zinn, J. S., & Aaronson, W. E. (1995). The Effects of Ownership, Operating Environment, and Strategic Choices on Nursing Home Efficiency. *Medical Care, 33*(10), 1001–1021. doi:10.2307/3766674

Salamon, L. M. (1994). The Rise of the Nonprofit Sector. *Foreign Affairs, 73*(4), 109–122.

Schatteman, A. M., & Waymire, T. R. (2017). The State of Nonprofit Finance Research across Disciplines. *Nonprofit Management and Leadership, 28*(1), 125–137. doi: https://doi.org/10.1002/nml.21269

Skelcher, C., & Smith, S. R. (2015). Theorizing Hybridity: Institutional Logics, Complex Organizations, and Actor Identities: The Case of Nonprofits. *Public Administration, 93*(2), 433–448. doi: https://doi.org/10.1111/padm.12105

Sloan, F. A. (2000). Chapter 21 Not-for-profit ownership and hospital behavior. *Handbook of Health Economics*, 1, 1141–1174: *Elsevier.*

Stone, M. M. (1996). Competing Contexts: The Evolution of a Nonprofit Organization's Governance System in Multiple Environments. *Administration & Society, 28*(1), 61. Retrieved from http://aas.sagepub.com.lib-ezproxy.tamu.edu:2048/content/28/1/61.full.pdf; http://aas.sagepub.com/content/28/1/61.full.pdf

Tacon, R., Walters, G., & Cornforth, C. (2017). Accountability in Nonprofit Governance: A Process-Based Study. *Nonprofit and Voluntary Sector Quarterly, 46*(4), 685–704. doi:10.1177/0899764017691637

Thornton, P. H., & Ocasio, W. (2008). Institutional Logics. In R. Greenwood, C. Oliver, K. Sahlin, & R. Suddaby (Eds.), *Sage Handbook of Organizational Institutionalism* (pp. 99–129). Thousand Oaks: Sage.

TOMS Company Overview. (2020). Retrieved from www.toms.com/corporate-info

Yan, W., Denison, D.V., & Butler, J. S. (2009). Revenue Structure and Nonprofit Borrowing. *Public Finance Review, 37*(1), 47–67. doi:10.1177/1091142108321239

Young, M. N., Peng, M. W., Ahlstrom, D., Bruton, G. D., & Jiang, Y. (2008). Corporate Governance in Emerging Economies: A Review of the Principal–Principal Perspective. *Journal of Management Studies, 45*(1), 196–220. doi:10.1111/j.1467-6486.2007.00752.x

3

UNDERSTANDING THE IMPACT OF POLITICAL POLARIZATION ON NONPROFIT AND PHILANTHROPIC PROGRAMS

Matthew Hale

Introduction

It is somewhat difficult to understate the massive upheavals taking place in the world of the last six years (2016–2022). While the Covid-19 global pandemic rightly took center stage, it always came with a belief and hope that one day it would end, and life would go back to something resembling the old normal. In contrast, the concurrent disruptions of polarized electorates and controversial leaders worldwide (the United States, Britain, Brazil, Israel, Austria, France, India all being prime examples) may ultimately have longer lasting impact on national and international organizations. In the United States, the insurrection on the US capital by supporters of President Donald Trump on January 6, 2021 and the Summer 2020 social movements and protester occupation of Portland, Oregon caused by the deaths of several African Americans at the hands of law enforcement, serve as vivid examples of the political, economic, and social divisions that exist in the United States. These divisions promise to reshape the social and political landscape long after Covid-19 fades into the history books.

Examining how these disruptions and upheavals will reshape society has become a virtual cottage industry. Certainly, this chapter will not attempt to replicate those efforts. However, the political polarization, the disruptions and calls for meaningful social and racial justice progress within the larger society, present those leading nonprofit academic programs with opportunities but also at times daunting and unprecedented challenges. Some of these challenges, pre-date the current political tensions but others have come to a head because of them.

The goal of this chapter is twofold. First, to identify ways that this social and political upheaval is manifesting itself in nonprofit academic programs. Second, to

DOI: 10.4324/9781003294061-4

suggest strategies and mechanisms that may help leaders of these program manage these turbulent times.

Political Polarization and Institutional Decline

There is little doubt that political polarization is a global phenomenon. Evidence from recent elections is emblematic of divided publics around the world. In 2020, the US Presidential election brought more people to the polls than ever before and while the Electoral college and even popular vote was not ultimately particularly close, the division within the American society remains clear. In Israel, the inability of any party to form a long lasting and stable parliamentary coalition led to an unprecedented four elections in less than three years. In Great Britain, social and economic division regarding their relationship with Europe, known as Brexit, was decided by less than a million votes out of almost 34 million cast, and ultimately led to a change in government leadership.

While polarization is a worldwide phenomenon, polling data from The Pew Research Center seems to suggest that the gap between liberals and conservatives, Democrats and Republicans is as deep seated and pernicious in America as it is elsewhere. So much so that Pew has called political polarization the "defining feature of American politics today" (Pew, 2014) (see www.pewresearch.org/topics/political-polarization/). A wide variety of Pew Research studies document this divide on traditional political questions such as Presidential approval ratings,[1] assessments of the news media,[2] and congressional leadership.[3]

However, additional Pew studies suggest that the deep partisan divide separating Americans on electoral politics goes beyond politics. For example, one Pew study found that

> Roughly four-in-ten registered voters in both camps say that they do not have a single close friend who supports the other major party candidate.[4]

Another Pew study found that

> Roughly eight-in-ten of those who support Biden (80%) and Trump (77%) say they fundamentally disagree about core values; only about one-in-five say their differences are limited to politics and policies.[5]

We have, of course, even seen wide partisan differences in responses to Covid-19 vaccines, masks, and opening of public schools.[6]

It is clearly troubling that this political divide exists at all. However, it is even more disconcerting that further studies from Pew suggest that these differences are ossifying and that they are ossifying[7] along racial and gender lines.[8]

Interestingly, one area where Americans find some common ground is the belief that as an institution higher education is in trouble. In 2019, The Pew Research

Center found that just 50% of the respondents felt that Higher Education was a positive influence on society. Almost four out of 10 respondents (38%) felt that institutions of higher education make a negative contribution to society.[9]

According to the study, while both Democrats and Republicans seem to increasingly hold negative views of higher education, why they hold these beliefs is different. Republicans who hold negative views of higher education most often cite the liberal bias of colleges as the primary reason. In contrast, Democrats tend to site the ever-increasing costs of higher education as their reason for viewing it negatively.

Polarization within Academia

The polarization in the larger society is no doubt taking place on college campuses, among, faculty, students, administrators, alumni, donors, and executive board members. It is rare that the politics of academia are portrayed in popular entertainment. However, the recent Netflix television show "*The Chair*" serves as some indication that social, class, age, and partisan divides and differences in approaches are real enough to warrant treatment in popular entertainment television. The program details the machinations of a new young department chair of an old and dying English Department. The series touches on many of the points I raise below, in particular tensions between faculty members in terms of politics but also in terms of race, gender, age, and most importantly perceptions about the value of long-standing institutions and management processes to the academic endeavor.

While I touch on many of these tensions below, the focus of this chapter is on two of these key tensions or poles within academia. The first is political divisions and specifically political divisions within the left or democratic end of the political spectrum. The reason for this focus is because, as we will see, that is where most people working in academia lie politically. There are clearly professors and certainly administrators who are Republican partisans, but they are the minority on most campuses. Focusing on this slice of the political spectrum also clearly dovetails with the second major tension in the chapter, namely differences between institutional/managerial approaches and critical theory approaches to the academic enterprise. In short, I argue that the tensions within the left/Democratic Party mirror tensions in the institutional/critical theory divide and that these are central tensions within academia writ large but also within our field of nonprofit management and philanthropic studies.

It is important to point out that these are not the only set of fault lines. In particular, as we see in *The Chair*, many of the division I discuss fall along age, race, and gender lines as well. Older, whiter, and more male professors and administrators who have always thought of themselves as generally progressive on a wide range of issues are increasingly finding themselves as uncomfortable defenders of the institutional status quo. Similarly younger professors and administrators who are more diverse in terms of race and gender, often see themselves as having moral responsibility to challenge and think critically about the institutional status quo. So while I have chosen to focus on the political and institutional divisions in this chapter it is important recognize that these other fault lines exist alongside those discussed in this chapter.

We Lean Left and It Is Ok

For many, the people working at and attending college and universities define the so-called "liberal-elite."The research on political viewpoints of professors seems to confirm this but offers some important caveats. A 2016 study (Langbert, Quain, & Klein, 2016) of 40 universities found that Democrats outnumbered Republicans 11.5 to 1. This ratio, however, varies by discipline with it dropping to 4.5 to 1 in economics departments and jumping to 33.5 to 1 in History departments. Similar findings from the Higher Education Research Institute and reported by Sarah Lawrence Professor Samuel Abrams suggest that this gap has steadily increased over time (Abrams, 2016). Interestingly, Abrams found the gap in New England colleges and universities at 28 to 1 compared to 6 to 1 nationally. Additional research on top universities in all 50 states by Langbert and Stevens (2020) suggests faculty members not only register as Democrats more but donate more to democratic campaigns. While it might be possible to quibble with the details, it seems that the premise that there are more left/Democrats than Right/Republicans among the faculty, staff, and administrators on college and universities is not a particularly controversial one.

However, I would suggest that within the seemingly "liberal" leaning professoriate there is a growing tension and divide that echoes a larger divide on the American left and the Democratic Party specifically. This is the growing division between centrist democrats and the progressive democrats. For reasons we will discuss later on it is this nuanced tension that will present significant challenges to nonprofit center directors, academic program directors, and department chairs. Before turning to this, however, it is important to note that the Republican side of the aisle may be as divided, if not more divided, than the Democrats. Trump Republicans and traditional Republicans are clearly two distinct and divided factions with the Grand Old Party (GOP). However, those divisions are less likely to play a role in the successful management of academic programs, hence the focus on the democratic divide.

Democrat vs. Democrat: Understanding the Fault Lines

To begin, it is also important to point out that the decision to use the term "Democrat" is more out of convenience than strict adherence or allegiance to the Democratic Political Party. It is also important to remember the truth behind two famous sayings about democrats. The first is from actor Will Rodgers who is widely quoted as saying "*I am not a member of any organized political party... I am a Democrat.*" The second is attributed to many people but most recently to Bill Clinton; "*Democrats need to fall in love; Republicans fall in line.*" The underlying truth behind each of these statements is that by history and perhaps by nature Democrats are less uniform in thought and less disciplined in action than Republicans.

There are many ways of looking at the divide and tensions within the Democratic Party. Some of the most interesting work in this area comes from popular pollsters such as 538 and Real Clear Politics. In an article entitled "*Why the Progressive Left Fits So Uncomfortably within the Democratic Party*" (2020). FiveThirtyEight writer and Data for Progress fellow Shom Mazumber uses principal component analysis and raw poll results to identify the fault lines within the Democratic Party. Mazumber explores the clustering of favorability rating of various actors within the Democratic Party. He identifies two clear clusters (the Establishment and the Progressive Left). He also found a third group, which he calls the Neoliberals. In the Establishment group, the higher favorability ratings clustered around party leaders such as Chuck Schumer, Nancy Pelosi, Barak Obama, and The Democratic National Committee. In the Progressive cluster, the greatest favorability ratings clustered around Alexandria Ocasio-Cortez, Black Lives Matter, Labor Unions, and the Democratic Socialists of America. While less strong, the third cluster centered on positive connections to Wall Street, (Conservative) Democratic senator Joe Manchin, The Ivy League, and Facebook.

This research suggests that one way of looking at the divide within the Democratic Party is through the lens of institutional support. In the establishment group and the neoliberal group there is (not surprisingly) a greater tendency to identify with and think positively toward individuals supported by existing institutions or those institutions themselves (Chuck Schumer, the DNC, and the Ivy League). In contrast, the progressive group identifies with those who challenge institutions (Ocasio-Cortez) or organizations acting outside the existing institutional structures (Black Lives Matter [BLM] and the Democratic Socialists of America [DSA]). There is a fair amount of research documenting a significant decline in the power of and trust in political institutions broadly (Gecan, 2018; Levinsky & Ziblatt, 2018; Klinenberg, 2019). This same work also shows that declining trust in institutions is not surprisingly mirrored by a greater willingness to openly question the processes of democratic institutions. So, in addition, to questioning Congress as an institution and institutional party leaders there is also a rising number of progressives who question the validity of traditional democratic processes and question the validity of things like the filibuster, seniority, single choice voting, life-time term limits for the Supreme Court and the Electoral college.

It is important to recognize that the framing of polarization in terms of institutional support and willingness to challenge or question the validity of institutional processes is not solely limited to the left/democratic side of the political spectrum. It is possible to argue that the same divisions are occurring on the right. As we saw in the January 6th attacks on the US capital clearly segments of the far right are as willing if not more willing than progressives to engage in serious challenges to existing institutions. The focus on left is simply because that side of the political spectrum serves as a more relevant heuristic in an academic setting.

How Institution Support Differences Matter

As a program director or administrator, it is helpful to develop heuristics to help us understand our environment. I suggest that the divide between democrats and how it relates to institutional support that is outlined above is happening in a non-political context of academic administration and program management. As such it is a useful heuristic to explore more deeply.

It is not hard to see how the tension between support and rejection of institutions and institutional figures within left/Democratic politics might plays itself out in the academic management of centers and programs. Just as Establishment Democrats support establishment leaders like Chuck Schumer and Nancy Pelosi, there are likely to be program stakeholders who support and show deference to institutional personnel, people like chairpersons, leaders within an academic senate, deans, provosts. Similarly, it seems that this group will be more likely to support ancillary academic institutions, like accrediting agencies or national associations. Finally, it is possible that this cluster of establishment academic stakeholders will support existing processes of the academy, things like tenure, the dissertation granting process, deference to established publishing venues, and traditional classroom lecture pedagogy.

In contrast, within the same academic enterprise, there are likely to be a cluster of individuals who are less tied or interested in supporting existing institutional structures. They are more likely to oppose and confront the directions from institutional leaders, question the value of accrediting associations, and more likely to challenge the traditional oversight process mechanisms within academia. For example, this group might be more likely to recognize and validate the transfer of scholarly knowledge outside of the traditional journal peer review process. This group might be more inclined to support and recognize service contributions to communities outside the university and not just within it. When it comes to institutional support and involvement with existing institutions a slightly different dynamic may occur. Institutional skeptics seem to either shun active participation within existing institutions or attempt to take them over in an attempt to redirect them to their liking (see Table 3.1).

TABLE 3.1 Institutional Supporters vs. Institutional Skeptics

Factors	*Institutional Supporters*	*Institutional Skeptics*
Leadership	Defer to Department Chairs, Deans, and University Administration	Argue with Department Chairs, Deans, and University Administration
Processes	Favor tenure, dissertation processes, traditional publish venues, accreditation, and traditional teaching pedagogy	Question and challenge process of tenure, dissertation processing, publishing, accreditation, and teaching
Institutions/ Structure	Support and play active roles in academic governance, national organizations, accrediting agencies	Dismiss, ignore, or attempt to take over these institutions

Managerialism/Establishment Democrats vs. Critical Theorists/Progressive Democrats

The political division described above may also be playing itself out another central tension within our field. This tension is between those who propose and advocate for a managerial, rationalist, capitalist, and business centric approach (Bishop & Green, 2009; Buchanon & Walker, 2018; Blessett, Gaynor, Witt, & Alkadry, 2016; Evans, Richmond, & Shields, 2005; Jenkins & Nowell, 2010; Salm & Ordway, 2010; Zanetti & Adams, 2000) to the nonprofit enterprise and those that argue the future of the field should move toward critical theorist, radical democracy, anti-capitalist, and the implementation of social justice frameworks (Mirabella & Nguyen, 2019; Giridharadas, 2018; Eikenberry, 2009; Eikenberry & Kluver, 2004; Eikenberry & Mirabella, 2018; Graefe, 2006; Hasenfeld & Garrow, 2012; Hvenmark, 2013; Maier, Meyer, & Steinbereithner, 2016; Mirabella, 2013; Nickel & Eikenberry, 2009; Sandberg, 2013).

In this volume, we have two excellent chapters discussing both perspectives. Fischer and Mayer focus on Managerialism. Mirabella, Nguyen, and Feit take a Critical Theory Perspective. As you review them both, notice how the authors frame the perspectives is reminiscent of the preferences identified in Table 3.1 toward institutions, process, and leadership.

Mangerialism/Establishment Democrats

Fischer and Mayer provide multiple definitions and approaches to understanding the concept of managerialism. One component of the definition is that managerialism requires that a great deal of faith and trust be placed in the manager. They cite Edwards (1998) and say that a central part of managerialism is…

> faith in the techniques of management science to resolve organizational problems, class consciousness among managers, and the belief in the manager

> as a moral agent seeking actions in accordance with the greatest good for society.

In essence then, managerialism requires that a high level of trust if not deference is given to the leaders and managers of an institution. This is not to say the manager is always "right" simply that the starting point of a managerialist framework is that manager is given the authority and autonomy to make the "best" decisions. However, the ideology of managerialism expands beyond support to managers but to support institutions and organizations.

> However, the ideology does not only function on managers, rather, it seeks to facilitate public belief in management. In this way, managerialism addresses the question of why organizational members, with the resources to resist the attainment of organizational goals, generally follow management.

Throughout the chapter, Fischer and Mayer describe the processes of managerialism as focused on "*efficiency*" and "*rationality*." They trace the lineage of managerialism to concepts of "*scientific management*." They argue that "*outcomes*" are the guiding goal of a managerial approach. These frames all focus on the attempt to systematize decision-making by managers of an organization on what is perceived as "*objective*" facts and processes.

When taking managerialism's implied trust in the leadership and management and the belief in process objectivity and "best practices" Fischer and Mayer cite Klikhauer (2013) as they describe managerialism as an ideology which permits

> technocratic managers to centralize decision making power.

Taken together, these examples suggest that a managerial approach to some extent requires a degree of trust in institutional leaders, institutional processes, and at a minimum tacit support for existing institutional structures. While there are of course exceptions, these structures tend to be hierarchical with ultimate decision-making authority residing in the University Administration and academic leadership. In essence then, it seems quite reasonable to argue that the managerial approach and the traditional, centrist, institutionalist democrat approach are quite similar. The same deference to centralized authority, trust in time tested processes, incrementalism, and desire for rationality that we see argued by centrist democrats is also evident in managerial approaches to public and nonprofit management education.

It is important to recognize that Fischer and Mayer and others rightly point to ways that as strictly conceived the managerial approach is imperfect when strictly applied to nonprofit enterprises. They point out that the diversity of the nonprofit sector strains the universalist conception of management. They also suggest that primacy of efficient outcomes and the moral agency given to managers in managerialism may be incomplete when applied to the nonprofit sector. In part, perhaps because of the inadequacies a great deal of attention has recently focused on alternative visions to the nonprofit teaching, namely critical theory approaches. We turn to those next.

Critical Theory/Progressive Democrats

As mentioned earlier, this volume has an excellent chapter on critical theory from Mirabella, Nguyen, and Feit. In it and in other writing, we can see several examples of how a critical theory approach to the field has tendency to challenge existing institutions in favor of reformulating them in less hegemonic, less patriarchal, and perhaps more democratic ways. In fact, by definition, a critical theory perspective on virtually anything, directly challenges that power and structure of existing institutions. In fact, the Stanford Encyclopedia of Philosophy uses the following definition.

> **Critical theory** is an approach to social philosophy that focuses on reflective assessment and critique of society and culture in order to reveal and challenge power structures.
>
> *Bohman, 2021*

When critical theory perspectives are used and explained within the context of nonprofit management education we see a similar attempt to frame the field in opposition to the existing institutional power structures. Eikenberry, Mirabella and Sandberg (2019) define "critical" as an effort

> ...to dig beneath the surface of (often hidden) historically specific, social structures and processes – such as those related to politics, economics, culture, discourse, gender, and race – to illuminate how they lead to oppression and then to also reveal ways to change these structures.
>
> *Eikenberry, Mirabella, & Sandberg, 2019*

The same authors defined the critical approach to nonprofits as

> ...a perspective that considers nonprofit and voluntary organizations and their management within the context of historically specific social structures and processes – such as those related to politics, economics, culture, discourse, gender, and race – and the political and changeable nature of these perspectives
>
> *Eikenberry, Mirabella, & Sandberg, 2019*

As with managerialism there is an important caveat and nuance. Critical theory perspectives do not appear to be against all institutions for all times. Instead, critical theory is generally conceptualized as critical of neoliberalism and the institutions created by neoliberalism. It seems likely that if institutional structures were created in more egalitarian and equitable ways and run similarly, they could be seen as acceptable to critical theorists.

In some ways part of the fundamental appeal and argument made by critical theory advocates is that managerialism (and neoliberalism) as an ideology and as a practice is contrary to the unique nature of the nonprofit enterprise. Mirabella and her colleagues cite Hvenmark (2013) to explain that by adopting the practices of managerialism nonprofits and civil society organizations,

> run the risk not only of losing track of their mission and goals, but also of losing touch with the values of democracy, solidarity, voluntariness, and civic engagement, and thus of diluting their organizational distinctiveness.
>
> *Hvenmark, 2013, p. 228*

While the work on critical theory perspectives is vast, growing and diverse it is possible to identify three important through lines of the work. The first is the idea that existing institutional structures are socially constructed and that they are therefore subject to change. The second is that those existing social structures and institutions *should* be challenged and ultimately changed. The third is that those of us in the nonprofit world have an obligation to construct our enterprises in ways that bring about or facilitate this change.

One (hopefully entertaining) way of showing the linkages between the progressive wing of the Democratic Party and these core critical theory ideas is by pointing to quotes from one of the de facto leaders of the progressive movement in American politics Alexandria Ocasio-Cortez.

On the social construction of and changeability of institutions.

> Capitalism has not always existed in the world and will not always exist in the world.

On the pressing need to change those institutions

> We have a political culture of intimidation, of favoring, of patronage, and of fear, and that is no way for a community to be governed.

Since Representative Ocasio-Cortez rarely speaks about nonprofits we can substitute in the Democratic Party with this quote

> It's time we acknowledge that not all Democrats are the same. That a Democrat who takes corporate money, profits off foreclosure, doesn't live here, doesn't send his kids to our schools, doesn't drink our water or breathe our air cannot possibly represent us.

This chapter has to this point, identified the growth in political polarization in American politics and highlighted a growing divided within the left/Democratic side of the political spectrum. Then the divisions within the left/Democratic side of the political spectrum were mapped to different preferences toward institutions and institutional power. Next, we overlaid these political divisions to a fundamental debate in the nonprofit field, managerialism vs. critical perspectives. The hope is that taken together, this will provide an academic leader with a useful heuristic device for understanding their diverse constituencies. In the final section of the chapter, we suggest another broad heuristic for trying to manage these diverse approaches.

What Is an Administrator to Do?

As noted, the purpose of this chapter is not to choose sides in the debates outlined in it. Taking this neutral position is often a good start in academic administration. This is because academic administration, like nonprofit and public administration, can suffer from the inability to punish and reward workers in meaningful ways. In addition, leadership of academic departments and programs is often conceptualized as a rotation between colleagues and not as permanent position. Because of this, academic administrators (at least at the department or program level) serve as almost as volunteer coordinators who focus on keeping as many workers as possible happy and content. This makes picking sides in debates perhaps more difficult than in situations where leaders may have more formal power to sanction and reward.

So how might an administrator respond to a polarized situation like the one described above? One strategy is to identify challenges faced by both "sides" in this potential conflict and work collaboratively on those conflicts. By reframing these tensions in overtly political terms it is perhaps easier to identify gaps or weaknesses in each position, which provides the administrator a place to start.

Ask the Institutionalist Why

A fundamental weakness of institutionalist, traditionalists, and managerialists is that they take the existing structures of governance as given and in general assume they are useful. While there are any number of possible reasons for this, two stick out.

History

One possible reason for support of existing institutions is personal history. Many with the traditional perspective have benefitted over the course of their careers from the existing power dynamics and structures. In essence, the "system" has by and large worked toward their self-interest. If you are successful at traditional modes of scholarship transmission (peer-reviewed articles and books) it may not strike you that more non-traditional forms of public scholarship can or should be seen as valid modes of scholarship transmission. We can also look at the self-interest rationale in a somewhat less self-interested way. If you have spent your career producing scholarship that relies on a common understanding of the value of institutional structures or managerial methods those who seek to undue or break down institutional structures may be seen as undermining or seeking to eliminate this previous work. As a result, some may cling to institutional beliefs not just because they have benefited from them but because they have based their scholarship on the underpinnings of existing institutions.

Institutions/Managers "Work"

A second reason for maintaining a pro-institution/managerial perspective is that strong, well-run institutions can and do accomplish tasks in an efficient manner. In academic settings, time spent on administrative tasks is often seen as time NOT spend on the core tasks of research or teaching. As a result, there is perhaps a bias among many academics toward getting the administrative tasks done as quickly as possible so we can get back to the so-called important things, like research and teaching. There is little doubt or argument that hierarchical strong process driven organization can make decisions faster than other organizational forms. The speed and efficiency in decision-making has value to many administering in an academic setting. However, it is of course also true that *faster, more efficient* decisions do not necessarily equal *better or more sustainable* decisions. It is also true that "who" institutions work for is a primary critique of them posed by the progressive/critical theory perspective. With these caveats, it is still possible that support for institutions and managerialism is driven by the belief that they offer the best option for accomplishing goals and objectives.

Looking at the institutionalist perspective through this political and personal lens leads to a way of challenging or pushing against this perspective by an academic administrator. Challenging this belief may simply be a matter of asking "why"? Why is this structure the best way to reach our common goals? Why is this way we have organized ourselves as an organization? Why do you individually support the status quo? By asking institutional/managerialist to explain why in any context it is possible to move the conversation and discussion away from unconditional support for existing structures or systems to perhaps acknowledgement that as they exist institutions and managerialism can have significant flaws. In addition, asking these "why" questions can lead an institutionalist to confront how they may have individually benefitted from existing structures possibly to the detriment of others "outside" the existing system. Similarly, asking versions of the "who" question to institutionalists can help move them toward new thinking on institutional structures and processes. Questions such as "Who are we?," "Who do we want to be?," and to the critical theorist challenge "Who do we serve?" may also be framing questions for the administrator to ask of institutionalists.

Ask the Non-traditionalist How

If history and self-interest help explain a traditionalist position, they may also help explain some of motivations behind critical perspectives. Critical theory perspectives are based, at least in part, on the idea that existing systems and structures exclude or prevent those "outside" of them from participating equally from societal benefits. Often the critical perspectives are articulated by those who have been (or feel they have been) excluded based on their race, gender, class, or other characteristics. As a result, if a traditionalist supports the system because they have historically benefitted from it; a non-traditionalist may oppose the system because they or a group they care about have NOT benefitted from or been oppressed by the existing system. In the political context, Alexandria Ocasio-Cortez was an under-employed bartender prior to becoming a Congresswomen. She grew up far from power and privilege and with that perspective she argues that the existing "system" fails to provide her and people like her with their fair share of societies benefits. It is not surprising that her own self-interest and history leads her to argue for the dismantling of the existing institutions and power structures.

Interestingly, there may be common ground and agreement by both institutionalist and institutional critics on whether or not institutions work to deliver benefits. I would argue both would agree that a well-run, well-managed organization or institution has the capacity to accomplish goals and tasks for its constituencies. Even as critics of existing institutions called for their dismantling, they recognize that strong institutions deliver benefits to a constituency in very efficient ways. The argument for dismantling existing institutions isn't that they don't work, it is that they work at maintaining structural inequalities and oppression.

It is here where; there may have an opportunity to move past the existing debates. One area that the critical/progressive position struggles is in providing sufficient explanation of "how" new less oppressive institutional structures will operate or be created. If we require an institutionalist to defend the "why" organizations are structured as they are; we should ask those with critical approaches to articulate "how" new ways of organizational structure will form and lead to more equitable outcomes? It is insufficient for an institutionalist to answer the why questions by saying the system works efficiently. Similarly, it is not enough for a critical theorist to say the existing system is corrupt, without providing some conception about how new institutional structures will be created and lead to broader or more equitable distribution of benefits.

A Case Example: Revising the NACC Curricular Guidelines

An admittedly anecdotal example of this "why" and "how" dynamic comes from recent experience of updating the NACC curricular guidelines (see Appendix). The NACC curricular guidelines were originally created in 2003, revised in

2007, and again in 2015. Historically, the process for revising the guidelines was driven by a core group of leaders in the field and through their affiliation with NACC. These core leaders attempted to cast a wide net for input on revising the guidelines through their existing networks. Although many attempts were made throughout this process to reach out widely and broadly beyond NACC, they were only somewhat successful. It is not that anyone was intentionally excluded from participating in the process of guideline revision. However, it is clear that in practice the people who gave feedback into the process tended to be those from established institutions and organizations who had easy access to the review process through existing personal and professional networks. As NACC was moving toward another revision in 2017–2018, the same iterative outreach process was initially put in place. Had that process continued, it is my belief that there would have been an updated set of curricular guidelines unveiled at the 2019 NACC conference in London. In essence, the traditionalist/institutionalist approach would have successfully delivered an outcome of moderate or incremental change in a timely and efficient manner.

The process, however, did not continue as it had in prior years. The primary reason for this was a group NACC board members and outside constituents asked "why?" Why is NACC doing this revision process the same way we have historically done it? In addition, this group asked "who" have we missed in the process of curricula guidelines revisions?

Upon reflection (and to be clear some raised voices) the primary answers to the "why" question were often ones of efficiency and expedience. As an organization, NACC felt a responsibility to update guidelines in a timely manner. Doing that in a time tested and reliable manner made sense. The old processes led to a clear and predictable outcome in a reasonable (by academic standards) time frame. However, those answers of predictability and expedience ultimately felt insufficient and inadequate.

As a result, the curricular revision process stopped for almost a year. Admittedly that year coincided with the Covid-19 Pandemic. Even so, the process was brought back on track by asking the question of "how" should we go about revising the curricular guidelines? The process of articulating how the new revision process would be accomplished was the subject of panel presentations at Association for Research on Nonprofit Organizations and Voluntary Action (ARNOVA) and NACC conferences as well as significant committee meeting discussions. The discussion on curriculum guidelines was enveloped in part on broader efforts by NACC to examine ways it as an organization could improve on its diversity and inclusion efforts. But ultimately, a new process for curriculum revision has been articulated and continues to be implemented. The process among other things involves using a group of masters level capstone students to help research new approaches toward curriculum guidelines and significant additional outreach toward new stakeholders within the nonprofit academic world that have not been part of the previous curriculum guideline revisions. Ultimately, the new curricular guidelines will be born from a process that is far more inclusive, transparent, open, and ideally that will mean that the guidelines will be even more universally recognized as the benchmarks in the field. However, that process will take time and a significant amount of effort.

This admittedly brief example shows a pathway for challenging both institutionalist and critics of institutions using the why and how heuristic. It also shows that managing and perhaps merging these two diverse perspectives can be a difficult and time-consuming process. On one hand there is no doubt that the traditional revision processes would have led to a faster and more efficient outcome. On the other hand, there is no doubt that the new process will lead to a more inclusive, comprehensive, and perhaps more sustainable outcome.

As we confront more tensions in our society and in our organizations like the ones articulated in this chapter we will continually struggle to identify where the balance is between getting something done and getting something done in an equitable and fair manner. Academic management of nonprofit programs and in fact leadership of nonprofit organizations has always been a matter of trying to apply strategies of "Yes/And" instead of "Either/Or." Asking the "why" to institutionalist and the "how" to critical theorist is one way of trying to live up to that ideal.

Notes

1 "Trump's Approval ratings so far unusually stable – and deeply partisan" Pew Research Center (August 24, 2020) www.pewresearch.org/fact-tank/2020/08/24/trumps-approval-ratings-so-far-are-unusually-stable-and-deeply-partisan/
2 "Partisans remain sharply divided in many views toward the news media" Pew Research Center (August 21, 2020) www.journalism.org/2020/08/31/partisans-remain-sharply-divided-in-many-views-toward-the-news-media-stark-differences-between-trumps-strongest-supporters-critics/
3 "Voters view of McConnel and Schumer are Negative and deeply divided by partisanship" Pew Research Center (October 12, 2020) www.pewresearch.org/fact-tank/2020/10/12/voters-views-of-mcconnell-and-schumer-are-negative-and-deeply-divided-by-partisanship/
4 "Few Trump or Biden supporters have close friends who back the opposing candidate" Pew Research Center (September 18, 2020) www.pewresearch.org/fact-tank/2020/09/18/few-trump-or-biden-supporters-have-close-friends-who-back-the-opposing-candidate/
5 "Amid Campaign Turmoil, Biden Holds Wide Leads on Coronavirus, Unifying the Country" Pew Research Center (October 9, 2020) www.pewresearch.org/politics/2020/10/09/amid-campaign-turmoil-biden-holds-wide-leads-on-coronavirus-unifying-the-country/
6 "Intent to Get a COVID-19 Vaccine Rises to 60% as Confidence in Research and Development Process Increases" Pew Research Center (December 3, 2020) www.pewresearch.org/science/2020/12/03/intent-to-get-a-covid-19-vaccine-rises-to-60-as-confidence-in-research-and-development-process-increases/#republicans-and-democrats-differ-over-outbreaks-threat-to-public-health

7 "In Changing U.S. Electorate, Race and Education Remain Stark Dividing Lines" Pew Research Center (June 2, 2020) www.pewresearch.org/politics/2020/06/02/in-changing-u-s-electorate-race-and-education-remain-stark-dividing-lines/
8 "Voters Rarely Switch Parties, but Recent Shifts Further Educational, Racial Divergence." Pew Research Center (August 4, 2020) www.pewresearch.org/politics/2020/08/04/voters-rarely-switch-parties-but-recent-shifts-further-educational-racial-divergence/
9 "The Growing Partisan Divide in Views of Higher Education" Pew Research Center" Pew Research Center (August 19, 2019) www.pewresearch.org/social-trends/2019/08/19/the-growing-partisan-divide-in-views-of-higher-education-2/

References

Abrams, S. J. (2016) "Professors Moved Left Since 1990s, Rest of Country Did Not." Heterodox Academy. https://heterodoxacademy.org/professors-moved-left-but-country-did-not (accessed December 2020). Google Scholar.

Bishop, M., & Greene, M. (2009). Philanthrocapitalism: How Giving Can Save the World. New York: Bloomsbury Press.

Blessett, B., Gaynor, T. S., Witt, M., & Alkadry, M. G. (2016). Counternarratives as critical perspectives in public administration curriculum. Administrative Theory and Praxis, 38(4), 267–284.

Bohman, J. (2021). "Critical theory", The Stanford Encyclopedia of Philosophy (Spring 2021 Edition), Edward N. Zalta (ed.). https://plato.stanford.edu/archives/spr2021/entries/critical-theory.

Buchanon, P., & Walker D. (2018). Giving Done Right: Effective Philanthropy and Making Every Dollar Count. New York: Hachette Book Group.

Edwards, J. D. (1998). Managerial influences in public administration. International Journal of Organization Theory & Behavior, 1(4), 553–583. https://doi.org/10.1108/IJOTB-01-04-1998-B007

Eikenberry, A. M. (2009). Refusing the market: A democratic discourse for voluntary and nonprofit organizations. Nonprofit and Voluntary Sector Quarterly, 38(4), 582–596.

Eikenberry, A. M., & Kluver, J. D. (2004). The marketization of the nonprofit sector: Civil society at risk? Public Administration Review, 64(2), 132–140.

Eikenberry, A. M., & Mirabella, R. M. (2018). Extreme philanthropy: Philanthrocapitalism, effective altruism, and the discourse of neoliberalism. PS: Political Science and Politics, 51(1), 43–47.

Eikenberry, A. M., Mirabella, R. M., & Sandberg, B. (2019). Reframing Nonprofit Management: Democracy, Inclusion and Social Change. Irvine, CA: Melvin and Leigh, Publishers.

Evans, B., Richmond, T., & Shields, J. (2005). Structuring neoliberal governance: The nonprofit sector, emerging new modes of control and the marketisation of service delivery. Policy and Society, 24(1), 73–97.

Gecan, M. (2018). People's Institutions in Decline. Chicago, IL: ATCA Publishers.

Giridharadas, A. (2018). Winners Take All: The Elite Charade of Changing the World. New York: Knopf.

Graefe, P. (2006). Social economy policies as flanking for neoliberalism: Transnational policy solutions, emergent contradictions, local alternatives. Policy and Society, 25(3), 69–86.

Hasenfeld, Y., & Garrow, E. E. (2012). Nonprofit human-service organizations, social rights, and advocacy in a neoliberal welfare state. Social Service Review, 86(2), 295–322.

Hvenmark, J. (2013). Business as usual? On managerialization and the adoption of the balanced scorecard in a democratically governed civil society organization. Administrative Theory and Praxis, 35(2), 223–247.

Jenkins, P., & Nowell, B. (2010). Humanistic perspectives on the policy and praxis of disaster management: Reflections on Freire and recovery post-Katrina. Administrative Theory and Praxis, 32(3), 431–437.

Klikauer, T. (2013). Managerialism. Hampshire, UK: Palgrave Macmillan. https://doi.org/10.1057/9781137334275

Klinenberg, E. (2019). Palaces for the People. New York, NY: Penguin Random House.

Langbert, M., Quain, A., & Klein, D. (2016). Faculty voter registration in economic, history. Journalism, Law and Psychology Econ Journal Watch, 13(3), 422–451.

Langbert M., & Stevens S. (2020). "Partisan Registration and Contributions of Faculty at Flagship Colleges". National Association of Scholars (January 17). www.nas.org/blogs/article/partisan-registration-and-contributions-of-faculty-in-flagship-colleges.

Levinsky, S., & Ziblatt, D. (2018). How Democracies Die. New York, NY: Crown.

Maier, F., Meyer, M., & Steinbereithner, M. (2016). Nonprofit organizations becoming business-like: A systematic review. Nonprofit and Voluntary Sector Quarterly, 45(1), 64–86.

Mazumber, S. (2020). "Why the Progressive Left Fits So Uncomfortably Within the Democratic Party". FiveThirtyEight Blog. https://fivethirtyeight.com/features/why-the-progressive-left-fits-so-uncomfortably-within-the-democratic-party.

Mirabella, R. (2013). Toward a more perfect nonprofit. Administrative Theory and Praxis, 35(1), 81–105.

Mirabella, R. & Nguyen, K. (2019). Educating nonprofit students as agents of social transformation: Critical public administration as a way forward. Administrative Theory and Praxis, 41(4), 388–404.

Nickel, P. M., & Eikenberry, A. M. (2009). A critique of the discourse of marketized philanthropy. American Behavioral Scientist, 52(7), 974–989.

Salm, J., & Ordway, J. L. (2010). New perspectives in public administration: A political process of education and leadership through mediation. Administrative Theory and Praxis, 32(3), 438–444.

Sandberg, B. (2013). The road to market. Administrative Theory and Praxis, 35(1), 28–45.

Zanetti, L. A., & Adams, G. B. (2000). In service of the Leviathan: Democracy, ethics and the potential for administrative evil in the new public management. Administrative Theory and Praxis, 22(3), 534–554.

Pew Research Center Studies

"7 things to know about political Polarization". (2014). Pew Research Center (June 12). www.pewresearch.org/fact-tank/2014/06/12/7-things-to-know-about-polarization-in-america/

"Amid Campaign Turmoil, Biden Holds Wide Leads on Coronavirus, Unifying the Country". (2020). Pew Research Center (October 9). www.pewresearch.org/politics/2020/10/09/amid-campaign-turmoil-biden-holds-wide-leads-on-coronavirus-unifying-the-country/

"Few Trump or Biden Supporters Have Close Friends Who Back the Opposing Candidate". (2020). Pew Research Center (September 18). www.pewresearch.org/fact-tank/2020/09/18/few-trump-or-biden-supporters-have-close-friends-who-back-the-opposing-candidate/

"In Changing U.S. Electorate, Race and Education Remain Stark Dividing Lines". (2020). Pew Research Center (June 2). www.pewresearch.org/politics/2020/06/02/in-changing-u-s-electorate-race-and-education-remain-stark-dividing-lines/

"Intent to Get a COVID-19 Vaccine Rises to 60% as Confidence in Research and Development Process Increases". (2020). Pew Research Center (December 3). www.pewresearch.org/science/2020/12/03/intent-to-get-a-covid-19-vaccine-rises-to-60-as-confidence-in-research-and-development-process-increases/#republicans-and-democrats-differ-over-outbreaks-threat-to-public-health

"The Growing Partisan Divide in Views of Higher Education". (2019). Pew Research Center (August 19). www.pewresearch.org/social-trends/2019/08/19/the-growing-partisan-divide-in-views-of-higher-education-2/

"Voters Rarely Switch Parties, but Recent Shifts Further Educational, Racial Divergence". (2020). Pew Research Center (August 4). www.pewresearch.org/politics/2020/08/04/voters-rarely-switch-parties-but-recent-shifts-further-educational-racial-divergence/

4

PHILANTHROPY AND VOLUNTEERISM

The Why and How of Philanthropic Studies

Patrick M. Rooney and Katherine Badertscher

Introduction

The interdisciplinary nature of the study of philanthropy is both a benefit and hindrance to students as it involves many ways to consider the topic across disciplines, professions, and applied fields.[1] The study of philanthropy integrates theory and practice, is morally complex, expresses human values, and seeks solutions to help create an ideal world. Humans want to be free from pain, live in security and peace, flourish in our careers, and give and receive love and companionship. How we navigate the complex world to fulfill these needs, however, is far from simple and filled with contradiction. The challenge, of both ideology and action, to reconcile self-interest with morality is universal among humans and across time and cultures.

Philanthropic studies, similarly, reflects not only on knowledge, but on action: *voluntary action for the public good*. This fusion of the pursuit of a deeper understanding with action, as Richard Turner notes, makes ours an "exemplar field … dedicated to improving the practices that make life better in the world."[2] The duality of giving coupled with service, of vision plus action, differentiates philanthropy from nonprofit management, philosophy, or other fields of study. This context makes it difficult to gain a full understanding of research, theoretical, and practical frameworks … hence the value of the philanthropic studies curriculum.

In his 1983 seminal essay for the *Independent Sector*, Robert Payton wrote:[3]

> Philanthropy is America's most distinctive virtue. There is no other aspect of American life that is so vast in scale, so rooted in tradition, so broadly supported by law and public policy or more gratuitously neglected by the educational community. The system of charity and philanthropy and

DOI: 10.4324/9781003294061-5

voluntary service is at work in almost every aspect of our lives. We give to it, and we receive from it. We use it to help others and to express our ideas about how life could be made better for all of us. Philanthropy is a subject that touches the life of every student and every faculty member at every American college. It is easily related to every discipline of the humanities and social sciences and to professional studies like medicine, law, and business. It could be taught, and in my opinion, it should be taught, but it is not.

Defining Philanthropy

This chapter builds on Payton's essay and presents a bold case for the broad sweeping concept of philanthropy far beyond just wealthy donors giving large sums of money to their favorite causes. We argue that philanthropy encompasses all manner of informal charity, volunteering, generosity, advocacy, and highly professional institutional structures with diverse missions.

The concept of philanthropy is an ancient one, literally translated as the "love of man" or "love of humanity." Philanthropy is often referred to simply as the giving of time, money, or other assets. However, Robert L. Payton and Michael L. Moody in *Understanding Philanthropy* define philanthropy more broadly as "voluntary action for the public good."[4] Each component of this phrase, "voluntary action" and "public good," must be present to complete the notion of philanthropy.

Voluntary Action

Voluntary action is a vast and complex concept that is central to our understanding of philanthropy. Volunteers not only perform much of the work of nonprofit organizations, they help to define them. Voluntary action is a characteristic of civil society, a key to a functioning democracy, and a powerful mechanism for social change.[5] Voluntary action includes a range of activities including buying private goods in the for-profit market, giving or volunteering formally through a nonprofit organization, or informally by helping or donating directly to another individual or group of individuals (but not mediated by a nonprofit).

Public Goods and the Public Good

Public goods are produced by both all levels of government and many types of nonprofits. Technically, public goods are non-rival (one person's consumption of the good does not rival or interfere with another person's consumption of the good) and non-exclusionary (once produced, the producer cannot exclude individuals from consuming it). The clearest example of a pure public good is national defense: once provided, it applies to all; and your "consumption" of it does not affect mine (and vice versa). Many other goods have aspects of pure public goods but with limitations (e.g., roads, bridges, parks – up to the point of congestion; or theatrical and musical productions – but these goods can be excluded even if their consumption is non-rival). Conceptually, public goods could be produced by the government, the philanthropic sector, or the market (but the inability to exclude non-payers makes public goods inherently unprofitable, so not likely provided by the market).

Therefore, voluntary action alone could be market-oriented, and public goods alone could be government based. It is the integration of these two concepts that defines philanthropy. Payton and Moody take care to note that philanthropic ideals and actions are continually contested and negotiated across cultures and over time. Dwight Burlingame amended the definition of philanthropy slightly to emphasize the actors' vision: "voluntary action *intended* for the public good."[6] In other words, intentions matter. One can easily imagine a donation or volunteer effort, which is intended to do well, but has a neutral effect – or worse. However, we would still consider this as a philanthropic act. Conversely, if somebody inadvertently achieves a public good (like) outcome, but their intention was self-serving, that would not really be philanthropy, but rather good luck (or bad luck – depending on their perceptions). Acting in one's self-interest does not necessarily lead to undesirable outcomes, just as acting altruistically does not assure positive consequences. Students best understand philanthropy when they take into consideration concepts of self, others, and communities, as the fluid roles in philanthropic exchanges mean that one moment one is a receiver and the next moment one may be a donor.[7]

There is a sense when combining voluntary action with public goods we create a new conception of "the public good" that is separate from the economic context. The idea of "the public good" suggests both an intentionality and sense of collective action toward a more positive future. We work "toward" the public good; we work "for" the public good when we engage in philanthropy.

Charity vs. Philanthropy

Around the world, many people find the term "philanthropy" problematic, as it does not capture a spectrum of generosity in its scope. To some, "philanthropy" implies an activity within reach of society's elite bestowing handouts upon the poor. Similarly, "charity" invokes images of the dependent poor receiving handouts from people of privilege. We agree that the terms "charity" and "philanthropy" may have similar goals, but have subtly different connotations. "Charity" implies the giver's altruism, direct personal gifts usually to the poor, and small handouts of an immediate or reactive nature. "Philanthropy" implies the giver's self-interest and values; indirect, systematic, institutionalized giving; and large-scale gifts that attract the public's attention. Charity is short-term in nature, while philanthropy is long-term and strives for systemic change or transformation. Schervish views philanthropy as a "social relation of care," an interactive process through which individuals and groups connect their sympathetic connection with others to courses of action that may meet others' needs.[8] These perspectives allow us to consider a wide range of interactions as philanthropy, from palliative measures to transformational interventions that alter social structures or injustices. Philanthropy, as we think of it, encompasses a continuum of giving from individual, charitable generosity to strategic, institutional grantmaking.

Philanthropy and Nonprofits

If we accept philanthropy as this proposed broad concept, it *encompasses* voluntary associations and the nonprofit sector as crucial organizational elements that provide structure and leverage to philanthropic values and ideals. The terms "philanthropy" and "nonprofit sector" are often used interchangeably, when in fact the two phenomena are not one and the same. Nonprofit organizations mobilize, harness, and organize philanthropic gifts of time and money for public purposes. Volunteering and donating are done with purpose via the nonprofit sector; philanthropic visions of the public good thus couple intention with action.[9]

Philanthropy, nonprofit sector, third sector, civil society are all related terms, but struggle to differentiate from each other. The group of organizations other than government (the state) or for-profit businesses (the market) is known collectively as the nonprofit sector, the charitable sector, the third sector, the voluntary sector, or the independent sector. The negative referent, "nonprofit," distinguishes organizations from profit-seeking businesses in the United States. Outside US borders, non-governmental organization (NGO) is the common term for the same organizations. NGO is the descriptive term used internationally to distinguish nonprofit organizations from the state, which so often dominates health, education, and social services. Some reject the notion of the nonprofit "sector" because boundaries between nonprofit, government, and business are indistinct and continually evolving. This point has merit, especially in view of complex healthcare holding companies that control both nonprofit and for-profit businesses or nonprofit organizations that receive virtually all their revenue from government contracts. Nonprofit organizations, however, do share defining characteristics: legal standing as corporations, voluntary association and participation, private or non-governmental status, self-governing, unclear lines of ownership, and the prohibition of distributing profits to owners or managers (nondistribution constraint).[10]

We assert that civil society is that part of society, separate from business, government, and family, in which people can freely associate and express their views without fear or coercion, although scholars don't agree on a precise definition of the abstract and broad concept of civil society. Civil society includes both formal and informal networks, associations, and social institutions. Michael Edwards, for example, describes civil society as a triad of interdependent components: associational life, "good society" and a public space. Associational life is a network of voluntary associations beyond government, business, and family. The phenomenon of association is crucial because it allows pluralism, enables multiple interests to be represented, fosters civic engagement, builds trust among citizens, and links society together to promote collective solutions. The "good society" protects individual liberties, and promotes citizens' egalitarian respect and tolerance for one another. A public space is a social space in which citizens can deliberate questions of public interest, build consensus, and negotiate peaceful solutions.[11] When the three elements are taken together, a definition emerges: a society is civil if it simultaneously cherishes and protects both individual and collective freedom.

Philanthropy is sometimes differentiated from the nonprofit sector in two regards. First, the philanthropic sector would include all nonprofits that rely on current or former charitable gifts as a part of their income (e.g., foundations of all types as well as organizations that receive charitable gifts such a congregations, museums, and some educational and medical nonprofits). Second, the nonprofit sector might include organizations that operate as not for profits, but may or may not raise money philanthropically (e.g., nonprofits funded by either earned income and/or governmentally funded contracts or grants).

Why Philanthropy?

With the definitions and boundaries of philanthropy explained we now ask, "Why Philanthropy?" Philanthropy is often a response to what Payton called the "human problematic," the vagaries of the human condition that we seek to improve. Philanthropy is one of many possible responses and solutions to human problems, and can compete, complement, or collaborate with self-help, mutual aid, business, or government systems. Governmental systems are best equipped to address issues when a consensus exists, thus government tends to gear solutions toward the majority of the populace (e.g., "the median voter theory"). Once a governmental system or solution is created, government is required to treat citizens equally under the law. Only government has the coercive power to redistribute income and wealth through taxation. The power to tax sometimes assures the possibility of equity of service or treatment delivery, equal access to services, and eliminates the potential problem of free riders.

Yet consider five types of governmental constraints that can lead to unsatisfied demands. Governments must provide goods and services uniformly to its citizenry. This *categorical* constraint allows little provision for niches or experimentation. Government responds to the majority of voters, known as the *majoritarian* constraint. A *time horizon* constraint inhibits governments from taking long-term views on issues, as most elected officials serve short tenures (normally two to six years per term), and thus maintain a short-term focus on satisfying voters. Governments are also constrained by *knowledge*. They are monolithic and hierarchical, and, therefore, cannot generate all possible relevant information and ideas to satisfy all consumers. Finally, the *size* constraint applies to governments that are large, intimidating, and often inaccessible, especially to underserved, underrepresented, or minority populations.[12]

Nonprofit management programs frequently approach the study of nonprofit organizations with these governmental constraints in mind. Government has historically supported the nonprofit sector through favorable tax treatment, service programs that promote volunteering (Peace Corps, AmeriCorps, VISTA), demand-side funding through grants and contracts, supply-side funding for users of nonprofit services (Medicare, Medicaid, student loans), and other regulatory policies that benefits all types of corporations. Missions rely on values and often seek to help those in need or change people and society, not merely produce goods or services. Payton and Moody summarize these broad defining features of the three sectors (see Table 4.1).[13]

While both government and nonprofit organizations work to serve the public interest, or toward some public or common goal, nonprofits create opportunities for social linkages, networks, and participation that are the essence of community. Nonprofits, in addition, have the flexibility to serve niches, experiment with partially tested social innovations, preserve cultural values, and act as crucibles of religious expression and sacred belief systems. Philanthropic studies, therefore, views nonprofits not only as organizations that are subsets of governmental aims, but begins with individual actors as the drivers that may choose nonprofits to harness and structure their giving, volunteering, and advocacy.

We also can explain philanthropy via the "demand-side" rationale. Philanthropy's benefits are myriad: it touches every human being in some way, is an essential tool in solving public problems, and is essential to democratic society. It fulfills an important role in the economy (producing greater job growth than the for-profit or government sectors for the last several decades). It is the backbone of the nation's health and educational systems, as well as arts and culture, human services, and international relief organizations. Frumkin's quadrants illustrate both the explanation (why they are formed) and the justification (why they continue to thrive) of nonprofits[14] (see Table 4.2).

The instrumental role of nonprofits, in particular, calls for nonprofit management to be an important curriculum for nonprofit staff and executives. Nonprofit organizations may also originate from the "supply side," with visionary leaders who identify a social issue and create local, grassroots networks. Networks then coalesce into formal nonprofit organizations that signal legitimacy and provide

TABLE 4.1 Defining Features of the Three Sectors

Sector	*Means*	*Ends*	*Defining Idea*
Government	Public Actors	Public Good	Power
Business	Private Actors	Private Good	Wealth
Nonprofit	Private Actors	Public Good	Morality

TABLE 4.2 The Four Functions of Nonprofit and Voluntary Action

	Demand-Side Orientation	*Supply-Side Orientation*
Instrumental Role	Service delivery Provides services, responds to market/government failure	Social entrepreneurship Creates social enterprise, combines commercial and charitable goals
Expressive Role	Civic and political engagement Mobilizes political advocacy, builds social capital	Values and faith Volunteers, staff, and donors express values and faith through work

Peter Frumkin, *On Being Nonprofit: A Conceptual and Policy Primer* (Cambridge: Harvard University Press, 2002), 25.

structures that outlive founders. Nonprofit organizations then deliver services, mobilize advocacy, and attract and retain human and financial resources for the long term.

The expressive purpose of philanthropy encompasses the broad, distinctive set of values and faith for which donors, staff, volunteers, and congregants strive. Those who donate money and time must be confident that philanthropic organizations are aligned with their individual values. If we accept these notions then we see that the study of philanthropy is distinct from nonprofit management. In a Venn diagram, one can imagine areas of overlap between the two, but also non-overlapping portions. If nonprofit management focuses on the nuts and bolts of managing nonprofits (e.g., budgeting, planning, HR) and philanthropic studies focused on the big questions such as "Why does anyone give at all?" Or, "Why do we have a philanthropic sector at all"? (as opposed to government provision of public goods and capitalistic provision of private goods). Similarly, both might include the art and science of fundraising and proposal writing.

Philanthropy, moreover, would include the "kitchen table charity" with its small budgets and volunteer-driven work. Philanthropy would also include the largest charities such as the American Red Cross, United Way Worldwide, Salvation Army, and even the world of commercial and community-based Donor-Advised Funds (DAFs). While nonprofit management might also be concerned about those larger, philanthropic-driven charities, nonprofit management would be concerned with nonprofits that are essentially the government outsourcing its work to agencies with earned income and/or government grants, but no philanthropic support, but philanthropic studies conceptually would ignore them. "For profits in disguise," or fake charities, which operate as nonprofits in name but are in place only to enrich its "owners/managers" rather than to serve the sector as a nonprofit might be interested in nonprofit management techniques but are clearly not interested in philanthropy as we have described it.

Philanthropic studies would be curious about volunteering as a philanthropic activity both formally (for a charity) and informally (helping others but not through a charity), but nonprofit management might in interested in the need for the management of volunteers in charitable organizations. Similarly, philanthropic studies would want to understand the motives for making and halting gifts both formally (donating to a charity) and helping others directly (whether homeless person on the street, a neighbor, or a family member). Nonprofit management programs would be concerned with the tracking and measuring of the gifts to charities and the costs of fundraising. That all said, we acknowledge that our friends and colleagues in nonprofit management programs may look at and define these boundaries differently, but these distinctions are how we organize our thoughts in explaining our philanthropic studies programs to current and prospective students.

Third-Sector Orientation

Philanthropic studies alumni believe that the nonprofit sector is best positioned to solve pressing social problems and feel a strong sense of belonging in philanthropy. The overwhelming majority (92.4%) strongly agree that they plan to spend their entire careers in the nonprofit sector. The majority (75.6%), moreover, strongly agree that they feel part of a family while working in the nonprofit sector.[15] The notion of the third-sector orientation, therefore, provides an important orientation for both philanthropic studies and nonprofit management. Scholars have theorized philanthropy as a sector of society that interacts with the business and government, and at times the family or household, sectors. A simple depiction of the three sectors is not uncommon (see Figure 4.1).

Van Til recognizes four sectors with distinct interactions among them[16] (see Table 4.3).

Rudolph suggests the sector roles are out of balance with everyday life, preferring this type of construction[17] (see Figure 4.2).

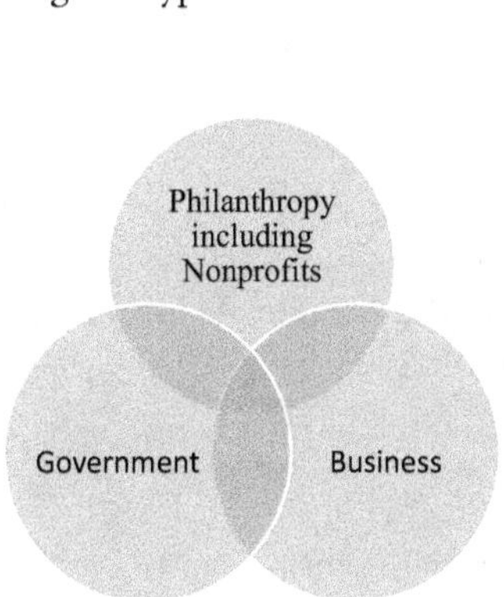

FIGURE 4.1 Depiction of the Three Sectors

TABLE 4.3 Transactions among the Sectors

GOVERNMENT regulates, subsidizes, and contracts with nonprofits	**BUSINESS (MARKET)** provides philanthropy through giving and employee volunteering (and creates wealth and expertise)
501c3 NONPROFITS attract tax-deductible contributions and volunteer time; provide services as government contractors	**FAMILIES, HOUSEHOLDS, NEIGHBORHOODS** donate to and volunteer for nonprofits

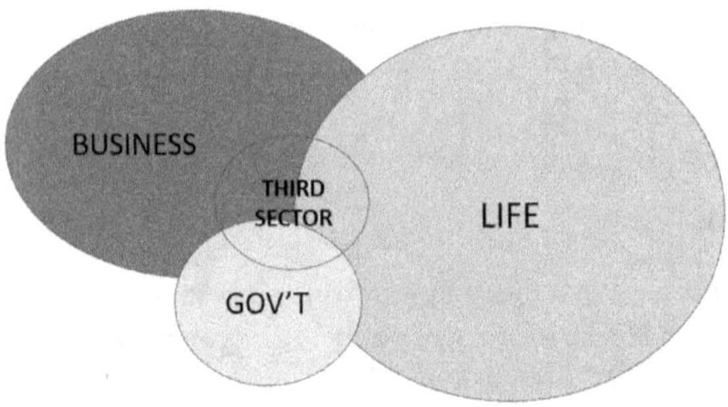

FIGURE 4.2 Sector Roles in Everyday Life

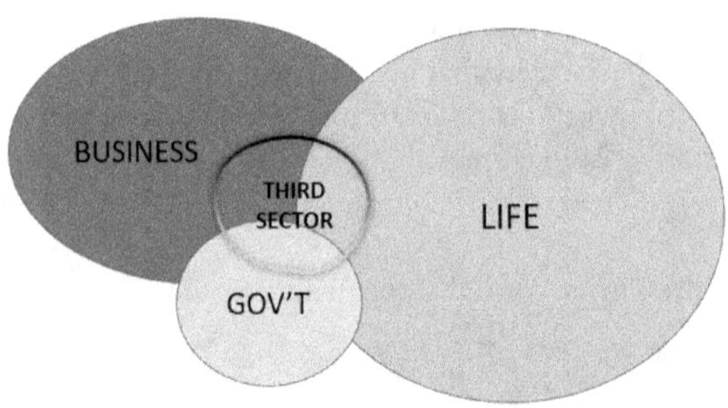

FIGURE 4.3 Sector Boundaries Are Blurry

Finally, scholars recognize that sectoral boundaries, definitions, and interactions are blurry, indistinct, and ebb and flow over time, causing the role of philanthropy, the third sector, to continually remain a fuzzy concept (see Figure 4.3).

The Emerging Field of Philanthropic Studies

Philanthropy's emerging definitions, disciplinary domain, and various characterizations of the third sector, therefore, give rise to a simultaneously emerging field of philanthropic studies.

The academic study of philanthropy has grown dramatically in its relatively short existence. Indiana University, the home to America's first school of Philanthropy, is among the founding members of the Nonprofit Academic Centers Council (NACC), which numbers 58 now and had approximately 100 attendees at its last two conferences. In addition, there are more than 1,200 members of the Association of Research on Nonprofits and Voluntary Associations, and 850 attendees at its last in person conference. This number does not include the many scholars in other disciplines, who do significant work in the area, but who tend to publish in more traditional disciplinary journals.

The field of philanthropy comprises a large, complex, heterogeneous body of work that includes both disciplinary and interdisciplinary research. Several refereed academic journals are devoted exclusively to this body of work including *Nonprofit and Voluntary Sector Quarterly*; *Nonprofit Management and Leadership*; *Voluntas*; *Philanthropy and Education*; *NonProfit Policy Forum*; *Journal of Philanthropy and Marketing*; and *The Foundation Review*, as well as scores of academic journals in disciplines that welcome scholarly research in these specialties. The Indiana University (IU) Press Philanthropy Series has published 43 books by both IU philanthropic studies faculty members and scholars from other institutions. The topics covered range from ethics and board governance to biographies of important figures and historical events in philanthropy.

Beyond the Sectors – The Case for Liberal Arts

The liberal arts were, are, and will continue to be the core of philanthropic studies curricula. Graduate cohorts include students who identify across a broad spectrum of roles in philanthropy: current or aspiring nonprofit professionals, donors, private and family foundation officers, seasoned board members, and full-time community volunteers. As such, graduate students in philanthropic studies hold and go on to pursue leadership positions that require a balance of analytical, emotional, ethical, and intra/interpersonal competencies.[18] Taken together, we construe this admixture of competencies as philanthropic leadership, which embodies the broader mission of the school, to improve philanthropy in order to improve the world. Leaders enact social changes in order to perpetuate and maintain philanthropy within changing economic, cultural, and political contexts. Other times, leaders enact social changes to evolve the ways that employees, volunteers, funders, boards of advisors, and the general public engage with the organization.[19]

Philanthropic studies do not encompass the full spectrum of NACC's domains.[20] More relevant, perhaps, is what philanthropy DOES include, that NACC does not contemplate.

Philanthropic studies, differentiated from nonprofit management, encompasses all aspects of voluntary giving (of money, time, and expertise), voluntary associations, and voluntary action in many societies throughout history. The nature of philanthropy varies according to national, historical, cultural, and social contexts. Far from being an isolated activity, philanthropy is ensconced in its conditions across time and place. Because scholarly study of philanthropy relies on many disciplines, the philanthropic studies domain includes the aspirations and traditions of people(s) around the world who seek to end suffering and improve communities. A comparative perspective, starting with the simple question "what is philanthropy?" is a crucial component of the curriculum.[21]

The field of philanthropic studies is based on the Association of American Colleges & Universities (AAC&U) description of liberal education as an approach to learning that empowers individuals and prepares them to deal with complexity, diversity, and change. It provides students with broad knowledge of the wider world (e.g., science, culture, and society) as well as in-depth study in a specific area of interest. A liberal education helps students develop a sense of social responsibility, as well as strong and transferable intellectual and practical skills such as communication, analytical and problem-solving skills, and a demonstrated ability to apply knowledge and skills in real-world settings.[22]

Martha Nussbaum's *Not for Profit* articulates persuasively that democratic societies need humanities education. She notes that education must prepare students to become active, critical, reflective, and empathetic community members.[23] These qualities align with those of thoughtful givers and receivers as well. It is easy to be distracted by the glitz of celebrity philanthropy and discouraged by the magnitude of the wealth of Warren Buffett, Bill Gates and Melinda French Gates, but every human being gives and receives throughout life. Thoughtful reflection on the ethical ideals, virtues, and responsibilities of giving and receiving increases the understanding of an individual's philanthropy, for students and scholars alike.[24] If schools or programs of philanthropy are to "move philanthropy forward," as our own school promises, it is imperative that they teach students how to see beyond blind spots in their worldviews.[25] Everyone acquires blind spots due to their upbringing, culture, ethnicity, religion, class, or gender as they walk through life, and often we are not even aware that those blind spots exist. Liberal arts coursework uniquely challenges students to pause, wonder, reflect, and ponder their own moral philosophy and how it fits into the world. It is therefore incumbent upon programs whose goal is to provide students a deeper understanding of voluntary action for the public good, and the onerous responsibility that philanthropy entails, to maintain this rich educational tradition.

Mark William Roche makes the case for liberal arts education in *Why Choose the Liberal Arts?* Roche's argument aligns with Nussbaum, as he demonstrates three primary values of liberal arts education: engaging the great questions, cultivating virtues, and forming character.[26] His argument beautifully applies to questions in philanthropy, in that these should be considered ideal goals for students in philanthropic studies programs. Liberal arts education gives students the joy of asking and exploring questions about the ultimate meaning of life, including *giving and receiving*. Philanthropic studies curricula bear a solemn obligation to equip students with the ability to recognize ethical questions, wrestle with them forthrightly, and make the wisest possible choices.

How Indiana University Approaches Philanthropic Studies

Students at all degree levels express personal philanthropic goals upon entering the program. The philanthropic studies curriculum guides alumni to become more informed donors and volunteers, to encourage others' philanthropy, and to reciprocate to those who may have contributed to their success in life. The curriculum prepares students to act responsibility for the public good through intentional, individual action whether informally or formally, personally or professionally. Philanthropic studies link intellectual inquiry with action in the world, as we say, "understanding philanthropy and improving its practice."

Our academic programs began with a face to face, two-year, full-time master's (MA) degree program. Soon thereafter, we added an Executive MA format in which students would take classes which had a remote (online) component but concluded with an intensive all day every day for a week (per course) format. This program was designed for more experienced students, who had at least five years of experience. Typically, they completed this part-time degree program in four years.

Subsequently, we created a traditional PhD program, which could be completed in four years (a relevant MA is required for admission), but most students take five to six years to complete. Many of our doctoral students have been offered their "dream job" before graduating, which tends to drive up the mean time to completion. This program is designed for individuals who aspire to become faculty members or researchers at universities and think tanks, etc. However, some of our doctoral students have entered this PhD program with the intention of being a leader in the philanthropic sector but were intellectually curious and wanted a deeper understanding of the sector both from a theoretical and a research methods perspective.[27]

Later, we offered a bachelor's (BA) degree, which has had adequate but lower than expected enrollments. Fortuitously, pre-pandemic, we initiated an entirely online version of our MA degree. The same faculty teach largely interchangeably in both, so the quality is comparable. There is a clear market demand for that, as we have seen the online enrollments growing dramatically pre-pandemic and certainly during the pandemic.

While our overall enrollments are relatively small for a school at a major research university, we know we are meeting a real demand. Virtually all of our students, who want a job are placed within six months of graduating (typically 96%–97%). Most of those who are not placed are not looking for a job for a variety of reasons. Many are placed before graduating. Even during the pandemic, 95% of our students were placed within nine months of graduation in an era of massive layoffs and record high unemployment rates. In addition, a recent survey of seven philanthropy and nonprofit management graduate programs conducted by a team of scholars from different schools and universities, they found that our alumni are more likely to be working in the nonprofit or philanthropic sector (75.5% vs. 70%) and a larger share of our alumni "strongly agreed the degree was worth" the time (55.5% vs. 42.2%) and money (45.1% vs. 32.9%) invested in it.[28]

We have quadrupled our faculty in the last 7 years since we became a school. Three lines were funded by the campus to help stand up the school. However, over half of our faculty have been funded by endowed chairs. Amazingly, none of the donors/funders had a prior relationship with the school, and only one had graduated from any IU campus.

Four faculty members have retired in the past 3 or 4 years and more are expected in the next two or three years. During the pandemic, all of IU imposed a hiring freeze, so these posts have not yet been replaced, but we expect that they will be over time. This is important both in terms of the quality and quantity of instruction, but also the impact of the research that is produced by the school's faculty and their contributions to the building of the field through professional service.

These changes are already manifesting themselves in differences in perspectives of what is "philanthropy" and what is or should be philanthropic studies between the "old guard" faculty and at least some of the more recent faculty hires. For example, as we (members of the "old guard") have discussed a more traditional view of philanthropy as "voluntary action for the public good," which has been held by the "old guard" for decades, it has become clear that at least some of the newer faculty hires view philanthropy as an element of social change and/or social justice – or that it should be. Hence, there is an active debate as to whether or not social change is a subset of philanthropy (old guard) or whether philanthropy is a subset of social change and/or social justice (at least for some of our new hires). This can be seen in the two versions of the Venn diagram below. This may be a normal evolution of a field or simply an academic debate among faculty committed to the school and its programs (see Figures 4.4 and 4.5).

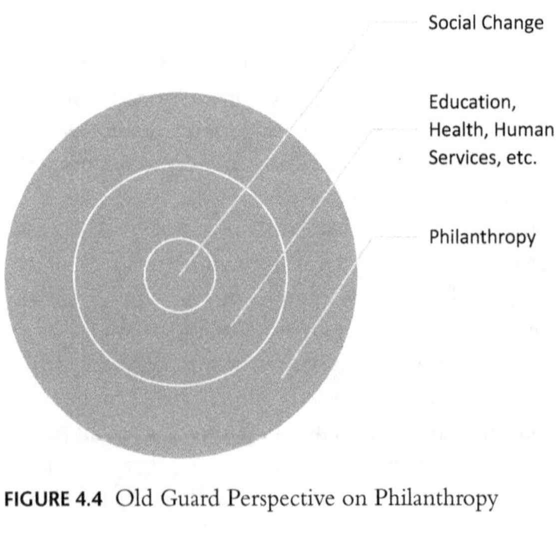

FIGURE 4.4 Old Guard Perspective on Philanthropy

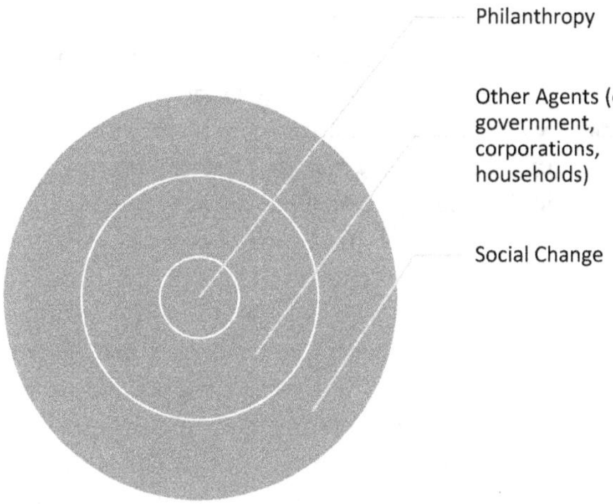

FIGURE 4.5 Changing Perspective on Philanthropy

The Future of Philanthropic Studies

As of 2020, our school has 20 core faculty members, although two faculty members are just now retiring. Nine of 20 faculty positions are endowed and held by either chairs, fellows, or directors. Two more chairs are fully funded and pending searches. At least two more will be funded by planned gifts. Extensive endowed funding exists for scholarships (and more committed in planned gifts) and operations. These endowments for chairs, scholarships, and operations provide some fiscal stability and guarantees our future at a minimal level, which would still be relatively large for our field. Rooney and Burlingame revealed in recent research about the sustainability of philanthropy and nonprofit management centers that significant amounts of endowed funds are often one of the key (if not the key) differentiating factors between centers that either survive – not to mention thrive – or die.[29]

With more retirements expected in the next few years, it becomes the duty and opportunity for the next generation of faculty to shape the destiny and future of the school. How philanthropy is defined by the faculty in the future will undoubtedly change. One thing that will remain abundantly clear is philanthropy has and will always have a distinct and important role in understanding society, the philanthropic or nonprofit sector, and our core values. Whether the boundaries between Philanthropic Studies and Nonprofit Management become more distinct or further blurred will be a fun, and, hopefully, intellectually important debate now and in the future.

We believe that philanthropic studies play a vital role in higher education, not in lieu of but alongside nonprofit management. Questions of who should give, how much, to whom, in what way, and why remain persistent.[30] Undergraduate and graduate students pursue degrees in philanthropic studies and nonprofit management programs for many similar and different reasons. Students will go on to pursue many different career paths. They may volunteer, pursue further graduate study, work in various capacities in nonprofit organizations, or work in business or government. Graduates represent the ideals of philanthropy and have tremendous responsibility to put their beliefs into action and improve the character of philanthropy in the world. The deep thinking, reflection, lingering over great works, and thoughtful conversation that liberal arts coursework provides fosters the development of students' value systems and empathy. These experiences, and the character they build, apply in the workplace, the congregation, and the home, and they endure for a lifetime. Regardless of their future paths, students will face choices about giving and serving virtually every day. As Amy Kass notes, "we are all, willy-nilly, called upon to give and to serve … as human beings who seek to promote the well-being of others." "We can choose or refuse to be philanthropic," she continues, "but we cannot choose whether or not to have such choices."[31] Because philanthropic studies consider giving beyond the boundaries of formal nonprofit organizations, such as informal, unintentional, or unrecognized action, we believe it is an important field of study that prepares citizens of the world.

Notes

1 Noah Drezner, "Setting the Mission and Vision for a New Journal within the Landscape of Our Field," *Philanthropy and Education* 1, v. 1 (Fall 2017): viii.
2 Richard C. Turner, "Philanthropic Studies as a Central and Centering Discipline in the Humanities," *International Journal of the Humanities* 2, no. 3 (2004), 2083.
3 Robert L. Payton (1927–2011) was the nation's first full-time professor of philanthropic studies and the first full-time executive director of the Indiana University Center on Philanthropy, housed in the Indiana University School of Liberal Arts at IUPUI.
4 Robert L. Payton and Michael L. Moody, *Understanding Philanthropy: Its Meaning and Mission* (Bloomington: Indiana University Press, 2008), 28.
5 Virginia A. Hodgkinson, "Individual Giving and Volunteering," in Lester M. Salamon, ed., *The State of Nonprofit America* (Washington, DC: Brookings Institution Press, 2002), 392.
6 Dwight F. Burlingame, "Nonprofit and Philanthropic Studies Education: The Need to Emphasize Leadership and Liberal Arts," *Journal of Public Affairs Education* 15, no. 1 (2009): 59–67.
7 Dwight F. Burlingame, "Altruism and Philanthropy: Definitional Issues," in *Essays on Philanthropy No. 10* (Indiana University Center on Philanthropy, 1993), 7–8.
8 Payton and Moody, *Understanding Philanthropy*, 6; Paul G. Schervish, "Philanthropy," in *Encyclopedia of Politics and Religion*," ed. Robert Wuthnow (Washington, DC: Congressional Quarterly, 1998), 600.
9 Payton and Moody, *Understanding Philanthropy*, 28.
10 Lester M. Salamon, *America's Nonprofit Sector: A Primer,* 2nd ed. (New York: Foundation Center, 1999), 10–11. An interesting counterfactual is in China with GONGOs – Government Owned Non-Governmental Organizations, which is inherently an oxymoronic notion by our Western definitions.
11 Michael Edwards, *Civil Society* (2004; Reprint, Cambridge: Polity Press, 2008).

12 Dennis R. Young, "Government failure theory," in J. Steven Ott and Lisa A. Dicke, ed, *The Nature of the Nonprofit Sector*, 2nd Edition (Boulder, CO: Westview Press, 2012), 151–154.
13 Payton and Moody, *Understanding Philanthropy*, 49.
14 Frumkin, *On Being Nonprofit*, 25.
15 Marlene Walk, Kerry Kuenzi, Mandi J. Stewart, and Ashabul Alam, "A Report for the Lilly Family School of Philanthropy at IUPUI," nonprofiteducationsurvey.com, 13.
16 Jon Van Til, *Civil Society: From Nonprofit Sector to Third Space* (Bloomington: Indiana University Press, 2000), 21.
17 Rudolph Bauer, "Intermediarity: A theoretical paradigm for third sector research," (Geneva: Third Conference of the International Society for Third Sector Research, 1998). Conference Paper, 8–11.
18 Heather L. Carpenter, "Philanthropy: Evidence in Favor of a Profession," *Foundation Review* 9, no. 4 (2017): 68.
19 Indiana University Lilly Family School of Philanthropy, Pre-Proposal: Professional Doctorate in Philanthropic Leadership, 2021.
20 Nonprofit Academic Centers Council (NACC) Curricular Guidelines – Graduate 3rd ed. (2015).
21 Michael Moody and Beth Breeze, *The Philanthropy Reader* (New York: Routledge, 2016), 3.
22 www.aacu.org/leap/what-is-a-liberal-education.
23 Martha C. Nussbaum, *Not For Profit: Why Democracy Needs the Humanities* (Princeton: Princeton University Press, 2010), 141.
24 Mike W. Martin, *Virtuous Giving: Philanthropy, Voluntary Service, and Caring* (Bloomington: Indiana University Press, 1994), 2.
25 Indiana University Lilly Family School of Philanthropy Web site, https://philanthropy.iupui.edu/about/founding.html.
26 Mark William Roche, *Why Choose the Liberal Arts?* (Notre Dame, IN: University of Notre Dame, 2010), 10–11.
27 We are currently in the developmental and final approval stages for a professional doctorate in philanthropic leadership (PHILD). It is planned to be a part-time (two courses per semester), three-year, online degree program for experienced practitioners, who are working full-time.
28 Marlene Walk, Kerry Kuenzi, Mandi J. Stewart, and Ashabul Alam, "A Report for the Lilly Family School of Philanthropy at IUPUI," nonprofiteducationsurvey.com, 14–15.
29 Patrick M. Rooney and Dwight F. Burlingame "Build It and They Will Come! Or, Built to Last? Key Challenges and Insights into the Sustainability of Nonprofit and Philanthropy Programs and Centers," *Journal of Nonprofit Education and Leadership*, 2020, Vol. 10, No. 4, 395–409.
30 Robert L. Payton, "Philanthropic Values," in *Philanthropy: Private Means, Public Ends*, ed. Kenneth W. Thompson (Lanham, MD: University Press of America, 1987), 43.
31 Amy A. Kass, *The Perfect Gift: The Philanthropic Imagination in Poetry and Prose* (Bloomington: Indiana University Press, 2002), 3.

5

PUBLIC SERVICE REFORM AND ITS IMPLICATIONS FOR NONPROFIT MANAGEMENT EDUCATION

Steven Rathgeb Smith

Nonprofit managers today face a turbulent and challenging environment due to the ongoing pandemic, fiscal austerity, competition for resources and staff from other nonprofits and increasingly from for-profit firms, and pressure to deliver greater programmatic impact and success. Thus, the appropriate education and training of nonprofit managers has never been more important. Nonprofit leaders now need to navigate a very complicated and shifting set of political, economic, and social pressures.

More recently, many scholars and policymakers have called attention to additional changes the public services that focus on collaboration and cooperation between government and nonprofit organizations as the increase in multi-sector partnerships coalitions and partnerships at the local, regional, and national level. This "new public governance" is reshaping the relationships of nonprofit organizations at the local and regional level and calling for new types of skills for nonprofit leaders (Phillips and Smith, 2011; 2015).

Indeed, nonprofit leaders need to have the capacity to create adaptive, flexible organizations to respond quickly to emergent challenges including the changing "value proposition" of membership, volunteering or donating to the organization. The economic challenges facing many nonprofits is also encouraging nonprofits to seek new types of collaborations with government, other nonprofits, and/or for-profit firms.

Importantly, this shifting fiscal, political, and social environment for nonprofits is also affecting nonprofits who do not receive government funding. Organized philanthropy including many small and large foundations are expecting that nonprofits demonstrate greater impact and provide more evidence for their programmatic success. Many foundations also expect their grantees to work closely with partners at the local level.

DOI: 10.4324/9781003294061-6

The rapidly evolving landscape for nonprofit organizations has direct implications for nonprofit management education. This chapter makes a case that the advent of public sector reform in the 1990s and thereafter has greatly contributed to the growth of the nonprofit sector and profoundly affected the management of nonprofit organizations, with important consequences for nonprofit management education.

The focus of this chapter is on graduate education for nonprofit managers especially in schools of public affairs and public policy, although the chapter has broader relevance for other types of nonprofit management education. In the chapter, I will argue that nonprofit management education should be integrated into the core curriculum of graduate programs in public administration, public policy, and social work. Further, nonprofit managers need to develop skills in strategic planning, program evaluation, flexible and accountable governance, and collaborative managerial styles. In this sense, nonprofit managers need many of the same qualities and skills that are valued other sectors, reflecting shifts in thinking about leadership of effective organizations (see Senge, Hamilton, and Kania, 2015; Kotter, 2007; Kettl, 2006).

Nonprofit Management Education and Public Service Reform

In the US context, nonprofit managers, prior to the 1960s, often lacked formal training or education in management. Often, they received a degree in social work, psychology, health care, or arts. They would then take a position in a nonprofit and then gradually assume more administrative responsibility. Some individuals may also have sought an MBA degree or graduate training in social work with a concentration in administration. Graduate training in public administration was overwhelmingly focused on the public sector, especially state and local government. The leading association, at the time for the public sector, the American Society for Public Administration (ASPA) had a nationwide network of local chapters that included public administration scholars and state and local public servants.

The growth of the federal government in the US in the 1960s, especially through new and expanded programs in education, social services, health care, and income support, created new incentives for change in the management education of the public and nonprofit sectors. In regards to the public sector, new federal funding of graduate education in public administration encouraged leaders at ASPA and more broadly the foundation and higher education community to create a new organization to improve the standards for the public sector workforce. The result was the creation of the National Association of Schools of Public Affairs and Administration (NASPAA) in 1970. The goals of the new association included setting education standards and providing incentives and encouraging the establishment of schools of public administration throughout the country (Henry, 2015). Due in part to the efforts of NASPAA and the broader changes occurring in federal policy and higher education, the number of public administration programs did indeed rise with many new master's in public administration programs established and new schools of public policy such as the Kennedy School of Government at Harvard and the Institute of Policy Studies at Duke founded in the 1970s. Importantly, eligibility for membership in NASPAA was limited to institutional members primarily departments and schools, rather than individual members.

Around the same time, the Association for Voluntary Action Scholars (AVAS) was established in 1971 to bring together scholars conducting research on voluntary organizations. The initial group of members were concentrated in the fields of sociology, social work, and political science; their research tended to focus on community organizations and voluntarism, rather than nonprofit management, broadly defined. To an extent, the founding of AVAS also represented the changes at the federal level. Many major federal initiatives in a wide variety of fields including health care, community mental health, pre-school, and social services were implemented through nonprofit organizations funded by government. Moreover, widespread support existed for community-based activism and political engagement through local organizations. For example, community action agencies, a high-profile, federal anti-poverty program were required to have community members on their boards of directors. The sharp increase in federal funding of nonprofits also led to a significant increase in the number of nonprofit organizations, especially nonprofits providing public services and nonprofit advocacy organizations striving to change public policy such as environmental groups. With more nonprofits and the growth of higher education in general, the founding of AVAS was a logical and predictable development.

The landscape of nonprofit management education began to change significantly in the 1980s with the establishment of nonprofit academic centers and programs at key universities such as Case Western Reserve University, the University of San Francisco, and Yale University. In general, these nonprofit-centered programs were initially funded from foundation grants and provided a programmatic vehicle to promote research and teaching on nonprofit organizations. At Yale, the Program on Nonprofit Organizations supported an extensive working paper and seminar series by scholars on nonprofit organizations and philanthropy. The Mandel Center on Nonprofit Organizations at Case Western, directed by Dennis Young, led to the creation of a new academic journal, *Nonprofit Management and Leadership*. The Center on Philanthropy at Duke University supported research and greater engagement between philanthropic leaders and scholars. In addition, the leading foundations including the Ford Foundation and the Rockefeller Brothers Fund, the Mott Foundation, the Carnegie Corporation, and Atlantic Philanthropies pooled their financial support to create the Nonprofit Sector Research Fund at the Aspen Institute in Washington, DC. Starting in the early 1990s, this Fund was critical to the growth and development of the research field on nonprofit organizations and philanthropy. Likewise, a major multi-year initiative of the Kellogg Foundation was to support the establishment and expansion of nonprofit academic centers such as the Mandel Center. The Ford Foundation, Atlantic Philanthropies, the Mott Foundation, and the Charities Aid Foundation provided the grant support for the establishment of the International Society for Third Sector Research in 1991, an international association of scholars studying philanthropy, nonprofits, and civil society.

This infusion of major foundation resources in the field created new research opportunities and facilitated the development of new curricular offerings on nonprofit organizations and philanthropy. The long-term growth of the nonprofit sector, especially through nonprofits providing public services through government contracts and grants, led more and more students to seek undergraduate and graduate education focused on nonprofits and philanthropy.

This shift was reinforced by the advent of the New Public Management (NPM) in the 1990s that has over time has had quite profound effects on the delivery of public services and the role of nonprofits. Starting in the mid-1980s, NPM replaced bureaucracy as the dominant point of reference of public administration (Hood, 1991; Rhodes, 1994). To exchange "hierarchy" for "the market" as the central mode of coordination constitutes the key idea of NPM, leading to the adoption of various market-oriented strategies including: government contracting with nonprofit and for-profit organizations, individual vouchers for housing and community care, greater competition for government funding, and much greater emphasis on performance management and accountability (Osborne, 2010; Phillips and Smith, 2015).

The widespread adoption of NPM strategies across the world has been facilitated by several political, economic, and social developments: government fiscal austerity; government and foundation support for social innovation; widespread concern among policymakers on the perceived ineffectiveness of many publicly supported programs; and interest in greater community and individual control for services. Also, many leading scholars of business administration have proposed that businesses adopt more collaborative and networked models of organization to enhance their likelihood of financial success (Senge, Hamilton, and Kania, 2015; Kotter, 2007; Porter and Kramer, 2011).

In many countries, the nonprofit sector benefitted significantly from this new public administration approach inspired by NPM (Zimmer and Smith, 2022). Traditional public services were increasingly provided by nonprofit organizations (Phillips and Smith, 2015) especially in countries where the provision of welfare services used to exclusively be a state/government affair such as post Second World War UK (Kendall, 2000). In other countries such as the US and the UK, new nonprofits were founded in fields such as community care or programmes such as child welfare that were previously the responsibility of the public sector (Smith and Lipsky, 1993). Also, countries including China created government-organized nongovernmental organizations (Gongos) or quasi-nongovernmental organizations (Quangos). From a legal perspective, they are private, nonprofit organizations but entirely funded by public money, and they represented a shift from public provision to the nonprofit sector. This shift was particularly evident in the countries of the former Soviet bloc that transitioned to liberal governments and market economies in the 1990s and thereafter. Indeed, many countries in Eastern Europe first created legal forms for nonprofits and thereafter legally "privatized" social service providers that were previously part of bureaucratic government and public administration. These modified social service providers were also subject to extensive control by the government (Freise and Pajas, 2004, p. 131). Also, in this period, globalization and the steep increase of global problems that can only be solved internationally triggered a foundation boom of nongovernmental organizations that soon were at least partially accepted as new players in the international arena (Joachim, 2014). In short, many factors contributed to a "global associational revolution" (Salamon, 1994) and a significant growth of the nonprofit sector worldwide in the 1990s and 2000s (Zimmer and Smith, 2022).

The implementation of NPM has varied in terms of the actual mix of policy strategies or "tools" that are employed (Salamon, 2002). But overall, nonprofits increased in scope and activity including many nonprofits that received public support. In addition, NPM encouraged a renewed attention to the co-production of services which generally refers to the active participation of service users and citizens with professionals and volunteers in the development and delivery of key public services. Co-production was initially used to refer to the reliance of street-level bureaucrats such as teachers and the police on citizens to actually produce education or policing (Parks et al., 1981; Brudney and England, 1983). More recently, co-production has received support from the NPM movement to encourage more efficiency, effectiveness, and innovation in the public services.

Nonprofit organizations are predictable and logical homes for expanded "co-production" because their community roots offer an opportunity for voluntarism and citizen participation (Bovaird, 2007; Alford, 2009; Smith, 2021) Many examples of co-production involving nonprofits exist: self-help programs for mentally ill and individuals with substance abuse; government contracting with a local community agency to support a clubhouse program for at-risk teenagers; and a parent education program to promote positive early child development (Smith, 2021). A major connecting thread for these various initiatives is joint production of services by professionals and citizens often in complicated collaborative initiatives.

Increasingly, many for-profit community firms are also offering various co-production options. For example, a for-profit agency for ex-prisoners on parole might rely heavily upon clients to help in their own readjustment to the community. Co-production through community organizations has also been facilitated by the greater utilization of vouchers which typically involve a government subsidy directly to an individual to purchase services from public or private organizations.

Vouchers for primary education or community care for older adults are good examples.

NPM-type strategies have also led to greater organizational complexity and fragmentation, given the growth of service agencies at the local level. Many new local programs are relatively small and may have overlapping missions. It also can be difficult to have substantial program impact with limited scope and resources. Many scholars of organizational management have also criticized isolated, "siloed" approaches to service delivery. Consequently, policymakers, scholars, and practitioners have observed that greater collaboration or joint action is required if services are to be more responsive and effective. Scholars refer to this new paradigm the "new public governance" to reflect that need to consider a more comprehensive approach to public services reflecting contemporary organizational complexity and programmatic design. Importantly, the pathway to increased participation and responsive public service provision facilitated through new public governance depends on horizontal partnership arrangements or relational governance (Phillips and Smith, 2011). This shift in thinking is represented in the multiplicity of partnerships, coalitions, and collaborative initiatives at the local, regional, and even national level. The new public governance also fits well with the attractiveness of nonprofit organizations as sites of civic engagement, building social capital, democratic participation, and co-production (Zimmer and Smith, forthcoming).

NPM and the new public governance have also greatly influenced the widespread support among public and private for greater accountability, performance, and evaluation for the public services (Phillips and Smith, 2015; Mirabella and Nguyen, 2019). Often this movement is called "pay-for-success" (PFS) (Corporation for National and Community Service, 2015). In brief, PFS seeks to link payment for services to the success of the intervention for clients and the broader community. Perhaps one of the most visible examples of this focus on performance management with regards to human services is the advent of social impact bonds (SIBs) – a form of PFS that has achieved wide attention in the US and abroad as an innovative strategy to achieve greater social impact. SIBs are complicated initiatives that depend upon private investors assuming the risk of social programs, with the government paying off those investments if and when the outcome goals are met. Private investors loan money to an intermediary (usually a nonprofit) which then sub-contracts with service providers (nonprofit and for-profit) who then deliver services with specific performance targets. The project is evaluated by independent researchers and the government sponsor repays the loan with interest to investors if the performance targets are met. SIBs illustrate the combination of NPM (performance contracts and private capital) and the new public governance (many stakeholders and horizontal relationships) (Zimmer and Smith, 2022).

SIBs also represent the widespread enthusiasm for social innovation and the mixing of the public, nonprofit, for-profit sectors. Not surprisingly, countless examples of mixed private-public ventures have also encouraged the movement of personnel between sectors. Whereas previously an individual civil servant might remain in a public sector position for their entire career, many public service-minded individuals now might work in a nonprofit organization or a for-profit social enterprise. Indeed, it is now not uncommon for individuals to work in all three sectors in a specific field such as home care, economic development, and child welfare.

Policymakers reinforced this shift to more involvement with the nonprofit sector with many different initiatives reflecting in part the interest in more local and effective strategies to address social problems. President Bill Clinton created the Corporation for National and Community Service in 1993 to further community service, especially through the nonprofit sector through its major service program, AmeriCorps. Through this program, the federal government supported the placement of primarily recent college graduates in a wide array of local community organizations. AmeriCorps continues to the present-day and one of its important legacies is the development of a nonprofit service infrastructure. Many leading nonprofit organizations including City Year, YouthBuild, Teach for America, and the Harlem Children's Zone have received substantial support from AmeriCorps, facilitating their overall service expansion.

In addition, President Obama created the Office of Social Innovation and Citizen Participation as a partnership between leading foundations and the federal government to support important and effective social innovations at the local level. One of the key goals of this new office was "outcomes-driven government and social sector" – another reflection of the ripple effects of NPM on government and the nonprofit sector. This priority for evidence-based solutions also translated into support for community-based initiatives that mixed public and private incentives. As part of its overall support of social innovation, the Obama administration also supported the growth of Program-Related Investments (PRIs) by foundations, a financial strategy that allows foundations to move beyond traditional grants to other types of financial support. The Obama Administration tried to encourage foundations to use PRIs more widely by simplifying IRS rules so foundations to provide credit enhancements, loan guarantees, lines of credit, even equity investments to achieve their philanthropic missions.

The enthusiasm for social innovation is also evident in Europe where government policymakers including at the European Union (EU) which has directly supported social innovation projects primarily through community-based nonprofits (Anheier, Krlev, and Mildenberger, 2019). Indeed, the EU has supported an impressive array of social innovation projects including place-based regeneration initiatives in the arts and culture field (Cancellieri et al., 2019). Many foundations have also directly supported many different types of social innovation including SIBs in partnership with national, state, and local governments.

Social innovation and the emphasis on performance by public and nonprofit organization is also reflected in the push for "collective impact." In brief, "collective impact" is an approach to evaluation and program accountability that calls attention to community-wide effects of public and nonprofit programs, especially in the fields of economic development, human services, and health care. By working together, local community organizations can achieve program synergy and a more profound impact on the local community. For instance, Kania and Kramer (2011) cite the example of Shape Up Somerville (a small city in Massachusetts) which is a city-wide public-private partnership focused on a comprehensive and successful effort to reduce childhood obesity. Part of the impetus behind collective impact is the dissatisfaction with the fragmented local service systems in many communities that creates serious obstacles to more enduring and substantial change in social problems. Collective impact also highlights the centrality of nonprofit organizations to local communities and the need for joint production of services in order to achieve greater program impact.

Nonprofit Management Education: Challenges and Opportunities in a New Organizational Landscape

Given the changes in the role and responsibilities of nonprofits at the community, regional, and national level, the education of nonprofit managers and more broadly individuals interested in working for social mission-related organizations has had to adapt and respond. One notable shift underway for many years has been in the education of students in schools of public affairs and public policy. Indeed, the need for change and its connection to public service reform was noted by the well-known scholar of nonprofit organizations and philanthropy, Lester Salamon (1996) at a 1996 conference on nonprofit management education. He observed that public administration teaching programs should undertake a "basic reconceptualization of what the nature of public administration has come to mean" (p. 12). He reiterated his call for curricular change and innovation at schools of public affairs in a 2004 keynote address at the annual meeting of the National Schools of Public Affairs and Administration which he urged schools to "devise a form of training that focuses on preparing people not for a particular type of organization – be it government, business, or nonprofit – nor with a particular technique, such as policy analysis, but for *a particular type of career*". Salamon called this career the "professional citizen". A central element of this needed curricular innovation for the professional citizen would be the integration of nonprofit-related issues into the core curriculum of masters-level programs (Salamon, 1996, 2005; Cohen and Abbott, 2000; Smith, 2008; Saidel and Smith, 2015).

In this vision, students would be educated to serve in a variety of social-mission oriented settings including: public agencies, nonprofit organizations, for-profit social enterprises, foundations, and corporate community affairs programs. He also observed that public service reform had increased the extent to which the purposes of government were accomplished through a variety of different "tools" including contracting, vouchers, tax credits, and loans. The effect was to increase the reliance of government on nonprofit and for-profit organizations to achieve public purposes. The various tools of government also have increased the complexity of local services, creating greater professionalization of public and nonprofit organizational staff (Smith, 2008).

These changes in the public services, broadly defined present important opportunities for nonprofit management education, especially in schools of public affairs and public policy. The potential pool of students interested in a master's in public administration or public policy for example has been enlarged, due to the growth of nonprofit organizations and the shift in the focus of many public service minded individuals. Whereas a person might have worked in the public sector to help at-risk youth or promote economic development, a person might now work in a nonprofit community organization.

Not surprisingly, perhaps, nonprofit graduate education for nonprofit managers expanded rapidly starting in the 1980s and thereafter to meet this growing demand (Mirabella and Wish, 2000; Mirabella, 2007; Young, 1999). Nonprofit management related courses within schools of public affairs and public policy increased sharply. Management content also increased in other graduate programs including social work and business (Mirabella and Wish, 2000). A few programs were also free-standing master's degrees in nonprofit organization or management in the mid-1980s and early 1990s. For example, the University of San Francisco created a Master's in Nonprofit Administration and Case Western Reserve University established a Master's of Nonprofit Organization degree. Seattle University launched a Masters in Nonprofit Leadership. These free-standing programs tended to be institutionally separate from regular departmental degree programs, although over time these degree programs were eventually incorporated into a regular university school or department.

More generally, though, the most common response of graduate programs was to add courses on nonprofit management and hire new faculty who specialized in nonprofit organizations and management. Many programs also created nonprofit concentrations and specializations; thus a student could receive a masters in public administration with a concentration in nonprofit management. Some graduate programs also created inter-departmental certificate programs that would allow students in many different departments such as social work, theatre, business administration could receive a nonprofit management certificate in addition to their master's in arts administration.

The growth of these programs was also fueled by the major influx of resources from foundations to create and support nonprofit academic centers and capacity building for nonprofit organizations. These centers would serve as hubs for research and teaching on nonprofit organizations and provide support for local nonprofit organizations on an ongoing basis. Many centers also organized regular conferences and non-degree educational and training opportunities for local nonprofit leaders. At the Evans School of Public Policy and Governance at the University of Washington, a one-week, Nonprofit Executive Leadership Institute for nonprofit executives was created. The McCourt School of Public Policy at Georgetown has a Nonprofit Management Executive Certificate program. Many other similar educational programs exist around the country.

The creation of these nonprofit centers raised the visibility of nonprofit management education and in turn spurred new programs and faculty hiring. The proliferation of these centers and the availability of foundation funding eventually led to the founding of the Nonprofit Academic Centers Council (NACC) in 1991. This new association promoted nonprofit research and education and eventually promulgated set of curricular guidelines for undergraduate and graduate study of philanthropy and nonprofit organizations (NACC, 2015).

The increase in nonprofit organizations and the pressure for more accountability and professionalization also led to the sharp growth in many different types of nonprofit training and educational apart from traditional graduate degree programs in public administration and social work such as extension schools, community colleges, and consulting firms. Also, nonprofit associations also became important, to varying degrees. The growth of nonprofits almost inevitably led to the creation of nonprofit associations at the local, state, and national level to represent the interests of nonprofits especially regarding government funding and regulation. Many state and local associations sponsor annual and/or regular conferences that provide various types of professional development opportunities for nonprofit leaders, staff, and volunteers. Larger nonprofit associations such as Maryland Nonprofits have a full menu of services including training, professional development, and conferences. Maryland Nonprofits (2021) even has a form of nonprofit accreditation called the "Standards of Excellence" whereupon nonprofits agree to abide by certain best practices, especially pertaining to governance and transparency. These standards have in turn created incentives for more professionalization, training, and consulting for nonprofit leaders.

In brief, the landscape of nonprofit management education has been drastically transformed in the last 30 years with a tremendously varied array of programs often vying with each other for students and resources, especially in major urban areas. Graduate programs in nonprofit management however arguably set the standard for the field and serve educational opportunities for nonprofit leaders. These programs, as noted, also support capacity building and training opportunities. Given the shift in careers of students interested in public service careers and the volatility of the nonprofit organizational landscape including increased competition for staff and resources, graduate programs in public affairs, public policy, social work, and business administration need to move toward a model of curriculum integration. Initially, many nonprofit management programs began with a single course or just a few courses. Many programs then added courses to create a concentration in nonprofit organizations. Often this concentration just reflected a few courses that were taken as part of master's program. This concentration could also sometimes be combined with a formal certificate in nonprofit management depending upon rules at the university or school.

However, many programs did not integrate nonprofit content into their core curriculum as suggested by Salamon (1996), Cohen and Abbott (2000), and others. Instead, the nonprofit courses tended to be quite separate and distinct from the rest of the curriculum. The reasons for the lack of curricular integration are numerous including the resistance of faculty in the core curriculum to changing their courses, resource constraints, and the difficulty of revising core curriculum. However, many schools did move to revise their core curriculum. In a study of nonprofit curricular integration, Saidel and Smith (2015) found that programs with greater integration were more likely to be accredited by NASPAA, suggesting the powerful isomorphic pressures exerted by NASPAA on their accredited organizations through their standards, annual meetings, committees, and publications including the *Journal of Public Affairs Education*. Programs are more likely to have more resources if they are accredited. NASPAA standards also evolved to reflect the changes in the public services and the recognition for the need curricular integration and greater focus on nonprofits through concentrations and specializations. A major shift in the accreditation standards occurred in 2009 when NASPAA moved from an input and process-based assessment process to mission-based. The practical consequences were to allow graduate programs in public administration and public policy to increase their curricular content on nonprofits because it was a reflection of their public service mission. Over time, the expectation has grown that NASPAA accredited programs will integrate nonprofit content into their core curriculum as reflected the latest revision of the NASPAA standards in 2019 (NASPAA, 2019).

To be sure, nonprofit curricular integration does not preclude the continuation of nonprofit concentrations and specializations, especially for students who want more intensive education in nonprofits and philanthropy. Moreover, a strong need will continue to exist for non-degree nonprofit management certificates, especially for individuals who may find themselves in leadership positions in nonprofit organizations without substantial background in key issues pertaining to nonprofits such as tax law, fundraising, and strategic planning.

Importantly, the education of nonprofit leaders should also reflect the reality of the public services today. The integration of nonprofit curriculum into courses such as public management, policy analysis, and program evaluation is an essential part of the graduate education for nonprofit leaders today. Yet, the advent of NPM and the more recent development of the new public governance also calls attention to the importance of training and education in the skills needed by students and practitioners committed to public service careers including leadership in nonprofit organizations. First, nonprofit management education should emphasize the acquisition of skills in negotiation, collaboration, and coalition building. As noted, nonprofits are in a complex mixed public/private organizational environment requiring joint action. This effort can take many forms: corporate partnerships, co-location of services, sharing administrative costs, integrating services, fiscal sponsorship, and participation in coalitions including advocacy. Many coalitions for example represent many different organizations who have a collective interest in public policy including funding and regulations. Many state and regional coalitions provide direct services including technical assistance to members agencies. In the US, the state coalitions are often members of the National Council of Nonprofits which advocates for the interests of member state associations at the federal level. It also provides technical assistance to member associations.

Knowledge of strategies for coalition building also fits the need for nonprofit managers to build a supportive community, especially in the current challenging fiscal environment. More specifically, nonprofits are often started by an initial public or private grant. And many nonprofits are highly dependent upon government contracts or a large foundation grant. However, this financial dependence creates significant risks for the organization. If a contract is reduced or delayed, it can lead to organizational cutbacks and turbulence. Further, the competition for government funds also means that nonprofits can benefit from community support. Indeed, long-term sustainability hinges on community support, broadly defined. Community members can be on the board of directors which can also forge cooperative social networks with the broader community. In essence, then, nonprofit leaders need the same facility with working with external groups as public sector personnel who often need to work closely with external groups to advance important public policy goals and objectives.

Building external support also highlights the strategic importance of governance and representation in nonprofits. As David Renz (2010) observed, governance in nonprofits has, until recently, been identified as the same as the board. Thus, nonprofit governance referred to board functioning, dynamics, and representation. The voluminous literature on governance often focused on strategies to improve board functioning and educating board members and nonprofit executives on the strategic and fiduciary role of nonprofit boards and their separation from the staff and ongoing operations. But the ripple effects of NPM and the emergence of the "new public governance" including more network approaches to program development, design, and implementation mean that nonprofit leaders need to think very differently about governance. The emphasis now shifts from the board itself or the board–staff relationship to the relationship between the board, staff, and the broader community of public, nonprofit, and for-profit organizations. In this environment, a premium also needs to be placed by nonprofit leaders on building individual and community support through philanthropic contributions, volunteering, and political support.

For students at graduate programs in public affairs and administration, this expanded and reconstituted vision of governance means the nonprofit leaders need to think differently about accountability and organizational performance. In an environment of collective impact, strategic alliances, and coalitions, nonprofit leaders need to understand that the success of the organization hinges upon productive relationships with other organizations and community leaders. As a result, governance design has become a crucial aspect of effective nonprofit leadership. In this context, design means the purposeful structuring of the relationships and the representation of different constituencies and individuals within overall governance. For example, many nonprofits participate in coalitions with other organizations such as coalitions to address substance abuse or homelessness. The success of these coalitions in achieving program impact can directly hinge on the ability of the coalition leadership to manage the representation of different interests. If representation is not perceived to be fair or accessible, then the coalition can struggle with the development of financial sustainability and effective programs. Nonprofits in a particular field increasingly need to collaborate with other organizations; thus, the management of the relationships requires skillful supportive attention.

Effective governance also requires appropriate and up-to-date by-laws that match well with the needs of the organizations. Many nonprofits are started by individuals passionate about a particular cause or issue such as helping at-risk youth, a new community theatre, or promoting economic development. When a nonprofit is initially incorporated, they are required to have by-laws; over time, though, these bylaws may seriously hamper the ability of the nonprofit to be nimble in responding to new trends and opportunities. Thus, by-laws and the overall governance structure needs to be periodically updated. This issue is more important than ever, given the uncertainty and turbulence in the environment of nonprofits.

Present and future nonprofit leaders then need to think broadly about governance including interorganizational relationships that are embedded in the design of programs. A nonprofit economic development organization cannot simply rely upon its own internal programs to be successful; instead, it has to work closely with other local public and private organizations. This basic approach applies in countless other program areas. To be sure, arts and cultural organizations may be staging their own exhibitions; nonetheless, these same organizations need the philanthropic and political support of the local community including foundations, business, the municipality, and the region. This effort also reflects the widespread interest and support for collective impact and services integration to overcome the tendency for program fragmentation at the local level and the so-called "silo" effect of many relatively small local organizations with relatively minimal impact. The vision of collective impact and services integration is that joint production of services will lead to more effective and impactful programs for the overall betterment of the community.

These collective and inter-organizational imperatives and the more competitive environment for resources, staff, and philanthropic contributions also suggests that students interested in graduate education in nonprofit management would benefit from a wholistic, integrated approach to management education that directly addressed leadership, stakeholder analysis, collaboration, diversity, equity and inclusion, program management and design, and building community and political support. Of course, current and future leaders can benefit from more specialized coursework on nonprofit and philanthropic topics such as federal tax law, state regulations, fundraising and capital campaigns, and advocacy. Certificate programs in nonprofit management for degree and non-degree students can be very helpful, especially for current nonprofit leaders. Nonprofit board members can also benefit from workshops and seminar on board governance and overall nonprofit management. Many graduate programs in public administration and public policy also have concentrations in nonprofit management that can be a great complement to the core, required courses. Indeed, the growth of these concentrations to be the most popular concentration in many schools reflects the longer-term ripple effects of the NPM and public service. Graduate programs that would have been almost entirely focused on state and local government service in 1990 are now primarily serving students interested in careers in nonprofits, foundations, and social enterprises.

With the advent of more competition in public services, the leadership and staff of public, nonprofit, and for-profit service organizations also need a new skill set that places greater emphasis on negotiation, strategic planning, networking, effective communication, and the assessment of program impact. Indeed, the demonstration of program impact by service agencies is increasingly critical to obtaining grants and contracts, especially from public funding bodies and foundations.

Given these accountability trends, the staff in public service organizations broadly defined need to have greater knowledge of program evaluation and greater sophistication in terms of their training in the assessment of outcomes and impact. Moreover, the trend toward big data and its use for program evaluation requires greater skill sophistication. The increasingly digital environment also necessitates that staff have the ability to present accessible and informative program and organizational data.

While these analytic skills are very important, the so-called "soft skills" of teamwork, partnerships, and collaboration are essential, especially given the emphasis on innovation and accountability. Many organizational scholars have noted the importance of horizontal networks and partnerships for innovation and organizational effectiveness (Senge, Hamilton, and Kania, 2015; Kotter, 2007; Porter and Kramer, 2011). Public service agencies in turn need to create governance structures that promote collaboration and innovation. Thus, program design, governance, and project management need ongoing emphasis and attention by leaders in public and nonprofit service organizations.

Conclusion

Public service reform in the last 30 years has over time transformed the public services, leading to extensive contracting with nonprofit and for-profit agencies, a wide variety of public-private partnerships, greater competition among service agencies, and much more emphasis on accountability, evaluation, and program impact. This transformation of the public services has in turn lead to fundamental changes in the education of students interested in public service careers. Students now demand greater course content on nonprofit management including certificate and specializations. At the same time, public service reform has blurred the boundaries between the public, nonprofit, and for-profit sectors. Social enterprises often combine a social mission with a reliance on fees and earned income. Nonprofit community agencies need to pay heed to financial sustainability and often actively compete with other local organizations for contracts, grants, and private donations. For-profit service agencies such as hospices, home health agencies, and job training organizations now dominate their service niches in many jurisdictions. Staff may now work in the nonprofit, for-profit, and public sector during their careers. Consequently, graduate programs in public affairs and public policy need to adapt their course content to provide a solid grounding in core management and leadership skills that can be valuable in different sectors. Thus, an integrated approach to nonprofit management education that includes content on nonprofit management in the core curriculum in graduate programs can be especially useful, especially given the growing emphasis on program impact, partnerships, and greater accountability. Nonprofit managers, like their counterparts on the for-profit sectors, also need to be effective advocates for their organizations in their local communities and with policymakers at different levels of government.

Finally, the pandemic has created a much greater demand for the services of many community organizations while at the same time has produced an enormous loss of income and services in other types of nonprofits such as arts and cultural agencies. Regardless of the course of the pandemic in the coming months and years, nonprofit organizations will very likely remain in a very turbulent and uncertain environment. Consequently, nonprofit leaders will need to be adaptive, flexible, and resourceful, requiring the building of important alliances and partnerships and fostering an internal culture supporting innovation and responsiveness. Graduate management programs thus have a great opportunity to educate future leaders of nonprofit organizations to effectively respond to the contemporary and future challenges facing their organizations and their local communities.

References

Alford, John. 2009. *Engaging Public Sector Clients: From Service-Delivery to Co-Production.* London: Palgrave Macmillan.

Anheier, Helmut K., Gorgi Krlev, and Georg Mildenberger (eds.). 2019. *Social Innovation: Comparative Perspectives.* London: Routledge.

Bovaird, Tony. 2007. "Beyond Engagement and Participation: User and Community Co-Production of Public Services," *Public Administration Review*, 67, 5: 846–860.

Brudney, Jeffrey and Robert E. England. 1983. "Toward a Definition of the Coproduction Concept," *Public Administration Review*, 43, 1: 59–65.

Cancellieri, Giulia, Alex Turrini, María José Sanzo Perez, Noelia Salido-Andres, Jeanet Kullberg, and Aurélie Sara Cognat. 2019. "Place-Regeneration Initiatives Driven by Arts & Culture to Achieve Social Cohesion," in Helmut K. Anheier, Gorgi Krlev, and Georg Mildenberger (eds.), *Social Innovation: Comparative Perspectives*. London: Routledge. pp. 79–103.

Cohen, Steven and Tracie Abbott. 2000. *Integrating Nonprofit Management Education into Graduate Programs in Public Policy and Administration*. New York: Columbia University School of International and Public Affairs. www.columbia.edu/~sc32/documents/Integrating%20Nonprofit%20Management.pdf

Corporation for National and Community Service (CNCS), Office of Research and Evaluation. 2015. *State of the Pay for Success Field: Opportunities, Trends, and Recommendations*. Washington, DC: CNCS.

Freise, Matthias and Petr Pajas. 2004. "Organizational and Legal Forms of Nonprofit Organizations in Central Europe", in Annette Zimmer and Eckhard Priller (eds.), *Future of Civil Society. Making Central European Nonprofit-Organizations Work*. Wiesbaden: VS-Verlag, pp. 129–146.

Henry, Lauren L. 2015. *Education for Public Service: The Growth of University Study of Public Administration and Public Affairs and the Origins and Founding of the National Association of Schools of Public Affairs and Administration*. Charlottesville, VA: NASPAA. www.naspaa.org/sites/default/files/docs/2019-02/Education%20for%20Public%20Service%20-%20Laurin%20Henry.pdf

Hood, Christopher. 1991. "A Public Management for all Seasons," *Public Administration*, 69, 1: 3–19.

Joachim, Jutta (2014), "NGOs in World Politics", in John Baylis, Steve Smith and Patricia Owens (eds.), *The Globalization of World Politics*. Oxford: Oxford University Press, pp. 347–362.

Kania, John and Mark Kramer. 2011. "Collective Impact," *Stanford Social Innovation Review* (Winter). www.ssireview.org/images/articles/2011_WI_Feature_Kania.pdf

Kendall, Jeremy. 2000. "The Mainstreaming of the Third Sector into Public Policy in England in the Late 1990s: Why and Whereofs," *Policy & Politics*, 28, 4: 541–562.

Kettl, Donald F. 2006. "Managing Boundaries in American Administration: The Collaboration Imperative," *Public Administration Review*, Special Issue (December): 10–18.

Kotter, John P. 2007. *Leading Change*. Cambridge, MA: Harvard Business School Press.

Maryland Nonprofits, 2021. *Standards of Excellence*. www.marylandnonprofits.org/what-we-offer/standards-for-excellence/

Mirabella, Roseanne M. 2007. "University-Based Educational Programs in Nonprofit Management and Philanthropic Studies: A 10-Year Review and Projections of Future Trends." *Nonprofit and Voluntary Sector Quarterly*, Supplement to 36, 1: 11S–27S.

Mirabella, Roseanne M. and Khanh Nguyen. 2019. "Educating Nonprofit Students as Agents of Social Transformation: Critical Public Administration as a Way Forward." *Administrative Theory and Praxis*, 40, 4: 1–17.

Mirabella, Roseanne M. and Naomi B. Wish. 2000. "The 'Best Place' Debate: A Comparison of Graduate Education Programs for Nonprofit Managers." *Public Administration Review*, 60, 3: 219–229.

National Network of Schools of Public Affairs and Administration (NASPAA). 2019. *Accreditation Standards for Master's Degree Programs*. www.naspaa.org/sites/default/files/docs/2019-10/NASPAA%20Accreditation%20Standards%20-%202019%20FINAL%20DRAFT%20no%20rationale.pdf

Nonprofit Academic Centers Council (NACC). 2015. *Curricular Guidelines: Graduate and Undergraduate Study in Nonprofit Leadership, the Nonprofit Sector, and Philanthropy*. www.nonprofit-academic-centers-council.org/NACC-WP/wp-content/uploads/2019/01/NACC_Curricular_Guidelines_100615-2.pdf

Osborne, Stephen P. 2010. "Introduction. The (New) Public Governance: A Suitable Case for Treatment?" in Stephen P. Osborne (ed.), *The New Public Governance. Emerging Perspectives on the Theory and Practice of Public Governance*. London: Routledge, pp. 1–16

Parks, Roger B., et al., 1981. "Consumers as Coproducers of Public Services: Some Economic and Institutional Considerations." *Policy Studies Journal*. 9, 7: 1001–1011.

Phillips, Susan D. and Steven Rathgeb Smith. 2011. "Between Governance and Regulation," in Susan Phillips and Steven Rathgeb Smith (eds.), *Governance and Regulation in the Third Sector*. New York and London: Routledge.

Phillips, Susan D. and Steven Rathgeb Smith. 2015 "A Dawn of Convergence? Third Sector Policy Regimes in the 'Anglo-Saxon' Cluster." *Public Management Review*, 16, 8 (November/December): 1141–1163.

Porter, Michael E. and Mark R. Kramer. 2011. "Creating Shared Value." *Harvard Business Review*, 89, 1/2 (January–February): 62–77.

Renz, David O. 2018. "Reframing Governance II." *Nonprofit Quarterly*, 17, 4: 50–53. https://nonprofitquarterly.org/reframing-governance-2/

Rhodes, R. A. W. 1994. "The Hollowing Out of the State: The Changing Nature of the Public Service in Britain." *The Political Quarterly*, 65, 2: 138–151.

Saidel, Judith and Steven Rathgeb Smith. 2015. "Nonprofit Management Education with Public Affairs Curricula: An Analysis of the Trend Toward Curriculum Integration." *Journal of Political Science Education*, 21, 3: 337–348.

Salamon, Lester M. 1994. "The Rise of the Nonprofit Sector." *Foreign Affairs*, 73, 4: 109–122.

Salamon, Lester M. 1996. "Nonprofit Management Education: A Field Whose Time Is Passed?" Paper prepared for delivery at the Conference on Nonprofit Management Education 1996: A US and World Perspective. Berkeley, CA.

Salamon, Lester M. (ed.). 2002. *The Tools of Government*. New York, NY: Oxford University Press.

Salamon, Lester M. 2005. "Training Professional Citizens: Getting Beyond the Right Answer to the Wrong Question in Public Affairs Education." *Journal of Public Affairs Education*, 11, 1: 7–20.

Senge, Peter, Hal Hamilton, and John Kania, 2015. "The Dawn of Systems Leadership." *Stanford Social Innovation Review*, 139, 1 (Winter): 26–33.

Smith, Steven Rathgeb. 2008. "The Increased Complexity of Public Services: Curricular Implications for Schools of Public Affairs." *Journal of Public Affairs Education*, 14(2):115–128.

Smith, Steven Rathgeb. 2021. "Governance Challenges in Co-Production," in Tony Bovaird and Elke Loeffler (ed.), *The Palgrave Handbook on Co-production*. London: Palgrave, pp. 595–611.

Smith, Steven Rathgeb and Michael Lipsky. 1993. *Nonprofits for Hire: The Welfare State in the Age of Contracting*. Cambridge, MA: Harvard University Press.

Young, Dennis R. 1999. "Nonprofit Management Studies in the United States: Current Developments and Future Prospects." *Journal of Public Affairs Education*, 5, 1: 13–23.

Zimmer, Annette and Steven Rathgeb Smith. 2022. *Nonprofits Contributing to Public Governance*. Cheltenham: Edward Elgar, pp. 327–351.

6

NONPROFIT MANAGEMENT

Beyond Managerialism

Robert L. Fischer and Duncan Mayer

Introduction

The nonprofit sector is an important economic and social force, accounting for a substantial portion of GDP and employment. At the same time, it is charged with providing a range of vital and otherwise highly valued services. The management of nonprofit organizations is important to the growth of the sector, the economy, and those that depend on the delivery of services. It is widely acknowledged that nonprofit organizations face unique managerial circumstances, as they actively engage with social conditions and economic markets under various constraints. Given the importance and complexity of nonprofit management, the training of nonprofit managers has become of increasing significance in the sector. University degrees, particularly post-baccalaureate training (e.g., masters degrees or certificates) in nonprofit management have proliferated and are increasingly common among organizational leadership (Kuenzi et al., 2020).

Despite the value in management education for the nonprofit sector, a unifying approach to education in nonprofit management is relatively recent, with the first guidelines appearing in the early 2000s and the first formal accreditation of educational programs more recently (*NACC Curricular Guidelines*, 2015; see Appendix). With the formalization of nonprofit management education, managerialism; the ideology, culture, and socialization of management, becomes particularly relevant. In this chapter, we discuss the existing understandings of managerialism, as well as its limits and applications in the education of nonprofit managers. This leads naturally to a discussion of the value proposition for management education in the nonprofit sector. In this approach we address two primary questions. First, to what extent has the development of nonprofit management education been influenced

DOI: 10.4324/9781003294061-7

by managerialist philosophies? Second, in what ways do the aims and goals of managerialism not apply as clearly in the nonprofit management context?

Defining Managerialist Thinking

Managerialism has a long history in management sciences and education; often, it is viewed as beginning with the reification of management and distinctions about the role of the manager. Although the practices related to managerialism were born in the for-profit arena (particularly in corporate/industrial practice and MBA programs), managers and educators quickly made the transition to promoting managerialism as it applies to the management of public organizations. Managerialism has been the object of interdisciplinary discussion for decades; however, understandings of managerialism vary considerably. Often it is seen as the ideological accoutrement to the practice of management (or the combination of the two). In one review, Edwards (1998) presents a composite definition of managerialism as an ideology which places the highest value on the pursuit of maximum output with minimum input (i.e., efficiency), faith in the techniques of management science to resolve organizational problems, class consciousness among managers, and the belief in the manager as a moral agent seeking actions in accordance with the greatest good for society. Klikauer (2013a) rather emphasizes the role of management technologies when they suggest that the

> central dogma of managerialism is that the differences between, for example, universities and car companies are less important than their similarities and that the performance of all organizations can be optimised by the application of generic management skills and knowledge.
>
> *p. 4–5*

This corresponds, historically, to the inception of the use of performance indicators, which permitted management to track operational and employee efficiency without a complete understanding of the specific tasks (Melo & Beck, 2014). The US public sector analogue to this phenomenon is seen clearly in the Kennedy and Johnson administrations (1960–1968), as the evaluation of the Great Society programs brought new emphasis on outcomes. These administrations also applied management principles more broadly, including in areas such as international trade and national defense (Scott & Hart, 1991).

More pessimistically, managerialism is often considered the ideological component of an effort to reallocate the locus of decision making in civil society, permitting technocratic managers to centralize decision making power (Klikauer, 2013b). Often such a movement is framed around the moral obligations of managers, who act in the best interests of their organizations, with the further assumption that organizational interests and societal interests coincide (Klikauer, 2013a; Scott &

Hart, 1991). A similar, although more recent framing maintains that organizations have a responsibility to society, termed corporate social responsibility. This framing suggests that organizations follow ethical principles and contribute to the good of their communities (Melo & Beck, 2014). Prior understandings weave these themes together, highlighting social progress as an outcome of economic productivity, and believing productivity is best achieved through the application of sophisticated technologies by a disciplined workforce (Terry, 1998).

The intellectual origins of managerialism are somewhat ambiguous, but have been presented as emerging from the changes during the industrial revolution (Melo & Beck, 2014), while others emphasize its connection to pragmatic and progressive philosophy (Scott & Hart, 1991). The influence of cultural values may explain the emergence of early proponents of managerialism and managerial science from the United States, given the prominence of rationality in western philosophy (Klikauer, 2013a, 2013b). Despite this ambiguity, there is reasonable consensus on the centrality of early management theorists such as Taylor, Drucker, and Fayol in concretizing and enacting managerialist beliefs (particularly the earliest works, such as Fayol, 1949; Taylor & Person, 1947).

The development of management science and formal schools of management were essential to the proliferation of managerialism, as education provided a legitimizing force for the field, as well as a platform for the development of professional identity among managers. It is then important to note that early management theorists were instrumental in the development of formal management training. Soon after its first dean visited one of Fredrick Taylor's long-term projects, the newly minted Harvard Business School included scientific management in its core curriculum (in addition to the development of a research laboratory), followed a few years later by Dartmouth's Tuck School of Business. This is notable as Taylor's approach to scientific management is largely inseparable from his contempt for labor and pursuit of efficiency (Hoopes, 2003). The institution of management sciences in the academy served to further support the desire for a scientific (and largely positivist) approach to management. This is distilled most clearly in Simon's (1997) landmark contribution (originally published in 1947) to organizational theory, which advanced a research agenda in management sciences that privileges positivism, rationality, and efficiency, while also providing a path for management's inclusion in the social sciences.

The role of managerialism in public management was solidified as Americans began to believe that government institutions should be managed rationally to increase efficiency. The natural place for the public sector to turn for "best practices" was the management of private corporations. Certainly, managerialism had taken root by the late 1800s as evinced by the passage of the Pendleton act, which established the civil service system, as well as the inception of scientific administration during the Wilson administration, during which Henry Gantt applied a refined version of scientific management to Naval production practices (Edwards, 1998; Hoopes, 2003; Scott & Hart, 1991). Some contemporary trends in the management of public organizations can be seen as resulting from the proliferation of managerialism, particularly as the function of the administrative state has shifted public organizations from facilitators to policy makers (Scott & Hart, 1991). For example, the New Public Management (NPM) movement has been reframed as a result of the proliferation of managerialism and a profit orientation (Klikauer, 2013a), others have emphasized the role of public entrepreneurs and innovation, dubbing NPM neo-managerialism (Terry, 1998). The influence of managerialism in public management is important to the study of its role in nonprofit management, as schools of public management as the fields are intertwined, and increasingly share in common management practices. Such shared experience is clear when common circumstances encountered by managers are considered, including provision and creation of goods under outcome ambiguity, non-distribution constraints, and delegation (Mitchell & Schmitz, 2018).

In addition to providing the grounds for a professional identity, managerialism may also implicitly set the agenda for management, including the design of organizational and managerial intervention around core values such as efficiency and rationality. Therefore, managerialism may define the means available to managers. However, the ideology does not only function on managers, rather, it seeks to facilitate public belief in management. In this way, managerialism addresses the question of why organizational members, with the resources to resist the attainment of organizational goals, generally follow management. When reference is made to managerialism in this chapter, we rely on the composite definition offered by Edwards (1998) including an emphasis on efficiency through the techniques of management science, the development of a professional identity, and the belief in the manager as a moral agent.

Emergence of Managerialism in Nonprofit Management Education

The Nonprofit Academic Centers Council (hereon, NACC) has been a dominant force in development of nonprofit management education. Founded in 1991 to support nonprofit education and research, NACC also began developing curricular guidelines in 2001 with quality indicators following soon after. Recently, NACC also began offering accreditation to masters programs in nonprofit and nongovernmental studies including management, social entrepreneurship, social-purpose organizations' leadership, as well as other programs in philanthropic studies. The curricular guidelines and quality indicators are central to the accreditation process, as accreditation emphasizes mapping between these and syllabi (Hale & Irvin, 2017). The NACC curricular guidelines provide a clear distillation of important features in nonprofit management and may therefore give some indication of the permeation of managerialism in nonprofit management education and philanthropic studies. See Appendix.

We examined the NACC graduate guidelines for evidence of our identified definition of managerialism discussed in the first section. To begin, evidence of facilitating a professional identity as a nonprofit manager is seen in the emphasis on history (2.1, 2.5, 3.1), socializing prospective managers into the philanthropic traditions and legacy. Understanding the history of the field/sector may support prospective managers in further developing their professional narrative and support a consciousness in the field. Indeed, a motivation of NACC and nonprofit research has been the creation of a unique professional approach and intellection (i.e., nonprofit first thinking) (Mendel, 2013). The document and accreditation efforts, in-themselves, represent an effort at demarcating the class of nonprofit managers from related fields of public/businesses administration and social work, and thereby facilitating a unique shared experience and identity among prospective nonprofit managers.

The emphasis on efficiency discussed in our review of managerialism is seen throughout the NACC competencies. There are times the emphasis on a particular dimension or channel to increase efficiency is explicit, such as in governance, the application of market principles, data management and technology, and assessment (5.5, 8.4, 15.4, 16.1). Relatedly, there is great emphasis on management technologies as a primary vehicle to achieve these ends, including outcome measurement, cost-benefit analysis, models of authority, strategic planning, and more (4.2, 5.1, 8.4, 9.1, 11.4, 12.6, 15.2–15.4, 16.1–16.4). The NACC guidelines similarly address the concerns around the manager as a moral agent, as they emphasize the creation of social value, and its role in facilitating trust, transparency, responsibility, and accountability while centering the organization's mission (1.2, 4.1–4.4, 11.1, 12.3).

The review reveals that all key aspects of managerialism are present, in some way, within the NACC guidelines. There is evidence that the NACC curricular guidelines address the ends (efficiency), means (management technology), justification (the manager as a moral agent), and identification (professional identity) for nonprofit managers. While the NACC guidelines exhibit many of the key characteristics of managerialist thinking and the influence of managerialist ideology, it does not necessarily follow that programs and students in nonprofit management ingest the most deleterious elements of managerialism. Rather, despite what appears to be the clear presence and the influence of managerialism in the NACC guidelines, there are unique circumstances in the nonprofit sector that provide context for managerialism, and ultimately complicate its interpretation. Further, none of the key characteristics of managerialism, such as the reliance of management technologies or an emphasis on efficiency, confirm the presence and influence of managerialism, which is a comprehensive ideology, rather than a set of actions or skills.

It is worth discussing the limitations of the construct of managerialism in the nonprofit sector. As suggested in Klikauer (2013a), a central feature of managerialism the belief that a set of skills and intellection transcend differences between organizations, however, the study of nonprofit organizations has generally belied this point. Indeed, the preceding quote is in stark contrast to Newman and Wallender's (1978) observation that the diversity of nonprofit organizations makes general management recommendations challenging, and that

> the differences between not-for-profit enterprises – for example a cancer research institute versus a Harlem street academy versus a cemetery association – are so great that their common characteristic of not seeking a profit becomes minor, at least with respect to managing them.
>
> *p. 25–26*

This emphasizes that nonprofit organizations are sufficiently different as to make the development of universally applicable management technologies challenging, as well as reiterating that nonprofit organizations differ dramatically from their for-profit and public counterparts.

Typical interpretations of efficiency involve maximum output for some minimum input. Here, we immediately encounter complications in the application to nonprofit organizations. Nonprofit organizations often manage (at least) two bottom lines, financial and social, with multiple constituencies vying for the organization to focus on a particular area of emphasis. Across constituencies within any given organization, there rarely exists a unifying conception of efficiency, or the most important inputs or outputs. In the nonprofit space, therefore, it remains an organizational decision to decide (1) to optimize efficiency, (2) the means, and (3) ends of this optimization, should it be decided on.

The role of the manager as a moral agent, a theme of which appears in several of NACC competencies, carries a different connotation in the nonprofit sector as well. While themes of social responsibility exist in the for-profit space, the interpretation changes in the nonprofit sector as organizations may arise through market failure, a primary form of which is contract failure, as the public may form or turn to nonprofit organizations as a result of lacking trust in for-profit enterprises (Steinberg, 2006). This shows that the role of the nonprofit manager as a moral agent is tempered by the constraints of the legal form and the organization's role in the market. Particularly, nonprofit organizations must maintain transparency, as their function is often catalyzed by public trust. Unilateral actions of nonprofit managers will be subject to the scrutiny of their board of trustees, other organizational members, and the public, many of whom are often highly invested. While exceptions exist, the nonprofit sector provides natural guardrails for organizations and managers to act in the interest of public welfare. Further, the motivations for the entrance of nonprofit managers differ from those entering the related management fields. A desire to help others and a high value for non-monetary returns have been shown to predict interest in employment in the nonprofit sector (Kuenzi et al., 2020; Tschirhart et al., 2008). Such motivations indicate that prospective nonprofit managers are exchanging some personal monetary benefit for a role that supports their social identity. This may suggest that once in the position, managers may avoid further departures from this social identity, absent other motivations (Akerlof & Kranton, 2010), including the undemocratic features of autocratic management described in managerialism.

Management Value in the Nonprofit Sector

Having acknowledged the uniqueness of nonprofit organizations, it is clear that management technologies developed in a for-profit context can rarely be adopted "off-the-shelf" by nonprofit managers. There are cases where such practices may work, although the success of implementing such interventions often depends on the size of the organization as well as the degree of centralization and bureaucracy (Beck et al., 2008). For example, there is some evidence that total quality management practices have been successful in the nonprofit context, however, its requirements, including ongoing training as well as measurement and continuous monitoring, may present a challenge for smaller organizations or those with few administrative staff (Kearns et al., 1994). Generally, larger nonprofit organizations of a certain structure may approximate for-profit counterparts well enough for successful implementation of management interventions developed in the for-profit arena, while smaller organizations may implement strategies restricted in larger settings, such as direct supervision (Beck et al., 2008).

The management context of the nonprofit sector is unique to the extent that any strategy may require substantial adaptation, or the development of new management interventions entirely. Some characteristics to consider include the ambiguity of core technologies, the strength of customer/consumer influence, employee commitment, the influence of resource contributors, and constraints on (dis) incentives (Newman & Wallender, 1978). A striking example is found in volunteer-dependent organizations, where the organization is reliant on labor which does not respond to monetary incentives. Rather, attracting and retaining volunteers may be contingent on the volunteer's experiences and the organizations adherence to the mission. The conditions faced by managers in volunteer-dependent organizations are, perhaps, a limiting case of those faced by nonprofit managers in other organizations, however, management practices must respond to the level of volunteer dependence (Guo et al., 2011). As in the preceding example, despite myriad limitations, management tools can still prove valuable for nonprofit managers. However, the ambiguity of many organizations' core technology as well as the investment of employees (e.g., multiple constituencies) may restrict over-emphasis on the easily quantifiable, leading an emphasis on adherence to the mission and its use as a management tool.

Considerations for the Field

The discussion of managerialist principles leads to consideration of the degree to which they align well with the nonprofit context and the decisions faced by nonprofit managers. Here we discuss the four primary components of the definition of managerialism (Edwards, 1998) and their applicability to the nonprofit context.

Focus on Efficiency

In the most general terms, the objective of increasing efficiency in organizations is widely held and transcends the context in which they operate (for-profit, governmental, nonprofit). However, in the for-profit context achieving efficiencies leads to a reduction in the cost of production, responding to a maximization of profit motive for the shareholders. This also leads to a willingness to invest in structures and staffing in the pursuit of efficiency. In the nonprofit context, there is no formal price incurred by direct consumers and funders may have fixed the allocation for a program. When efficiencies are achieved in production of a program or service, this may lead to an expansion of service provision without any additional resources. While this is desirable and may be consistent with a nonprofit's mission, it may lead to no additional income to the organization. This suggests that nonprofits may experience difficulty in securing resources for the pursuit of efficiency, as achieving efficiencies may not allow the organization to divert savings to such aims.

Use of Management Techniques

Managerialism places great emphasis on the use of management technologies for problem-solving. Such technologies include systematized ways of thinking and acting ideally coupled with an infrastructure that has the capacity to carry out these approaches over time. While for-profits have the ability to attract equity to invest in such infrastructure, this is much less the case for nonprofits. In fact, the downward pressure on "overhead" expenses by nonprofits make investments in management infrastructure and supports very challenging. Nonprofits may be successful in attracting capacity-building investments from selected funders but these are often time-limited and narrow in scope (e.g., fundraising capacity, data management systems). This is exacerbated by the interest of many funders to pay only for client-facing program operations rather than core organizational operations, among which management would be a central cost. It is worth noting that low-cost management technologies are accessible to many nonprofits (e.g., strategic planning, program logic models) but the longer-term value of these may be limited by insufficient infrastructure.

Manager as Moral Agent

The managerialist aim of the moral agency of managers places emphasis on managers acting in the best interest of their organization, which is seen as aligned with the best interest of society. Arguably, nonprofit managers seek to serve their organization's mission, which is defined in terms of social benefit. However, managerialist goals related to efficiency and use of management techniques could well run counter to other methods seen as better delivering on mission. For example, mission goals related to community-engaged service delivery and co-creation of programming could necessarily require approaches alternative to those in the managerialist toolkit. In the nonprofit sector, the agency of the manager is also directly influenced by the role of the board of directors and the volunteers that the organization engages in its work. Nonprofit managers must propose and implement approaches under the oversight of the board, who bring their own views about how best to achieve mission and seek to guard against mission drift. Further, while paid staff can be seen as carrying out the aims of management, volunteers offer a more fluid workforce who engage in activities based on self-motivation and commitment. Nonprofit managers will need to consider how managerialist aims can best be communicated and carried out by these unpaid staff, to the extent that they are central to program delivery.

Professional Identity of Managers

Managerialism's tenet of evoking a sense of professional identity among managers (or class consciousness) has limited applicability in the nonprofit context. Those serving in nonprofit management roles often have a stronger identity as a nonprofit professional than as a manager, focusing more on their commitment to social betterment and social justice than organizational performance. Within nonprofit management roles, arguably the strongest identity may occur for those in fund development or fundraising roles, which are focused on the attraction of resources rather than the management of operations. Within the nonprofit context, there may well be a sense of otherness for managers, in that they may be seen as helping the nonprofit "run more like a business" in order to achieve greater sustainability. This suggests that nonprofit managers may well have a unique identity, but they may experience some challenges aligning it with the nonprofit context in which they serve.

Conclusion

Nonprofit management education has been substantially influenced by managerialist approaches following their application in the for-profit and governmental sectors. This is evident in the creation of curricular approaches to the education of nonprofit managers and the development of related competencies. Though managerialism has provided a useful framework for the development of the field, there has been less consideration of the limits on its applicability in the nonprofit sector context. The limits we highlight suggest that while managerialist thinking has some value for nonprofit managers, more attention is needed on how to adapt these approaches to the realities of nonprofit organizations. This could involve reassessing the goals underlying managerialism and/or developing new approaches that better match the nonprofit context.

References

Akerlof, G. A., & Kranton, R. E. (2010). *Identity economics: How our identities shape our work, wages, and well-being*. Princeton University Press.

Beck, T. E., Lengnick-Hall, C. A., & Lengnick-Hall, M. L. (2008). Solutions out of context: Examining the transfer of business concepts to nonprofit organizations. *Nonprofit Management and Leadership, 19*(2), 153–171. https://doi.org/10.1002/nml.213

Edwards, J. D. (1998). Managerial influences in public administration. *International Journal of Organization Theory & Behavior, 1*(4), 553–583. https://doi.org/10.1108/IJOTB-01-04-1998-B007

Fayol, H. (1949). *General and industrial management*. Pittman.

Guo, C., Brown, W. A., Ashcraft, R. F., Yoshioka, C. F., & Dong, H.-K. D. (2011). Strategic human resources management in nonprofit organizations. *Review of Public Personnel Administration, 31*(3), 248–269. https://doi.org/10.1177/0734371X11402878

Hale, M., & Irvin, R. A. (2017). A position paper on accreditation on nonprofit/philanthropy university curricula. *Journal of Nonprofit Education and Leadership*. JNEL Special Issue (1), 126–137. https://doi.org/10.18666/JNEL-2017-V7-SI1-8248

Hoopes, J. (2003). *False prophets: The gurus who created modern management and why their ideas are bad for business today*. Basic Books.

Kearns, K. P., Krasman, R. J., & Meyer, W. J. (1994). Why nonprofit organizations are ripe for total quality management. *Nonprofit Management and Leadership, 4*(4), 447–460. https://doi.org/10.1002/nml.4130040407

Klikauer, T. (2013a). *Managerialism*. Palgrave Macmillan UK. https://doi.org/10.1057/9781137334275

Klikauer, T. (2013b). What is managerialism? *Critical Sociology, 41*(7–8), 1103–1119. https://doi.org/DOI: 10.1177/0896920513501351

Kuenzi, K., Stewart, A., & Walk, M. (2020). Nonprofit graduate education: Who gets the degree and why? *Journal of Public Affairs Education, 26*(1), 11–30. https://doi.org/10.1080/15236803.2018.1482107

Melo, S., & Beck, M. (2014). Managerialism: A historical overview. In S. Melo & M. Beck (Eds.), *Quality management and managerialism in healthcare* (p. 31). Palgrave Macmillan UK. https://doi.org/10.1057/9781137351999

Mendel, S. C. (2013). A field of its own. *Stanford Social Innovation Review, 12*, 2.

Mitchell, G. E., & Schmitz, H. P. (2018). The nexus of public and nonprofit management. *Public Performance & Management Review, 42*(1), 11–33. https://doi.org/10.1080/15309576.2018.1489293

NACC curricular guidelines. (2015). Nonprofit Academic Centers Council.

Newman, W. H., & Wallender, H. W. (1978). Managing not-for-profit enterprises. *The Academy of Management Review, 3*(1), 24. https://doi.org/10.2307/257573

Scott, W. G., & Hart, D. K. (1991). The exhaustion of managerialism. *Society, 28*(3), 39–48. https://doi.org/10.1007/BF02695594

Simon, H. A. (1997). *Administrative behavior, 4th edition*. Free Press.

Steinberg, R. (2006). Economic theories of nonprofit organizations. In W. W. Powell & R. Steinberg (Eds.), *The nonprofit sector: A research handbook* (2nd ed., pp 117–139). New Haven, CT: Yale University Press.

Taylor, F. W., & Person, H. S. (1947). *Scientific management*. New York, Harper.

Terry, L. D. (1998). Administrative leadership, neo-managerialism, and the public management movement. *Public Administration Review, 58*(3), 194. https://doi.org/10.2307/976559

Tschirhart, M., Reed, K. K., Freeman, S. J., & Anker, A. L. (2008). Is the grass greener? Sector shifting and choice of sector by MPA and MBA graduates. *Nonprofit and Voluntary Sector Quarterly, 37*(4), 668–688. https://doi.org/10.1177/0899764008314808

7

TEACHING ACCOUNTING AND FINANCIAL MANAGEMENT ON CHARITABLE ORGANISATIONS

Paul Palmer

Where Do You Begin?

Traditionally with the literature, but I am also going to suggest you should consider who the students you are going to teach are and what they really want and need to know. Two major theoretical contributions underpin the distinctive financial nonprofit literature. The first is in accounting and reporting and draws upon the pioneering work of Vatter (1947) fund theory of accounting which links to the Legal and Regulatory Framework and underpins Stewardship Theory. The second is the economic concept of nonprofit distribution (Hansmann 1980, 1987; Rose-Ackerman 1986; Steinberg and Gray 1993). Both provides a conceptual framework to engage students when dealing with nonprofit financial management and issues associated with endowment asset management.

The other key starting point is what the students themselves need. Unlike professional qualification studies or MBAs with accrediting organisations, which are prescriptive in what should and must be covered, there was nothing of this kind with nonprofits in the early 1990s – the Nonprofit Academic Centre Council (NACC) Curriculum guidance and now accreditation was still to arrive! I therefore had considerable freedom over what areas I should cover. This enabled me to design modules and even whole courses that met the needs of students and their organisations from a grounded, bottom-up perspective. When designing the first charity accounting course I spent three years working with the UKs then Charity Finance Directors Group. This was a membership charity that had been established by the leading charity finance practitioners and met under the auspice originally of the Institute of Chartered Accountants in England and Wales. Attending their meetings, discussing and knowledge exchanging with members from all types of charitable organisations and undertaking small practitioner

DOI: 10.4324/9781003294061-8

focused research projects enabled me with an insight of how to fuse traditional for-profit accounting and finance courses that I had been teaching with distinctive aspects of charity finance – fund accounting, nonprofit distribution – but also issues and topics that these prospective students were dealing with on a daily basis. Some of these topics also embraced wider issues that you would never see in traditional finance courses such as social policy, community stakeholder analysis, and practical management issues of engaging with a volunteer board that may have little financial knowledge or interest. This allowed me to introduce students to use the lens of critical accounting studies, which challenges the perspective that accounting is a neutral free discipline. We are therefore equipping students to have challenging insights rather than just professional and practical application.

My first charity finance course was targeted at finance professionals, some of whom were qualified accountants. Later I started developing finance modules for those working in charities but not in finance; initially fund raisers, but then senior staff some of whom were in the Chief Executive role. Then followed finance courses for those working in grant making charities which extended into philanthropists keen to understand charity finance to enhance their personal giving decisions and, most recently, then staff in sub-sectors like arts charities or those working in organisations (NGOs) with operations overseas. Could a one size course fit all?

The answer was not a simple "yes" or "no" but a complexity of different issues. On the "yes" side I do believe there is a common body of knowledge that anyone studying nonprofits should have. This is now formulated in the NACC curriculum guidance. Directly related to developing a finance course was to distinguish and segment the needs of qualified finance professionals from those with some or no financial background. Then to further divide those professionals with charity accounting and finance experience from those transferring into charities with little or no practical experience. This segmentation analysis meant I could overcome class teaching management issues where an introduction course on charity finance was not viewed as too simple, or "I already know this" by those qualified and experienced.

Utilising the Advanced Prior Learning (APL) and Advanced Prior Experience and Learning (APEL) schemes (that benchmark both education and experience against curriculum) I was able to identify appropriate exemptions and construct modules focusing on different topics in accounting and financial management. This was not to exclude those with finance experience from attending introductory modules but to manage expectations. Those applicants who were professionally qualified and experienced felt that their qualifications and experience were being recognised but had a choice. They could still attend but if they did so I briefed them on how to enhance their own learning and add value. This involved asking them to take on a leadership role in being peer mentors to those in the class who had no finance knowledge and indeed "phobias" about numbers. This leadership role had a further value in breaking down the barriers that often emerge in organisations between finance and operations. The educational experience for both sets of students was a "win-win" for all. The accountants reflecting in their learning log books that they now fully understood what had been sometimes hostile encounters with staff back in their charities. They now had an insight into these issues and been equipped to overcome these barriers. Finally, this approach and learning reflections opened up a rich possibility of using diversified teaching methods which we explore later.

A Core Body of Knowledge – Does It Have to Start with Financial Accounting?

I believe it does, but this is not about double entry book keeping. The accountants are already versed in for-profit techniques so no need to go over these subjects. But what about the non-accountants? How much of the valuable time and resource did I wish to spend on financial accounting which these students will never use? Instead I take the view that it is about equipping those students for their future roles in being empowered to understand a set of financial accounts. To enable them to critically appraise and ask questions. To resolve the time resource question, I run a separate optional session on Introduction to Accounting which takes students through a simple business starting trading and explains a Profit and Loss Account, Balance Sheet, and most importantly define terminology, for example what an accrual is. I then begin my course with an overview of charity finance and the similarities and then differences to private and public sector practices. The key principle for students to understand is that unlike a for-profit organisation, for charitable organisations there "… are restrictions on what an organisation may do with any surplus (profit) it generates" (Weisbrod 1988, p.1). This concept underpins the entire financial reporting and regulatory framework and subsequent discussions on tax. It enables discussion on stewardship theory and governance while also giving context to what should be the financial objectives of a charity and its approach to risk and the holding of reserves. It provides a context to financial planning and the sustainability of the organisation.

Financial Accounting and Regulation

International Accounting Standards have increasingly moved to the fore in for-profit accounting, providing a consistency in company reporting and auditing. In contrast nonprofit's reporting requirements vary considerably globally. These include a lack of guidance or standards for nonprofit organisations to follow in reporting for grants and donations received, or for subsequent expenditure, for example, makes reporting to supporter's problematic. Mack et al. (2017) review of the accountability and regulation literature assumes high level of ability and facility, in order to compare charities and ensure accountability. This research analysed financial reporting requirements applicable to charities in four jurisdictions (Australia, England, Ireland, New Zealand) using case study analysis which compares the actual financial statements of four charities operating in the same field and with similar levels of total income. The authors highlight common issues and implications in terms of the concepts underpinning not-for-profit organisation (NPO) financial reporting and argue the case for harmonised international NPO accounting standards. Their call has in-part been answered with the IFR4NPO project, which seeks to address gaps in nonprofit financial reporting guidance for small and medium organisations. A consultation paper articulating possible solutions and developing guidance on specific topics was released in early 2021 for public comment submissions (IFR4NPO 2021).

In preparing the paper, those attending the consultation meetings with little or no knowledge of the UK often expressed surprise when they find out how advanced UK Accounting and Regulation standards for charities are. In 1981 research into the top 53 charities was undertaken by academics for the Institute of Chartered Accountants in England and Wales (Bird and Morgan-Jones 1981) which found complete inconsistency in charity accounts and financial reporting. This was later followed by a series of exposure drafts beginning in 1984 by the then UK Accounting Standards Committee. An exposure draft is a document published by the Financial Accounting Standards Board (FASB) to solicit public comment on a proposed new accounting standard. These standards were initially advisory and research studies showed were not being complied with by the majority of charities (Palmer and Randall 2002). This state of affairs was replaced by a truly radical transformation in charity accounting culminating in the 1995 Statement of Recommended Practice (SORP) – accounting by charities. As I commented at the time "During that time the SORP changed radically from a rather latitudinarian document into a strongly prescriptive one" (Williams and Palmer 1998, p.265). Despite the term recommended the Charity SORP is a mandatory requirement for larger charities in law.

The radical change was to turn away from the hybrid income and expenditure statements modelled on a for-profit accounting format and instead embrace a fund accounting approach with a Statement of Financial Activities (SOFA) which essentially amalgamated the old income and expenditure account with the reconciliation and analysis of the movement of funds. The main purpose of the SOFA is to bring together all transactions in a single statement so as to present a complete picture which will give a true and fair view of the charity's affairs. Reviewing the history of the SORP enables me to engage students in a number of discussions. First the recognition that the financial position of a charity is quite different to that of a business venture where profit is the main motive. As I wrote in 2002:

> A business raises capital which it uses to generate profits, which it either then distributes to those who contributed to the capital, or retains in order to expand its profit-making capacity. On the other hand, a charity administers

> funds received for the purpose of its charitable objectives. Historically, accounting by charities has been based on a commercial-type profit-and-loss presentation where a surplus or a deficit on the income and expenditure account did not necessarily reflect the actual position of the charity.
>
> *Palmer and Randall 2002, p. 62*

This proposition encourages reflection and the opportunity to point to the class options for additional reading and viewing accounting. Utilising a critical accounting lens to consider why the SORP and regulatory regime was developed in the late 1980s and early 1990s. Here, drawing upon policy studies and context, I encourage students to think about the changes in the UK State as it embraced market economics. The re-emergence of philanthropy with donor tax reliefs and the opening of former public statutory run services to instead be outsourced to both private and charitable organisations as contracts and open to competition. Accounting standards then move on from being seen as neutral technical and created in isolation statements; instead they are integral to a more complex policy picture, which are used to ensure compliance to that policy.

The next part of the course focuses on technical explanation, viewing the students who are managers in the charity sector as to what they need to understand as users of accounts, e.g. the meaning of restricted funds. The drawing up of accounts are instead in a separate module for accountants and finance staff. This understanding of accounts normally involves about six hours of contact time comprising a mixture of teaching methods including work book type exercises and group discussions. In this part of the module we cover:

- Introduction to the basics of accounts, cash compared to accruals accounting, and key pieces of jargon
- Charity accounts and the SORP
- Going concern assumption and reserves
- Risk and other key policies/statements
- Impact of Covid-19 – introduced this year given the insolvency statement issues that some charities are facing.

Usually face-to-face teaching but during Covid, and with the University closed, we have instead used Teams and Zoom, etc., for this year and taught it online with breakout rooms for small group discussions and short pre-recorded lectures followed with live questions and answers on each topic.

Once students are equipped or empowered with this technical application it means we can then focus on them understanding and using financial accounts for decision-making. This is of particular value to students studying courses in grant making, social investment, and philanthropy who are assessing grant applications, contracts, etc., as it enables them to assess a charity's financial position as well as governance and other reporting requirements. Pre-reading of a real charity's accounts are given to students and we then go through the accounts page by page asking critical questions. This is where I utilise guest lecturers from auditor firms to give expert insights. In my text book the *Good Financial Management Guide* (Palmer et al. 2014 I signpost students to both ratio analysis for charities and my own check list for understanding a charity's accounts as well as other guides produced by accounting firms.

We conclude the financial accounting and reporting session with a focus on charity law, an appreciation of charity tax including donor reliefs and a guest lecture, usually from the former Chief Executive of the Charity Commission, the regulator who is a Chartered Accountant and had worked previously as a Finance Director in, respectively, a large International Aid Charity and then the largest children's services charity in the UK. This last lecture on enhancing public trust through better financial reporting brings together all the different elements that have been covered.

Costing and Financial Management

The next component of the course features on Financial Strategy, Management Accounting, and Understanding Core Costs. In these sessions we again utilise a combination of critically questioning – what should be the financial objectives of a nonprofit? How to ensure financial sustainability and balance immediate need expenditure requests. Costing behaviour and methodologies including understanding fixed and variable costs, breakeven analysis, and constructing cash flow budgets are explored. This provides the foundation for students to understand the importance of full cost recovery, how to apply it, and then use it in negotiations.

Traditional costing adopts a cost centre approach but for charitable organisations there are a number of different issues that we explore. First, that charitable organisations are very poor at costing their work; the cost involved in operating and providing good management is often underestimated, not properly identified or even ignored. This attempt to do "quality" on the cheap can easily lead to a long-term crisis. Second, many organisations that have adopted a cost-centred approach have found that the true cost of providing a service or activity is greater than the funding being offered. How do you use this information? For example, does it empower the managers to be more assertive when negotiating with funders or the charity may take the strategic decision to subsidise and/or fundraise to cover the loss? Finally, there are internal organisational issues where people in one cost centre are more "profitable" than another centre. Cost accounting and absorption are management tools that allow decisions to be made about priorities; they are not concerned with assigning value to an activity. This gives an early opportunity to raise with students the issue of value and how it can be measured in non-financial terms? A topic we explore later in the module when we return to the theme of the absence of a bottom profit line objective.

After covering off the weaknesses of the absorption costing model we then explore the advantages of a full cost recovery model linking to sustainable funding to cover not just project costs but also a fair proportion of overheads. How it can be used to monitor overhead costs and consider their efficiency over time and finally, why full cost recovery makes sense. How can you make rational decisions and future plans without knowing the true cost of a project or service, and how this impacts overheads and free reserves?

Once we have gone through technical costing exercises including why charities have different rates, i.e. the nature of their maturity and by what they do, we can then enter into discussions about competitive environments, decision-making, and how full cost recovery can facilitate strategic decision-making. We also explore the politics and power of commissioners (Commissioning in the UK is the process of procuring services. It is a complex process, involving the assessment and understanding of a population's health or other needs, the planning of services to meet those needs and securing services on a limited budget, then monitoring the services procured) and the ethics around "low balling" where an organisation deliberately reduces the cost to win a contract using comparative advantages of scale or other sources of income to cross subsidise.

In the Absence of the Bottom Line

Profit is the dominant motive and the primary performance indicator in for-profit organisations, but what should it be in a Charity? This question opens the conversation with students. There is an extensive literature to draw on and direct students to with a range of techniques from cost benefit analysis to Triple bottom-line (the economic, environmental, and social) which provide a comprehensive approach to looking at value. How to measure value, and determine which techniques to use for impact measurement and evaluation, are increasingly becoming important focuses in a course on finance for nonprofits. A leading model is Social Return on Investment (SROI), a capacity-building and measurement framework that meets these needs. Explaining and illustrating how SROI has been used through real life impact case studies which incorporate social, environmental, and economic impacts for a range of stakeholders. This lens of analysis encourages students to think in a new way about value and enables a mode of decision-making that is informed by the things that matter to people and communities. It also provides a conduit to social bonds and mixed motive investing as opposed to conventional Investment Management (Salway et al. 2020).

How do you teach a course on investment management for organisations fortunate to have endowments or hold long-term investments as part of their reserves policy? There is a long history and a complex, highly analytical literature to draw upon. However, as with teaching tax and similar to financial accounting, I take the view that students who are general managers in charities need an appreciation and not an in-depth understanding of portfolio theory and asset management. This means focusing on understanding the different asset classes, strategic vs. tactical decision-making, correlations, terminology, and benchmarks. There is also the distinctive issue relating to ethical investment and a legal underpinning of how that relates to charities and exclusion now challenged by the emergence of pro-active Ethical, Social, and Governance (ESG) funds that are changing the investment universe and previous assumptions on negative returns. The vast majority of charities in the UK appoint a discretionary investment manager, so how to appoint an investment manager and measure their performance is the management issue to focus on. This focus also offers more creative teaching delivery options which I cover later.

Over the years there are a variety of other topics that I have covered according to contemporary interest or have been consistently in the curriculum. For example, Social Enterprise initially featured as a topic but this has now moved in its own right to a separate module. Mergers and Acquisitions has stayed throughout and again provides an opportunity to knowledge exchange between conventional for-profit literature and the differences when applied to nonprofit organisations and alternatives to full scale merger like collaborative working.

Diversified Teaching Methods and Assessments

Conventional finance and accounting teaching assessed by an exam does have its place particularly, as we discuss later, with advanced applications and the need for financial leaders in nonprofits to demonstrate their professional competence. But, there is the opportunity for more creative educational approaches. For example, in investment management I have persuaded investment managers specialising in the sector to run investment games where students are involved in a group exercise to compete against each other by managing their own portfolios. Providing an insight into how assets are allocated and tactical decisions happen. I have run "beauty parades" on how to appoint auditors, bankers, investment managers, and other outsourced services using practitioners as consultants and for mock pitches where they have been interviewed by students as commissioners. Guest lecturers, who are the actual leaders in the real case studies the students have studied, add value through further insights that the written word can never give where students are able to ask questions.

Perhaps the most innovative teaching method and one that brings this module to an end is a session on Turnaround Management. After a conventional introduction, students are allocated into a "role play" with a scenario and parts based on a real example of a charity that is on the brink of insolvency. Students are allocated all the roles including trustees, senior staff, the bank that has lent money, and the auditors. They enact through various rounds of the charity's journey until reaching a conclusion on either solvency and continue to operate or insolvency and closure. Professionals including the turnaround practitioners act as mentors and observers. At the end of the exercise a forensic debrief is followed where students can reflect on their decision-making and consequences. Finally, the real-life example and what happened is given. The role play involves all students and additional topics around mindset and skill challenges. These are almost always the causes of failure induced by control and influence weakness. These disseminations enable a knowledge transfer into the wider literature on ailing organisations where boards that are focused on solving the challenges of the past and unable to think outside a narrow set of frames (Gavetti and Rivkin 2005; Gavetti and Warglien 2015).

The educational philosophy is on "bottom-up", what do the students need to learn as opposed to a "top-down" generic accounting module? This approach enables an opportunity to use more innovative assessment methods. For exams I have taken a real set of charity accounts and altered them with mistakes and provided a scenario. This is then set as an "open exam" providing the accounts and scenario, but not the questions, three weeks in advance. Students can do some preparation, including as in real life on reviewing the accounts with an accountant. But under exam conditions providing a time frame and some element of stress in then answering the questions as they would have to do, if for example they were assessing the organisation for a grant. One of the most added value elements has been in setting a course work which plays to the student's strengths and time by letting them identify, seek approval, and then explore a financial issue within their own organisation. Although having to still write a conventional essay with appropriate literature this exercise also provides an opportunity for an inhouse consultancy exercise that benefits the student's charity. Some of these essays have subsequently been published in practitioner journals like *Charity Finance*.

Advance Application and Deep End learning

The module I have been describing has been focused on the needs of the non-finance student who is in operations, project, or a general manager to Chief Executive in their charity. For those students who are finance staff or associated professionals providing services to the sector a different focus is required. For example, financial accounting moves into the actual doing. Why advanced knowledge on tax with computations is also required. My role in these modules moves into being more a facilitator, utilising leading experts in each of these specialised fields. Supporting professional study but underpinning with guidance on theory, literature, and context. A primary motive in developing these courses was to encourage the charity sector to develop its own staff and offer career advancement opportunities rather than being an "importer" of personnel. A second reason was to support the pioneering work of David Billis who established the first ever Masters degree in nonprofits in 1987 (Palmer and Bogdanova 2008) and identified a distinct body of knowledge and practice in nonprofits. Linking the MSc in Charity Accounting and Financial Management to the leading chartered accountancy organisation – the ICAEW – to create a post qualification certificate in charity finance, provided a professional qualification for charity finance staff.

This sends a clear signal to employers that the financial issues of charities are not a hybrid or small-scale activity. Having the professional qualification provides a legitimation and a signal to trustees on the competence of appointing that person who has undertaken a rigorous course and professional examination.

We begin the financial management for charities module by exploring the ICAEW Framework (2017). The lead authority of the report facilitates students through the research that underpins the framework and draws out the similarities and differences between for-profit finance functions and those in charities. Developing wider management issues include focusing on the finance leader role in the charity, including the issue of how to "manage up" and engage with a trustee board of unpaid volunteers, whose primary interest is the work of the charity. As a recent research report for the Charity Commission by the Centre for Charity Effectiveness found, the vast majority of trustee boards inevitably rely on one or two of their number to oversee finance (CCE 2017). We also pick up on topics such as internal control and audit, risk frameworks, forecasting methods, and capital project assessment.

Further finance course module is a management development experience which enables finance students to undertake a field work placement in another charity. Chartered accountants with extensive work experience can obtain an APEL exemption and instead provide a reflective CV for their assessment. This module is particularly beneficial for those who are career transitioning into the sector or those whose experience is limited to just one or two organisations. Drawing upon a "Deep learning" philosophy (Palmer and Grant 2018) students spend five days working on a finance project and then write it up as a consultancy report. They have a mentor during the experience drawn from a panel of senior finance directors or partners in accountancy firms who head up the charity department providing audit and other services to charities. These students maintain a log on their experience and reflect in a learning focused assignment on their experience and future career development plan.

Financial Education for Other Stakeholders – What About the Volunteers?

This chapter has focused on the development needs of paid staff in nonprofit organisations. Volunteers are not excluded; indeed, a pleasant surprise one year was finding the former auditor of the World Bank now in his 70s undertaking the MSc course and contributing authoritatively to class discussions as well as providing inspiration to younger course members. As the cited Taken on Trust research found, there are a small number of volunteer trustees who take responsibility for finance. Research for the Chartered Institute of Management Accountants (Palmer et al. 1999) focused on the need for trustees for accountancy education. This research explored the extent and nature of management information needs of trustees, as perceived by selected trustees of smaller charities. The study discovered the existence of an "expectations gap" between what charity trustees are supposed to do and what they can actually achieve. The "voluntary" principle for charity boards has faced increasing challenges and a recent report by the Public Administration and Constitutional Affairs Committee (2016a, 2016b) on the collapse of Kids Company, a prominent children's services charity, has added further pressure for financial education. However, the High Court ruled against the UK insolvency service disqualifying the trustees with the Judge citing the voluntary principle as an important factor in their ruling not to have the trustees disqualified (High Court 2021).

Providing further education resources, however, goes beyond courses and the academic literature. There is a richness of resources for those interested in charity finance, many of which are free to download. For example, the accounting and investment management firms' websites and regulators which in the UK includes the Charity Commission as well as the UK Tax Office (HMRC), where they can find authoritative guidance, research reports, and case studies. There are also the respective professional accounting institutes, umbrella organisations like the Charity Finance Group and in the UK a monthly journal called *Charity Finance* which focuses on publishing short but applied articles written by practitioners and charity finance leaders.

Concluding Comments

In essence accounting and financial management are applied practical subjects and students attending postgraduate and executive courses are seeking tuition to enable them to understand finance which they may have to manage. However, just a practice focused course is little more than rote training. Little long-term value is achieved by not giving a policy framework, context, and skills to continue further education and development. Nonprofit finance courses needed to be grounded in nonprofit theory to add value and showcase distinctive applications. However, these courses need to be "bespoke tailored" with practitioner focused case study examples, crafted to meet their interests and learning needs. A one size fits all approach is not appropriate.

References

Bird, P and Morgan-Jones, P (1981) Financial Reporting by Charities. London: Institute of Chartered Accountants in England and Wales.

CCE (2017) Taken on Trust: the awareness and effectiveness of charity trustees in England and Wales https://city.tfaforms.net/4722960.

Gavetti, G and Rivkin, J (2005), How Strategists Really Think. Harvard Business Review, 83(4), p.54–63.

Gavetti, G and Warglien, M (2015), A Model of Collective Interpretation. Organization Science, 26(5), p.1263–1283.

Hansmann, HB (1980) The Role of Nonprofit Enterprise. In The Economics of Nonprofit Institutions. ed. S Rose-Ackerman. Oxford: Oxford University Press.

Hansmann, HB (1987) Economic Theories of Nonprofit Organisations. – In, The Non-Profit Sector – A Research Handbook. ed. WW Powell. Murray, MA: Yale University Press.

High Court (2021) Judgement 12 February 2021. www.judiciary.uk/wp-content/uploads/2021/02/Official-Receiver-v-Batmanghelidjh-judgment-120221.pdf.

ICAEW (2017) The Finance Function. A Framework for Analysis. London: ICAEW.

IFR4NPO (2021) www.ifr4npo.org/consultation-paper/.

Mack, J, Morgan, GG, Breen OB, & Corder, CJ (2017) Financial Reporting by Charities: A Matched Case Study Analysis from Four Countries. Public Money & Management, 37(3), p.165–172.

Palmer, P and Bogdanova, M (2008) The British Are Not Coming! UK Higher Education and the Nonprofit Sector. Non-profit Management and Leadership, 19(1), p.79–99.

Palmer, P and Grant, P (2018) Enhancing the Academic Prestige of Nonprofit Studies: Can Impact Case Studies Help? Journal of Nonprofit Education and Leadership, 8(4), p.358–374.

Palmer P, Harrow, J, and Vincent, J (1999) Management Information Needs and Perceptions in Smaller Charities: An Exploratory Study. Financial Accountability & Management, 15(2), p.155–172; [Peer Reviewed].

Palmer, P and Randall, A (2002) Financial Management in the Voluntary Sector. London: Routledge.

Palmer, PW, Young, F, Finlayson, N, and Rajani Y (2014) The Good Financial Management Guide for the Voluntary Sector. ed. Updated edition. London: NCVO Publications.

Powell, W W (1987) The Non-Profit Sector – A Research Handbook. Murray, MA: Blackwell.

Public Administration and Constitutional Affairs Committee (2016a). The collapse of Kids Company: The full Report from The Public Administration and Constitutional Affairs Committee. https://publications.parliament.uk/pa/cm201516/cmselect/cmpubadm/433/43302.htm February 2016.

Public Administration and Constitutional Affairs Committee (2016b). The collapse of Kids Company: Lessons for charity trustees, professional firms, the Charity Commission, and Whitehall, 1 February 2016. https://publications.parliament.uk/pa/cm201516/cmselect/cmpubadm/963/963.pdf

Rose-Ackerman, S (1986) The Economics of Non-profit Institutions. Oxford: Oxford University Press.

Salamon, L and Anheier, H (1994) The Non-profit Sector Cross Nationally: Patterns and Types. In Researching the Voluntary Sector. Eds. S Saxon-Harrold and J Kendall (p.147–163; 2nd ed.). Tonbridge: Charities Aid Foundation.

Salway, MPP, Grant, P, and Clifford J (2020) Demystifying Social Finance and Social Investment. Oxford: Routledge.

Steinberg, R and Gray, B H (1993) The Role of Nonprofit Enterprise in 1993: Hansmann Revisited. Nonprofit and Voluntary Sector Quarterly, 22(4), p.297–316.

Stone, M and Crittenden, W (1993) A Guide to Journal Articles on Strategic Management in Nonprofit Organisations 1997–1992. Nonprofit Management and Leadership, 4(2), p.193–212.

Vatter, NJ (1947) The Fund Theory of Accounting and its Implications for Financial Reports. (Reprint edition 1978). New York: Arno Press.

Weisbord, BA (1988) The Nonprofit Economy. London: Harvard University Press.

Williams, S and Palmer P (1998) The State of Charity Accounting – Developments, Improvements and Continuing Problems. Financial Accountability & Management, 14(4), p.265–279.

Young, DR (1993). The First Three Years of NML: Central Issues in the Management of Nonprofit Organisations. Nonprofit Management and Leadership, 4(1), p.3–19.

8

LEGAL PERSPECTIVES IN NONPROFIT EDUCATION

Robert M. Pallitto

It is a challenge for educators to find the right level of detail and complexity at which to teach law to non-lawyers. I encountered this challenge when I began teaching "Issues in Nonprofit Law" to graduate students in public administration about ten years ago. There are excellent textbooks available for that class, and sections of those texts cover such topics as the history of charities and the tests for tax-exempt status thoroughly and effectively without reference to court decisions. But the course has "law" in its title and course description, and sooner or later we come around to talking about the interpretation of a statute, or the scope of a constitutional right. At such points, the textbooks cite court decisions. How are students to understand them? More fundamentally, is it even necessary for students to know how to read a court opinion?

Legal education as undertaken in American law schools is quite different. It is a specialized pursuit, primarily involving the reading and discussion of court decisions over the course of three years of full-time study. Upon completion of a law degree, most students sit for a bar exam in the state where they plan to practice. It is also common for recent graduates to be hired by large law firms where they receive mentoring, something like apprenticeship, from more senior attorneys before they are allowed to manage cases on their own; this process can start even before graduation with "summer associate" positions that turn into offers for full-time work.

There is good reason for the years of preparation and training that precede entry into the legal profession. It is necessary to acquire a specialized form of thinking in order to practice law, and attaining that skill requires more than mere familiarity with legal terms and concepts. As with other forms of learning, the mastery of legal reasoning develops over time as comfort with the subject matter grows through constant practice. Anyone who has struggled through the intricacies of pendent jurisdiction in civil procedure class or toiled to differentiate remedies under the Uniform Commercial Code in contracts can attest to how much

DOI: 10.4324/9781003294061-9

one relies on the preceding intellectual groundwork necessary before becoming conversant with such complex subject areas. But lawyers and judges are not the only professionals whose work touches the domain of law. Business ownership, management, civil engineering, and public administration, to name just a few roles, bring people into contact with the law, and those roles can all be performed more effectively by someone who has a basic understanding of how the law works. This cross-disciplinary knowledge, albeit in a less intricate or comprehensive form, is needed in the same way that some lawyers are obliged to acquaint themselves with fundamental concepts of medicine, engineering, or forensic analysis.

There is certainly a significant amount of law-related content in existing public administration curriculum. Fremont-Smith's (2004) work, *Governing Nonprofit Organizations*, for example, cites many court decisions, contains a section on interpreting the tax exemption portions of the federal tax code, and details enforcement of state and federal law governing nonprofits. Similarly, the entry in *Global Encyclopedia of Public Administration, Public Policy, and Governance* (Mead, 2018) concerning legal issues in nonprofit organizations divides the subject into organizational, tax-exemption, and operations issues. The entry also provides a description of nonprofit legal structure – that is, the legal forms that nonprofits can take (corporation or trust). The curricular guidelines provided by the Nonprofit Academic Centers Council (see Appendix) for teaching public administration specify legal content that should be taught: legal frameworks, rights and duties of actors in the system, tax implications, advocacy and lobbying restrictions, risk management, reporting requirements, and fiduciary duties. Clearly, then, there is no shortage of legal material in public administration curriculum. The question is how deeply the material should be studied and how best to do that.

I maintain that public administration students should be able to state a disputed legal issue and explain the way a court resolved it. This ability in turn requires them to be able to read and understand a court decision. It is common in some undergraduate classes (business law, for example) to ask students to "brief" a case by following a set formula (Issue/Rule/Analysis/Conclusion, for example). The formulaic method, however, runs the risk that students will fill in the blanks with language they do not yet understand. As a result, briefing (particularly at the undergraduate level) does not always lead to positive learning outcomes. Instead, I favor a more content-specific approach that signals to students what they should be looking for in each part of the opinion and allows them to explain it in their own words. Graduate students are better-equipped to adopt this approach as compared to undergraduates. At a general level, the learning outcomes are:

- To obtain a basic knowledge of how courts work
- To identify the constituent parts of a court opinion
- To be able to cite a court opinion for the proposition of law it establishes
- To identify policy issues affecting public administration as those issues arise in court rulings.

The first step toward reaching these objectives is to provide an overview of the US court system, state and federal, as well as the source of judicial power (Article III of the US Constitution in the case of the federal courts) and courts' role in a system of separated and balanced powers. That overview can be conveyed to students with the use of organizational charts[1] and a cite to constitutional text. Next, a brief explanation of what an appeal is, and how it differs from a trial proceeding, helps students to recognize what they are reading, since the vast majority of published opinions that public administration students will read come from appellate courts rather than trial courts. With that introduction, they are ready to analyze the text of an opinion.

I have developed a guide for reading court opinions that helps to identify signposts common to all such texts. For instance, the facts of the case and the procedural history are sometimes set off by an identifying heading, but even if no heading is present the reader can examine content to locate them. Procedural history starts with the nature of the claim and where (in what forum) the case was brought. The statement of facts is often prefaced by a phrase such as, "This case arose...." Both facts and procedural history are always found at the beginning of the opinion, so even if those signposts are not present in a given case it is a simple matter to locate the corresponding material.

In order to make sense of a court opinion students must be able to articulate what issue the court is being asked to decide. A signpost in this regard is a phrase like, "The question presented is," or "We are asked to decide...." Once the legal issue has been identified, it should be articulated in one's own words, avoiding legal jargon. I encourage students to ask "so what" questions as they work to come up with their answers to this query. Why does the case matter to the parties? Why should anyone care about it? What is at stake?

The ruling, or "holding" is the court's resolution of the matter. The holding will often be announced explicitly with a statement such as, "We hold that...." The final sentence of the opinion will indicate how the court disposed of the case after deciding the question at issue. Was it dismissed? Affirmed? Reversed? Sent back to the lower court with instructions? Students can check their understanding of the ruling by making sure that that understanding accords with the disposition contained in that final sentence. If the last word in the opinion is "reversed," for example, they must confirm that their articulation of the ruling actually says the court disagreed with the previous ruling below. Once again, students should state the result in language they are comfortable with and can explain. It should not be cribbed from a Wikipedia entry.

The holding in the case can be cited by public administration students in the same form that law students and lawyers use, e.g., *The Supreme Court held in Texas v. Johnson that flag burning is protected speech under the First Amendment.* After citing a ruling, they can then discuss its importance for their field. In what follows, I present and summarize two Supreme Court decisions that I use in teaching my nonprofit law class. Both were handed down in the past dozen years. Their subject matter and level of complexity are different from one another, but they both bear directly on the field of public administration. They contain useful teaching material pertaining to how courts operate, and each one also serves to introduce a policy issue as well. For each one, I have listed specific learning outcomes that track the more general outcomes stated above.

Case # 1: *Humanitarian Law Project v. Holder*[2]

First filed in 1998, this case spanned three presidential administrations and the terms of five attorneys general before the Supreme Court conclusively resolved it in 2010. Originally, *Humanitarian Law Project* (HLP) involved a challenge by a nonprofit to a federal antiterrorism law that made it a crime to provide "material support" (including humanitarian assistance) to designated terrorist organizations. HLP members sought to give training in peaceful dispute resolution, as well as other forms of help, to the Kurdistan Workers' Party in Turkey and the Tamil Tigers in Sri Lanka. However, they did not want to run afoul of the law, so they sought a determination of its constitutionality. They believed that the law violated the First Amendment's guarantees of freedom of speech and association, and also that it was too vague. The progress of the case was complicated by the 9/11 terror attacks, which prompted the passage of subsequent legislation amending the original law.

A majority of the Court rejected all of the constitutional challenges HLP raised in this case, leaving the "material support" prohibition in place for the future and making it clear that the forms of assistance plaintiffs wished to provide would be illegal.

HLP v. Holder is a complex and at times highly technical opinion. Not all of the lengthy decision is worthwhile to analyze in detail in a non-law class. Nonetheless, it offers four instructive points for students of public administration:

1. It provides an example of an *advance challenge* to a law's application, as HLP sought to know beforehand whether their proposed conduct would be criminally punishable if they went ahead and engaged in it
2. It shows how the Court goes about determining the scope of *constitutional freedoms*
3. It illustrates the *institutional deference* the Court allows to congress and the executive branch
4. It outlines a form of *legal jeopardy* that NGOs and nonprofits potentially face.

Advance Challenge

Ordinarily, courts will not engage with a dispute until it is ripe for decision. There must be an actual, as opposed to potential, legal conflict at the moment a complaint is filed. It would be reasonable to ask, then, why the Court agreed to hear and decide this case. After all, the plaintiffs (HLP and individual US citizens) had not yet been charged with a crime; they were asking the courts to tell them whether *future conduct they wished to engage in* would be considered a crime. The Supreme Court found that the plaintiffs faced a "credible threat of future prosecution," and in view of that threat the Court agreed to hear the case as an "advance" or "preenforcement" challenge. They relied on previous decisions in reaching this conclusion, and with that threshold question out of the way they could proceed to the "merits" of the case, or the actual challenge itself.

Constitutional Freedoms (Free Speech and Association)

The merits here involve constitutional rights – specifically, the rights to free speech and association that are protected by the First Amendment to the US Constitution.[3] Fast-forwarding to the conclusion, we see that these challenges were rejected: the "material support" law was found to be constitutional. But why? The Court explained how prior decisions differentiate speech from acts, or conduct. In short, some activities consist only of speech, while others have both an expressive aspect as well as a conduct aspect to them. The kinds of assistance plaintiffs wished to provide to the Kurdistan Workers' Party (PKK or Partiya Karekerên Kurdistanê) and the Tamil Tigers contained elements of both: advocacy for the organizations' political causes (expressive), and training (conduct). Since both were present, the Court had to apply a more stringent analysis than would be required in instances of pure conduct. Under this stringent test, the government's interest in fighting terrorism was found to be strong enough to justify restraints on speech and association. The lesson here is that even when a constitutional right is recognized and comes into play, as free speech did here, that is no guarantee that the plaintiff asserting that right will prevail. The right to free speech can be overridden by a sufficiently strong countervailing interest. From this result, we are reminded that no constitutional right is absolute; all of them are analyzed through constitutional doctrine developed in previous cases. Here national security concerns form a boundary delimiting the right to free speech.

Institutional Deference

In large part, the Court ruled as it did on the constitutional question because it felt the need to defer to the "political" branches – the legislative and executive – in the matter of foreign policy generally and combatting terrorism in particular. American constitutional law is replete with such expressions of deference by the courts, with perhaps the most notorious being the refusal to condemn race-specific internment of Japanese-Americans in *Korematsu v. US.*[4] These arguments are usually predicated on the claim that congress and the president (through Cabinet members) have access to more complete information and are also constitutionally entrusted to make political judgments such as the one at issue here. As a result, the argument goes, courts should not interfere with the performance of these political roles by the political branches. Of course, the rejoinder to that call for deference, as the dissent in *Korematsu* reminded us, is that Courts are responsible for taking the measure of constitutional rights when they are asserted, as here. Seen that way, deference can amount to abandonment of the courts' own constitutional role. Institutional deference is an issue worth exploring and discussing in the context of a case like this one.

Legal Jeopardy

The policy issue here is rather starkly posed: nonprofit administrators could wind up in prison, under the HLP ruling, for humanitarian advocacy and assistance to an entity designated as a terrorist organization, even if that advocacy or assistance is entirely peaceful and does not promote violence in any direct way. Public administrators must be aware of this ruling as a matter of prudent self-interest. Moreover, they need to consider how the limitations created by the HLP ruling affect an organization's work in the contemporary world: what can be done and how money can be raised and spent (and for what causes or beneficiaries).

Case # 2: *Frank v. Gaos*[5]

Frank v. Gaos was decided by the Supreme Court in 2019. In contrast to *HLP v. Holder*, the *Gaos* decision is undramatic. Rather than determining criminal liability for supporting terrorist organizations (the issue in HLP), *Gaos* involved a class of plaintiffs who sued Google for alleged violation of privacy laws. The Court sent the case back down to the trial court, directing that body to determine whether the plaintiffs actually had the right to bring suit in the first place. Notwithstanding its lack of drama, the case provides three useful teaching material for a graduate public administration class:

1. It exposes students to issues of *procedural law*
2. It explores the concept of *legal standing*
3. It introduces the doctrine of *cy pres* in connection with charitable gifts and bequests.

Procedural Law

The procedural history of a case involves determining what claims were raised, in which court, and what happened at each level (trial, appellate, highest court in system) as the courts disposed of the case. As stated above, procedural history is typically set forth alongside the basic facts of the case in an appellate opinion. Knowing that, students new to reading caselaw can separate the parts, study them, and focus on gaining a precise understanding of each. Here, the matter commenced with the filing of a *class action*. A class action involves an individual plaintiff (or several of them) bringing suit on behalf of a *class* of unnamed plaintiffs whose circumstances are similar. Suing on behalf of a class offers advantages to litigants and courts alike: it makes litigation feasible for aggrieved individuals who might not be able to afford legal counsel (the attorney's fees are usually paid by the defendant if the suit is successful), and for courts it is far more efficient to manage one suit with a class of plaintiffs than to handle and decide multiple individual suits. It is useful for students to know what class litigation looks like, as the class action approach is often used in impact litigation to accomplish large-scale changes in the law.

The subsequent procedural turns of the *Gaos* case are also instructive. The complaint was dismissed, re-filed, and eventually settled. Ordinarily, a lawsuit that is settled by consent of the parties would not produce a published opinion, much less a Supreme Court decision, because the settlement obviates the need for a court to decide anything. Here, though, another dispute arose when some class members objected to the terms of the settlement. As a result, the question of the settlement's validity eventually reached the Supreme Court. The Court decided that the matter had not been properly analyzed by the courts below, and so the lower court ruling was "vacated" and had to be reconsidered in accordance with the Supreme Court's instructive guidelines. In a sense, the resolution was a non-resolution: in fact, the Court expressly declined to express any view on what the ultimate outcome of the case should be. It is worth emphasizing to non-lawyers that not every Supreme Court ruling provides a final resolution of the underlying dispute.

Legal Standing

Legal standing – the right to stand before a court and raise a claim – is a bottom-line requirement for initiating legal action. A party who lacks standing may not bring a lawsuit, and there is a basis in common sense for this requirement. Courts perform the institutional role of settling disputes and providing relief to people who have been harmed through the wrongful acts of others. If I did not suffer a harm, it is inappropriate for me to complain to a court and seek redress. Unlike the legislative and executive branches in a democratic system of separated and balanced powers, courts are limited in their capacity to act: they can only decide what is brought before them; they do not seek or reach out for cases to hear. If there is no harm, or if the harm did not affect the person who has brought suit, then the court must dismiss that suit. Standing law can be complicated and technical, and there are some standing issues presented by the *Gaos* case that are difficult to teach to non-specialists. Nonetheless, the case is a useful teaching tool because it introduces the concept of standing and shows students how a case outcome can turn on an issue that is not central to the subject-matter of the case. The substance of *Gaos* is a privacy question: did Google violate a federal communications statute by storing user data? Yet the decision we read in class disposes of the matter by focusing not on the underlying privacy question, but on whether the parties should have been allowed into court (i.e., whether the plaintiffs had legal standing) in the first place. The lesson here is that substance and procedure interrelate in the process of litigation; in view of that relationship, it is important to pay attention to both.

Cy Pres

Cy pres is a term originating in the French language that is usually translated as "near this."[6] In US law, the *cy pres* doctrine is applied in cases where a gift or bequest has become impossible to fulfill. By reformulating the terms of a gift as nearly as possible to the original, a court can keep the gift from failing entirely. Some cases where *cy pres* has been applied involved racially discriminatory gifts or bequests, which courts are unable to enforce because they violate law or public policy, or both. In all *cy pres* cases, regardless of the reason a court is applying the doctrine, there is a potential conflict between honoring the intention of the person making the gift/bequest on the one hand, and the public good on the other. Thus, *cy pres* use invites controversy over whether the proper balance has been struck in a given case. Since *cy pres* usually arises in connection with charitable gifts and bequests, nonprofit and public leaders are bound to encounter a *cy pres* issue sooner or later.

In the *Gaos* case, the proposed settlement sought to use *cy pres* to award a portion of monetary relief ($5 million, to be precise) to nonprofit organizations that promote and advocate for individual privacy rights. Some of the class plaintiffs objected to a portion of the settlement being used that way. In the end, the entire settlement was called into question when the Supreme Court sent the case back down for further consideration, but that ruling functioned to thwart the use of *cy pres* to benefit nonprofit advocacy on privacy issues. It also cast a shadow over future cases where a nonprofit organization might serve as conduit for settlement funds directed at the public good.

Conclusion: What Is to be Learned from the Caselaw Approach?

It is necessary at this point to tie together the general learning outcomes set out at the beginning of this chapter with the more specific discussion points generated by the *HLP v. Holder* and *Frank v. Gaos* cases. Students gain practice identifying the component parts of a court opinion and articulating them. I chose recent cases decided by the Supreme Court because they are noteworthy, they were widely discussed in the press, and they contain clearly identifiable legal issues. Those characteristics make *Frank* and *HLP* suitable for students learning to read and interpret this kind of document. It is easier to state a ruling on free speech (the issue in *HLP*) than one deciding a more obscure or technical point of law.

As for the *Frank* case, while the ruling concerns standing, which is less obvious and familiar, it goes to the *nature* of courts: what is their appropriate role and who can access them. Thus, *Frank* provides both the opportunity to introduce a fundamental point about the role of courts and a bridge to understanding more technical rulings in subsequent course readings.

By covering the basic parts of a court opinion and teaching students how to read them, I can also demonstrate the interrelatedness of procedure and substance. In both *HLP* and *Frank*, there are procedural matters that the Court must address before reaching the substance (free speech rights in the former and internet privacy in the latter). Can the Court even hear the "advance challenge" in *HLP* since no crime has yet been committed? Can the plaintiffs even "get in the door" to stand before the Court and press their claims in *Frank*, or are they ineligible to do so? Procedural questions intertwine with substantive ones in numerous ways, and sometimes even determine whether the substantive issues can be reached at all. It is important for students to see and appreciate the substance/procedure relationship.

Courts decide fundamental rights issues that shape the experience of living under a government. They delimit the boundaries separating the individual from the state. Thus, all of us have a stake in knowing and understanding what caselaw says and how it evolves from one case to another. Rulings that bear on public administration hold a particular importance, of course, for our students since those cases will impact students' professional lives directly. The limits on humanitarian aid and the scope of *cy pres* are vivid examples presented by the sample cases I have discussed here. Students cannot afford to ignore those developments. Yet future nonprofit and public leaders are not mere passive consumers of this knowledge; they also have the potential and the obligation to shape the discussions about future policy directions. Since courts are able only to decide the matter brought before them, there is an opportunity and a responsibility for other actors in the public, private, and nonprofit sectors to raise issues of concern in public policy debate and litigation and to contribute their insights in pending disputes. That input can be provided far more effectively if the legal dimensions of public policy issues are understood. For those seeking to contribute to policy debates such as the ones touched on here, the ability to read and understand caselaw is vital.

Notes

1 The National Center on State Courts (www.ncsc.org) offers a number of such charts.
2 561 US 1 (2010)
3 The plaintiffs also claimed that the "material support" statute was unconstitutionally vague, but the Court disposed of that argument relatively quickly.
4 323 US 214 (1944).

5 586 US ___ (2019).

6 The entire phrase from which the name of the doctrine is derived is *cy pres comme possible*, or "as near this as possible."

References

Fremont-Smith, M. (2004). Governing Nonprofit Organizations. Cambridge: Harvard University Press.

Mead, J. (2018). Legal Issues in Nonprofit Management. In: Farazmand A. (eds) Global Encyclopedia of Public Administration, Public Policy, and Governance. Cham: Springer. https://doi.org/10.1007/978-3-319-31816-5_3584-1

9

TEACHING ABOUT NONPROFITS

The Global Dimensions[1]

John Casey

This chapter begins with a note about the challenges for global nonprofit pedagogy posed by the diversity in nomenclature and academic disciplines used to frame discourses about the sector. It then outlines the three key perspectives in creating curricula content that addresses the global dimensions of the nonprofit sector. First is the comparative perspective that focuses on differences between national nonprofit sectors. Second is the globalization perspective that focuses on the cross-border dynamics that are increasingly affecting almost every nonprofit. Third is the international perspective that focuses on the role of international nonprofits in global dialogues, governance, and service delivery. Finally, the chapter concludes with an outline of the global content in the Curricula Guidelines of the Nonprofit Academic Centers Council. This chapter is written by an educator based in the United States, but the insights should help inform anyone teaching about the sector in education and training programs around the world.

Diversity in Nonprofit Discourses

As the latter sections in this chapter demonstrate, global pedagogy requires an understanding of the variations in nonprofit collective activity around the world. Before we analyze those dynamics, it is necessary to underscore the diversity in the vocabulary used to describe the sector and in the intellectual homes of nonprofit studies. How the sector and its organizations are conceptualized and identified in different polities will determine the content of academic programs and shape researchers' and students' understanding of how nonprofits operate.

DOI: 10.4324/9781003294061-10

Different Nomenclature

We work with a potpourri of terms to describe and frame our understanding of the sector. In the United States, *nonprofit* is the most commonly used term to describe the sector and its organizations – hence its use as the dominant term in this chapter. Concurrently, cognate terms such as *third sector, civil society, nongovernmental, non-state, philanthropic, community, social,* and *voluntary* are also used in the United States and elsewhere. These terms may be rooted in somewhat divergent conceptual lenses, but their differences are often more symbolic and cultural than substantive. Different organizations, disciplines, polities, and authors simply have their own preferred jargon.

Within the United States, the two largest national associations representing the sector are the *National Council of Nonprofits* and the *Independent Sector*; the academic association is the *Association for Research on Nonprofit Organizations and Voluntary Action*; and the two leading industry publications are *Nonprofit Quarterly* and *Chronicle of Philanthropy*. Since 1997, the United States Agency for International Development (USAID) has published regular reports on the nonprofit sector in Europe and Eurasia initially titled *The Nongovernmental Organizations (NGO) Sustainability Index*, but a new series on Sub-Saharan Africa launched in 2009, was titled *The Civil Society Organizations (CSO) Sustainability Index*, and in 2012 all the USAID reports switched to the CSO designation. A 2009 report to the US Congress by the Congressional Research Service was *An Overview of the Nonprofit and Charitable Sector*; while a 2010 federal legislative proposal was the *Nonprofit Sector and Community Solutions Act*.

This multiplicity of vocabulary extends to the global arena. Globally, one of the most widely employed terms is *third sector,* which is now less often used in the United States, even though it featured prominently in the seminal 1974 Filer Commission report (Filer Commission, 1975). The *International Society for Third Sector Research* is the leading association for nonprofit academics from around the world and it is the preferred term – in English or in translation in other languages – to describe the sector in many countries. The Spanish translation *tercer sector* is widely used in those countries where that language is spoken.

The other two most commonly used terms at the international level are *NGO* (the acronym is more widely used than the original long form, *nongovernmental organizations*) and *CSO*. The preference for these two terms reflects their focus on differentiating nongovernmental activity from actions on behalf of states. They are relatively neutral terms that can describe international and domestic activities under a range of regimes, without the additional baggage inherent in terms such as *nonprofit, voluntary, community,* or *charity*.

To complicate matters somewhat, the term *international* (e.g., as in *international NGOs – INGOs*) is often parsed, with some commentators preferring the term *transnational* (e.g., *transnational NGOs – TNGOs*) to emphasize the cross-border dynamics of their work. Moreover, in many developing countries there is often a division between *I/TNGOs*, a designation reserved for larger organizations originating in the global North, or large local organizations funded primarily from external sources, and the more autochthonous, local-level forms of collective action, which are instead referred to with other terms such as *community-based* or *rights-holders* organizations. In this approach, *NGOs* and *civil society* are seen as Euro-centric and colonizing concepts, with somewhat limited application to the global South.

Finally, when working with languages other than English, there are a myriad of additional challenges generated by translations and by the cultural nuances inherent in the use of any term. The media in Poland commonly refers to nonprofits as *organizacje społeczne* (social organizations), but as it is the same term used by the former communist regime for party-based mass movement organizations, it is now generally avoided by those working in the sector (who often use the English loanword *organizacje nonprofit*).

Different Disciplines

In the United States and other English-speaking countries, many current educational programs in this field are stand-alone nonprofit or philanthropy programs, and when they are embedded in other programs, they are generally in public administration, business studies, or social work. All heavily emphasize the governance and voluntary provision of public goods dimensions of nonprofit studies.

Elsewhere, the related studies are equally embedded, institutionally and intellectually, in academic departments such as sociology, political science, economics, and public law, which put more emphasis on social dynamics, structural inequalities of power and economic relations, or legal authority and legitimacy. Some openly reject what they perceive as the neoliberal, managerialist approach of the English-speaking academy. As Della Porta (2020) notes, there has been both an *NGOization* of social movement organizations (SMOs) and a *SMOization* of NGOs, but some disciplines continue to focus almost exclusively on the political bargaining, conflict, and transgressive facets of the sector.

In many countries, there are also parallel organizational concepts that may not be always deemed as analogous to the nonprofit sector as it is studied in the United States. Perhaps, the most glaring examples are the *social economy* organizations in Continental Europe that clearly operate in a nonprofit space, but with different traditions and logics from nonprofits in most English-speaking countries. Equally, there may be indigenous collective structures that do not fit neatly in classifications originating in other countries. Some of these are highlighted in the following sections.

Comparative Perspective: Understanding the Differences between National Sectors

Nonprofits have become central to policymaking, the promotion of civic action, and the delivery of new quasi-public services in almost every country in the world (Casey, 2016; McCarthy et al., 1992; Salamon et al., 2017; also see the references in the sections below on the research projects and cultural frames). In industrialized democratic countries with a longer history of independent associational life, the nonprofit sector has expanded and become a more integral element in the development and delivery of public goods and services. In developing countries and those with authoritarian or single-party regimes, a nascent sector has more openly been pushing against previous constraints and opening up spaces of alternate service delivery and civic participation, often in concert with authorities that previously had spurned them and continue to constrain them to a limited sphere of approved activities.

The increase in the activity of nonprofits is in part a spontaneous phenomenon – the bottom-up growth in social action, activism, and civic participation. It is also the consequence of deliberate, top-down, developmental policies by governments that see nonprofits as instruments for achieving their own objectives, by the for-profit business sector seeking to demonstrate its adherence to corporate social responsibilities, and by the growing nonprofit sector itself that seeks to perpetuate and expand its activities.

No single ideology has dominated the discussions in favor of expanding nonprofit activities. Conservatives consider them a key source of nongovernmental initiatives for counter-balancing state power and introducing market forces into the delivery of public services. Progressives see them as the embodiment of grassroots activism that can help ensure that social services are effectively delivered to those most in need. Paradoxically, the growth of the nonprofit sector has been characterized as both the death knell for the welfare state and its salvation (Ullman, 1998). Nonprofits give organizational form to sentiments such as the distrust of governmental institutions and the yearning for arenas for independent action, which neither the political right nor the left necessarily monopolize. As trust in the capacity of governments to deliver services and to create change wanes, nonprofits are seen to offer an alternative pathway for addressing societal challenges.

The nonprofit sector is immensely heterogeneous, spanning everything from large, multi-billion dollar, mainstream, professionalized institutions that function similar to for-profit firms and have close relations to governments and corporations, to small, hardscrabble all-volunteer organizations providing shoestring mutual aid or pushing for systemic change from the fringe. Definitive global figures on the extent of the nonprofit sector are not available as there is no single international repository of comprehensive statistics. The BRIDGE project, an attempt to provide unique identifiers to nonprofits around the world, catalogued more than 3 million organizations before the effort collapsed in 2020 due to lack of funding and the complexities inherent in the project (BRIDGE, 2020).

Studies on nonprofit sectors at national levels document the increases in numbers and salience within countries. The growth may not be constant – in any country there are spurts and contractions that reflect the short-term impacts of political transitions, economic cycles, and changing legislation or regulations – but the upward trend is the norm around the world. Table 9.1 gives examples of typical growth narratives in various countries and regions.

Some governments and elites fear the rise of the nonprofits, as they constitute a potential threat to their hegemony, while others promote a state-centric model of policymaking and service delivery that restricts the operational space afforded to nonprofits. Many regimes continue to erect significant institutional barriers

TABLE 9.1 Growth Narratives

Country/Region	*Narrative*
India	The number of [nonprofits] formed after 1990 has increased manifold, and the pattern of increase over the years is almost the same in all the states. There were only 144,000 societies registered till the year 1970, followed by 179,000 registrations in the period 1971 to 1980, 552,000 registrations in the period 1981 to 1990, 1,122,000 registrations in the period 1991 to 2000, and as many as 1,135,000 societies registered after 2000 (Government of India, 2009).
Sub-Saharan Africa	In the post-independence period, advocacy, development, and human rights organizations emerged across the continent. In addition, [nonprofits] increasingly played a critical role as service providers. Indeed, some commentators described their growth as an "explosion of associational life in Africa" (International Center for Not-for-Profit Law, 2011).
Catalonia, Spain	The [nonprofit sector] has witnessed a long growth period over the last decades which has resulted in a considerable increase in both their number and size, as well as in their social impact (TercerSector.net, 2011).
Saudi Arabia	In recent years, the Saudi Arabian people have increasingly called for expanded civic rights. In response, the government has offered slow, incremental moves towards reform. In 2006, the Ministry of Social Affairs first proposed a draft law to provide a unified framework for governing civil society organizations. In 2008, the Shura Council approved a revised version. Seven years later, in 2015, the Cabinet approved a new Law on Associations and Foundations. For the first time in the Kingdom's history, the law provides a legal framework to govern the establishment, operation, and supervision of associations and foundations (International Center for Not-for-Profit Law, 2019).

to contain and channel the expansion of nonprofits, and they occasionally resort to hard power repression against nonprofits seen as threats to state power. The Carnegie Endowment for International Peace reports a "viral-like spread" of new laws restricting foreign funding for domestic nonprofit and a shrinking of the political space for independent civil society (Carothers & Brechenmacher, 2014). Transitional and emerging countries have witnessed a growth in a wide range of nonprofits, but they are also the epicenters of closing spaces and associational counterrevolutions as governments tighten restrictions on foreign funding and seek to fetter any domestic operations perceived as threats to the current regime.

The Challenges of Documenting and Comparing National Nonprofit Sectors

The origins, functions, and modes of operation of the nonprofit sector in each country reflect its unique social, economic, and political history (Anheier & Salamon, 1998; Casey, 2016; DiMaggio & Anheier, 1990; Kramer, 1981; McCarthy et al., 1992). Historical path dependency is a well-established concept in social sciences and in nonprofit studies: Salamon and Anheier (1998) speak of "social origins" and "nonprofit regimes" while Anheier and Kendall (2001) identify "national scripts." Despite an increasingly common global discourse about the growth of the nonprofit sector and its increasing role in service delivery, policy-making, and economic life, fundamental historic variations between sectors the different countries persist. Any contemporary growth is grafted onto distinctive national rootstocks.

The legal definitions and structures of these nonprofit organizations vary considerably from country to country. Forms of incorporation differ between common law, civil law, and religious law, and there are wide variations in tax exemptions, incentives for donations, and oversight structures. In many countries, there is a large informal sector as a result of bureaucratic barriers to incorporation or because of government restraints on nonprofit activities. Alternatively, organizations that might otherwise operate as nonprofits choose to register as business entities to avoid scrutiny. In the most repressive and authoritarian countries, nonprofits, particularly those promoting human rights and democracy but also any not submitting to strict control by the regime, are under siege and workers in the sector operate under constant threat of violence and incarceration.

Research on nonprofits offers multiple examples of the challenges of documenting and comparing sectors, and of interpreting long cultural histories of associative life through the lens of contemporary conceptual frameworks. Key concepts such as civil society and social capital may inform our understanding of the nonprofit sector around the world, but attempts to apply them in different cultural contexts are often fraught. The Chinese *guanxi* and Melanesian *wantok* both describe traditional relationship networks that help individuals and groups articulate their interests, and are often equated to the Western concept of social capital.

However, they are also seen, primarily by external commentators, as corrupting influences that potentially generate cronyism and nepotism.

Deciding which organizations to include in counts of the nonprofit sector is in itself a conundrum. Japan is often characterized as having a comparatively small nonprofit sector, a ranking based on the relatively low number of entities incorporated under a landmark 1998 law on nonprofit organizations, and the fact that very few of these organizations are eligible for tax deductible donations. However, Japan has a long history of local communal life with neighbors taking an active part in the maintenance of public spaces and ensuring the well-being of neighbors. The formal structures of this neighborhood life are associations known as *jichikai (*also rendered in English as *chihi-kei*, and usually translated as neighborhood or community associations*)*, which are present in almost every locality. Neighbors pay dues and the association provides sanitation, security, recreation, and welfare activities, as well as institutional links to local government (Applbaum, 1996).

Participation in the *jichikai* is voluntary but there is strong cultural pressure to belong and nonparticipation would leave one branded as an outsider, particularly in rural areas and older urban neighborhoods. Nonetheless, they are often overlooked in research on nonprofits in Japan, with many observers regarding the *jichikai* more as part of the government apparatus because of their institutional links. They are generally regarded as conceptually separate from modern independent nonprofits in Japan, even though analogous neighborhood organizations with similar goals and activities would be considered the core of the community-based nonprofit sector in many other countries.

Path dependency and social origins approaches to the study of nonprofits are based on understanding how the history of each polity has conditioned current dynamics. In industrialized countries, guilds and fraternal societies that once dominated the associative sector have become a shadow of their former selves; mutual financial institutions such as local savings and loans societies have amalgamated and de-mutualized; and trade unions, mainstream religions, and political parties have all seen membership plummet. In developing countries, traditional associative structures based on ethnicities, religions, kinship, localities, or trades are being swept away as "modernization," "development," and "globalization" (all highly contested concepts) take hold. Political transitions transform former clandestine opposition networks into new legal organizations, or simply foster new spaces of independent, non-state action.

In the cultural frames described below, historical change is a constant theme in the analysis of the forces that have created the contemporary sectors. National narratives from around the world describe "new" or "modern" sectors that reflect the recent changes. Although collective voluntary action has a long history within each national context, the contemporary nonprofit sector is clearly distinct from earlier structures that were rooted in faith-based organizations, political parties, labor movements, or other traditional bonds. In the narratives of the contemporary dynamics of a wide range of countries, the nonprofit sector is cited as larger, more influential, and more integrated into national policymaking and service delivery than any time in recent history.

National and Regional Profiles and Comparative Research Projects

For those seeking to teach about the global and comparative dimensions of the nonprofit sector, there is an extensive body of research and documentation that can be used to generate curricula content. The major sources of documentation and data that explore the contours and operations of the nonprofit sector in countries and regions include:

- The seminal Johns Hopkins University *Comparative Nonprofit Sector Project* that began in 1991 bills itself as the largest systematic effort to analyze the private nonprofit sector around the world. It has operated in more than 45 countries, and has generated, several books and more than 60 published working papers (https://ccss.jhu.edu/research-projects/comparative-nonprofit-sector-project/).
- As a result of a collaboration between the Johns Hopkins project and the UN Statistics Division, a methodology was created to generate standardized and comparable statistics for national nonprofit sectors. Originally titled a *Satellite Account on Nonprofit and Related Institutions and Volunteer Work*, it is now referred to as the *Third or Social Economy Sector Handbook Project* and has been implemented in 27 countries (https://ccss.jhu.edu/research-projects/un-tse-sector-handbook/).
- CIVICUS, the global civil society alliance, along with regional partners, publishes a *Monitor* tracking civil space (https://monitor.civicus.org/)
- The International Center for Not-for-Profit Law publishes a range of country-level resources, including the Civic Freedom Monitor (www.icnl.org/resources/civic-freedom-monitor), the *Digital Legal Library* (www.icnl.org/resources/library), and the *Country Notes* series published in collaboration with the Council on Foundations (www.cof.org/country-notes).
- *USAID CSO Sustainability Index* is now published in collaboration with the nonprofit FHI (www.fhi360.org/resource/civil-society-organization-sustainability-index-reports).
- UK Charities Aid Foundation publishes an annual *World Giving Index* based on data from the *Civic Engagement Index* of the *Gallup World View* poll, as well as country-level reports on philanthropy (www.cafonline.org/about-us/publications).
- A newly emerging project, GRNDS, is an open register of national data sources about domestic nonprofits around the globe. Each country's record contains a comprehensive list of the forms and fields the national government collects from nonprofits (www.grnds.org/).

- There is a long list of other indicators published by various research institutes and think-tanks that either directly address the nonprofit sector or focus on related social political and economic dynamics. These include: *Big Mac Philanthropy Index; Cingranelli-Richards Human Rights Dataset; Edelman Trust Barometer; Fragile States Index; Human Freedom Index; Global Philanthropy Environment Index; Legatum Prosperity Index; Values Surveys; World Bank Indicators Database; Worldwide Governance Indicators.*
- Profiles of the nonprofit sector in any country or region can easily be found through keyword searches in academic databases, on research websites such as Academia and ResearchGate, or using general search engines.

The Cultural Frames

Using research such as that listed above, various researchers have identified overlapping cultural frames (or models, or patterns) that represent archetypes of the dynamics of national nonprofit sectors operating under different political, economic, regulatory, and social regimes. Table 9.2 summarizes the characteristics of a typical set of frames.

TABLE 9.2 The Key Parameters of the Cultural Frames

Frame (Examples)	*Economic Parameters*	*Regulatory Parameters*	*Social Parameters*
Liberal (United States, UK) Democratic, pluralist. High level of contracting of public services to nonprofits. Philanthropic provision of collective goods and services supplement lower level of government services.	High-Income Countries	Low barriers to sector entry. High tax incentives for charitable donations by individuals and corporations.	Strong culture of philanthropy and medium to high trust in nonprofits.
Corporatist (Germany, Belgium) Democratic corporatist. Dominated by subsidiary relations between political and social actors.	High-Income Countries	Low barriers to sector entry. Tax incentives for donations by individuals, but more restricted incentives for corporations.	Long history of philanthropy and cooperative structures. Taxation burden constrains philanthropic culture. High participation in expressive and recreational nonprofits.

(continued)

TABLE 9.2 Cont.

Frame (Examples)	*Economic Parameters*	*Regulatory Parameters*	*Social Parameters*
Social Democratic (Sweden, Demark) Democratic, State-centered social-democrat. State dominates delivery of public services and collective goods.	High-Income Countries	Low barriers to sector entry. Limited incentives for donations for individuals and corporations.	Welfare State and taxation burden constrain philanthropic culture. High participation in expressive and recreational nonprofits. Philanthropy often focused on international causes.
Emerging (Mexico India) Democratic, or incomplete transition to liberal, corporatist or social democratic models.	Middle-Income Countries	Recently established processes for sector entry and incentives for donations according to emerging model. Limited capacity to enforce regulations.	Small but growing non-profit sector. Growing local philanthropy, but low trust in nonprofit capacity, and concerns about corruption. Instability if there is withdrawal of international funding.
Developing (Rwanda Bangladesh) Democratic or semi-authoritarian. Low level of public services, many supported by international aid and philanthropy and implemented by international nonprofits.	Low-Income Countries	Medium to high barriers to incorporation of indigenous organizations. Oversight of operations of foreign nonprofits. Limited capacity to enforce regulations.	High incidence of funding by foreign donations. Tension between indigenous and international nonprofits. Low trust in all public and nonprofit institutions, concerns about corruption.
Authoritarian (China, Kuwait) Single-party, authoritarian.	Low-, Middle-, or High-Income Countries	Limited rights of association and assembly. High barriers to incorporation of independent organizations. Growing nonprofit sector restricted to "non-political" activities.	Membership in regime-sponsored organizations confirms allegiance to hegemonic party. May have dissident nonprofit sector in exile.

Source: Based on the cultural patterns in Casey (2016).

These cultural frames provide a useful conceptual lens for studying nonprofit sectors around the world, but they should be used with caution and caveats. Any one country may have elements of different frames, or a sector that may be moving between the frames. All nonprofit sectors are in constant evolution, in both their metrics and in how they are perceived by researchers and the public. This evolution may be the result of incremental changes in the factors that determine the national scripts or it may be marked by sudden shifts.

Globalization Perspectives: The Internationalization of Domestic Nonprofits

The primary focus of the literature on the international dimensions of the nonprofit sector is on those organizations created deliberately to work in the international arena. Equally significant, are the increasing international contacts and collaborations between nonprofits in different countries, as well as the domestic nonprofits that are expanding their operations internationally. Contacts between domestic organizations often lead to international outreach work; domestic nonprofits may create new separate international affiliates to extend their work abroad; and many international organizations foster the creation of new domestic organizations around the world to promote local ownership.

International Contacts and Cooperation between Domestic Nonprofits

There are almost endless iterations of the increasing incidence of international contacts and collaborative relations between organizations that continue to maintain a primarily domestic focus. In a globalizing world, with its ease of online communications and the relatively low cost of travel, there are few nonprofits anywhere in the world that have not entered into some exchange with counterparts in other countries, even if it is as modest as entertaining foreign professionals on fact-finding tours, visiting foreign counterparts while travelling, or participating in international forums of organizations working in the same field. While individually each of these contacts may appear to have little transcendence, their cumulative effect is a greatly enhanced international dialogue on nonprofit policy and practice.

For domestic nonprofits from industrialized democratic countries, their international contacts may be primarily for professional development and understanding of international good practice. It may also stem from a desire to create international solidarity networks to facilitate advocacy work in global arenas, or from an entrepreneurial interest of exporting an intervention model and brand. Nonprofits in developing and authoritarian countries have additional incentives for international outreach as they face the challenge of few domestic sources of funding, and their activities may be proscribed by the authorities. Many nonprofits in aid-recipient nations receive the majority of their funds from external sources and often look to external supporters to help ensure a certain measure of protection for their work. To survive and thrive they must have the capacity to plug into international networks. Casa Amiga, a nonprofit that supports victims of gender violence in Ciudad Juarez, Mexico, lists on its contributors page the Consulates of Canada, Holland, and the United States, multilateral institutions such as the European Union and the Inter-American Development Bank, as well as numerous philanthropic foundations and multinational corporations from Europe and the Americas (Casa Amiga, 2019). External support is not without peril, and in recent years a number of governments have moved to restrict external funding of nonprofits, branding it as foreign interference in internal affairs.

Networks, Movements, Coalitions, and Collaborations

Casual or sporadic international contacts are often the precursors to more stable relationships between nonprofits in different countries. There is a continuum that moves from loose, informal networks with fluid membership and participation to stable alliances, often coalescing around an anchor organization. Some of these alliances are formally constituted organizations created specifically to manage relations between collaborators in different countries and to lobby on their behalf, so in effect they should be categorized as international nonprofit membership organizations, but many others are more informal. A network secretariat may be housed in one of the more active promoters, or the network may operate without a fixed central coordinating body.

There are also global political and social movements that generally eschew traditional organizational structures. The anti-or alter-globalization movement, the solidarity campaigns that support indigenous struggles or nationalist movements such as the Zapatistas in Chiapas, Mexico, and the contemporary Occupy movements, often operate at the margins of the more formal nonprofit sector. They generally have a looser structure, both within the individual member entities and in the networks they create, and some may deliberately shun any attempt to define them as part of the nonprofit sector. Nevertheless, they are often supported by existing organizations formally constituted in their own countries as nonprofit organizations and may generate new nonprofits to carry on the work of the movement.

The North–South dimensions of networks present particular challenges with the richer, more powerful Northern elements often accused of speaking on behalf of the South. Increasingly, Northern domination is being tempered by more independent ownership in the South through the emergence of stronger indigenous nonprofits. The conduct of North–South collaborations continues to be controversial, with claims that they do little more than whitewash ongoing power differentials and that they are often used to shift blame for failures to Southern partners that cannot meet the terms imposed by Northern partners (Abrahamsen,

2004). The challenges can also be more prosaic – the founding statute of a network or federation may state that each member pays its own way to the international general meetings, a reasonable provision when all members were from the economic North, but this becomes less viable when organizations from poorer nations join.

Power imbalances and cultural differences can also lead to inequities in participation. An observer at the nonprofit forums that ran parallel to the 1992 UN Earth Summit conference remarked, "the Africans were watching, the Asians listening, the Latin Americans talking, while the North Americans and Europeans were doing business" (Colás, 2002, p. 154). Arguably, little has changed in the last three decades.

The Internationalization of Domestic Nonprofits

Many formerly domestic organizations that have chosen to go global, either by extending membership across borders, seeking to replicate abroad the work they do domestically, or by merging with similar organizations in other countries. These efforts transcend the networks addressed in the previous section, as they go beyond international contacts meant primarily to strengthen existing domestic activities. Instead, there is a deliberate choice to internationalize the work of an organization.

The size and economic power of US nonprofits often means that a nominally domestic organization becomes in effect the international organization for its field. The Muscular Dystrophy Association, based in Tucson, Arizona, which focuses on supporting research on neuromuscular diseases around the world, was founded in the 1950s as the Muscular Dystrophy Association of America. It evolved into its current international identity in the 1970s as it increased its work with other countries.

These dynamics may lead to possible demarcation disputes with existing international associations or other large national associations that are operating internationally. The National Association of Schools of Public Affairs and Administration (NASPAA), the US and Canada professional association for university public administration programs, changed its name in 2013 to the Network of Schools of Public Policy, Affairs, and Administration, and adopted a new tagline, *The Global Standard in Public Service Education*, after receiving a growing number of requests for membership from foreign programs. At the same time, there is also the Brussels-based International Association of Schools and Institutes of Administration (IASIA – tagline Improving Public Administration Worldwide) that brings together universities and other public sector training institutions and professional associations from around the world (NASPAA is a member of IASIA, along with the American Society for Public Administration and a number of US universities). In 2012, IASIA created its own accreditation system, the Commission on International Accreditation of Public Administration Education and Training.

More common than a large organization from one country acting as the de facto international organization are the various iterations of the establishment of global brands and franchises such as the Teach for America and Repair Cafes. Historic organizations, such as the Mission Societies and the Red Cross, and the service clubs Lions, Rotary, and Kiwanis, are early exemplars of global brands, but the last decades have witnessed an explosion of these dynamics as the transaction costs of the cross-border pollination of brands has decreased. Expatriates and "returnees" who have lived or worked abroad also colonize new territories with familiar nonprofit brands. In 2018, a branch of Toastmasters, the California-based public speaking club, was established in Ramallah in the West Bank by young Palestinians who had spent time in the United States.

A global brand might also be created simply by using the coda "without borders." Inspired by the objectives and evocative name of Médecins Sans Frontières (Doctors Without Borders), there are currently more than 50 organizations and networks that use those words in their name (or close variants such as "without frontiers"). They include Librarians Without Borders, Bikes Without Borders, and Geeks Without Frontiers. Some are single international organizations, while others are global networks of national organizations that share that name. Similar replications of brands are a combination of the spontaneous adoption of approaches by those who have heard about the work being done in other countries, and a direct strategy of expansion by some organizations.

The globalization of nonprofit brands can also be driven by the global aspirations of their commercial sponsors. The Australian clothing brand Cotton On, through its affiliated Cotton On Foundation, has established charitable projects around the world. It is the lead sponsor of the New York-based Global Citizen project, which runs online anti-poverty campaigns and has organized solidarity concerts in New York's Central Park.

The International Perspective: The International Nonprofit Sector

Just as nonprofits have become increasingly influential at national levels, there has been a corresponding escalation of international dimensions of the third space that operates between the expanding intergovernmental structures and the global marketplace for transnational and multinational businesses (Anheier, 2014; Batliwala & Brown, 2006; Boli, 2006). As evidenced in previous section, there is no "red line" that clearly distinguishes the international activities of domestic nonprofits, from the deliberately international nonprofits. Instead of distinct categories, there is a continuum of internationalness, based on the founding intentionality of the organization, its mission statement, and its operations.

International nonprofits operate globally much like multinational business corporations. There is variety of structural models that combine international headquarters with a network of locally incorporated branches, affiliates, or franchises and, like multinationals, they seek favorable legal environments for incorporation. Holland is often the legal home of choice because of its favorable corporate laws and tax environment. Greenpeace, which describes itself as an international nongovernmental organization with offices in 39 countries, was founded in Canada, but now bases its international secretariat in Amsterdam, where it is formally registered as Stichting Greenpeace Council (*stichting* is the Dutch word for foundation). Oxfam International, which describes itself as an international confederation of 20 independent national Oxfam organizations, was founded in the UK and maintains its international secretariat in London, where it operates as a foreign corporation registered in Holland as Stichting Oxfam International.

In addition to the prominent humanitarian aid, human rights and environmental organizations – such as Oxfam, Amnesty International, and Greenpeace – that tend to dominate any discourse about international nonprofits, there are also thousands of other organizations working in a wide range of fields. Given the considerable national variations in political regimes and service delivery models, the nonprofit legal structure has become a "flag of convenience" for a wide range of international dialogues, exchange, and collective action in fields as diverse as culture, recreation, academia, and technology support. TechSoup Global is a nonprofit network of more than 70 organizations around the world (some using the TechSoup brand while others use pre-existing identities from before their joining the network) that provides technology capacity-building to the nonprofit sector in their countries and regions.

There are also a significant number of nonprofit international professional and trade associations with either member national associations or individual members from around the world. Like most of their domestic counterparts, they function as autonomous nonprofits that foster the members' interests by providing a range of services, including acting as clearing houses for information and research on good practice, and advocacy work to promote policies and practices favorable to members.

The Rise of the International Nonprofit Sector

Since 1907, the Union of International Associations has documented the growth of intergovernmental and international nongovernment organizations. The Union was established in Brussels, Belgium, which at the beginning of the twentieth century was host to one-third of the then existing 150 international organizations (primarily intergovernmental organizations dominated by the European powers of that era). The Union was an outgrowth of the International Institute of Bibliography, founded in 1895, which had developed the Universal Decimal Classification system for libraries (Union of International Associations, 2012). Figure 9.1 shows the growth of both intergovernmental organizations (IG) and international nongovernment organizations (INGO) since 1909 as documented in the Union's Yearbook.

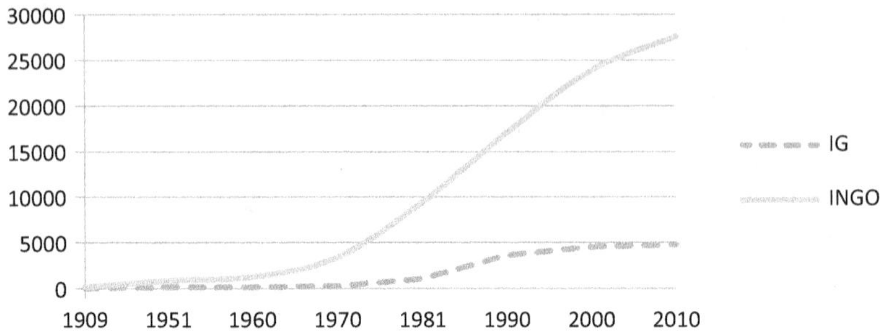

FIGURE 9.1 Growth in International Organizations

Note: does not include inactive organizations registered in the database.

Source: Union of International Associations (2012).

The database of the Union records the year of founding of international nongovernmental organizations. The first entry is for the Sovereign Constantinian monastic order founded in 312; the second is the Order of St Basil in 358. There is a steady trickle of organizations founded in the fourth to eighteenth centuries, almost exclusively religious, including Muslim Sufi tariqas after the ninth century. There were also a few early fraternal organizations, universities, scientific and academic associations, mercantile organizations, and performing arts groups. It was not until the mid-1800s that secular international nonprofits – advocacy, social welfare, professional, cultural, and recreational organizations – were founded in greater numbers than faith-based organizations.

The secular independent international nonprofit sector began to emerge in significant numbers through social movements focused on humanitarian and human rights, including anti-slavery and women's suffrage. While more avowedly secular, many of these new organizations had identifiably faith-related roots. A number of now emblematic international nonprofits appeared in the mid-1800s, albeit in original forms that do not necessarily correspond with their current focus – the Young Men's Christian Association (YMCA) was founded in London in 1844 as an evangelical organization, and the Red Cross in Geneva in 1863 to minister to soldiers wounded on European battlefields.

While some of the earliest organizations continue to exist, it was the early 1900s that saw the first surge of truly modern international nonprofits, instantly identifiable as such to contemporary observers. The importance of the work of international nonprofits was acknowledged in the 1945 Charter of the UN. The term "nongovernmental organization" (and the acronym NGO) is commonly regarded as having come into widespread use through its inclusion in Article 71 of Chapter 10 of the Charter, which established a formal Consultative Status for organizations that were not agencies of member governments. In the first years of the UN there were only some 50 NGOs with Consultative Status, and now there are currently almost 6,000 (United Nations, 2020).

The earliest NGOs with Consultative Status reflected both the primarily European, UK, and US origins of the first international nonprofits, and the diversity of what constitutes the nongovernmental sector. They included the Howard League for Penal Reform, the oldest penal reform charity in the UK established in 1866; the International Air Traffic Association founded in the Hague in 1919; the International Association of Schools of Social Work, founded at the First International Conference of Social Work in Paris in 1928; Pax Romana, the international Catholic movement for intellectual cultural affairs, first founded as a student lay Catholic association in Switzerland in 1921; and the International Bar Association, founded at an international meeting of jurists in New York in 1947.

Religious faith continues to be an important impetus in international nonprofits. The modern nonprofit sector may be more secular and universalist than earlier iterations, but religion is still a key part of the sector. Large historic faith-based entities, such as the Salvation Army, Islamic Relief, and Jewish World Service, as well as networks such as APRODEV (the association of development agencies affiliated with the World Council of Churches), continue to be major players in the international nonprofit scene, and the foundation story of a significant percentage of contemporary organizations includes narratives of faith-based inspirations. The YMCA evolved its focus and mission from the aggressive evangelism of its origins to its current focus on social responsibility, and a similar description could be also applied to many of the historic religious nonprofits.

International Nonprofits and Global Civil Society

There is no global government or executive body that legislates and regulates affairs or exercises the coercive powers equivalent to national governments. Yet public and private affairs are increasingly global, so regulation is effected through international governance "regimes" (Karns et al., 2015), "systems" (Willetts, 2011), or "triangles" (Abbott & Snidal, 2009) constructed by a patchwork of processes and institutions that include intergovernmental institutions, for-profit industry self-regulation, and international nonprofits. The treaties and conventions that emerge from the UN and the dozens of other multilateral and regional institutions, combined with the protocols and agreements from global summit meetings and conferences, constitute the dense networks of regulation and oversight that is the basis of international law. But their powers fall far short of those exercised by sovereign nations within their own borders, particularly in matters of enforcement. The global governance organizations that develop and administer the patchwork are continually negotiating their legitimacy and authority and so potentially conferring considerable political space to non-government actors.

Scholars continue to debate whether globalization is leaving nation-states behind as the highest legitimate level of power, a position they have held since the modern concepts of national sovereignty emerged from the Westphalia peace treaties of the 1640s (Walzer, 1998). For much of the twentieth century, the debates focused largely on intergovernmental relations and the possible emergence and merits of a global government. More recently, however, the focus has broadened to include analyses of the multilayered and multifaceted governance of international rulemaking and the processes of global governmentality. Nonprofits are seen as an integral element of the construction of global governance from below, as intergovernmental and multilateral institutions increasingly incorporate a broader range of non-government actors into the processes for policy development and legitimation (Jönsson & Tallberg, 2010; Karns et al., 2015).

Are international nonprofits part of an emerging global civil society that constitutes a truly new institutional realm with an increasingly autonomous role in global governance, as the "authentic" voice of world public opinion? Or, are they unrepresentative artifacts, bound to the donor elites, narrow interests, or national governments that created them and facilitated their growth? Keane (2003) argues that a global civil society is emerging and it is a new "society of societies," but that it is still evolving and that its salience will depend on its ability to become more democratic, better integrated into governance institutions, and more invested with universal values. However, others argue that international nonprofits continue to primarily represent the interests of their donors and sponsor governments over those of their putative constituencies or beneficiaries, and their authority to represent anyone is often called into question. The mandate of international nonprofits is ambiguous at best given that their combined claimed membership is less than the population of a small country, and the internal governance processes of most organizations are less than democratic (Archibugi, 2008).

The debates around the existence of an autonomous global civil society focuses particularly on the role of nonprofits as opinion-makers and as rule-makers through their work in promoting, developing, and supervising international norms, standards, and regulations in fields such as environmental issues, human rights, the empowerment of women, corporate social responsibility, election monitoring, prison reform, and post-transitional justice. Even though they have limited formal legal standing in the international arena, nonprofits can be advocates for new standards and watchdogs for their implementation and oversight. Nonprofits shape international events by identifying problems that might otherwise be ignored, articulating new values and norms to guide international practice, building transnational alliances, disseminating social innovations, helping negotiate resolutions to transnational disagreements, and mobilizing resources to intervene directly to address problems.

Arguably, the international nonprofit that has the greatest impact on the everyday lives of the global population is the International Organization for Standardization. Commonly known as ISO (not an acronym, but short name adopted to avoid confusion between the acronyms in different languages), it is the most widely accepted international standard-setting body. ISO describes itself is an independent, nongovernmental organization made up of members from the national standards bodies of 165 countries. Member associations reflect the political administrative arrangements of their nations – some are government agencies, some are quasi-governmental administrative bodies, while others are voluntary associations (ISO, 2020).

ISO began in 1926 as the International Federation of the National Standardizing Associations, with a focus on mechanical engineering, but was disbanded during the Second World War. It was reorganized in 1946 under its current name when delegates from 25 countries met in London and the restructured organization began operations in February 1947. The Central Secretariat, now in Geneva, Switzerland, coordinates the system, which comprises some 20,000 ISO standards, in areas as diverse as freight container dimensions, ISBN numbers on publications, the pictograms used to mark "This Way Up" on packages, and the sizes for screw threads. The ISO 9000 series is widely accepted as the standard for quality management in private, public, and nonprofit organizations.

The ISO is a nonprofit, nongovernmental organization, so it has no enforcement powers and the adoption of its standards is voluntary. However, many standards, particularly those concerned with health, safety, or the environment, have been incorporated into the legislation and regulatory frameworks of many countries. Other standards, such as the sizes of connectors for electronic devices, have become so universal that they in effect become gatekeepers for market entry.

Concluding Remarks: Developing Curricula Content for Global Nonprofit Pedagogy

The purpose of this chapter has been to highlight the complexities of nonprofit contexts around the world and to explore the three perspectives that must be addressed in global nonprofit pedagogy. Currently, nonprofit educators often gloss over the profound differences in how the nonprofit sector operates in different countries; they may pay insufficient attention to the globalization dynamics that now impact many even seemingly domestic organizations; and they tend to focus primarily on the subset of high-profile humanitarian aid, human rights, and environmental organizations and all but ignore the much wider range of nonprofits that increasingly drive global exchanges and rulemaking.

To be useful to educators and students, the material presented still has to be distilled into curriculum content. Each program must decide how to incorporate this content into core courses or into separate more deliberately comparative and international nonprofit courses. The global dimensions have implications for courses that focus on the sector as a whole, or on any of the sub-disciplines such as advocacy, fundraising, government relations or leadership and management.

The Curricular Guidelines of The Nonprofit Academic Centers Council (see Appendix; NACC) – itself a good example of a formerly US-focused nonprofit that has in the last decade become increasingly global – provide a roadmap for the design of global content. The Third Revised Edition of the Graduate Curricular Guidelines has a "more pronounced global and international perspective" (NACC, 2015, p. 3) than previous iterations. The first two guideline focus on global issues.

Other guidelines also address global contexts. While there has been a genuine intent to ensure that the NACC guidelines are applicable in the widest possible range of cultural, political, and discipline settings there is no escaping the fact that they primarily reflect the circumstances most common in English-speaking, multi-party, common law countries. Nonprofit programs that hew most closely to content based on the concepts of nonprofit, philanthropy, and voluntary action can easily follow the NACC guidelines. Programs based on other terminology, more steeped in other academic traditions, or operating under different regimes will need to adapt the approaches to their own realities. For some it may be as easy as simply substituting the local terminology for those currently in the guidelines. For others it may require a more profound rewriting according to the context in which they are operating.

Note

1 This chapter is based on material from *The Nonprofit World: Civil Society and the Rise of the Nonprofit Sector* by John Casey. Copyright © 2016 by Lynne Rienner Publishers, Inc. Used with permission of the publisher.

References

Abbott, K. W., & Snidal, D. (2009). The Governance Triangle: Regulatory Institutions and the Shadow of the State. In W. Mattli & N. Woods (Eds.), *The Politics of Global Regulation*. Princeton University Press.

Abrahamsen, R. (2004). The Power of Partnerships in Global Governance. *Third World Quarterly*, *25*(8), 1453–1467.

Anheier, H. (2014). *Nonprofit Organizations: Theory, Management, Policy* (2nd ed.). Routledge.

Anheier, H., & Kendall, J. (Eds.). (2001). *Third Sector Policy at the Crossroads: An International Non-Profit Analysis*. Routledge.

Anheier, H., & Salamon, L. M. (Eds.). (1998). *The Nonprofit Sector in the Developing World: A Comparative Analysis*. Manchester University Press.

Applbaum, K. (1996). The Endurance of Neighborhood Associations in a Japanese Commuter City. *Urban Anthropology*, *25*(1), 1–37.

Archibugi, D. (2008). *The Global Commonwealth of Citizens: Toward Cosmopolitan Democracy*. Princeton University Press.

Batliwala, S., & Brown, L. D. (2006). *Transnational Civil Society: An Introduction*. Kumarian Press.

Boli, J. (2006). International Nongovernmental Organizations. In W. W. Powell & R. Steinberg (Eds.), *The Nonprofit Sector: A Research Handbook* (2nd ed., pp. 333–351). Yale University Press.

BRIDGE. (2020). *BRIDGE Project – Shut Down*. www.bridge-registry.org/

Carothers, T., & Brechenmacher, S. (2014). *Closing Space: Democracy and Human Right Support Under Fire*. Carnegie Endowment for International Peace.

Casa Amiga. (2019). *Financiadores*. www.casa-amiga.org.mx/index.php/Contenido/financiadores.html

Casey, J. (2016). *The Nonprofit World: Civil Society and the Rise of the Nonprofit Sector*. Kumarian Press, Lynne Rienner Publishers, Inc.

Colás, A. (2002). *International Civil Society: Social Movements in World Politics*. Polity Press.

Della Porta, D. (2020). Building Bridges: Social Movements and Civil Society in Times of Crisis. *Voluntas*, *31*(5), 938–948.

DiMaggio, P., & Anheier, H. (1990). The Sociology of Nonprofit Organizations and Sectors. *Annual Review of Sociology*, *16*, 137–159.

Filer Commission. (1975). *Giving in America: Toward a Stronger Voluntary Sector: Report of the Commission on Private Philanthropy and Public Needs*. Commission on Private Philanthropy and Public Needs.

Government of India. (2009). *Compilation of Accounts for Non Profit Institutions in India in the framework of System of National Accounts (Report of Phase-1 of the Survey)*. National Accounts Division Central Statistical Organisation Ministry of Statistics and Programme Implementation.

International Center for Not-for-Profit Law. (2011). NGO Laws in Sub-Saharan Africa. *ICNL: Global Trends in NGO Law (Online)*, *3*(3). www.icnl.org/knowledge/globaltrends/GloTrends3-3.htm#_ftn4

International Center for Not-for-Profit Law. (2019). *Civic Freedom Monitor – Saudi Arabia*. www.icnl.org/resources/civic-freedom-monitor/saudi-arabia

ISO. (2020). *ISO - About us*. ISO. www.iso.org/about-us.html

Jönsson, C., & Tallberg, J. (Eds.). (2010). *Transnational Actors in Global Governance: Patterns, Explanations, and Implications*. Palgrave Macmillan.

Karns, M. P., Mingst, K. A., & Stiles, K. W. (2015). *International Organizations: The Politics and Processes of Global Governance* (3rd ed.). Lynne Rienner Publishers, Inc.

Keane, J. (2003). *Global Civil Society?* Cambridge University Press.

Kramer, R. M. (1981). *Voluntary Agencies in the Welfare State*. University of California Press.

McCarthy, K., Hodgkinson, V. A., & Sumariwalla, R. D. (Eds.). (1992). *The Nonprofit Sector in the Global Community: Voices from Many Nations*. Jossey-Bass.

NACC. (2015). *NACC Curricular Guidelines*. National Academic Centers Council.

Salamon, L. M., & Anheier, H. (1998). Social Origins of Civil Society: Explaining the Nonprofit Sector Cross-Nationally. *Voluntas*, *9*(3), 213–248.

Salamon, L. M., Sokolowski, S. W., & Haddock, M. A. (2017). *Explaining Civil Society Development: A Social Origins Approach*. Center for Civil Society Studies, John Hopkins University.

TercerSector.net. (2011). *Temes Clau per Enfortir Les Organitzacions No Lucratives*. www.tercersector.net/?p=640&lang=ca

Ullman, C. (1998). *The Welfare State's Other Crisis: Explaining the New Partnership Between Nonprofit Organizations and the State in France*. Indiana University Press.

Union of International Associations. (2012). *Yearbook of International Organizations*. Brill.

United Nations. (2020). *United Nations Civil Society Participation – Consultative Status*. https://esango.un.org/civilsociety/displayConsultativeStatusSearch.do?method=search&sessionCheck=false

Walzer, M. (1998). *Toward a Global Civil Society*. Berghahn Books.

Willetts, P. (2011). *Non-Governmental Organizations in World Politics: The Construction of Global Governance*. Routledge.

10

NONPROFIT LEADERSHIP TEACHING AND LEARNING

Takeaways from Two Rounds of NACC Accreditation

Stuart C. Mendel

Introduction

I have long held the view that teaching *leadership* to those seeking careers as nonprofit managers in North America is essential knowledge for thriving, high performing, and enduring third sector institutions in the United States. Drawing on the dedicated thinking for the field in the years since the Filer Commission (1975), it is accepted convention in graduate education that nonprofit and philanthropic institution leadership has nuance and complexity that is all its own. Also, given what nonprofit executives tell us about leadership-intense initiatives like forming meaningful and important partnerships (2018), there is little disagreement that leadership characteristics are more a mosaic reasonably mastered as they ripen with time and experience than a set of learned skills taught in the classroom.

Those of us who teach, study, mentor others, and run nonprofit organizations can point to as many ten nonprofit and philanthropy first conditions to navigate in nonprofit leadership performance:

- the authority of volunteers in governance necessitating skills of diplomacy both up and down an organizations hierarchy;
- due-care for the culture and values flowing from governance that require steady tending;
- decision-making that values pragmatism over dogmatism;
- tolerance for ambiguity and imprecision to effectively solve problems;
- vigilance for shifts in public policy and private sector political economy;
- respect for the limits set for charitable organizations by law;
- deference for the limits of resources;

DOI: 10.4324/9781003294061-11

- comprehension that operational resiliency is a best practice and is at odds with principle–agent relationships drawn from public and philanthropic funding sources;
- openness to "work arounds" as signal to warrant innovation practices in management, public policy or other aspects of the operating environment;
- necessary endorsement by third parties as a desired outcome of collaboration and partnership.

The takeaway for nonprofit academic programming is that although we talk about it a lot, nonprofit organization *leadership* is hard to teach and hard to learn in the classroom (Eich, 2008; Janson & McQueen, 2007; Sergiovanni, 2007; Giloth, 2007, Adler, 1996).

For those accepting the challenge of instruction, existing interdisciplinary leadership theory seems ill-suited to the task of nonprofit settings. Seemingly, few if any unaltered public sector and private business leadership principles port across the nonprofit academic programs of higher education (Parris & Peachey, 2013; Podolny, Khurana, & Hill-Popper, 2004).

Those learning are wise to appreciate that nonprofit sector leadership pedagogy is typically left to individual instructors who rely heavily on case study, field work, scenario assessment, their own and student experiences as leadership practitioners, and in the work of reflective contemplation.

These same sentiments apply to other aspects of nonprofit pedagogy, an observation supported through review of syllabi for nearly all 16 NACC Curricular guideline categories. As a system for replicable learning, that is difficult to teach and to learn in the classroom, nonprofit pedagogy, and specifically as illustrated by leadership subject matter is much like Saxe's (1816–1887) version of Blind Men and the Elephant: the students and others are in the darkness as to just what leadership as a whole concept, really is.

The elephant maybe an overly simplistic allegory but the phenomenon is not.

It is the purpose of this chapter to express common approaches for teaching and learning nonprofit and philanthropy first principles in nonprofit management graduate programs and professional development settings. This discussion will focus on *leadership* knowledge content as a model for the larger pedagogy milieu of all 16 NACC Curricular guideline subject categories.

Leadership as a Nonprofit and Philanthropy First Field of Its Own

Simply put, leadership where volunteerism sets the conditions for legitimacy of the thing being led requires a skill set not comparable to leadership necessary in public institutions or private business settings (Brudney, 2016; Smith, & Shen, 1996). The skills, perceptions and influences volunteers contribute to governance, strategy, resources – sustainability, ethos, and culture and nonprofit organization tendency to derive legitimacy from external stakeholders point to the basis for nonprofit first leadership practices branded on principles of adaptability, flexibility, and rapid response (Worley & Lawler, 2014; Brinckerhoff, 2009). Often overlooked in the scholarly literature as the defining feature of nonprofit life, the nature of volunteers (Bell, Bell, & Elkins, 2005) and their influence on an organization has application to the other curricular subject topics included in the NACC Curricular Guidelines.

For these reasons, it's not a big leap to conclude that teaching leadership to nonprofit graduate students requires a pedagogy and approach drawn on the fuzziness of volunteerism which is a different premise from those of public and private sector actors.

Others seem to agree.

First, respected thinkers grounded in nonprofit first perspectives have well-established that nonprofits and philanthropic institutions in the United States are neither businesses nor government in design or purpose; succeed or fail in ways that differ from those of public institutions and private business; are restrained in their cross-sector contributions to wealth creation, public agency, and public value; and operate within the limits of their mission (Goldman, 2008; Farmer & Fedor, 1999; Drucker, 1989; Commission on Private Philanthropy and Public Needs, 1975).

Second, *leadership* has a subject-durability in scholarly research literature that is undiminished since the earliest writings for the field A google scholar search for nonprofit and philanthropic sector leadership articles, for example, produces roughly 30,900 leadership-friendly titles spanning publication dates at the time of this writing (February 2022). Scrutiny of *leadership* also extends to nonprofit subsectors such as social welfare organizations, operating foundations, intermediary organizations, and many of the remaining tax-exempt categories recognized by the US Internal Revenue Service (Internal Revenue Service, 2020).

Third, *leadership* applied to scholarly inquiry beyond North American nonprofit organization settings has also been a focus for civil society institutions (Mitchell, 2013; Van Til, 2000, 1988). A vast pool of writing has been published centered on leadership subject matter for within the frame of the independent sector, social sector, third sector, nongovernmental sector, voluntary sector, charitable sector, and social enterprise organizations (Salamon, 2010; Hesselbein, 2002).

Fourth, *leadership* as a theme of comprehensive nonprofit management pedagogy has been a dedicated category among the NACC Curricular Guidelines in both undergraduate (number 7) and graduate curricular subject matter (number 5 and number 12) since their respective inception. Without exception, nonprofit academic graduate programs participating in the first two years of the NACC Accreditation project have made provision in their finite curricular space for the leadership subject matter. Some of these academic programs go even farther in using the term in their program titles and degree nomenclature.[1]

Finally, those who create policy for, work in, and care about nonprofit organizations or may otherwise be experienced executives of the sector sustain an awareness that nonprofit organization *leadership* is "a field of its own (2013)."

What the NACC Accreditation Project Data Tells Us About *Leadership* in the Curriculum

Evidence that many nonprofit graduate management programs credit *leadership* as a distinct and important aspect for nonprofit performance is plentiful. Table 10.1 draws on materials submitted in the general data collection of the NACC Accreditation pilot project which took place during 2019 and 2020. Observers will note from the table, 9 of the 11 programs include some derivation of *leadership* as an overarching program purpose. 30 courses apply the term *leader or leadership* to course titles or as a central theme for focus. Five of the 11 graduate degrees had *leadership* in the name, while three institutions had the term in the college or school title.

Table 10.2 paraphrases the much longer mission statements of the same 11 academic programs examined in Table 10.1. The detail illustrates the variety of uses and emphasis of the terms: leaders, leading, or leadership. Nine of the 11 programs employ some derivation of the term leadership to describe the overarching purpose of a program. The two remaining programs do not explicitly use the leadership terms but do offer courses dedicated to lead, leading, or leadership as instructional outcomes.

Table 10.3 draws on curricular maps completed by each of the 11 programs in which institutions plotted specific courses where leadership was at least one subject theme. All 11 programs offered at least a single course invoking the term leadership either in the course title and within the course description and learning outcomes. Six of the programs offered two or more courses involving leadership subject matter.

Table 10.4 lists those courses drawn from the accredited programs whose syllabi described leadership as a central theme of course subject matter. These courses were included for comparison in this table to reveal potential for a common leadership text and theoretical underpinnings used by faculty across institutions. The review does not account for changes to readings from year to year, but rather for a single offering of the course.

TABLE 10.1 Summary of Institution Participating in NACC Accreditation

Institutions	*Leadership in academic unit name*	*Leadership in degree name*	*Leadership mission Statements*	*Leadership titled courses*		*Service learning or capstone*
				Required	*Elective*	
11	3	5	9	17	13	11

TABLE 10.2 Academic Program Mission (Paraphrased for Summary)

1	To prepare students with knowledge of core competencies of nonprofit management in order to achieve their organization mission; enhance their employment opportunities or advance in their organization; make a career change while developing **leadership** skills and enhancing the field of public service.
2	To provide graduate students with professional, intellectual, and personal skills and knowledge that prepare them for real world application of diverse and advanced nonprofit management and **leadership** theories and practices.
3	To drive transformation in the sector where students can come for cutting-edge professional development and to meet and network with peers and share their experiences and ideas.
4	To integrate theory, research, and service into nonprofit management education that promotes ethical **leadership**, and the effectiveness, and sustainability of civil society organizations.
5	To train students for **leadership** of ground-breaking, fearless, and effective nonprofit and philanthropic endeavors.
6	To educate effective administrators by providing the essential **leadership** value mindset and managerial organizational competencies.
7	To provide students with the essential theoretical and practical knowledge and skills needed to be successful in managing and **leading** nonprofit sector organizations.
8	To build confident and ethical nonprofit **leaders** who transform themselves, their organizations, and their communities.
9	To prepare students for careers or advancement in the nonprofit and philanthropic sectors through classroom study, applied research, professional development, and field experience.
10	To explore both theory and the practice of management and **leadership** in the nonprofit sector.
11	Prepares working professionals to advance their careers in service and **leadership** through academic excellence, innovation, and a strong commitment to equity and inclusion.

TABLE 10.3 Course Title and Required (R) or Elective (E)

Leadership & Ethics in the Nonprofit Sector	E	Examines **leadership** and ethical questions encountered in the nonprofit organizations.
Leadership Capstone/Public Management Seminar	R	Application of **leadership** principles to field work.
Nonprofit **Leadership**	R	Theoretical and applied knowledge about concepts of **leadership, leadership** styles and situations, communication skills, techniques of inspiration, motivation, conflict resolution, negotiating and building consensus, coping with change, and fostering innovation.

TABLE 10.3 Cont.

Fundraising **Leadership**	R	**Leaders** foster and support a culture of philanthropy across an organization and its constituencies. Students will learn to analyze trends, assess opportunities, develop effective and ethical strategies, integrate fundraising into the larger strategic vision of the organization, and inspire others to action.
Leading Staff	R	Best practices for implementing the management competencies needed to lead staff, political realities of staff operations, fostering creativity, coaching for excellence, achieving diversity, nonprofit aspects of personnel recruitment, administration, retention and evaluation policies and procedures, laws, and regulations.
Executive **Leadership** of Nonprofit Organizations	R	No description
Strategic Management and **Leadership** for Nonprofit Organizations	R	No description
Leadership, Team Building, and Effective Management	R	No description
Nonprofit Ethical **Leadership**	R	Nonprofit **leadership** from an ethical and social sector value perspective.
Strategic Planning	R	No description
Nonprofit Board Governance	R	No description
Managing Nonprofit Organizations	R	This course will cover principles of effective management in nonprofit organizations, focusing on **leadership**, governance, legal structure and standards, strategic communications, volunteer administration, and the role of nonprofits in solving some of society's greatest problems. This course will not only provide a "how to" in managing nonprofit organizations, but will provide some of the research and theory on issues facing nonprofits, and help students approach problems from a strategic perspective grounded in both theory and practice. In doing so, we will use real world examples and experiences to ensure that academic lessons translate to the nonprofit experience.
Nonprofit **Leadership** Dialogues: Key Issues in the Nonprofit Sector	E	Understand: the social impact sector, its scope, and the character of entities that comprise it (service areas, missions, structure); how the sector intersects with government and business; that success in achieving an organizational mission depends on effective **leadership**, well-managed operations, and sustainable finances; become familiar with issues facing.

(*continued*)

TABLE 10.3 Cont.

		nonprofits and develop a working understanding of how **leaders** effectively address challenges; learn from nonprofit **leaders** by asking questions about their work, their organization, and their career; Advance thinking about career goals and expand professional networks for career growth and work collaboration; gain insight into personal needs for development.
Nonprofit Organization and Management	R	To gain an understanding of organizational theories and how they explain organizational behavior. To develop knowledge of the variability of **leadership** styles and organizations and their impact on organizational performance. To become aware of the dilemmas of managing nonprofit organizations.
Organizations, **Leadership** and Change	E	This module provides a theoretical foundation for the rest of the program, covering the core approaches to organization, change and **leadership** theory and their practical application in non-profit organizations. Understanding organizations and their development within an ethical framework is a vital element of a **leader** and manager's toolkit and central to their ability to manage change.
Nonprofit Administration and Theory	R	This course explores theories and research related to the administration of nonprofit organizations. Students will spend time solving case studies on a range of topics such as mission statements, structural analysis, and human resource management among others.
Nonprofit Governance and Decision Making	R	This course analyzes the role and organization of the Board of Directors as the legal and **practical head** of a nonprofit organization and its oversight of management. Students will use case studies on topics relevant to the Board and present an analysis of the governance of a nonprofit organization.
Leading from Within	E	This course is designed to celebrate the framework that makes this University superior to other universities. Principles, such as spreading knowledge, thinking critically, embracing personal standards, being socially responsible, and becoming **leaders** in a quest to improve society, are course learning objectives.

TABLE 10.4 Required Textbooks in Selected Leadership Course

Course Name	*Required readings*
Leading from Within	• Muller (2000): Sabbath; 2. Bennis & Thomas (2002): Geeks and Geezer – Harcadd Business • George (2007): True north: Discover your authentic leadership
NP governance and leadership	• Bolman, L.G. & Deal, T.E. (2013). Artistry, choice, & leadership: Reframing organizations (5th ed.). San Francisco, CA: Jossey-Bass • Renz, D.O.(Ed.), & Herman, R.D. (2010). The Jossey-Bass handbook of nonprofit leadership and management (3rd ed.). San Francisco, CA: Jossey-Bass

TABLE 10.4 Cont.

Course Name	*Required readings*
	• Trower, C.A. (2013).The practitioner's guide to governance as leadership: Building high-performing nonprofit boards. San Francisco, CA: Jossey-Bass
Nonprofit Administration and Theory (Online)	• Ralph Brody. (2014). Effectively Managing Human Service Organizations, Fourth Edition. Thousand Oaks: Sage Publications • Robert Egger. (2004). Begging for Change. New York: HarperCollins Publishers, Inc. • Norman Dolch, Julianne Gassman, Ann Marie Kimell, Stephanie Krick, Regan Schaffer, Sue Ann Strom, Susan Cruise, and Ronald Wade. (2013). Leadership Cases in Community Nonprofit Organizations. Debuque, Iowa
Organizations, Leadership and Change	• Adair, John (2010) Strategic Leadership • Kogan Page Hudson, M (2002) Managing Without Profit, Directory of Social Change
Nonprofit Ethical Leadership	• The course requires reading articles and reports central to the topics of each session
Nonprofit Management: People, Programs & Policies	• Renz, David & Associates. The Handbook of Nonprofit Leadership and Management (2016)
NONPROF 740 – Executive Leadership of Nonprofit Organizations	• Bolman, L., & Deal, T. (2013). Reframing Organizations: Artistry, Choice and Leadership. 5th edition. San Francisco: Jossey-Bass • Gallos, J. (2008). Leadership: A Jossey-Bass Reader. San Francisco: Jossey-Bass • Perry, J. (ed.) (2010). Public and Nonprofit Leadership. San Francisco: Jossey-Bass
Nonprofit Leadership	• Dugan, J. P. (2017). Leadership Theory: Cultivating Critical Perspectives. San Francisco: Jossey Bass • Lowney, C. (2003). Heroic Leadership: Best practices from a 450-year-old company that changed the world. Chicago: Loyola Press • Northouse, P.G. (2018). Introduction to Leadership. Los Angeles: Sage Publications

Findings

Despite all the energy exerted and interest in tracing the contours of "leadership" principles we consider part of nonprofit management pedagogy, the four data tables illustrate the many ways instructional content of leadership knowledge and instruction varies greatly across the compared academic programs. It is not a stretch to observe:

- few if any textbooks are common across the inter-institutional leadership syllabi;
- course learning goals stated in each institution are difficult to distill as transferable nonprofit and philanthropic first principles;
- common core archetypes and characteristics for leadership instruction are not easily discernable (Mendel, 2016, 2014; Mason, 1984, p.13).

Five practical findings and observations support the view that leadership knowledge is an education priority for teaching and learning nonprofit management. For example:

- The designers of the 11 graduate degree programs in nonprofit management participating in the Accreditation pilot project value leadership as a subject for their curriculum as reflected syllabi and program nomenclature.
- Concepts identified in the "lead, leaders, leadership" cluster of epistemologies is such that the terms do not convey a single discernable pattern for learning outcomes.
- Program missions reflect institutional-framed ambitions for an array of leadership concepts found in Table 10.2, while course syllabi learning aspirations paraphrased in Table 10.3 reflect a multiplicity of outcomes. It worthy of note in comparing the two tables that the way nonprofit academic programs teach leadership differs across all the programs and between the courses.
- The multiplicity of required course textbooks signals an absence of a unified theory for leadership in the management of nonprofit organizations.
- Course syllabi content and methodology establishes that students, like nonprofit executives and leaders learn from practical experience performing the work in the field, and from one another in unstructured interactions and networking social settings.
- There are distinctions for nonprofit and philanthropy first teaching and learning that are worthy of our attention as we build the field of nonprofit epistemology and nonprofit sector education. Understanding these norms for a field will propel scholars, teachers, learners, and doers toward the next generation of nonprofit management theory and practice.

Nonprofit and Philanthropy First Leadership Instruction Transferable Norms

The leadership pedagogy illustrates the artistry in teaching and learning-norms across nonprofit and philanthropy first management academic programs. We are reminded that "nonprofit and philanthropy first" refers to knowledge content drawn from the perspective and experience of nonprofit sector actors. This characteristic is essential in institutional learning environments where most of the knowledge materials, underlying theory and research and graduate academic programs compete with the public management and private business administration perspectives (Mendel, 2014; 2015).

As described elsewhere (Mendel, 2015, pp. 3–4) countervailing conditions set a tension for differences in nonprofit pedagogy within their academic hosts. Sometimes the countervailing tensions rise to the level of paradox. For example, public administration or business management programs do offer nonprofit concentrations or specialties but are less likely to explore nuance required for well-functioning volunteer run organizations. Nonprofits are typically cast as subordinate to those disciplines in the sense that public managers and business administrator use nonprofits as agents for their own achievement outcomes. For the purpose of this discussion, we focus on two conditions.

1. The origins and emphasis of the varied leadership curriculum arise with the tradeoffs required of nonprofit program design to align with the values and ethos of the individual University institutions housing them. The specific institution-centered ballet necessary for nonprofit content to fit within a particular academic college or school does not set conditions for standardized readily transferable pedagogy from institution to institution.
2. Since nonprofit executives tell us that they learn more from shared experiences (Mendel & Brudney, 2018), use of approaches such as cases and scenario analysis presented for illustration, introduces randomness and unpredictability for teaching and learning subject matter. This characteristic of the field also does not create conditions for transferrable learning across institutions. Consequently, theory derived from observation (peer to peer learning) rather than theory-led pedagogy more typical of social sciences graduate education are also a seeming characteristic of nonprofit subject matter teaching and learning.

The design norms described in the paragraphs of above differ only as they are shaped by the norms common in each institution. Although likely true of other leadership disciplines, another norm for nonprofit and philanthropy first learning is that they draw on practice to inform theory development. Put another way, the nonprofit first teaching and learning norms rely on a logic paradigm centered on practice that informs theory, rather than the inverse (Mendel, 2018).

Drawing on earlier scholarship published in the *Journal of Nonprofit Education and Leadership* (Vol. 8, Issue 4, 2018) depicting how nonprofit educators might craft case-studies from applied research, it is established an inductive/deductive system of theory development that reflects principles useful for nonprofit and philanthropy first instruction and learning (Mendel, 2018) is a norm of the field.

Together, these concepts can be attributed to three more distinctive characteristics of nonprofit and philanthropy first teaching and learning perspectives.

- First, tacit knowledge and sharing of tacit knowledge is a distinct characteristic of nonprofit leadership subject matter course design. This approach explains for example reliance on case studies, guest lectures and the anecdotal source material from the stories shared, small group discussion and assignments replicating committee work as common design features.

- Second, educators in nonprofit management graduate curriculum typically transfer of knowledge from existing leadership theories of public and private sector management and administration rather than bound in nonprofit first theory. Tacit learning would flip this by virtue of nonprofit first learning principles. Nonprofit leadership based on the tacit knowledge of the student learner is inductive, drawing on experience and contemplation of that experience. The instruction pedagogy follows the path of theory development culminating in a theory proof and a deduced confirmation.
- Third, in nonprofit organization strategic decision-making, planning and operations, the stakes are high because organizations are fragile by way of a dependence on external policy environments, donor intention, mission, and the particulars of mission fulfillment within the bounds of volunteer governance and in many cases, volunteer labor. Consequently, leadership in nonprofit settings is typically situational, precarious, and fleeting.

Experiential Knowledge and Tacit Knowledge

Nonprofit executives consistently report the best sources of learning arise through their own experiences and through those shared by others (Mendel, 2018, p. 5,11; Mason, 1984, p. 8). This is not surprising considering that most nonprofit students have sensitivity of the vagaries and trade-offs necessary for a career as a nonprofit executive (Brown & Yoshioka, 2003). Among those trade-offs are expectations for duties flexibility, commitment to mission, and the quirkiness volunteer-derived legitimacy bestows on a nonprofit.

The tacit knowledge (Carnevale & Stivers, 2019) experienced nonprofit executives bring to academic programs as students has been an important aspect in teaching and learning *leadership.* Nearly all NACC accreditation institutions shared that a segment of their student enrollments are returning to school to advance their careers or add to their knowledge. In fact, the Charities Masters Programme of the City University of London is completely part time to accommodate working professionals who comprise their full enrollment complement.

Making space for tacit knowledge in course delivery may well be among the most distinctive qualities for teaching graduate nonprofit management to those seeking careers in nonprofit sector life. This approach is consistent with the diversity of primary texts, reliance on supplementary readings, and the challenges for instructors to craft an alchemic blend of theory with practical application across the nonprofit graduate management pedagogy. Through this lens it is not surprising that the program mission statements depicted in Table 10.2 and nonprofit first leadership courses listed in Table 10.3 display and are designed to answer the big questions for teaching and learning nonprofit and philanthropy first subject matter:

- Just what is it that students who become nonprofit executives need to know about leadership?
- What are the best practices for navigating the perils, pitfalls, eddies, and currents of nonprofit organization life?
- What constitutes a successful leadership run and how can it be preserved, replicated, and advanced?
- Who really leads when volunteers are the authority and governors?

Among the NACC Accreditation program participants, leadership course syllabi allocate considerable space for peer discussion, small group work approximating work-place committees, case study illustration and analysis, field work-placements, and structured debate parsing conceptual theory with practical experience. These approaches acknowledge the value of personal experience and the random nature of volunteerism. Examples are in the use of case study materials; committee simulation in small group discussion in real time and as assigned work; in collaborative written assignments; and self-directed field work or technical assistance under the direction of a nonprofit staff person.

The course study materials described in NACC accreditation participant syllabi rely on primary and tacit learning source materials. Some of these materials find their way into the scholarly literature as published cases or memoir type reflections by experienced nonprofit executives. The literature is too numerous to cite in this small space but some examples are readily found in places like the *Journal of Nonprofit Education and Leadership* for example Doug Eadie's interview of his colleague Jim McGuirk (Eadie, 2011); the past President of NASPAA Jeffrey A. Raffel's memoir depicted within a frame of career long leadership development (Raffel, 2019); Lilly Cohen and Dennis Young's presentation of short leadership bios of nonprofit sector movers and shakers (Cohen & Young, 1989); and Patricia Libby and Laura Deitrick's "Cases in nonprofit management: A hands-on approach to problem solving" (2016).

Teaching and Learning Insight, Wisdom, and Good Judgment

It is generally accepted that few nonprofit management graduate students enter the field without predetermination. Nearly all the participating NACC Accreditation project programs point to their student enrollments as diverse in terms of age and career maturity. Many students entering nonprofit and philanthropy first graduate management programs have prior exposure to nonprofit life as one or some combination of a volunteer, board members, paid staff, donor, or recipient of programming. Even students enrolling directly from undergraduate degree completion typically know something about the field, either as a reflection of their career track due-diligence, personal idealism to give back to society, or through a search for meaning.

As the NACC-accredited institutions share in their webpage marketing and background materials, the typical nonprofit management graduate student enters the field of study with a deliberate purpose and nor do they begin their work with a blank slate of expectations. In other words, the students who purse nonprofit knowledge do so without passivity for the field but with purpose and deliberate goals in mind tempered by experience and passion.

Since the learning aspect of nonprofit and philanthropy first pedagogy is not carried out passively, case studies, management dilemmas, group discussions, and committee projects all simulate practical experience in the classroom. Knowledge transfer through these methods build essential skills drawing on the wisdom of others. For example, learners with experience in nonprofit life already know that nonprofit organizations are fragile. Some aspects of fragility arise with the nature of their funding revenue and expense overhead and a plethora of other reasons too numerous to list. Over-arching this learning is the pragmatism required of leaders and managers that volunteers pervade every aspect of a nonprofit organization. Experienced nonprofit stakeholders who become graduate students carry the knowledge into the classroom that the margin for error in leading, managing, and operating a nonprofit is slim.

While teaching theory can make refence to the challenges familiar to students, the vigor and manner in which the operations and management dilemmas are overcome – or not – tend to have lasting value for the learner. For instructors and course design, we glean from the NACC accreditation leadership syllabi several common characteristics: learning from others; contemplation of that learning; and action drawn from that learning. This sequence sets the conditions for teaching and learning outcomes thru shared wisdom and vetted models for making good judgments.

Since so much of nonprofit life requires a comfort with the fuzzy presence of volunteers in a variety oftentimes concurrent, boundary spanning roles – authority figures, content experts, external funders, and laborers – teaching and learning outcomes must account for what is necessary to know, and, how to effectively apply that knowledge.

Another way to depict these necessary aspects of teaching and learning is knowledge transfer between instructor and student that draws on wise council and mutual mentorship in sharing knowledge. Teaching in nonprofit leadership pedagogy sets the conditions for mutuality in the classroom among instructors and learners. Clues to the presence of mutuality as a distinctive characteristic of nonprofit and philanthropy first pedagogy is reflected by the lack of common canon, and the diversity of course readings and texts across courses and institutions.

Conclusions

Drawing on these observations from the NACC-accredited institutions, several nonprofit and philanthropy first teaching and learning methods are discernable as underlying ethos for teaching and learning in nonprofit and philanthropy first classroom. Teaching and learning outcomes of students should include lessons derived through wisdom and good judgment achieved by leadership practices. A few illustrative examples of nonprofit and philanthropy first shared learning drawing on mutuality of experience may be:

- Flexibility, adaptability, and the practice to take in new information, revisit old decisions as circumstances dictate.
- Use core values to maintain consistency of approach and mission focus even as tactics shift.
- Value team, partnership, shared vision, and maintain their attainment as a priority.
- Gain a comfort through reflection as managers and leaders with the paradoxes of leadership, the dilemmas those paradoxes drive.

Reflections for Further Study

As the field of nonprofit pedagogy advances, it is our job collectively to push forward the sharpened themes for nonprofit teachers and learners. Toward this end, educators can draw on lessons learned from leadership in nonprofit academic programs. Among the more salient developments is that teaching and learning nonprofit subject matter for this field channels experiences of executives sharpened in the field of practice; eagerness to learn from one another; and preference for realistic problem-solving exercises using case studies, group assignments, and field work to the classroom.

One parting thought is the role conceptual pragmatism overlays on the standard social science logic model for teaching and learning nonprofit management subjects. Starting with practical experience to then guide development of theory, is atypical in the academy but essential for the workplace. In this respect research lags behind practice and it behooves educators of the field to adjust their approach accordingly.

Note

1 Participating Institutions in the NACC Accreditation pilot project, year 1 and 2: Arizona State University, Master of Nonprofit Leadership and Management; Case Western Reserve University, Master of Nonprofit Organizations; City University of London – Sir John Cass Business School Charities Masters Programme; Grand Valley State University, Masters of Philanthropy and Nonprofit Leadership; Louisiana State University Shreveport, Master of Science in Nonprofit Administration; Regis University, Master of Nonprofit Management; Seattle University, Master of Nonprofit Leadership; University of Oregon, Master of Nonprofit Management; University of San Diego, Master of Arts in Nonprofit Leadership and Management; University of San Francisco, Master of Nonprofit Administration; University of Wisconsin Milwaukee, Master Science in Nonprofit Management and Leadership. Source: www.nonprofit-academic-centers-council.org/accreditation/nacc-accredited-programs-pilot-year-one-2018-2019/ as found on April 15, 2020.

References

Adler, G. (1996). When a new manager stumbles, who's at fault? Harvard Business Review, 74(2), 22.

Bell, J. R., Bell, R. R., & Elkins, S. A. (2005). Embedding ethical frameworks in the leadership system of not-for-profits: The special case of volunteers. SAM Advanced Management Journal, 70(4), 29.

Brinckerhoff, P. C. (2009). Mission-based management: Leading your not-for-profit in the 21st century (Vol. 231). John Wiley & Sons.

Brown, W. A., & Yoshioka, C. F. (2003). Mission attachment and satisfaction as factors in employee retention. Nonprofit Management and Leadership, 14(1), 5–18.

Brudney, J. L. (2016). Designing and managing volunteer programs. The Jossey-Bass Handbook of nonprofit leadership and management, (Eds. David O. Renz, & Robert D. Herman), 688–733. New York: John Wiley & Sons.

Carnevale, D. G., & Stivers, C. (2019). Knowledge and power in public bureaucracies: From pyramid to circle. Routledge.

Cohen, L., & Young, D. R. (1989). Careers for dreamers & doers: A guide to management careers in the nonprofit sector. Foundation Center.

Commission on Private Philanthropy and Public Needs. Giving in America: Toward a Stronger Voluntary Sector. Commission on Private Philanthropy and Public Needs (1975). www.ulib.iupui.edu/special/collections/philanthropy/mss024

Drucker, P. F. (1989). What business can learn from nonprofits. Harvard Business Review, 67(4), 88–93.

Eadie, D. (2011). Astor Services's Jim McGuirk talks with Doug Eadie about Chief Executive Leadership. Journal of Nonprofit Education & Leadership, 2(1), 1–5.

Eich, D. (2008). A grounded theory of high-quality leadership programs: Perspectives from student leadership development programs in higher education. Journal of Leadership & Organizational Studies, 15(2), 176–187.

Farmer, S. M., & Fedor, D. B. (1999). Volunteer participation and withdrawal. Nonprofit Management and Leadership, 9(4), 349–368.

Giloth, R. (2007). Nonprofit leadership: Life lessons from an enterprising practitioner. iUniverse.

Goldman, A. (2008). Company on the couch: Unveiling toxic behavior in dysfunctional organizations. Journal of Management Inquiry, 17(3), 226–238.

Golensky, M., & Hager, M. A. (2020). Strategic leadership and management in nonprofit organizations: Theory and practice. Oxford University Press.

Hesselbein, F. (2002). Hesselbein on leadership. John Wiley & Sons.

IRS: Exempt Organization Types. (March 31, 2020; 8:20 p.m.) www.irs.gov/charities-non-profits/exempt-organization-types

Janson, A., & McQueen, R. J. (2007). Capturing leadership tacit knowledge in conversations with leaders. Leadership & Organization Development Journal Sept 25 Issue, 646–663.

Lewis, H. (1975). Management in the nonprofit social service organization. Child Welfare, 54(9), 615–623.

Libby, P., & Deitrick, L. (2016). Cases in nonprofit management: A hands-on approach to problem solving. SAGE Publications.

Mason, D. E. (1984). Voluntarism. In Voluntary Nonprofit Enterprise Management (pp. 1–12). Springer.

Mendel, S. C. (2014). A field of its own. Stanford Social Innovation Review, 12(1), 61–62.

Mendel, S. C. (2015). Nonprofit first: the promise and potential of the nonprofit academic centers council. Journal of Nonprofit Education and Leadership, 5(1), 30–36.

Mendel, S. C. (2016). Nonprofit First as grounding for nonprofit studies pedagogy, research, service to the community accreditation and national rankings in Will Brown & Matt Hale, editors. Special Issue: Papers From the Nonprofit Academic Centers Council (NACC) July 2015 Conference. The Journal of Nonprofit Education and Leadership, 6(3), 5–13.

Mendel, S. C. (2018). Writing nonprofit first cases for research and instruction. The Journal of Nonprofit Education and Leadership, 8(4), 342–357.

Mendel, S. C., & Brudney, J. L. (2018). Partnerships the nonprofit way: What matters, what what doesn't. Indiana University Press.

Mitchell, G. E. (2013). The construct of organizational effectiveness: Perspectives from leaders of international nonprofits in the United States. Nonprofit and Voluntary Sector Quarterly, 42(2), 324–345.

Parris, D. L., & Peachey, J. W. (2013). A systematic literature review of servant leadership theory in organizational contexts. Journal of Business Ethics, 113(3), 377–393.

Podolny, J. M., Khurana, R., & Hill-Popper, M. (2004). Revisiting the meaning of leadership. Research in Organizational Behavior, 26, 1–36.

Raffel, J. (2019). Lessons Learned: A Memoir of Leadership Development. Washington D.C.: NASPAA Press.

Reimnitz, C. A. (1972). Testing a planning and control model in nonprofit organizations. Academy of Management Journal, 15(1), 77–87.

Saxe, J. G. (1816). The Blind Men and the Elephant, poem based on an Indian fable. New York: Wentworth Press.

Salamon, L. M. (2010). The changing context of nonprofit leadership and management. In The Jossey-Bass Handbook of nonprofit leadership and management, 77–100. New York: John Wiley & Sons.

Sergiovanni, T. J. (2007). Rethinking leadership: A collection of articles. Corwin Press.

Smith, D. H., & Shen, C. (1996). Factors characterizing the most effective nonprofits managed by volunteers. Nonprofit management and Leadership, 6(3), 271–289.

Van Til, J. (1988). Mapping the third sector: Voluntarism in a changing social economy. Foundation Center.

Van Til, J. (2000). Growing civil society: From nonprofit sector to third space. Indiana University Press.

Williams, R. W., & Leonard, R. L. (1962). Financial reporting by nonprofit organizations. Journal of Accountancy (pre-1986), 113(000004), 46.

Worley, C. G., Williams, T. D., & Lawler III, E. E. (2014). *The agility factor: Building adaptable organizations for superior performance.* John Wiley & Sons.

11

PREPARING THE NEXT GENERATION OF NONPROFIT AND COMMUNITY LEADERS

A Pedagogical Framework

Jaclyn Le, David W. Springer, and Charlee Garden

Introduction

Preparing the next generation of nonprofit and community leaders is more important now than ever. Leadership development in the nonprofit sector is often seen as a luxury that comes after meeting community needs and providing programs or services. We believe that a leader is a catalyst for change, takes personal and social responsibility to work with others for a common good, and is guided by core values and ethics. Preparing, supporting, and nurturing nonprofit and community leadership is not a luxury. Our communities need authentic, values-based leaders who are committed to social change and social justice.

One of higher education's fundamental responsibilities is to develop leaders prepared for a rapidly changing world of increasing complexity and entrenched social and economic challenges. In many ways, a crisis and failure in leadership led to the problems that nonprofit and community organizations must now address. The systematic oppression of Black, indigenous, and other communities of color was the result of intentional choices made by some leaders in the world. To undo these actions and reimagine new systems, we need different leaders. Leadership pedagogy of the past needs to be reimagined to meet current and future challenges that nonprofit and community leaders face. Leaders need to be more self-aware, inclusive, and empathetic.

The purpose of this chapter is to offer a tailored pedagogical framework to guide how nonprofit and community leaders are prepared for their work ahead. We offer several teaching tools and examples that support self-reflection and raise self-awareness so that students may better understand their impact as leaders.

Why do we need to refine how we think about and teach leadership?

DOI: 10.4324/9781003294061-12

First, everyone has the capacity to lead. Leadership can be taught, and our students can matriculate from our programs empowered to lead from where they are, given their unique strengths. We need leaders from different personal and professional backgrounds with diverse lived experiences and values that enable them to center the people and communities they seek to serve. Our role as educators is to enable and empower all of our students to see themselves as leaders.

Second, nonprofit and community leaders have a unique role to play in cultivating a civil society, which refers to the space for collective action around common purposes and shared values. A civil society is nurtured and made more robust to the extent that we work collectively to promote social and economic justice, advance equal participation in democracy, protect the independence of associations and the structures of communication, and build a strong foundation for cross-sector collaboration. Efforts to cultivate a civil society require leaders to actively engage with economic, political, private, and social systems. Nonprofit and community leaders need to be viewed as equal peers to mayors, CEOs, and university deans. They have to be prepared to engage with people from all walks of life, from different sectors, and with different values.

The Future of Nonprofit and Community Leadership

The model of American leadership has changed over the last decade. Political polarization, economic stratification, and racial inequity intensified, causing government, corporations, and the social sector to redefine what leadership looks like. Clearly, the old guard of leadership is inadequate for meeting today's challenges. No singular type of leadership will be sufficient in solving the toughest problems we face. Instead, today's leaders are expected to bring a diversity of perspectives and experiences.

The treatment of Barack Obama and Kamala Harris is a prime example of how expectations of leadership have changed. President Obama made history as the first Black president of the United States; however, his Blackness, while historic, was often downplayed to avoid triggering those who still expected the president to act like the 43 that came before him. The 2008 election stirred a debate and created a false narrative about a "post-racial" society in which differences do not form the basis of prejudice and discrimination (Bhopal, 2018). This "post-racial" myth erased the value of diversity and made it invisible altogether.

In contrast, the election of Kamala Harris as the first woman as well as the first Black and South Asian person to the position of Vice President of the United States has been heralded in a different way. Her diversity has not only been recognized but also celebrated. News articles chronicled her blended family and embraced her life experiences as reflecting those of many Americans previously unrepresented in the highest levels of government (Bennett, 2021). For many, Kamala Harris's ascent to the White House brought hope that her background and life experiences would lead to an entirely different way of governing - one that is more tolerant, inclusive, and representative of the people.

This change in the leadership model is also seen in corporate America as well as the nonprofit and philanthropic sectors. In 2018, California Governor Gavin Newsom mandated gender diversity on the boards of directors of all publicly traded corporations in the state (California Senate Bill 826, 2018). Every public company in California is required to have at least one woman on its board. In 2020, a report from Echoing Green and the Bridgespan Group highlighted racial disparities in philanthropic funding for nonprofits led by people of color (Dorsey et al., 2020). Efforts to diversify nonprofit leadership are more prominent now than ever. For example, organizations such as the New Philanthropists, a nonprofit in Austin, Texas, with a mission to create more racially diverse and inclusive nonprofit boards, focus on building a leadership pipeline of people of color. These efforts, and others, are driven, in part, by the lack of diversity among philanthropic leaders who make decisions about funding. Unconscious biases guide who is viewed as a nonprofit leader, how funders interact with grantees, and how success is measured. In every corner of society, there is a clear need for a new vision of what leadership looks like and what it can be.

Core Beliefs About Leadership

The field of leadership studies has three branches (Roberts, 1981) with three corresponding lenses for teaching leadership: teaching "about" leadership, teaching "for" leadership, and teaching "practical wisdom" (Perruci & Hall, 2018). The first branch approaches leadership as an intellectual field of study. The second branch is competency-based, with a focus on the practical skills and competencies one needs to be a leader. The third branch, leadership development, is a blend of the first two, integrating knowledge and experience to cultivate wisdom. Our approach to teaching leadership most closely aligns with the practical wisdom branch, with a focus on leadership as a way of being and developing a personal philosophy of leadership.

More specifically, our approach to teaching leadership and developing the next generation of philanthropic and nonprofit leaders is based on five core beliefs about leadership. These core beliefs were born from our professional backgrounds and our lived experiences.

Leadership Is a Way of Being, Not a Position or Job Title

Leaders are often portrayed as people in authoritative positions with corner offices, management responsibilities, or power. But viewing leadership only from the top of the organizational chart shortchanges the impact that each one of us can have in our communities and for the world around us. Everyone can lead from where they are. There are millions of opportunities each day to demonstrate leadership (Dudley, 2010). The challenges that we face require everyone to step up and recognize the impact that each person can have on each other and our communities.

There Is No "Right" Way to Lead

Effective leadership is based on our individual strengths, values, and lived experiences. If leadership is a way of being, then we should expect over seven billion unique leadership styles. Everyone has their own way of being a leader. When leaders are able to identify their values and build on their strengths, they can have the most impact on others and their communities (Williams & Weber, 2019). Therefore, leadership theory and pedagogy should empower people to discover and develop their own leadership philosophy. Indeed, the future of leadership research and theory development is likely going to be multidisciplinary, emphasize the co-creation of leadership, and have an emergent and shared nature (Lord, 2017). While every leader has a unique way of leading, it is also important to note that different contexts and situations may lend themselves to certain practices or actions over others. There is significant literature about leadership practices that are correlated with success. We believe that specific practices and actions that leaders employ may vary, but their values and core leadership philosophy should be consistent across all contexts. There is no "right" combination of values and attributes that fit every leader. Therefore, those who teach leadership should facilitate, not prescribe.

Learning Leadership Is a Personal Journey

Authentic leadership is a personal craft. Developing a leadership philosophy that is true to who we are requires an understanding and exploration of our values, strengths, and beliefs (Ryan, 2016). With thoughtful intentionality and mindfulness, everyone can develop a personal leadership philosophy that integrates their values, draws upon their lived experiences, and is informed by leadership theories that resonate with them. Accordingly, we fully integrate design thinking (cf. Burnett & Evans, 2016), positive psychology (cf. Nettle, 2005; Raghunathan, 2016), and ethics (cf. McManus, Ward, & Perry, 2018; Schwartz & Sharpe, 2010) into our leadership classes and workshops.

Leadership Is Not a Fixed Target

Each person's leadership skills and capacity can be developed and can evolve over time. There is no such thing as a fully developed leader. There is not a finite amount of information to learn before someone is considered a leader. Over time, a person's leadership abilities can grow and evolve as their values and experiences change. The goal of leadership development is to raise self-awareness, increase understanding of leadership moments, and expand a person's choices in those moments.

Becoming a Leader Requires Intentional Practice

Applied practice is the bridge between philosophy and impact (Lanik, 2018). Leadership requires intentional and applied practice in both big and small moments. Like athletes and musicians, nonprofit and community leaders have to practice. To be a catalyst for change, leaders must intentionally apply their leadership philosophy in their work, relationships, and communities. As educators, we should not expect our students to emerge as fully formed and enlightened leaders by the end of a class. Figuring out what works for each leader is often about trial and error. Leaders experiment and fail as they apply their leadership philosophy in real moments and situations.

Creating a Personal Philosophy of Leadership

Everyone has the capacity to lead, yet each of us leads differently. We are drawn to particular theories and frameworks of leadership that resonate. We lean on our own strengths to impact others within our sphere of influence. And we are driven by our values, culture, and lived experiences. Who we are and what we believe is core to how we behave as leaders. Though contexts and situations may change what actions we take, the values and experiences that undergird our approach to leadership remain constant.

In light of this view of leadership, we believe in the potential of a transformational learning experience by providing students with scaffolding and opportunities to reflect upon and refine their guiding personal philosophy of leadership. This, in turn, enhances students' capacity to work in concert with others on substantive issues to catalyze change in their communities or agencies. A personal philosophy of leadership can act as a north star to guide how leaders respond to their environment and take action to better their teams and communities. In short, we have to know who we are and what grounds us before we can truly lead.

There is an important role for leadership theory in this work. The field of leadership research and studies lacks an integrative theory. One review (Dinh et al., 2014) identified nearly 70 separate theories examined by leadership researchers published in major journals since 2000 (Lord, 2017). In the face of this theoretical proliferation, it can be a daunting task to wade our way through leadership theories and narrow them down for ourselves and our students. Three of our personal favorites include Authentic Leadership (George, 2003; George & Sims, 2007; Terry, 1993), Servant Leadership (Greenleaf, 1970; 1977), and Transformational Leadership (Burns, 1978; Kouzes & Posner, 2017). It is beyond the scope of this chapter to provide a detailed exposition on each of these theories of leadership.

Rather, we offer an example of theory in action below through sharing the story of Celena.

Leadership is not a simple intellectual or theoretical exercise. In fact, some research suggests that the development of leadership identities may be one way to increase leadership capacity and skills (Day & Dragoni, 2015). True leadership is complex - navigating ambiguity in real time, treating others with compassion, living with intention, learning and growing from our mistakes, and supporting others to do the same. It's messy. This raises important questions: What do we do when the type of leader we want to be does not align with how we want to lead? How do we thoughtfully examine those growing edges? There are many ways to help ourselves and our students courageously explore the gap between our espoused philosophy of leadership and our behaviors in action. The case example below of Celena offers how one might respond to these and similar questions.

Theory in Action: Celena

The best way to illustrate the power of a personal philosophy of leadership is through an example of how a nonprofit leader applies their values and experiences in their daily work. An experience undergone by Celena Mondie-Milner, the Executive Director of New Student Services (NSS) at The University of Texas at Austin (UT), illustrates the guiding forces of values and philosophy in successful leadership.

Celena and her team of 14 NSS staff are renowned for hosting a world-class dynamic, impactful orientation where new Longhorn students learn to navigate UT and make lasting friendships. While she and her team have done this successfully for years, there is still an eight-month investment of energy and time in co-creating the orientation with the 80 student leaders and student mentors that participate each year.

At a mid-March 2020 Zoom meeting, Celena and her team were newly navigating remote work and quickly realizing that they needed to onboard 10,000 incoming students in this new virtual environment, while retaining the same high standards for impact and connection as in their in-person orientations. Most of the tools and resources the NSS team had relied on for a successful orientation were no longer available. Celena worked with a coach who helped her to reflect on her values as a leader and to envision the impact she wanted to have on her team and others around her. Celena's coach facilitated her learning by prompting her to answer questions such as "what do you imagine you hear or see on the Zoom," and "what could you imagine thinking or feeling if you were on the team, knowing that most of what you relied on to be successful in the past was no longer available to you?"

For Celena, while the challenge was unprecedented, she handled the moment itself with the same (extra)ordinary leadership style and values that she handles every moment with: perseverance, positivity, and the commitment to do whatever it takes to be successful. By reflecting on her values and the impact that she wanted to have on her team, Celena could respond to the situation with a clear understanding of what she needed to do and how she needed to communicate with others. With her transparent style, Celena clearly communicated the challenge, her vision, and her high expectations for an impactful 2020 orientation series. If anything, she communicated that it was even more important that they delivered this year. Due to the pandemic and rising racial tensions, incoming students needed orientation. They needed to connect and belong to something bigger than themselves, to be part of a university that changes the world.

To know Celena is also to know that she is a humble, hall-of-fame track star and that her leadership values and style solidified with one swift decision. During one of her first races, Celena was in her starting position when the gun went off and she fell flat on her face. She remembers watching the other runners begin their race while she was on the ground looking up at the crowd. She spotted a young boy she had a crush on who was laughing at her fall. Instead of this keeping her on the ground, she made a split-second decision and got up to prove him wrong. Despite her fall and late start, Celena ended up winning the race. This lived experience guided the way that Celena responded to crisis and uncertainty. As in that youthful moment when Celena looked up from the track, her 2020 conviction that the NSS team could, would, and should dig deep and figure out how to make orientation amazing was palatable. She didn't know how they would do it. No one did. But she invited the team to believe they could do it, and was willing to work with them to figure it out.

This crisis situation drew on Celena's core values and convictions as a leader. The combination of her belief in the importance of a dynamic student experience and her values of tenacity and hard work drove the success of the orientation. Celena's example shows that crises are not, in fact, the time to determine a leader; crises are moments when a leader's cultivation of values and philosophy pays off. Because of Celena's clear communications, conviction in her values, and decisiveness in a time of chaos, the student leaders on her team were successfully onboarded. The student leaders and mentors held dynamic orientations that allowed new students to create lasting relationships, even in a virtual environment.

Truth Reflections

As Celena's story highlights, we believe that growth as a leader requires personal and professional reflection, an understanding of one's strengths and growing edges, opportunities to try out new ways of leading, and space to lean into leading with intention. In this spirit, one of the authors (Springer) developed an assignment for his graduate seminar, Leadership as a Catalyst for Community Change, called

TRUTH Reflections. The assignment in the syllabus is included below (see Box 11.1), followed by an exemplar reflection submitted by an MPAff student, Britt Havey Dewitt (see Box 11.2).

BOX 11.1 DESCRIPTION OF *TRUTH* REFLECTION ASSIGNMENT IN SYLLABUS

Living and Leading Your *TRUTH* (Think, Reflect, Understand, Try Out, Heed the Call)

TRUTH Reflections provide a regular opportunity for you to do five things:

- *Think* critically about the readings and class discussion;
- *Reflect* on class material in a personal way to explore what resonates with you;
- *Understand* more deeply how lessons learned might apply to your own way of leading;
- *Try Out* new ways of thinking and leading; and
- *Heed the Call* – lead and live with intention and passion.

We will plant seeds (ideas and behaviors) through this class to live and lead with intention. Some you may plant and water now. Some you may decide to plant in the future, during a different chapter of your life. A portion of the class is devoted to planting seeds for leading through honest reflections with the class material and lessons. The idea here is for us to apply what we learn in class to our lives, to try them on, to see what resonates. We'll balance out-of-class seed planting with in-class instruction. Key strategies for *TRUTH* Reflections are listed below, and I hope that we generate other ideas and strategies together.

TRUTH Reflection Journal: Each week, you'll submit a brief, private, personal reflection that will only be seen by the professor. These will be one to two paragraphs, and may be a targeted reflection on class readings, class discussion, or other experiences from outside of class. Reflections will be relevant as long as they map onto the topics and themes that we examine in class. Use the TRUTH acronym to help you shape your reflections. I'm interested in how you are reflecting and changing as a result of taking this class. There will be about ten of these reflections over the course of the semester. You get two free passes at times of your choosing, where you may skip two weeks of submitting a reflection journal.

BOX 11.2 *TRUTH* REFLECTION ENTRIES FROM BRIT HAVEY DEWITT, MPAFF STUDENT ENROLLED IN PROFESSOR DAVID SPRINGER'S GRADUATE SEMINAR (*LEADERSHIP AS A CATALYST FOR COMMUNITY CHANGE*) AT THE UT AUSTIN, LBJ SCHOOL OF PUBLIC AFFAIRS. FALL, 2020.

Week 8 of Semester: "What are your top five strengths that you can lean into as a leader, and your top five core values that serve as a compass to live with intention?"

I feel most energized, happy, and satisfied in roles where my strengths and core values are aligned. Specifically, the roles where I was convening stakeholders at multiple levels of the system allowed me to leverage my strengths while keeping me excited and purposeful. In all four coalitions I helped lead in Colorado, we were working together towards a common goal related to social justice – educational equity, rights for immigrant and refugee families, and diversifying the teacher pipeline. We achieved real wins in those areas by playing on individual strengths and rowing in the same direction together.

The core values that serve as my compass are:

1. **Service** – Serving others is the North Star that keeps me purposeful, humble, motivated to stay on the path. My commitment to making an impact guides my career decisions, the people I surround myself with, and how I spend my time outside of work.
2. **Justice** – There is too much injustice in the world to stand idle. Achieving an equitable, inclusive, and healing future for all requires a lifelong commitment to question, analyze, and challenge oppressive systems and my own socialization, privilege, and biases.
3. **Community** – Meaningful change moves at the speed of relationships. I should always strive to promote togetherness, acceptance, and belonging, staying focused on the strength of our collective potential. Together, we have everything we need.
4. **Courage** – Being an effective leader and fighting injustice requires courage. I need to stand up and speak up, both for myself and others, even when it's uncomfortable. Being a brave leader means engaging in challenging conversations, giving and taking honest feedback, admitting when I'm wrong, and creating space for change.
5. **Growth** – As I progress on my journey, I will continue to face challenges and have blind spots. Rather than being a perfectionist who's discouraged by failure, I need to remain humble, vulnerable, and reflective so I can

learn from my mistakes and improve. I think I'll always be a work in progress and am committed to ongoing personal, interpersonal, and professional growth.

According to StrengthsFinder, my top five strengths are Learner, Achiever, Restorative, Strategic, and Individualization.[1] Leaning into these strengths can make me a better servant leader. My Learner and Strategic traits help me navigate and persevere through complicated problems. I enjoy diving deep into new subjects, letting my curiosity guide me. My Restorative and Achiever strengths help me move from identifying challenges to achieving solutions. Although my top four strengths fall in the executing and strategic thinking domains, my next three strengths fall under relationship building. My strengths in Individualization and Includer helped me learn what makes others tick, what makes them unique, and what they all have in common. I want everyone around me to feel included, valued, and appreciated. Together, my strengths and values allow me to thrive in roles where I build diverse coalitions, help solve complex problems, and move the group towards a shared vision.

Week 10: Are there two or three key principles or ideas from the readings – either in our class or from outside of class – that you'd like to weave into your personal philosophy?

1. **Servant leadership** – The leadership style that is most aligned to mine is Robert Greenleaf's Servant Leadership.[2] Laub's definition of servant leadership is "an understanding and practice of leadership that places the good of those led over the self-interest of the leader.... and the sharing of power and status for the common good." At a young age, I learned to put the needs of others first, prioritizing those who are subject to inequalities. From community organizing to teaching, I've served others in every position I've held. While my roles and responsibilities will evolve, I will continue to practice servant leadership, no matter where I am. As Taylor, Pearce, and Louw discuss, leadership development is a life-long process. The work is never finished nor is my personal growth as a leader.[3]
2. **Social Justice Leadership** – Just as important is Social Justice Leadership, which draws upon theory and systemic inequality analysis. Paulo Reglus Neves Freire's Critical Consciousness Model, Bobbie Harro's Cycles of Socialization and Liberation, and Barbara J. Love's Liberatory Consciousness Framework have been constructive frameworks for conceptualizing how to move towards healing and liberation individually

and as a society.[4][5][6] While there are some differences across the frameworks, all require one to develop awareness and critical analytical skills to 1) know the structural features of oppression; 2) analyze our own socialization within oppressive systems, and 3) take action against them. Vital to this process is the analysis step, which is often overlooked. I've made the mistake of moving from awareness to action too quickly rather than taking the time to listen and reflect. I still have work to do to unravel my own socialization and internalized assumptions. Being an ally is an ongoing, lifelong commitment that I see as critically embedded in my leadership philosophy and across my home, community, and career.

[1] Rath, Tom. (2007). Strengths finder 2.0. New York: Gallup Press.
[2] Greenleaf, Robert. (1977). Servant Leadership. New York: Paulist Press.
[3] Taylor, S., Pearse, N., & Louw, L. (2013). Development of a Philosophy and Practice of Servant Leadership Through Service Opportunity.
[4] Freire, Paulo Reglus Neves. (1970). Pedagogy of the Oppressed. New York: Seabury.
[5] Harro, Bobbie. (2000). The cycle of liberation.
[6] Love, Barbara. J. (2013). Developing Liberatory Consciousness. Routledge: New York.

A Lab for Intentional Practice

While the *TRUTH* assignment presents a tool for intentional reflection and deepening the understanding of one's strengths and growing edges, we also offer a teaching practice to spark interpersonal awareness in the classroom setting. One of the authors (Garden) refined the methodology for Leadership Labs, a pedagogical practice that spurs students to practice expanding awareness and intentionality in the moment, and offered it as a course at the LBJ School of Public Affairs at The University of Texas at Austin. Leadership Lab is based on the Human Interaction course at the Stanford Graduate School of Business. Yale School of Management also offers a version of this course.

Leadership Labs is akin to having a live executive coach support you in navigating real-time, authentic conversations with a learning cohort. The content for the course is each participant's here-and-now experience. Students in the class gather together in a circle. When the "lab" portion of the class begins, students are encouraged to only discuss their present thoughts. No models, no intellectualizing, no there and then. When we strip away the external content, it accelerates the learning of who we are and how we impact and influence others.

Focusing on the present raises students' awareness about how their words and actions affect others in the lab in each moment. It also pushes students to better understand themselves and their reactions to others in the lab. Because there is no time to plan what is said or how a scenario will unfold, the lab heightens the intensity of the moment, forces students to be present, and requires them to apply their philosophies without filter. This venue for learning is complex and messy - just like it is within a nonprofit organization or community setting. There is not always a direct path from A to B. Even perfectly practiced skills may not work when other humans are involved. Participating in the lab builds tolerance for discomfort and increases the ability to communicate in a more engaged and authentic manner.

Box 11.3 illustrates how this holistic approach to learning and personal change can happen in a facilitated Learning Lab session. In this example, the role of the educator is to facilitate and call attention to different dynamics that unfold during the lab. The educator's mindset during the lab is to simultaneously be very challenging and very supportive. Note that the tension and struggle that emerged in the example most likely wouldn't unfold or linger within an organization for an extended amount of time, but having lived the experience in the space of leadership lab offers participants more access to their choices in the organizational setting.

The lab setting accelerates and intensifies interpersonal dynamics. We believe that this can be an instructive practice in preparing nonprofit and community leaders because they are put in a setting where their personal leadership philosophies and values have to be applied and refined in a real-time setting.

BOX 11.3 LEARNING LAB EXAMPLE

A white male student opened the group by unintentionally attributing an insightful comment made by one Asian woman to the other Asian woman in the group. That action spurred a conversation about who mattered, who was seen, and who had influence in the group. During the aftermath of that exchange, one of the two women revealed that even though she had a distinctly different personality and features from the other Asian woman, professors and students called her by the other woman's name on a daily basis as if the two women were interchangeable. She shared that it happens so often that she doesn't even bother correcting people anymore. Others in the lab listened to the pain of her experience of not being seen or recognized. The young man who made the original mistake apologized, but what the woman wanted was to be seen. She wanted him to really listen and imagine what it might be like to have his best thoughts and ideas attributed to someone else. She insisted he walk in her shoes. He said, "I can see how you are upset." She responded, "That is not what I am asking for. Try again. Step into my world, feel what I feel."

On that note, lab ended for the day. The real-world payoff happened the next day when a professor once again called the woman the wrong name. She replied with a strong, clear voice, "My name is..., and I am here."

Applying a Personal Leadership Philosophy

One of the authors of this chapter (Le) was a student in leadership courses taught by the other co-authors (Springer and Garden) at the LBJ School of Public Affairs. She developed her personal leadership philosophy through this coursework, which provided the tools and resources for her to examine her values, strengths, and beliefs. The exercise of developing a personal leadership philosophy allowed Jaclyn to take an intentional approach to understanding her leadership strengths and challenges. Her instructors provided her with the information, tools, and safe space needed for genuine reflection and practice in applying her leadership philosophy.

When Jaclyn first crafted her personal leadership philosophy, she drew from her top strengths identified through Gallup's *StrengthsFinder 2.0* tool (Rath, 2007). As a Relator, Jaclyn's leadership philosophy is heavily focused on connections and relationships. The role of the course instructors was to provide information, such as readings and discussions with nonprofit leaders, as inputs to the students' sense-making and self-reflection. Drawing from the readings and assignments in the courses, Jaclyn identified her strengths and drew on varied literature to inform her philosophy. Her leadership practice centers on developing deep and genuine connections with her colleagues and clients. She considers herself a servant leader because of her personal and core belief in service to others, which is driven by her lived experience as the daughter of Vietnamese refugees. Supporting and serving communities at the margins is a deep driver of Jaclyn's work in the nonprofit sector focused on education and workforce development opportunities. Putting other people's experiences at the center of the work is a hallmark of servant leaders (Greenleaf, 1977). Furthermore, Jaclyn's leadership philosophy is also focused on systems leadership, which is focused on fostering collective action toward solving systemic challenges (Senge et al., 2015). This has informed her professional experiences, which focus on creating more equitable systems and creating the conditions necessary for lasting social change.

Taking the Leadership Lab course provided an environment in which Jaclyn had to apply her leadership philosophy in an intentional manner. The self-reflection required to craft a personal leadership philosophy is important, but learning how to live and practice that philosophy can be challenging. What the Leadership Lab practice provided was a safe, simulated space to try out her leadership philosophy.

The instructor of the Leadership Lab was responsible for creating a safe environment where students like Jaclyn could take risks and put their leadership philosophies in action. For example, Jaclyn was able to practice developing meaningful relationships and creating connections among others in the lab in a real-time setting while also benefiting from facilitated learning. The lab also allowed other students to observe how their actions and behaviors affected others while also raising their levels of self-awareness and understanding. This elevated level of learning was made possible by an instructor who created an intentional space for practice, guided students in deep self-reflection at the end of each lab session, and encouraged students to find ways to practice what they learned in the lab setting in real-life situations and environments.

In the nonprofit world, Jaclyn's leadership philosophy is applied on a daily basis in many big and small moments of her career. She is a nonprofit and public sector leader at the Texas Higher Education Coordinating Board. In her role, Jaclyn works with businesses to better invest in their workers and partner with higher education and workforce systems to support learner and worker mobility. She draws on her strengths as a relator and a connector to bring together stakeholders across different sectors and organizations to co-create solutions that will increase opportunities for students and result in more equitable education and workforce outcomes.

Her passion for nonprofit and community work is driven by her personal background and values. Jaclyn uses her lived experiences growing up in a working class, immigrant community to remind herself about the purpose of her work. One example of how her personal and professional experiences are blended is a project that Jaclyn led to develop best practices for companies to support immigrant and refugee employees. She strives to center all of her professional work on the people that she aims to serve - people similar to her parents and neighbors that shaped her growth and development. These values and experiences are core to Jaclyn's leadership and allow her to make a unique contribution to her organization every day.

Summary

Our intention for this chapter is threefold. First, we want to honor your commitment to preparing the next generation of nonprofit and community leaders. If you are reading this chapter, you already care. You are not alone in this work. Many educators around the globe are willing to share our best practices to make all of us better. Our second intention is to expand the traditional view about what it means to be a leader and who can lead. No one type of leadership is going to be sufficient in solving our complex challenges. Going forward, effective leaders will represent a range of diverse perspectives, experiences, and styles. And finally, we hope to inspire you to experiment with new methodologies for learning. We believe the old way of teaching isn't going to create the new way of leading. We invite you to shift from teaching leadership competencies to developing leadership capacity and practical wisdom.

We shared some of our favorite practices with you. Of course, you are free to use and adapt them, but more importantly we hope they serve as a catalyst in re-imagining what is possible for you and how you cultivate leaders. Ideally, we all will invest in sharpening and refining our own leadership philosophy, and will then enjoy using that philosophy to guide our approach to leading (teaching) in the classroom.

References

Bennett, J. (2021, January 17). Kamala Harris will make history. So will her 'big, blended' family. *New York Times*. www.nytimes.com/2021/01/17/us/kamala-.

Bhopal, K. (2018). *White privilege: The myth of a post-racial society*. Bristol, UK: Policy Press.

Burnett, B., & Evans, D. (2016). *Designing your life: How to build a well-lived, joyful life*. New York, NY: Alfred A. Knopf.

Burns, J.M. (1978). *Leadership*. New York, NY: Harper & Row.

California Senate Bill 826. (2018). https://legiscan.com/CA/bill/SB826/2017.

Day, D.V., & Dragoni, L. (2015). Leadership development; An outcome oriented review based on time and levels of analysis. *Annual Review of Organizational Psychology and Organizational Behavior, 2*, 133–156.

Dinh, J.E., Lord, R.G., Gardner, W., Meuser, J.D., Liden, R., & Hu, J. (2014). Leadership theory and research in the new millennium: Current theoretical trends and changing perspectives. *The Leadership Quarterly, 25*(1), 36–62.

Dorsey, C., Bradech, J., & Kim, P. (2020). Racial equity and philanthropy: Disparities in funding for leaders of color leave impact on the table. *Echoing Green and the Bridgespan Group*. www.bridgespan.org/insights/library/philanthropy/disparities-.

Dudley, D. (2010). *Everyday leadership* [video]. TED. www.ted.com/talks/drew_.

Freire, P.R.N. (1970). *Pedagogy of the oppressed*. New York, NY: Seabury.

George, B. (2003). *Authentic leadership: Rediscovering the secrets to creating lasting value*. San Francisco, CA: Jossey-Bass.

George, B., & Sims, P. (2007). *True north: Discover your authentic leadership*. San Francisco, CA: Jossey-Bass.

Greenleaf, R. (1970). *The servant as leader*. Westfield, IN: The Greenleaf Center for Servant Leadership.

Greenleaf, R. (1977). *Servant leadership: A journey into the nature of legitimate power and greatness*. New York, NY: Paulist Press.

Harro, B. (2000). The cycle of liberation. *Readings for diversity and social justice* (pp. 52–58). New York, NY: Routledge.

Kouzes, J.M., & Posner, B.Z. (2017). *The leadership challenge* (6th ed.). Hoboken, NJ: John Wiley & Sons.

Lanik, M. (2018). *The leader habit: Master the skills you need to lead--in just minutes a day*. New York, NY: AMACOM.

Lord, R.G. (2017). Leadership in the future, and the future of leadership research. In B. Schyns, R.J. Hall, & P. Neves (Eds.), *Handbook of methods in leadership research* (pp. 403–429). Northampton, MA: Edward Elgar Publishing.

Love, B.J. (2013). *Developing liberatory consciousness*. New York, NY: Routledge.

McManus, R.M., Ward, S.J., & Perry, A.K. (Eds.) (2018). *Ethical leadership: A primer.* Northhampton, MA: Edward Elgar Publishing.

Nettle, D. (2005). *Love and work in happiness: The science behind your smile.* New York, NY: Oxford University Press.

Perruci, G., & Hall, S.W. (2018). *Teaching leadership: Bridging theory and practice.* Northampton, MA: Edward Elgar Publishing.

Raghunathan, R. (2016). *If you're so smart, why aren't you happy?* New York, NY: Portfolio/Penguin.

Rath, T. (2007). *Strengths finder 2.0.* New York: Gallup Press.

Roberts, D. (1981). *Student leadership programs in higher education.* Carbondale, IL: ACPA Media, Southern Illinois University Press.

Ryan, L. (2016, April 1). Can leadership skills be taught? *Forbes.* www.forbes.com/sites/lizryan/2016/04/01/can-leadership-skills-be-taught/?sh=6d075f8d6579.

Schwartz, B., & Sharpe, K. (2010). *Practical wisdom: The right way to do the right thing.* New York: NY: Riverhead Books.

Senge, P., Hamilton, H., & Kania, J. (2015). The dawn of system leadership. *Stanford Social Innovation Review,* Winter, 27–33.

Taylor, S., Pearse, N., & Louw, L. (2013). Development of a philosophy and practice of servant leadership through service opportunity. *Proceedings of the European Conference on Management, Leadership & Governance,* 283–289. Academic Conferences and Publishing International Limited, Reading, UK.

Terry, R.W. (1993). *Authentic leadership: Courage in action.* San Francisco, CA: Jossey-Bass.

Williams, R. & Weber, K. (2019). *Learning to lead: The journey to leading yourself, leading others, and leading an organization.* Austin, TX: Greenleaf Book Group Press.

12

CRITICAL PEDAGOGY AND NONPROFIT MANAGEMENT EDUCATION

Refocusing Our Classrooms Toward Transformation and Liberation

Roseanne Mirabella, Khánh Nguyễn, and Maureen Emerson Feit

> The United States is alone among developed countries in insisting that while human rights are of fundamental importance, they do not include rights that guard against dying of hunger, dying from a lack of access to affordable healthcare, or growing up in a context of total deprivation.
>
> *Professor Philip Alston, United Nations Special Rapporteur on extreme poverty and human rights December 15, 2017*

At the request of the federal government, Professor Alston was in the United States to explore whether the persistence of extreme poverty undermines human rights. Noting dramatic cuts to both taxes and welfare, he observed the important role played by civil society groups in stepping in to provide basic services, like the community health initiative in Charleston that provides free health care services through a network of volunteers, the communities in Puerto Rico who rebuilt in the aftermath of Hurricane Maria, and indigenous groups that advocated for and led the redesign of an advanced and responsive health care system in Alaska. In each instance, nonprofit organizations were at the center of efforts to address growing income gaps and retraction of government services and protections. In his report, Professor Alston also called out the dominant myths of neoliberal policies that maintain the status quo, privileging some while marginalizing others including a "reliance on criminalization to conceal the problem… the gendered nature of poverty… racism, disability, and demonization of the poor… confused and counterproductive drug policies… the use of fraud as a smokescreen… privatization… and tax, healthcare and welfare reform" (Alston, 2017, Section 4). The

DOI: 10.4324/9781003294061-13

increasing proliferation and *acceptance of* these neoliberal myths and policies has compromised the ability of nonprofit providers to perform adequately their social justice advocacy function.

Professor Alston's observations rang true during the coronavirus pandemic, where we saw the impact of neoliberal policies on those already living at the margins of society, including communities of color, women, the elderly, and those living with disabilities (Mirabella et al., 2020). He found the United States has "many fewer doctors and hospital beds per person than the OECE average" (Alston, 2017, n.p.), which led to a critical shortage of ICU beds to deal with COVID patients. Minoritized communities are more likely to work in higher-risk environments and to experience chronic illnesses that increase complications from COVID-19 (Wen & Sadeghi, 2020). As Professor Alston suggest, the neoliberal myths marginalizing these individuals basically denied them the right to protection from COVID in the workforce and care if they became ill.

The energized civil society groups that Alston spoke with during his visit were the first line of defense during the pandemic, providing a safety net and advocating for families and individuals just as they have in previous emergencies in response to hurricanes, wildfires, and tornadoes (Cavaliere, 2020; Gajewski, Bell, Lein & Angel, 2011; Garcia & Chandreasekhar, 2020; Lu & Li, 2020; Ollove & Hamdi, 2021). The leaders of these nonprofit organizations had to respond to community needs even as they faced threats to their financial and organizational health wrought by the COVID lockdowns (Deitrick et al., 2020; Johnson, Rauhaus, & Webb-Farley, 2020; McMullin & Raggo, 2020; Mirabella et al., 2020). Were our third sectorleaders educated in nonprofit management education (NME) programs prepared to meet these challenges?

Previous studies have found that most NME programs are cast within a traditional managerial approach rather than approaches that would promote social change (Mirabella et al., 2019; Mirabella & Nguyen, 2019; Mirabella & Eikenberry, 2017a; Mirabella, 2013). Our current pedagogical approaches largely favor conventional understandings of nonprofit management embracing values of accountability and efficiency over those that emphasize community action for social change (Blessett, 2018).

In this chapter, we bring a critical lens to traditional curricular approaches to philanthropy and nonprofit curriculum in higher education to explore the following questions. What are the curricular models currently being used to educate future leaders of philanthropic organizations? To what degree do our education programs currently reflect what the literature deems are important aspects of critical pedagogy that are designed to equip students to enact social change and social justice in their work? What curriculum should exist to prepare students as community organizers and social change agents?

The chapter proceeds as follows. We first review the literature of critical pedagogy to familiarize the reader with curricular approaches outside the mold of traditional management education. This is followed with a description of data collection methods including an analysis of courses offered, course descriptions, and course syllabi of philanthropy and nonprofit management programs in business schools, schools of public administration, and social work schools, in addition to examine free-standing programs in nonprofit management and leadership. We conclude by suggesting changes to curriculum that will shift the conversation from individual rights to community responsibilities, reforming curricular discourses to include voices of marginalized groups and communities.

Critical Pedagogy

A critical pedagogical approach to education allows participants to acquire a critical consciousness through a radically democratic process (Brown, 2004; Canaan, 2005; Dehler, 2009; Giroux, 2011; Jones & Calafell, 2012; Marshall, 2004; McLaren & Jaramillo, 2007). Critical pedagogy does not reside in a singular body of work. Instead, with different paradigms and lived experiences, scholars and practitioners have proposed and debated a rich array of approaches to education that promotes the development of critical consciousness (Ellsworth, 1989; Freire, 1973; Furman & Gruenewald, 2004; Giroux, 2020; hooks, 1984; and Smith, 2013). Critical pedagogy departs dramatically from traditional education that primarily trained students for employment. As Giroux (2011) contends, traditional

> classrooms too often function as models of social, political and cultural reproduction, particularly when the goals of education are defined through the promise of economic growth, job training, and mathematical utility… limited to the propagation of a culture of conformity and the passive absorption of knowledge (8).

reflecting a "neoliberal pedagogy," that now dominates all levels of education. Following a Freirean tradition, we understand critical pedagogies as processes that examine and challenge the political and social influence of schooling governed by dominant society ideologies (Brown, 2004; Duncan-Andrade & Morrell, 2008; Furman & Gruenewald, 2004; Zembylas et al., 2014), especially neoliberalism.

Education has the potential to be a political act of liberation toward a free, just, and equitable world. Freire (1973) rejected the "banking model" of education as a static process where one individual (the instructor) bestows a gift to another (the student). He argues, along with hooks, for "the importance of an educational system that counteracts the propagation of ideological elements in a racist, sexist, and classist society by interrogating the political implications of externally imposed curriculum standards, banking pedagogical approaches, and hierarchical arrangements within educational settings" (Brown, 2004, 86). Dialogue plays a key role in unlocking the democratic essence of critical pedagogy and praxis. As

Hooks (2003) states "talking to share information, to exchange ideas is the practice both inside and outside academic settings that affirms to listeners that learning can take place in varied time frames [...] and that knowledge can be shared in diverse modes" (44). In contrast to traditional approaches, critical pedagogy emphasizes spaces of deliberation and shared power where participants engage with one another to further each other's critical consciousness. Scholars, practitioners, and community members all play a critical role in exploring and dismantling oppressive paradigms that perpetuate inequalities (Furman & Gruenewald, 2004; Lopez-Littleton, V, 2016; Rusch, 2004; Zembylas et al., 2014) and push the boundary of possibilities for educational transformation.

For Freire, critical pedagogy operates also through problem posing methods that center the realities faced by students and their relationship with the world (Pace & Merys, 2015). According to Freire (1973), critical consciousness describes a process of creative thinking and power in which trust is developed among educators, students, and community members, as they work in partnership with one another to dismantle oppressive structures through reflection and discussion of the historic, social, and political context of their geographic location. Lopez-Littleton advances the importance of critical dialogue in public administration [and nonprofit] classes, advancing an argument for the creation of "brave spaces," an environment where students can be confident in their ability to engage in discussions around controversial issues (2014, 286). In an ideal process, students and teachers become co-investigators, moving through a learning cycle that begins with a "sharp and intentional awareness" of context and experience, continues with a commitment to action and reflection, and ends with a time for self-assessment by both student and teacher (Pace & Merys, 2015, 244). By situating knowledge within the lived experiences of students, and centering the experiences of those historically marginalized, the classroom becomes a space where knowledge is debated, dismantled, and reconstructed (Brown, 2004; Jones & Calafell, 2012; Lopez-Littleton, 2016; Smith, 2013). Knowledge is no longer a set of abstract theories emanating from the ivory tower of academia, but rather embodied in the lived experienced of communities traditionally excluded in academic spaces as experts in their own lives. Participants are now active advocates in their own educational liberation rather than passive observer of history. Freire's emphasis on praxis and transformative action provides pathways for students and teachers to critically consider reality, they develop their power to challenge inequalities, dismantle oppressive systems, and posit new forms of social relations (Ablett & Morley, 2019).

Each of these elements are essential for nonprofit leaders – attention to power and inequality, critical engagement with the legacy and persistence of oppression, focus on dialogue and democracy in our pedagogy, and a commitment to a critical reflective practice but have been absent from traditional NPE curriculum that are primarily "cast as a science and as a tool of neoliberal power structures" (Mirabella & Nguyen, 2019, 391).

> More than a quarter of all courses within these academic programs contain curriculum related to acquiring and managing resources – fund development, financial management, and social entrepreneurship and innovation … Fewer than 10% of the courses offered within universities with an NMPS concentration focus exclusively on advocacy, ethics, social justice, human rights, and democracy, courses that would connect students and faculty to the moral issues of our time, and discourses central to pedagogies of freedom and democracy.
>
> *Mirabella & Nguyen, 2019, 391*

Critical pedagogical approaches to nonprofit management higher education programs would counteract the movement of traditional Nonprofit Management and Philanthropic Studies (NMPS) toward managerialism and professionalization (Mirabella & Eikenberry, 2017b, 26), developing and sustaining educational spaces that support all participants as they reflect and share with one another on how their ideas and actions are the products of the historical, social, and political contexts of their geographic locations. And, by developing spaces through which all participants can engage in critical reflection, students acquire new ways of exploring, developing, implementing, and reflecting new possibilities that move beyond the social oppression of the patriarchal, neoliberal, and Eurocentric systems in ourselves, our organizations and our systems. It is imperative for nonprofit leadership, philanthropic, and leadership education programs to support strategic, reflective, and critical thinking (Deaton, Wilkes, & Douglas, 2013; Hopkins, Meyer, Shera, & Peters, 2014; Lopez-Littleton, 2016; Mirabella, 2013) to equip students to imagine and create a more just, participatory, and sustainable sector.

Methodology

Drawing on the database of graduate programs in nonprofit management and philanthropic studies developed by Mirabella (www.academic.shu.edu), we examined current pedagogical approaches of 65 universities offering concentrations in nonprofit management and philanthropy. We compiled a list of more than 1600 courses offered that focus primarily on nonprofit organizations and philanthropy, coding each course with a generic course title and labeling each as either a required or elective course. For example, we assigned the generic code "Fund Development" to a course on "Annual Giving and Donor Relations," which was also coded "E" as an elective course within the curriculum. This coding mechanism provides a count of courses currently offered within nonprofit and philanthropic studies programs with the assumption that those deemed most important by faculty as essential to a student's education are courses that are required rather than offered as electives.

Findings

A summary of the schools with nonprofit management and philanthropic studies concentrations by institutional located are displayed in Table 12.1. Location within the academy of these programs gives us an indication of the intellectual space that might be readily accessible by educators and students adopting critical pedagogical approaches. For example, there might be more access by students to interdisciplinary content within a College of Arts and Sciences than might be possible within a professional school such as business or public administration. Collaboration across disciplines is essential as critical pedagogy strives to serve students' needs across a wide spectrum including "cultural, linguistic, social political [and] economic" (Duncan-Andrade and Morrell, 2008, 30).

We categorized and assigned a generic course title to the close to 1700 courses offered within the NMPS programs. Seven courses account for 50% of all courses offered by these programs (Table 12.2). Courses in fund development and nonprofit management are the most frequently offered courses (12% and 10%, respectively) followed by courses in financial management and social entrepreneurship (7% and 6%). Given that nonprofit organizations and their funders are increasingly "devoted to business principles embedded in a structure of 'social enterprise'" (Cohen, 2014, n.p.) it is not surprising to find that three of the four courses most often offered in these programs contain curriculum related to acquiring and managing resources. This finding also relates to the structure of nonprofit funding and the precarity of funding models. While addressing mechanisms for raising funds in our nonprofit programs is essential, we would argue that our financial management and fundraising courses should embrace an interdisciplinary approach raising sociological questions about structure of funding and inequality.

NMPS programs are comprised of a variety of required and elective courses ranging from skills needed for managing nonprofit organizations to strategies for collaborating with other organizations. About one-quarter of the almost 1700 courses offered by these programs are required. Figure 12.1 shows the

TABLE 12.1 Graduate Programs in Nonprofit Management and Philanthropic Studies by Institutional Location

Institutional Location	*Number of Programs*
College of Arts and Sciences	13
School of Business or School of Business & Public Administration/ Nonprofit Management	13
Other College*	13
School of Public Affairs and Administration	21
School of Social Work	7

* Includes the Lilly Family School of Philanthropy and other schools such as a College of Education or Health and Leisure Services.

TABLE 12.2 Courses in NMPS Programs by Generic Course Title: Top 50%

Generic Course Title	*% Of All Courses*
Fund Development	12%
Nonprofit Management	10%
Financial Management	7%
Social Entrepreneurship and Innovation	6%
Program Design and Evaluation	5%
Nonprofit Marketing	5%
Philanthropy and Nonprofit Organizations	5%

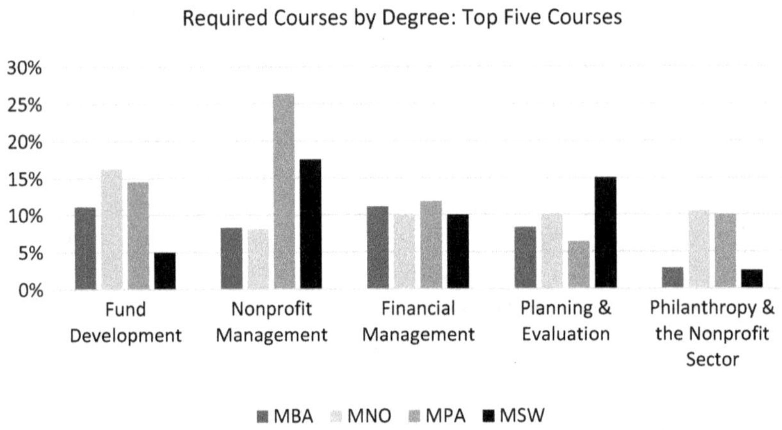

FIGURE 12.1 Top Five Required Courses by Degree

distribution of the generic identifier for the top three required courses of the most frequently offered graduate degrees in nonprofit management and philanthropic studies: Master of Business Administration (MBA), Master of Nonprofit Organizations (MNO), Master of Public Administration (MPA), and Master of Social Work (MSW). Courses in fund development and nonprofit management make up more than a quarter of all required courses, which is not surprising given that they comprise 22% of all courses, both elective *and* required. A course in fund development is most often required course by programs leading to the MNO, while programs leading to the MPA and MSW more often require a course in nonprofit management. Additionally, programs offering the MSW are slightly more likely to require a course in planning and evaluation. While few of the programs leading to the MBA and MSW require a course in philanthropy and the nonprofit sector, in contrast with the MNO and MPA degree programs where 10% of the programs require this course.

Among the courses required within these degree programs are the six courses in Figure 12.2 that fall within the middle range of all required courses.

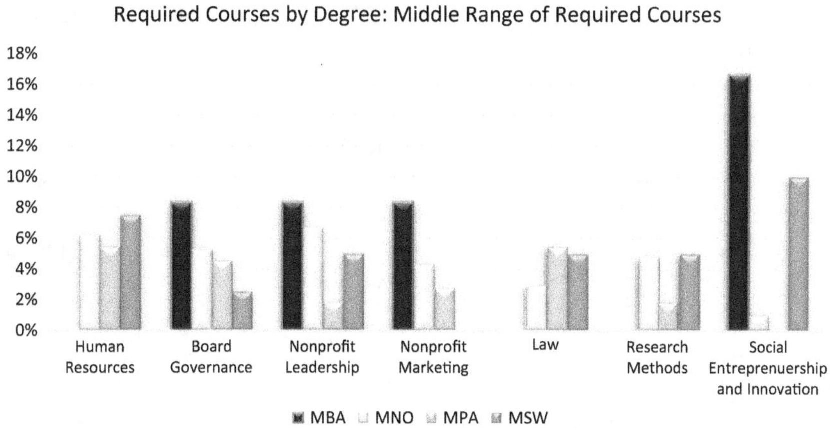

FIGURE 12.2 Middle Range of Required Courses by Degree

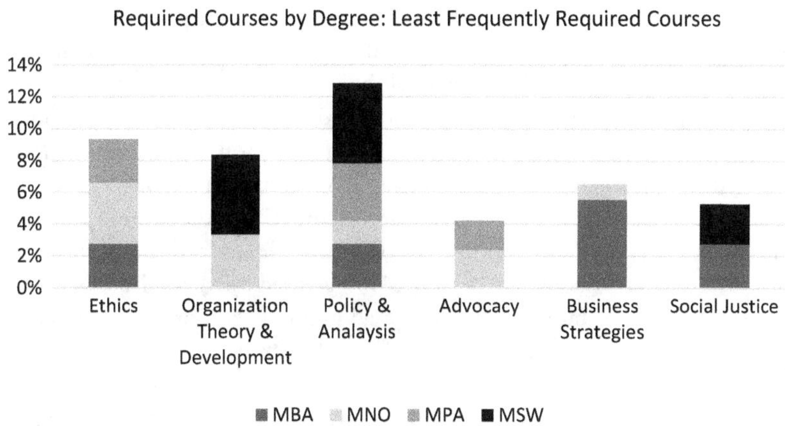

FIGURE 12.3 Least Frequently Required Courses by Degree

Not surprising given their dominance among social entrepreneurship programs (Mirabella & Eikenberry, 2017a), social entrepreneurship and innovation courses are most often required by programs leading to the MBA comprising 17% of all courses within these degree programs with 10% of the courses required by MSW programs likewise requiring a course in social entrepreneurship. MBA programs more often require a course in nonprofit marketing and board governance, about 8% each of all required courses within this degree program.

The courses in Figure 12.3 comprise fewer than 5% of all courses required by degree. Although few programs require a course in ethics, we know from previous research programs often infuse principles of ethics in leadership courses or other courses in the curriculum (Kennedy & Malatesta, 2010; Zhang et al.,

2012). Three percent of the courses required by MNO degree programs and 5% of the courses required by an MSW degree program are a course in organization theory and development, while none of the nonprofit management and philanthropic degree programs leading to the MBA or MPA require this course. It is important to highlight two categories for their relevance to our discussion of critical pedagogy: advocacy and social justice. Of the 407 required courses within these degree programs there are only seven required courses in advocacy, 2% of all required courses in MNO and MPA programs and only two required courses in social justice, one course each within the MBA and MSW degree programs.

Our analysis highlights current pedagogical approaches in NMPS favoring conventional economic understandings of nonprofit management within a neoliberal structure privileging content that creates technical experts to manage nonprofit institutions in service to the state (Giroux, 1997, 264) with little, if any, attention paid to issues of culture or community. More than a quarter of all courses offered within these degree programs cover material related to acquiring and managing resources, with another 20% or so focused on managing organizations and people. The curricular offerings of NMPS programs are quite standardized (Figure 12.1) with most of the courses shaped by what Giroux refers to as a "corporate-based ideology that embraces standardizing the curriculum, supports hierarchical management, and reduces all levels of education to job training sites" (Giroux, 2011, 10). In contrast, we find little NMPS curricular content focused on social justice, advocacy or social change (Figure 12.3) "that would connect students and faculty to the moral issues of our time, discourses central to pedagogies of freedom and democracy" (Freire, 1998 as cited by Mirabella & Nguyen, 2019, 391). Schools of business and public administration more often reflect a neoliberal understanding of the sector and its relationship with liberal democracy and market value, while schools of social work are more apt to emphasize curricular models that focus on community organizing, building social capital, and political engagement. However, our analysis has shown that most curricular offerings in professional education programs for future nonprofit leaders, regardless of degree or institutional location, are cast within a 'culture of positivism' favoring the status quo (Kincheloe, 2008, 79). As Giroux highlights, "the reign of neoliberalism and corporate culture" has blurred the boundaries between commercial culture and public culture (2011, 113). Universities have rushed to embrace the logic of industrial management "while simultaneously forfeiting those broader values both central to a democracy and capable of limiting the excesses of corporate power" (ibid). In the next section we turn to a discussion of critical pedagogy suggesting changes to curriculum that highlight the importance of shifting the conversation from individual rights to community responsibilities, reforming curricular discourses to include voices of marginalized groups and communities through the adoption of post-colonial frames, feminist ethics, and critical race theory (CRT).

Critical Pedagogy for Nonprofit Management and Philanthropic Studies

> We clearly live in a divided nation, a divided world. If we are to make inroads that will transcend this divide, our discourse of critical pedagogy must shift into another register, forming itself around new axes of commitment and solidarity and understanding...
>
> *McLaren and Jaramillo, 2007, 198*

Over ten years ago, McLaren and Jaramillo made these remarks about living in a divided nation and a divided world. Princeton Historian Daniel T. Rodgers calls what we are living through the *Age of Fracture*, beginning in the 1960s and continuing today (Tomasky, 2019, 195). The fracture is political and economic and has sorted Americans into the have and the have nots, and our great divisions are based on who is in and who is out. McLaren and Jaramillo's call to be oriented for a discourse of critical pedagogy is more essential now than ever. We must "explicitly integrate" critical pedagogy into our nonprofit classrooms (Mason, McDougle & Jones, 2019, 411) encouraging students to interrogate post-colonial exploitation of marginalized people, including people of color, those who are poor, women, members of the LGBTQI+ community, and the disabled, and to reposition the way they think about leadership shifting the conversation from individual rights to community responsibilities, from consumerism to democratic participation for all. In previous works, we proposed critical pedagogies for NMPS to reframe authority, embrace interdisciplinarity, include feminist theories of management and support praxis (Mirabella, 2013), outlining ways forward toward critical pedagogy to "transform curricular discourses" to center voices of marginalized groups and communities (Mirabella & Nguyen, 2019, 388). Here we turn our attention to an intersectional CRT, post-colonialist frameworks, and feminist ethics of care to reposition nonprofit organizations and their leaders to pursue a praxis designed to shift the conversation from individual rights to community responsibilities.

Blalock suggests we begin this process with the intentional incorporation of a social justice lens into our classrooms. Knowledges that were previously subjugated become centered "problematizing power" hidden in mainstream disciplines (2018, 55). Many of us were taught to view curriculum as objective and neutral, instructed by our colleagues to park our opinions outside the door before entering the classroom. CRT, post-colonial perspectives, and feminist theories tackle this myth head on challenging the status quo and providing space in the curriculum for exploration, critique, and transcendence of mainstream theories (Feit, Blalock & Nguyen, 2017, 62). Rather than pursuing a "managerialist agenda" privileging effectiveness in managerial practices, Goldman recommends adopting an "anti-performative stance ... to address issues of inequality, dominance, and oppression in the organisational context to create a better form of organization" (2020, 50), recognizing that organizations, including nonprofit organizations, are "sites of conflict" with "dehumanizing features" that must be exposed through exploration of what was heretofore considered "seemingly mundane" (Gonzales, Kanhai, & Hall, 2018, 546). What was once deemed sensible within traditional managerial education is reconfigured as claims previously marginalized are used to interrogate these sensibilities (Goldman, 2020, 54) and students are given opportunities to think more "imaginatively about how organisation and organising can be undone and reconfigured otherwise" (Rumens, 2017, 238). The ultimate end of integration of critical pedagogy in nonprofit curriculum "is the fight for social change" (Dixson, 2018, 233). Toward this end, we propose several critical frames to incorporate in the nonprofit management classroom, CRT, post-colonial frames, and feminist ethics of care.

Critical Race Theory

CRT provides a much-needed lens on the realities and complexities of power and identity in the history, structuring, and practice in nonprofit and voluntary organizations (Feit, Philips & Coats, 2021; Feit, 2018; Nickels & Leach, 2021; Willner, 2019). Originally developed by legal scholars and activists dedicated to the study and transformation of race, racism, and power (Delgado & Stefancic, 2017), CRT scholars have developed an extensive scholarship across multiple disciplines that challenges the claims of objectivity in American liberalism and the myth of meritocracy in US education (Ladson-Billings, 2011). Delgado and Stephancic identify the core tenets of CRT to include a recognition that: the concepts of race and races correspond to no biological reality; rather they are historically specific social constructions that society "invents, manipulates, or retires" as needed; racism is deeply ingrained in the both the founding and everyday business of the United States; colorblind concepts of equality make racism difficult to address; racism advances the interests of white elites and working-class whites; race intersects with other forms of identity such as gender, class, and sexuality and those who have experienced racism have important and unique perspectives on the systems that perpetuate oppression (36). CRT scholars have developed a rich body of scholarship that has direct application for nonprofit organizations and voluntary associations.

This includes a close examination of the ways nonprofit organizations participate in the making and remaking of race and racism in the United States. In their study of the role of nonprofits in the US census, for example, Feit, Philips, & Coats (2021) use CRT to reexamine the mediating role of nonprofits as buffers, bridges, and builders of representative democracy in relation to racialized projects of the state, paying close attention to ways nonprofit staff participate in transforming socially constructed categories of race and gender into seemingly objective facts. And it includes an attention to the ways in which nonprofits operate as "white space" (Anderson, 2015; Suarez, 2020) and nonprofit staff perpetuate white supremacy in their work. As Hecker argues, CRT can surface the often unspoken "rules, norms, and cultures" of white supremacy that equate whiteness and masculinity with an assumed superiority in public and nonprofit organizations (269). Willner applies the concept of interest divergence, a key tenet of CRT, to highlights how managerialism may serve to preserve racial and other social inequalities even in nonprofit organizations that are explicitly focused on social justice (Willner, 2019). Self-reflection and self-discover is imperative for the purpose of learning about one own bias. Before attempting to create a space for others to talk about racism, white scholars must allow time for themselves to unlearn their biases to rediscover the truths about education and the nonprofit sector through a CRT lens. Before attempting to create a space for others to talk about racism, white educators in particular need to understand white entitlement "that [they] are either not consciously aware of, or can never admit to ourselves" (Reilly, 2020, 47), White scholars must allow time for themselves to engage the scholarship of CRT, reflect and unlearn their own biases, and practice the skills needed to move students out of their comfort zones and confront racism in themselves and their organizations.

Even as we urge educators to critically engage with whiteness and masculinity, we also acknowledge the ways that an overemphasis on whiteness can re-center the power relations that critical pedagogy is focused on dismantling. As Leonardo (2004) emphasizes, when scholars and educators address an imagined white audience, racial understanding "proceeds at the snail's pace of the white imaginary" (268). Counter-storytelling, another key tenet of CRT, emphasizes the need to center and engage the voices and experiences of people too often excluded or discounted in our curricula and may offer a corrective to the current state of nonprofit education (Nickels & Leach, 2021; Reilly, 2020). As Solorzano and Yosso explained (2002), counter-storytelling is a tool use for "exposing, analyzing, and challenging the majoritarian stories of racial privilege" (32). By listening and uncovering the hidden stories that recount individual's experience of racism and sexism, the process challenges white supremacy by juxtapose the story with the majoritarian stories of neutrality, colorblindness, and "common sense." Thus, counternarratives can "inform social actions that can lead to change" (Dixson, 2018, 233) building on efforts to "incorporate marginalized and muted voices" into the nonprofit discourse (Nickels & Leach, 2021, 12). As CRT scholars have argued, the goal of education is to understand the theoretical underpinnings of race and oppression and their intersection with systems, and to use these ideas to work toward change (Crenshaw et al., 1995; Willner, 2019).

Post-Colonial Frames

The analysis of nonprofit curricular content revealed our embrace of managerialist paradigms that continue the exploitation of historically marginalized people, previously colonized through genocide (see Smith, 2016), enslavement and imperialism, by perpetuating hegemonic discourses (Gyamera & Burke, 2018, 462). Sefa Dei problematizes European and American definitions of progress and modernity, what he refers to as "colonial and post-colonial diseases," that have had "far-reaching consequences for human subjects and local communities" (2019, 43). Higher education with its culture of whiteness has

> become entrenched within colonial and imperial systems of education, founded on ideologies and hegemonies of neoliberalism. The problem is that, when we become so accustomed to the agenda of neoliberalism, it becomes invisible and natural. The virtues of personal agency, individual self-determination, freedoms and liberty, choice, free markets, deregulation, competition, individualism, privatization and so forth are extolled without acknowledging the emptiness of such rhetoric when disconnected from broad questions of social justice, equity, community development, social and institutional responsibility and institutional accountability to the most disadvantaged segments of our communities (44).

A post-colonial perspective can educate our students on the ways in which nonprofits and nongovernmental organizations perpetuate the exploitations inherent to imperialism, nationalism, and nativism (see Fanon, 1961) and reinforce representations of non-European culture and thought that have long been used to justify European and American imperialism (see Said, 1978). Employing a critical lens will help students understand who these representations benefit, who has perpetuated these representations, and who continues to benefit from their retellings, a process Goldman refers to as "denaturalisation," a mechanism to "upset the apple-cart" of long-held claims and promote alternative views (2020, 51). Coloniality created relationships of power through hegemonic narratives that continue long after colonial occupations or enslavements (Sefa Dei, 2019, 47). The classroom becomes a space to "create dissensus" challenging narratives long held by those in the dominant group (53), not simply replacing one set of beliefs with another, rather a constant churning of consensus and dissensus. In effect, the end state of decolonized management education may be similar Derrida's gift, something that is never full achieved but rather something for which we continually strive (Mirabella, 2013).

Feminist Ethics of Care

Our course analysis showed that fewer than 5% of the required courses offered in our nonprofit management programs cover ethics, advocacy, and social justice, while fund development, financial management, and nonprofit management are among the most required courses in our programs. As Blalock (2018) suggests, the curricular frame for nonprofit instruction courses in our nonprofit curriculum focus much more on cost-savings and efficiency than on social justice (2018,

51). She and others have called for contrasting the ideas of marketization, cost-savings, program evaluation, and bureaucratization with social ethics and social justice frameworks in our scholarship, teaching, and praxis (see also Coule, Dodge & Eikenberry, 2020, Mason, McDougle, & Jones, 2019; and Mirabella & Nguyen, 2019). These new ethical frames will "aim to help students realize a counter-discourse of care" (Sandberg & Elliott, 2019, 299) strengthening our curriculum and our students' ability to serve others.

> Care is a feminist, not a "feminine" ethic, and feminism, guided by an ethic of care, is arguably the most radical, in the sense of going to the roots, liberation movement in human history. Released from the gender binary and hierarchy, feminism is neither a women's issue nor a battle between women and men. It is the movement to free democracy from patriarchy. … Patriarchy is an order of domination elevating some men over other men and all men over women. Becoming a "real man" or "good woman" means internalizing its binary and hierarchy. The psyche must resist this implantation.
>
> *Gilligan, 2014, 101–102*

As we have proposed elsewhere, "[a] revaluing of care and recognition of the importance of care in the work our students do will bring about a transformation in both our curriculum and ultimately the sector" (Mirabella, 2013, 99) to center a discourse of care in our nonprofit management classrooms, acknowledging "the place of the affective in higher education" (Sandberg & Elliott, 2019, 299).

Relatedly, Boyd and Sandell suggest we cease thinking about our work as "civil engagement," with its focus on producing better citizens inadvertently attaching it to neoliberal structures and process, instead proposing that we refer to it as "critical engagement" to interrupt "structuring binaries, foreground social justice, and challenge neoliberal ways of thinking" (2012, 262). In effect, a feminist ethics of care disrupts structures of white supremacy and patriarchy through a "comprehensive and nuanced examination of gender, race and their intersections" (Oliphant, Allard, & Lieu, 2020, 99).

Conclusion

Our review of the current curriculum of education programs for future leaders of nonprofit organizations highlights approaches favoring conventional economic understandings of nonprofit management within a neoliberal structure privileging content that creates experts ill equipped to understand issues of culture, inequalities, and marginalization of communities. Our courses are quite standardized, supporting hierarchical management, with little curricular content focused on social justice, advocacy, or social change. We argue for changes in NMPS to shift the conversation from individual rights to community responsibilities, reforming the curriculum by adopting critical pedagogies that center voices of marginalized groups and communities, preparing future nonprofit leaders as community organizers and social change agents, thereby providing them with the knowledge to enact social change and create more equitable communities through their work.

References

Abel, C. F. (2014). Toward a theory of social justice for public administration: How public administration might be informed by catholic social theory. *Administrative Theory & Praxis, 36*(4), 466–488.

Ablett, P., & Morley, C. (2019). Social work as revolutionary praxis? The contribution to critical practice of Cornelius Castoriadis's political philosophy. *Critical and Radical Social Work*, 7(3), 333–348.

Alston, P. (2017). "Statement on Visit to the United States," United Nations Human Rights, Office of the High Commissioner. Retrieved from https://www.ohchr.org/en/statements/2017/12/statement-visit-usa-professor-philip-alston-united-nations-special-rapporteur.

American Academy of Arts and Sciences. (2017). Humanities Indicators. Retrieved from https://humanitiesindicators.org/content/indicatordoc.aspx?i=34.

Anderson, E. (2015). The white space. *Sociology of Race and Ethnicity, 1*(1), 10–21. https://doi.org/10.1177/2332649214561306.

Arday, J., Zoe Belluigi, D., & Thomas, D. (2021). Attempting to break the chain: reimaging inclusive pedagogy and decolonising the curriculum within the academy. *Educational Philosophy and Theory, 53*(3), 298–313.

Arevalo, J. A. (2020). Gendering sustainability in management education: Research and pedagogy as space for critical engagement. *Journal of Management Education, 44*(6), 852–886. https://doi.org/10.1177/1052562920946796.

Blalock, A. E. (2018). Incorporating critical qualitative inquiry in nonprofit management education. *Administrative Theory & Praxis, 40*(1), 43–59. https://doi.org/10.1080/10841806.2017.1420839.

Blessett, B. (2018). Symposium on cultural competence, accountability, and social justice: Administrative responsibility and the legitimacy of united states democracy. *Public Integrity, 20*(4), 321–324.

Blessett, B. Gaynor, T. S. Witt, M., & M. G. Alkadry. (2016). Counternarratives as critical perspectives in public administration curriculum. *Administrative Theory & Praxis, 38*(4), 267–284.

Boyd, N. A., & Sandell, J. (2012). Unpaid and Critically Engaged: Feminist Interns in the Nonprofit Industrial Complex. *Feminist Teacher, 22*(3), 251. https://doi.org/10.5406/femteacher.22.3.0251.

Brookfield, S. (1994). Tales from the dark side: A phenomenography of adult critical reflection. *International Journal of Lifelong Education, 13*(3), 203–216.

Brookfield, S. (2009). The concept of critical reflection: Promises and contradictions. *European Journal of Social Work, 12*(3), 293–304.

Brown, K. M. (2004). Leadership for social justice and equity: Weaving a transformative framework and pedagogy. *Educational Administration Quarterly, 40*(1), 77–108.

Canaan, J. (2005). Developing a pedagogy of critical hope. *Learning & Teaching in the Social Sciences, 2*(3), 159–174.

Cavaliere, P. (2020). *Nonprofit organizations in post-disaster recovery: a study of advocacy activities in Hurricane Sandy's aftermath in New Jersey* (Doctoral dissertation, University of Delaware).

Clayton, J., Donovan, C., & Merchant, J. (2016). Distancing and limited resourcefulness: Third sector service provision under austerity localism in the northeast of England. *Urban Studies, 53*(4), 723–740.

Cohen, R. (2014). Can philanthropic oligarchy nurture economic justice? *Nonprofit Quarterly*, Retrieved from https://nonprofitquarterly.org/2014/04/07/can-philanthropic-oligarchy-nurture-economic-justice/.

Coule, T. M., Dodge, J., & Eikenberry, A. M. (2020). Toward a typology of critical nonprofit studies: A literature review. In *Nonprofit and Voluntary Sector Quarterly*. https://doi.org/10.1177/0899764020919807.

Crenshaw, K., Gotanda, N., Peller, G., & Thomas, K. (Eds.). (1995). *Critical race theory: The key writings that formed the movement*. New York: The New Press.

Currie, G., & Knights, D. (2003). Reflecting on a critical pedagogy in MBA education. *Management Learning, 34*(1), 27–49.

Darby, S. (2016). Dynamic resistance: Third-sector processes for transforming neoliberalization. *Antipode, 48*(4), 977–999.

Davis, J. Stolberg, S. G., & T. Kaplan. (2018). Trump Alarms Lawmakers With Disparaging Words for Haiti and Africa. *New York Times*. Retrieved from www.nytimes.com/2018/01/11/us/politics/trump-shithole-countries.html?hp&action=click&pgtype=Homepage&clickSource=story-heading&module=a-lede-package-region&region=top-news&WT.nav=top-news.

Deaton, A. V., Wilkes, S. B., & Douglas, R. S. (2013). Strengthening the next generation: a multi-faceted program to develop leadership capacity in emerging nonprofit leaders. Journal of Nonprofit Education and Leadership, *3*(1): 34. Accessed February 28, 2022. https://search.ebscohost.com/login.aspx?direct=true&AuthType=sso&db=edsgao&AN=edsgcl.425460048&site=eds-live

Dehler, G. E. (2009). Prospects and possibilities of critical management education: Critical beings and a pedagogy of critical action. *Management Learning, 40*(1), 31–49.

Dehler, G. E., Welsh, M. A., & Lewis, M. W. (2001). Critical pedagogy in the new paradigm. *Management Learning, 32*(4), 493–511.

Deitrick, L., Tinkler, T., Young, E., Strawser, C. C., Meschen, C., Manriques, N., & Beatty, B. (2020). Nonprofit Sector Response to COVID-19. Nonprofit Sector Issues and Trends. 4. Retrieved from: https://digital.sandiego.edu/npi-npissues/4.

Delgado, R. & Stefancic., J. (2017). *Critical race theory: An introduction* (3rd Edition). New York: New York University Press.

Dixson, A. D. (2018). "What's going on?": A critical race theory perspective on Black Lives Matter and activism in education. *Urban Education, 53*(2), 231–247. https://doi.org/10.1177/0042085917747115.

Dodge, J., Holtzman, R., van Hulst, M., & Yanow, D. (2016). What does it mean to teach 'interpretively'? *Learning and Teaching. 9*(1), 73–84.

Duncan-Andrade, J. M. R., & Morrell, E. (2008). *The art of critical pedagogy: Possibilities for moving from theory to practice in urban schools* (Vol. 285). New York: Peter Lang.

Eikenberry, A. M. (2009). Refusing the market: A democratic discourse for voluntary and nonprofit organizations. *Nonprofit and Voluntary Sector Quarterly, 38*(4), 582–596.

Eikenberry, A. M., & Kluver, J. D. (2004). The marketization of the nonprofit sector: Civil society at risk? *Public Administration Review, 64*(2), 132–140.

Eikenberry, A. M., & Mirabella, R. M. (2017). Extreme philanthropy: Philanthrocapitalism, effective altruism, and the discourse of neoliberalism. *PS: Political Science & Politics*, *5*(1), 1–5.

Ellsworth, E. (1989). Why doesn't this feel empowering? Working through the repressive myths of critical pedagogy. *Harvard Educational Review*, *59*(3), 297–325.

Fanon, F. (1961). *The wretched of the earth*. Trans. Richard Philcox (2004). New York: Grove Press.

Feit, M. E. (2018). Addressing racial bias in nonprofit human resources. In A. M. Eikenberry, R. M. Mirabella & B. Sandberg (Eds.). *Reframing nonprofit organizations: Democracy, inclusion and social change*. Irvine, CA.: Melvin & Leigh.

Feit, M., Blalock, A. E., & Nguyen, K. (2017). Making diversity matter in a nonprofit accreditation process. *Journal of Nonprofit Education and Leadership, Special Issue*, 59–68.

Feit, M. E., Philips, J. B., & Coats. T. (2021). Tightrope of advocacy: Critical race methods as a lens on nonprofit mediation between fear and trust in the U.S. Census. *Administrative Theory & Praxis*, DOI: 10.1080/10841806.2021.1944586.

Finley, L., & Esposito, L. (2020). The immigrant as Bogeyman: Examining Donald Trump and the Right's anti-immigrant, Anti-PC rhetoric. *Humanity & Society*, *44*(2), 178–197.

Freire, P. (1973). *Education for critical consciousness* (Vol. 1). New York: Bloomsbury Publishing.

Freire, P. (1998). *Pedagogy of freedom: Ethics, democracy, and civic courage*. Lanham, MD: Bowman & Littlefield Publishers, Inc.

Furman, G. C., & Gruenewald, D. A. (2004). Expanding the landscape of social justice: A critical ecological analysis. Educational Administration Quarterly, *40*(1), 47–76.

Gajewski, S., Bell, H., Lein, L., & Angel, R. J. (2011). Complexity and instability: The response of nongovernmental organizations to the recovery of Hurricane Katrina survivors in a host community. *Nonprofit and Voluntary Sector Quarterly*, *40*(2), 389–403.

Garcia, I., & Chandrasekhar, D. (2020). Impact of Hurricane María to the civic sector: A profile of non-profits in Puerto Rico. *Centro Journal*, *32*(3), 67–88.

Gilligan, C. (2014). Moral injury and the ethic of care: Reframing the conversation about differences. *Journal of Social Philosophy*, *45*(1), 89–106. https://doi.org/10.1111/josp.12050.

Girei, E. (2017). Decolonising management knowledge: A reflexive journey as practitioner and researcher in Uganda. *Management Learning*, *48*(4), 453–470. https://doi.org/10.1177/1350507617697867.

Giroux, H. A. (1997). *Pedagogy and the politics of hope: Theory, culture, and schooling*. Boulder, CO: Westview Press.

Giroux, H. A. (2006). Academic freedom under fire: The case for critical pedagogy. *College Literature*, *33*(4), 1–42.

Giroux, H. A. (2011). *On critical pedagogy*. New York, NY: The Continuum International Publishing Group.

Giroux, H. A. (2020). *On critical pedagogy*. London; New York, NY: Bloomsbury.

Goldman, G. A. (2020). Using the critical management studies tenet of denaturalisation as a vehicle to decolonise the management discourse in South Africa. *African Journal of Business Ethics*, *14*(1), 42–61. https://doi.org/10.15249/14-1-272.

Gonzales, L. D., Kanhai, D., & Hall, K. (2018). *Reimagining Organizational Theory for the Critical Study of Higher Education*. https://doi.org/10.1007/978-3-319-72490-4_11.

Gover, A. R., Harper, S. B., & Langton, L. (2020). Anti-Asian hate crime during the COVID-19 pandemic: Exploring the reproduction of inequality. *American Journal of Criminal Justice*, *45*(4), 647–667.

Gyamera, G. O., & Burke, P. J. (2018). Neoliberalism and curriculum in higher education: a post-colonial analyses. *Teaching in Higher Education, 23*(4), 450–467. https://doi.org/10.1080/13562517.2017.1414782.

Hasenfeld, Y., & Garrow, E. E. (2012). Nonprofit human-service organizations, social rights, and advocacy in a neoliberal welfare state. *Social Service Review, 86*(2), 295–322.

Heaney, M. T. (2020). Protest at the center of American politics. *Journal of International Affairs, 73*(2), 195–208.

Heckler, N. (2019). Whiteness and masculinity in nonprofit organizations: Law, money, and institutional race and gender. *Administrative Theory & Praxis, 41*(3), 266–285. https://doi.org/10.1080/10841806.2019.1621659.

hooks, b. (1984). *Feminist theory: From margin to center.* London: South End Press.

hooks, b. (1994). *Teaching to transgress: Education as the practice of freedom.* New York: Routledge.

hooks, b. (2003). *Teaching community: A pedagogy of hope.* Routledge: New York and London.

Hopkins, K., Meyer, M., Shera, W., & Peters, S. C. (2014). Leadership challenges facing nonprofit human service organizations in a post-recession era. *Human Service Organization; Management, Leadership & Governance, 38*(5), 419–422.

Howard, C., & Brady, M. (2015). Teaching social research methods after the critical turn: challenges and benefits of a constructivist pedagogy. *International Journal of Social Research Methodology, 18*(5), 511–525.

Hvenmark, J. (2013). Business as usual? On managerialization and the adoption of the balanced scorecard in a democratically governed civil society organization. *Administrative Theory & Praxis, 35*(2), 223–247.

Johnson, A. F., Rauhaus, B. M., & Webb-Farley, K. (2020). The COVID-19 pandemic: a challenge for US nonprofits' financial stability. *Journal of Public Budgeting, Accounting & Financial Management, 33*(1), 33–46.

Jones Jr, R. G., & Calafell, B. M. (2012). Contesting neoliberalism through critical pedagogy, intersectional reflexivity, and personal narrative: Queer tales of academia. *Journal of Homosexuality, 59*(7), 957–981.

Kadi-Hanifi, K. (2009). Using critical pedagogies from adult education to inspire and challenge higher education students. *Learning and Teaching, 2*(1), 80–103.

Kennedy, S. S., & Malatesta, D. (2010). Safeguarding the public trust: Can administrative ethics be taught? *Journal of Public Affairs Education, 16*(2), 161–180.

Kester, K. (2019). Reproducing peace? A CRT analysis of Whiteness in the curriculum and teaching at a University of the UN. *Teaching in Higher Education, 24*(2), 212–230.

Kincheloe, Joe L. (2008). *Critical pedagogy.* New York: Peter Lang Publishing, Inc.

Ladson-Billings, G. (2011). Race to the top, again: Comments on the genealogy of critical race theory. *Connecticut Law Review, 43*(5), 1439–1458. Available at: https://search.ebscohost.com/login.aspx?direct=true&AuthType=sso&db=edshol&AN=edshol.hein.journals.conlr43.50&site=eds-live. Acesso em: 28 fev. 2022.

Landreman, L. M., Rasmussen, C. J., King, P. M., & Jiang, C. X. (2007). A phenomenological study of the development of university educators' critical consciousness. *Journal of College Student Development, 48*(3), 275–296.

Leonardo, Z. (2004). The color of supremacy: Beyond the discourse of 'white privilege.' Educational philosophy and theory, *36*(2), 137–152.

Lopez-Littleton, V. (2016). Critical dialogue and discussions of race in the public administration classroom. *Administrative Theory & Praxis, 38*(4), 285–295.

Love, J. M., Gaynor, T. S. and Br. Blessett. (2016). Facilitating difficult dialogues in the classroom: A pedagogical imperative. *Administrative Theory & Praxis, 38*(4), 227–233.

Lu, Y., & Li, Y. (2020). Cross-sector collaboration in times of crisis: findings from a study of the Funing tornado in China. *Local Government Studies, 46*(3), 459–482.

Lynn, M. (1999). Toward a critical race pedagogy: A research note. *Urban education, 33*(5), 606–626.

Maier, F., Meyer, M., & Steinbereithner, M. (2016). Nonprofit organizations becoming business-like: A systematic review. *Nonprofit and Voluntary Sector Quarterly, 45*(1), 64–86.

Marshall, C. (2004). Social justice challenges to educational administration: Introduction to a special issue. *Educational Administration Quarterly, 40*(1), 3–13.

Mason, D. P., McDougle, L., & Jones, J. A. (2019). Teaching social justice in nonprofit management education: A critical pedagogy and practical strategies. *Administrative Theory & Praxis, 41*(4), 405–423. https://doi.org/10.1080/10841806.2019.1643615.

McLaren, P., & Jaramillo, N. (2007). *Pedagogy and praxis in the age of empire: Towards a new humanism.* The Netherlands: Sense Publishers.

McMullin, C., & Raggo, P. (2020). Leadership and governance in times of crisis: A balancing act for nonprofit boards. *Nonprofit and Voluntary Sector Quarterly.* https://doi.org/10.1177/0899764020964582.

Meer, N. (2018). "Race" and "post-colonialism": should one come before the other? *Ethnic and Racial Studies, 41*(6), 1163–1181. https://doi.org/10.1080/01419870.2018.1417617.

Mirabella, R. M. (2013). Toward a more perfect nonprofit: The performance mindset and the 'gift'. *Administrative Theory & Praxis. 35*(1), 81–105.

Mirabella, R. M., & Eikenberry, A. M. (2017a). The missing "social" in social enterprise education in the United States. *Journal of Public Affairs Education, 23*(2), 729–748.

Mirabella, R. M., & Eikenberry, A. (2017b). A critical perspective on nonprofit accreditation. *The Journal of Nonprofit Education and Leadership,* (Special Issue I). https://doi.org/10.18666/JNEL-2017-V7-SI1-8235.

Mirabella, R. M., & Nguyen, K. (2019). Educating nonprofit students as agents of social transformation: critical public administration as a way forward. *Administrative Theory & Praxis, 41*(4), 388–404.

Mirabella, R., Carpenter, H., Dolch, N., Hoffman, T., & H. Wise. (2020). *Nonprofit crisis management: Response to COVID-19.* Champaign, IL: Sagamore Publishers.

Nadan, Y., & Stark, M. (2016). The pedagogy of discomfort: Enhancing reflectivity on stereotypes and bias. *British Journal of Social Work, 47*(3), 683–700.

Nickel, P. M., & Eikenberry, A. M. (2009). A critique of the discourse of marketized philanthropy. *American Behavioral Scientist, 52*(7), 974–989.

Nickels, A. E., & Leach, K. A. (2021). Toward a more just nonprofit sector: Leveraging a critical approach to disrupt and dismantle white masculine space. *Public Integrity, 23*(5), 515–530.

Oliphant, T., Allard, D., & Lieu, A. (2020). Addressing patron-perpetrated sexual harassment in libraries: Four propositions for intersectional feminist anti-violence education in LIS. *Journal of Contemporary Issues in Education, 15*(1), 95–109.

Ollove, A., & Hamdi, S. (2021). Activating the local food system in emergency food response. *Journal of Agriculture, Food Systems, and Community Development, 10*(2), 1–3.

Pace, T., & Merys, G. (2015). Paolo Freire and the Jesuit tradition: Jesuit rhetoric and Freirean pedagogy. *Traditions of Eloquence: The Jesuits and Modern Rhetorical Studies, 3*(2), 54–67.

Reilly, R. C. (2020). Pay attention to what is behind the curtain: Interrogating whiteness using contemplative practices in graduate management education. In E. Sengupta, P. Blessinger, & C. Mahoney (Eds.), *Civil society and social responsiblity in higher education* (pp. 45–60). Bingley: Emerald Publishing.

Reny, T. T., & Barreto, M. A. (2020). Xenophobia in the time of pandemic: othering, anti-Asian attitudes, and COVID-19. *Politics, Groups, and Identities*, 1–24. https://doi.org/10.1080/21565503.2020.1769693.

Rothstein, R. (2014). Modern segregation. *Economic Policy Institute*. (Retrieved from www.epi.org/publication/modern-segregation/).

Ruggunan, S., & Spill, D. (2014). Critical pedagogy for teaching HRM in the context of social change. *Journal of Business Ethics*, *8*(1), 29–43.

Rumens, N. (2017). Queering lesbian, gay, bisexual and transgender identities in human resource development and management education contexts. *Management Learning*, *48*(2), 227–242. https://doi.org/10.1177/1350507616672737.

Rusch, E. A. (2004). Gender and race in leadership preparation: A constrained discourse. *Educational Administration Quarterly*, *40*(1), 14–46.

Said, E. (1978). *Orientalism*. New York: Pantheon Books.

Sandberg, B. (2013). The road to market. *Administrative Theory & Praxis*, *35*(1), 28–45.

Sandberg, B., & Elliott, E. (2019). Toward a care-centered approach for nonprofit management in a neoliberal era. *Administrative Theory & Praxis*, *41*(3), 286–306. https://doi.org/10.1080/10841806.2019.1621661.

Schwartz, J. M. (2014). Resisting the exploitation of contingent faculty labor in the neoliberal university: the challenge of building solidarity between tenured and non-tenured faculty. *New Political Science*, *36*(4), 504–522.

Sefa Dei, G. J. (2019). Neoliberalism as a new form of colonialism in education. In S. Chitpin (Ed.), *Confronting educational policy in neoliberal times* (pp. 40–58). New York: Routledge. https://doi.org/10.4324/9781315149875-4.

Smith, A. (2016). Heteropatriarchy and the three pillars of white supremacy: Rethinking women of color organizing. In INCITE (eds.), *The color of violence: The INCITE anthology* (pp. 66–73). Cambridge, MA: South End Press.

Smith, N. L. (2013). (Re) Considering a critical ethnorelative worldview goal and pedagogy for global and biblical demands in Christian higher education. *Christian Scholar's Review*, *42*(4), 345.

Solorzano, D. G., & Yosso, T. J. (2001). Maintaining social justice hopes within academic realities: A Freirean approach to critical race/LatCrit pedagogy. *Denver University Law Review*, *78*(4), 595–622. Available at: https://search.ebscohost.com/login.aspx?direct=true&AuthType=sso&db=edshol&AN=edshol.hein.journals.denlr78.32&site=eds-live. Acesso em: 28 fev. 2022

Suarez, C. (2020, January 27). The nonprofit sector as white space. *Nonprofit Quarterly*. https://nonprofitquarterly.org/nonprofit-sector-white-space/.

Tinning, R. (2002). Toward a "modest pedagogy": Reflections on the problematics of critical pedagogy. *Quest*, 54(3), 224–240.

Tomasky, M. (2019). If we can keep it: How the republic collapsed and how it might be saved. New York: Liveright Publishing.

Warren, J. T., & Hytten, K. (2004). The faces of whiteness: Pitfalls and the critical democrat. *Communication Education*, 53(4), 321–339.

Wen, L. & Sadeghi, N. (2020, July 20). Addressing racial health disparities in the COVID-19 pandemic: Immediate and long-term policy solutions [Blog]. Heath Affairs. www.healthaffairs.org.

Willner, L. (2019). Organizational legitimacy and managerialism within social justice nonprofit organizations: An interest divergence analysis. *Administrative Theory & Praxis*, *41*(3), 225–244.

Zelizer, J. E. (2017). Blowing up the Deficit is Part of the Plan. *The Atlantic*. Retrieved from www.theatlantic.com/politics/archive/2017/12/blowing-up-the-deficit-is-part-of-the-plan/548720/.

Zembylas, M., Bozalek, V., & Shefer, T. (2014). Tronto's notion of privileged irresponsibility and the reconceptualisation of care: implications for critical pedagogies of emotion in higher education. *Gender and Education*, *26*(3), 200–214.

Zhang, Y., Zhang, Y., Lee, R., & Yang, K. (2012). Knowledge and skills for policy making: Stories from local public managers in Florida. *Journal of Public Affairs Education*, *18*(1), 183–208.

13

DIFFERENT APPROACHES TO APPLIED NONPROFIT MANAGEMENT

Pier C. Rogers and Monika Hudson

Introduction/Background

The invitation to write this chapter is a good fit for me as an educator who has chosen to focus on applied nonprofit management education. Since 2007 I have served as Director of the Axelson Center for Nonprofit Management at North Park University. The Center's mission is to educate nonprofit professionals and volunteers – through professional development programming. The Center is part of the School of Business and Nonprofit Management (SBNM) (where I also serve as a faculty member) at North Park University, which offers degrees or graduate certificates in nonprofit management, business, and more. In November 2020, I began a two-year term as the governing board President of ARNOVA (the Association for Research on Nonprofit Organizations and Voluntary Action), which has been my professional association home since the early 1990s.

I entered the world of academe after six years of work as a nonprofit sector professional. Following those professional work experiences and two master's degrees, I sought to "know more" about nonprofit management, which led me to pursue a doctoral degree.

My quest for gaining knowledge and a deeper understanding of the nonprofit sector led, a few years after completing my PhD, and conducting program research and development in a community college setting, to a full-time nonprofit management faculty position at the New School University in New York City. During my time there, I realized that my orientation as a practitioner competed with the more traditional faculty route of publishing and seeking a tenured faculty position. Despite having successfully completed a doctoral program, and securing a faculty position, I was drawn to more practical considerations about nonprofit management education. At the same time, I also began to meet other faculty – from around

DOI: 10.4324/9781003294061-14

the world – in the nonprofit research association – ARNOVA – and learned more about the range of disciplines and programs where faculty interested in nonprofit studies, practice, and research were located.

As the years passed, and I struggled to find research topics that were both of interest to me and acceptable in the more traditional world of academic research, I discovered that I embodied a tension between what was considered more in alignment with theoretically based research design as opposed to that designed for practical application, to which I was more committed.

Over the years, I made several career choices in an effort to reconcile that tension. Ultimately, my move to Chicago to lead the Axelson Center at North Park University presented the opportunity for me to exercise my interests, live in that tension, contribute my unique voice and perspective to the scholastic and practitioner landscapes as well as to maintain and grow my network within the field of both nonprofit academics and nonprofit professionals in ways that are increasingly satisfying.

Through my role as Director of the Axelson Center, I am able to personally achieve the best of both worlds – of nonprofit practice and academe. In directing the Center, I can focus on what practitioners need and deliver programming that evolves to meet their needs of growing their management and leadership capabilities in the context of their organizations. I have the flexibility of utilizing practice-based research, feedback from participants where they prioritize their content area interests, as well as including literature that is beyond peer-reviewed options in the development of programs and conferences. Through my faculty role with SBNM, I can engage with practitioners through teaching, but in a university that stresses teaching over research. Since I am an administrator with a faculty role, I do not have the usual research and service commitments. However, outside of my formal role with the university, I have chosen to engage in practical research interests with other colleagues – in and out of ARNOVA – in areas including diversity in nonprofit leadership, and innovative mindset in nonprofit organizations.

Chapter Approach

Arriving at a place that allows me personal and professional satisfaction in combining nonprofit management education with a more practical approach leads to examining some features of such applied programs. I will discuss key considerations in developing applied programs, innovative approaches that are supported in an applied setting, and evidence-based examples that utilize those approaches. I offer guidance for others seeking to create or expand an applied program. The focus will center more on best practices with program description, content development, instructional design, curriculum, faculty tips, students, rather than on the funding or overall administration of such programs.

What Does "Applied" Mean?

For the purposes of this discussion, key features of applied nonprofit management are the involvement of educational experiences, often outside of the classroom setting, where students are called to reflect upon and utilize concepts that were first presented in a more theoretical fashion. Students are expected to utilize those teachings and essentially practice them in a live setting, or with actual organizations. Sometimes collaboration between students and organizational entities may be involved in the learning experience. Typical "applied" educational experiences might be internships, service-learning projects, travel abroad activities, or specific classroom assignments created for this purpose.

There are some criticisms of applied learning pedagogy, where it is said that students can too easily take their single experience as an indicator of "truth" and continue to believe that their single experience is generalizable to all (Ash & Clayton, 2009). In these instances, the missing element was said to be reflection on the learning process itself – to guide students in raising questions about the learning experience itself, so that they are learning also to become more self-directed and critical thinkers on their own.

In the discussions here, "applied" education will be understood even more broadly. It is not just the usual experiential learning opportunities of internships, service learning, trips, projects, but will include the lens that is incorporated into the instructional design and used, as well as the approach itself, inclusive of who is teaching and who is learning. The ideas of teacher as learner, student as co-collaborator in learning, content as evolving and drawn from practice, not just from theory are also themes that fit well in applied nonprofit management education. Observations about the faculty and about the students, and how an applied program has perhaps a different opportunity to engage with them will be included. Also, some theoretical paradigms may be "applied" in nature. For example, critical theory (Coule, Dodge et al., 2020); participatory action research (PAR) (defined in the related section of this chapter; Kemmis et al., 2013); human-centered design (Cottam & Leadbeater, 2004; Bevan et al., 2007), are a mixture of theories, approaches to teaching/learning, to research, and to problem-solving. They come from different disciplinary backgrounds but offer fascinating entry points to our task of examining "applied" learning in the nonprofit management space.

Each of those areas will be discussed later in this chapter and considered for use to foster learning in an "applied" fashion. Key features held in common across each approach will be highlighted including the engagement with real world situations, people, organizations, communities – often at the start of the learning, research, or educational process. Examples of the practical uses of each of these approaches will be presented as well.

For the purposes of this chapter, applied nonprofit management programs can offer the traditional internships, service-learning projects, and classroom assignments. The program might be non-credit, or traditional credit-bearing in structure. An opportunity exists, though, to center the program on learning processes that do utilize both teacher and student as learners, and that draw upon theory and practice that utilize and are informed by real-world situations.

Features to Consider in Developing/Expanding an "Applied" Program

Before considering examples of approaches to the study of the content areas in applied programs, it will be helpful to explore some key questions that address the overall structure of the program itself.

- Is the nonprofit program established as credit or non-credit?
- Is the focus on theory; to what extent is "practice" and "best practices" a part of what is provided?
- What is the process for curriculum review/acceptance?
- Is conducting research an expectation?
- What is the degree of budgetary control?
- What autonomy exists to secure speakers; or are they only part of the university faculty?
- What type of students are targeted? Nonprofit professionals or younger individuals (undergrad); or just starting graduate school?
- Demographics of students?
- Faculty experience and demographics?

An applied program that offers a non-credit component may offer greater flexibility in that the curriculum may be developed outside of the traditional university curriculum review process. Such flexibility allows for topic offerings that may be designed to be short-term, and narrowly focused, like "Preparation for Giving Tuesday," or "Culturally Responsive Evaluation," or "The Essentials of Major Gifts: Trends, Prospecting, Planning, and Solicitation."

The questions above are pertinent for pursuing an "applied" approach, especially in the context of a more traditional nonprofit management program (where there are more constraints on curriculum, faculty selection, traditional student population, and budget.)

The Axelson Center, as part of the SBNM, is an example of an applied nonprofit management program.

Several factors contribute toward this reality: the Axelson Center programs are non-credit, therefore outside of the traditional curriculum approval process of higher education; the students are practicing nonprofit professionals and volunteers and bring their experiences and questions; and the Axelson Center is committed to continuing improvement and innovation in program development – within a particular framework; and the Axelson Center seeks to draw from its constituents, including its Advisory Board of civic leaders, when engaged in program planning.

As a non-credit program, though, the Axelson Center is able to develop program content in creative and innovative ways, and is not constrained by the traditional university curriculum approval process, although all its programs fit within the "Hallmarks of Nonprofit Managerial Excellence[SM]" framework, which includes learning areas of: mission/program; leadership and governance; strategy and innovation; human resources; financial strength and performance; resource generation and external relations; and accountability and integrity (Axelson Hallmarks, 2006). Having practitioners as students affords the possibility for engaging in real-world problem solving in the classroom context. The commitment to continuing improvement and innovation translates to program development that evolves and considers current trends, and demands of constituents for content areas, although the Axelson Center always makes such choices utilizing the "Hallmarks" as a curricular framework.

Significance Concerning Students

An applied nonprofit management program offers a chance to engage students in different ways. There is an opportunity to help them think critically to analyze their experience, and then to connect it with the theoretical and practical concepts being explored. In and of itself, this approach is not necessarily different from one in a program that is not applied in focus. What can be different is the emphasis on utilization of the learning – in immediate organizational practice, and the engagement of the student's background and context with the faculty in the learning process. Where programs do not have an intentional applied dimension, the learning of theory and coverage of key literature in each area may be the priority.

In addition, other demographic qualities can make a difference – so that considering race, gender, age, sexual orientation, etc., or the student's educational background – is often important – perhaps more so than in a more traditional program where theory rather than practice is the focus.

Students who choose a more applied nonprofit management program option may bring more professional experience. A student's understanding of what they may encounter in an applied program may also differ from their expectations of a more theoretically based program. In an applied program, a student may believe that their own experiences – that include various aspects of their personal and professional identity, their professional experiences, and challenges, will be acknowledged and addressed in the classroom. In that case, gender, race, class, age, disability, sexual orientation may also be factors to be considered – on both the part of the student and of the faculty.

Students in an applied program may ask the faculty to specifically offer guidance for issues in their own organizations or seek insights into leadership matters that are impacted by race, gender, and other characteristics of identity. This can happen in any program, but perhaps more in instances where practice is a greater focus of learning.

A friend who taught business at a small, private, liberal arts college in the Midwest found herself constantly coming up against students challenging her capabilities as an older, African American woman who had worked in the corporate sector, run her own consulting business, later earned a doctorate in business, and then entered a faculty role. She was teaching entrepreneurship (in a very practical and applied manner), and the younger, predominantly white, undergrad students continuously challenged her expertise as their professor. They were expecting more traditional, theoretically based learning, and she challenged them to be innovative, and she refused to just give them theory, but required their critical thinking and often setting aside of preconceptions about themselves, about her, about conceptions of entrepreneurship and what it might be used to accomplish.

She chose to leave that setting, moved to another university, and taught in a program where the students were older, and from more diverse racial/ethnic backgrounds. The university she moved too also placed a high value on diversity, inclusion, and equity. In that setting, she was received in a much more welcoming fashion, as were her efforts to teach entrepreneurship in ways that encouraged students to create a business model for themselves. Keep in mind that she had previous experience teaching millennials at other universities, so there were other factors at play, some of which may have been the values and culture of the institution itself.

The point here is that "seeing" your students – in all their complexities – and in recognition of their level of experience and their backgrounds can be quite helpful in designing course content, overall programs, and more. For applied programs, especially in nonprofit management, where the application of what is learned is often in an organizational context that is comprised of racially diverse individuals and is often located in racially and otherwise diverse communities, these considerations may be even more significant. To not address them in an applied program would leave students less prepared, and arguably miss opportunities and strategies that might be more effective if the lens that allowed for demographic realities were acknowledged, and actively taught.

The demographics of students may mean that programs are called upon to address more practical issues at earlier points than not. For example, students of diverse race/ethnic backgrounds may express deeper concerns about the extent of diversity among their student colleagues, as well as among the faculty (and possibly administration) of the institution. In an institution designated as "Hispanic-serving," for example, students may expect that there are a substantial number of Hispanic faculty and administrators. Current issues (e.g., politics, race, climate change, social justice, etc.) may be raised in programs with an "applied" emphasis, with the expectation that they will be discussed in the classroom, since the students may work in nonprofit organizations whose missions may focus on such issues. In more traditional programs, students may not have the same level of expectation for addressing current issues or organizational challenges.

Faculty Considerations

If students in applied nonprofit management programs have a greater expectation for faculty to bring practitioner expertise into the teaching experience, there are practical implications for bringing on faculty and speakers.

It seems that faculty with practice backgrounds (perhaps in addition to their academic knowledge), can draw upon that practice perspective, and perhaps allow for more flexibility in cultivating a two-way learning relationship that is important in applied programs. This might derive from the faculty person's realization that the student who may also be a practitioner has comparable experience to draw upon.

Where students may expect more experienced-based faculty, the institution is then challenged to draw faculty into its ranks who meet both the traditional academic requirements (e.g., doctoral degree), but also provide depth of experience. When seeking to meld those two – within a given discipline, say marketing for nonprofit organizations, there are greater challenges. Including the value for diversifying the faculty ranks (in terms of race, gender, etc.) provides an additional element that requires significant attention. Strategies are available but require intentionality in execution.

When a program is non-credit professional development (as is the Axelson Center), there may be greater opportunities for creativity in developing a pool of faculty. Learning about professionals who have become (or are becoming) experts in their work, and who come from a range of diverse backgrounds (i.e., race, gender, etc.), and who serve in a range of communities and organizations becomes the order of the day.

Some possible strategies for finding and vetting faculty might involve:

- Attending other conferences and programs, and hearing speakers whose expertise fits what is sought.
- Getting to know local nonprofit Eds and some of their senior staff members.
- Seeking out local nonprofit consultants to learn more about individuals, their expertise and backgrounds.
- Getting to know local foundation leaders (who might offer their expertise, or their networks).
- Seeking connection with appropriate professional associations;
- Engaging in discussion with potential speakers/faculty to learn more about their values and approach to teaching/learning, and sensitivity to effective communication with the students.
- When engaging a new topic, explore with the speaker to ensure agreement on learning objectives; and then work jointly to develop a session description to further ensure a common understanding of what will be delivered.
- When engaging a new speaker, seek references from trusted partners; research any online examples of the speaker's other engagements; request video clips for examples.

- One of the benefits of adjunct faculty is the opportunity to engage practitioners – who have demonstrated expertise in their field but may not have pursued the doctoral level educational credentials often necessary for full-time faculty positions.
- There is always the intentionality, as well, for paying attention to the gender, race, sexual orientation, disability, age range of individuals – in addition to their expertise, their strengths in terms of teaching, and the respect they may have in given communities and networks. Not being afraid to be intentional about making selections to ensure representation in any of the categories that are valued by the given program is critical to reaching the desired end goal of a diverse, representative team of speakers/faculty. (Of course, learning about these demographic characteristics can only be done when individuals openly present themselves with such identities.)

Ultimately, an applied nonprofit management program may allow or encourage the development of educational opportunities that emerge in concert with what is "needed" by students, in this instance, nonprofit professionals. By listening to those who work or volunteer in the sector, in combination with disciplinary knowledge and tracking research and trends in the field, applied nonprofit management can offer a wide range of learning and experiential opportunities. To consider the value of learning from and with the community outside of the university, along with the exchange of knowledge offered by the existing faculty of a university is an opportunity not all programs or universities pursue.

Opportunities for Innovation in Applied Nonprofit Management

The personal journey that led me to an applied nonprofit program formed the backdrop for this discussion of key elements of an applied program, as well as practices and values that support an applied approach for nonprofit programs.

In the early part of this chapter, we touched on framing the possible content in "applied" nonprofit management and offered ideas about student and faculty considerations. At this point, the discussion will move to questions of theoretical approach to learning and teaching in applied nonprofit management.

If you are developing a new nonprofit program or department, or are considering making changes to an existing program, consider your perspective. What do you bring – assumptions, experiences? What are you interested or willing to offer – perhaps outside of your body of knowledge – to provide your students a "stretch" educational experience – so they may insert themselves into their learning experiences as they are exposed to points of view, and bodies of knowledge, and experiential exercises that they may not have anticipated as they pursue learning within the field of nonprofit studies.

Another important consideration is how you plan to be innovative. What questions do you need to ask to offer an approach that embodies commitment to continual learning – for yourself as well as your students? The spirit of learning from all directions facilitates innovation.

Perhaps it is easier for "applied" nonprofit management programs to be open to their external environments and figure ways to include new content areas that are drawn from experiences occurring within the sector and larger society. If the applied program is non-credit in its structure, that may also increase the opportunity for such a program to be designed in ways that are more focused on engaged learning between student, faculty, organization/community, and may have an opportunity to be more innovative, if the program/curriculum design has more flexibility.

Given the opportunity to be innovative within applied nonprofit management education, why not start with figuring best ways to utilize a "DEI" (diversity, equity, inclusion) lens? These terms will be defined shortly. Applied nonprofit management education offers an opportunity for choosing to be intentional about diversity, inclusion, and increasing equity.

Enhancing DEI

Diversity, equity, inclusion. The conception of DEI has become so varied that it requires clarification here.

In searching for a way to establish common terminology, I uncovered the work of the D5Coalition. This organization defined DEI terms as:

> Diversity: "… a value that brings unique perspective or life experience to the decision-making table, but focuses particularly on racial and ethnic groups including Asian Americans and Pacific Islanders, Hispanics/Latinos, African Americans and other blacks, and American Indians and Alaska Natives; LGBT populations; people with disabilities; and women;"
>
> Equity: "…a means of promoting justice, impartiality, and fairness within the procedures and processes of institutions or systems, as well as in their distribution of resources;"
>
> Inclusion: "…the degree to which individuals with diverse perspectives and backgrounds are able to participate fully in the decision-making processes of an organization or group."
>
> *D5 Coalition, pp. 7–8*

If we accept the premise that the nonprofit sector is mission-oriented, there is an opportunity to focus on DEI in a variety of ways. The education of nonprofit leaders, then, should as a matter of course, address diversity, equity, and inclusion. Those who work in the sector come from diverse backgrounds.

Nonprofit organizations exist within diverse communities. Part of an applied nonprofit educational program, in its engaged learning between faculty and student, with an intention that the learning is practice-based, needs to ensure that students are prepared to work in those environments more effectively; therefore, agility with DEI is a necessity, and requires thoughtful and persistent attention. The question of "why DEI" must be addressed; however, that question is often overlooked.

I have heard stories of nonprofit agencies having mixed success in operationalizing the DEI conceptions. Some organizations have taken an educational approach, hoping that different workplace outcomes would result from "diversity training" provided; often the training is a "one size fits all" approach, which is poorly suited for the given organization or its goals, illustrating the absence of asking the "why DEI" for the given organization.

Some nonprofits have gone a step further to adjust power dynamics, taking from some groups and giving to others. The result-resentment all around. Other DEI strategies included research and data-gathering, but with limited use of the information found. As a result, the general systems, cultures, power dynamics in nonprofit agencies often remained unchanged. Again, the "why DEI" was most likely ignored.

At minimum, these approaches have not dealt with (1) underlying fears about change; (2) unacknowledged assumptions of superiority and inferiority; and (3) the natural desire for a quick "fix" that typically does not allow time to include all key players (Rogers, P., Oct. 2016).

The efforts to attain a "quick fix" with "off the shelf" DEI trainings, or adding readings to course syllabi, or appointing someone (more often a person of color) to "lead" any DEI initiatives, generally do not adequately focus on the intended outcome of the effort. Is it change? Or is it simply to "check off the box" that the matter has been addressed so that people can move on.

Ben Fong, in a *New York Times* (Nov. 18, 2020) opinion piece, raised several key concerns about universities and their engagement in the DEI space.

He was critical in many ways, expressing a "…danger that universities will equate teaching about DEI to doing the work necessary…." Fong observed, "If we free ourselves of the notion that education is social change, then we can begin to think of education about social change" (Fong, *NYT*, Nov.18, 2020).

A concluding point was offered:

> The liberal arts classroom is a unique space within which students can engage with the strategies, conflicts, tactics and historical conjunctures of movements that changed the United States for the better. There is a place for education in the fight for racial justice, provided education itself is not confused for the fight.
>
> *Fong, NYT, Nov. 18, 2020*

Suffice it to say that DEI is an important topic for consideration about how best to address such issues in designing courses, exercises, and the overall educational approach. When it comes to how will "applied" nonprofit management programs adequately address DEI, there is no single answer. Several examples follow of some strategies used to engage students, faculty, and outside organizations in addressing DEI in a manner that seems to consider some of the concerns Fong raised.

In response to the challenges of Covid-19 and social injustice, faculty have been required to be innovative in meeting the demands of online learning and retaining student engagement. Some examples of best practices for experiential learning and student engagement in antiracism education were found that were used in a Midwestern urban university with a 50-year history providing quality and equity-focused education to 11,000 predominantly diverse, underrepresented, and first-generation students. One faculty member designed a transformative learning assignment in an undergraduate asynchronous online diversity course which incorporated an innovative curriculum in antiracism and diversity agility. In the Double Pandemic Research Assignment (Williams, 2020), each self-directed student team was assigned an individual antiracism topic to research, zoom record an instructional training of 15 minutes for their student peers, and create two probing questions for critical thinking and discussion. The instructor provided student teams with a comprehensive collection of resources compiled by Stamborski, Zimmermann, and Gregory (2020). The resulting mixed media presentation for eight individual teams was loaded to the learning platform and required viewing for all students. Further, it created a platform for student leadership, rich content exploration and growth as each team became the subject matter expert, and the opportunity to reflect on how this learning would apply to their real workplace and life experiences.

Members of learning communities who engage in expanding their diversity agility and relational propensity must first examine their own beliefs, values, assumptions, unconscious bias, and mental models. Another best practice assignment designed to address this internal work necessary to build inclusive work environments introduced students to a proven systematic process by Byron Katie (Katie, 2012). Her effective technique poses four questions inviting a level of inquiry that in a short time dismantles beliefs that stand as obstacles or unexamined mental models. Students were taught to inquire:

> Is it true? Can you absolutely know its true – what is the evidence?; And what if the opposite was true?: How do you react when you believe that thought?; Who would you be without that original thought? (In other words, has your life been expanded or constricted by that thought?).

The lesson as applied, invites students to identify a situation or belief related to diversity and use the technique to inquire and examine that thought. For the first time, many students experience authentic self-monitoring and reframing new possibilities which directly impact their application to how they see themselves at work and in society.

These exercises are experiential in focus and are designed to help students begin to raise questions about belief systems, as they engage in conversations about diversity, equity, and inclusion. Rather than trying to force students to adopt any given way of thinking or believing, the intent is to help center them in "where they are" and begin to explore that in a critical fashion – for learning purposes.

In my role as director of the Axelson Center, I have worked with my team over the years in ever evolving strategies to address DEI in our programming. Some of those strategies include:

- After leading a workshop on diversity issues in 2008 where the panel outnumbered participants, we pivoted and began addressing diversity issues in the context of breakout sessions of the Axelson Center's annual conference. That strategy offered more choice, and supported the growing interest in the topic, which was evidenced by the fact that those sessions were always full.
- All programs are consistent in modeling the diversity we seek by ensuring racial and gender representation in speakers. This requires cultivating an ever-evolving network of speakers, which has been grown over time, and must be infused with new people, so as not to always rely on the same "diverse" individuals. That requires ongoing attention to building relationships and encouraging all staff to become involved in activities in the local community. This method has been intentional, is also tied with staff professional development, but is not always supported within higher educational institutions.
- The Axelson Center has begun to integrate a "DEI lens" on all work. That means including considerations that address race, gender, sexual orientation, and other "differences," regardless of whether the topic is DEI.
- In the fall 2018, the Axelson Center planned an entire conference on diversity issues entitled, "Embracing Inclusive Leadership: Uncommon Conversations about Diversity," featuring keynotes from principals at the Building Movement Project to present findings from the report "Race to Lead: Confronting the Nonprofit Racial Leadership Gap." Other panels included: "Candid Conversations: A White Guy's Perspective on Advancing Equity"; "Creating Brave Space: Storytelling and Performance to Advance Dialogue on LGBTQ & Inclusion" and more.
- "Axelson Access" programs are designed as strategic conversations that address pressing issues. Examples include: "From Moments to Movements: Racial Justice for Nonprofits"; "Black Philanthropy Matters" – with Dr. Tyrone Freeman, author of *Madam C.J. Walker's Gospel of Giving*, and Angelique Power, President/CEO of the Field Foundation.

What follows is an exploration of several different approaches to teaching and learning – based on theory – and used in a range of applied fashions. Ways to engage with research – from an applied vantage point – is also considered.

A Sample of Theoretical Paradigms Used as a Basis for Applied Learning

The three paradigms discussed here offer approaches or processes – to developing knowledge and understandings that engage with the learner and are iterative. There is an underlying assumption that the focus of learning or experience can change and should be considered in the approach to the learning, and that what is learned is malleable and not static. There are also strategies embedded in some of the paradigms that fully embrace individuals who are not professional researchers, but who may "live" the experiences, as valued partners in generating and using or applying the knowledge.

Critical Theory here refers broadly to an approach that "...signifies a fundamental, often historically specific critique that is attentive to the conditioning effect of social, economic, cultural, political structures – such as capitalism, patriarchy, or imperialism – on orthodox practice and understanding". [(p. 2 – Coule, Dodge et al. (2020) Toward a Typology...]

In nonprofit studies, it is referred to more as critical nonprofit scholarship – one that examines several areas of scholarship within the nonprofit field, but with this critical approach that questions power relationships and agency. Such an approach probes more deeply and reveals some assumptions that may have not previously been examined.

Eikenberry, Mirabella, and Sandberg presented this critical theory approach in its application to nonprofit studies in "Reframing Nonprofit Organizations: Democracy, Inclusion, and Social Change." The "Companion Instructor's Guide," written by Hazelton along with the relevant chapter authors, offers numerous examples of assignments and discussion questions to guide teaching with this "critical" lens.

In an instructor's guide dealing with nonprofit critical pedagogy by Hazelton et al. (Nov. 29, 2020), a point is made that should not be overlooked – a value for appreciating the humanity and significance of the student learner, and the willingness of the instructor to examine his/her own assumptions and biases and engage in the learning as well. The critical pedagogical approach is "interactive and co-productive" (p. 5 Hazelton et al., Nov. 2020 updated version)

The authors promote an approach that encourages students to ask questions as a key method of engagement (p.2 Hazelton et al.). An example of a student exercise included in the chapter on "performance assessment" is:

- Have students watch author Chimamanda Adichie's TED talk on the danger of a single story (www.ted.com/talks/chimamanda_adichie_the_danger_of_a_single_story) and then ask students to contemplate how particular metrics and particular notions of program or organizational effectiveness might tell "a single story" about a program's beneficiaries. The instructor can ask students to engage in a think/pair/share exercise to facilitate dialogue on this topic (pp. 24–25, Hazelton et al.).

Critical pedagogy, as the authors describe, would be useful in any classroom setting. In essence, it seems to be another form of critical thinking that is often presented as a desired outcome of a liberal arts education. Sometimes the terminology, i.e., critical theory, becomes the focus, instead of on the learning process itself, and may get in the way of greater consideration of ways in which it is useful – as a tool to encourage and facilitate critical thinking.

When considering approaches that might be especially effective in an applied nonprofit management program, critical pedagogy, which is essentially a means to encourage critical thinking, is one of them.

Participatory Action Research

In exploring the use of PAR, Dr. Monika Hudson, Associate Professor at the University of San Francisco School of Management, discussed PAR and its application to a research project with a local church in San Francisco. The exploration of PAR and its use in this case study presents an example of how practice-focused research might be applied to a nonprofit educational program in management. Dr. Hudson contributed the following to this section on PAR.

Theoretical Framing – Community

According to Dr. Hudson, community-engaged learning involves a course-based, experiential approach premised on "reciprocal learning" among three parties: students, instructors, and the associated community-based assignment (Bringle & Hatcher, 1999; McCarthy, 2004; Senge et al., 2005). If the conversation is just between students and respective instructors, there are some relatively straightforward ways of determining if and how much learning occurred. However, it is more difficult to identify and evaluate what, if anything, communities learn from engaging with students and instructors in this effort, or what the mutuality of learning is among all three parties, particularly if there is a desire to maintain university-community partnerships.

Determining whether "reciprocal learning" occurred requires a theoretical framework, data collection, exploratory findings, and a multi-phased effort that could only be addressed through a mixed-methods, triangulated approach (Creswell et al., 2011). The faculty member who led this project concluded that a collaborative effort between students, nonprofit organizations, and instructors, embedded in the inherent definition of PAR, could reveal benefits achieved from a community partner's engagement in mutual learning, collaborative instruction, and enhanced research capacity.

PAR is defined as an approach to community research that emphasizes both participation and action. Practitioners of PAR believe it is not enough to simply gain new knowledge; they must consequently act upon the same. PAR emphasizes collective inquiry and experimentation grounded in experience and social history. Research based on PAR principles makes sense of the world through collective efforts to transform it as opposed to simply observing and studying human behavior and views about what constitutes reality.

Fortunately, this design also aligned with the intentions of the church's social justice group that reached out for university assistance. As a result, it was relatively easy to develop a project timeline, recruit student members, and develop an overall research plan with mutuality and critical self-reflection as integral components of the project.

Case Study: Community-Directed Needs Assessment

Members of a church in the San Francisco Tenderloin neighborhood requested assistance with a needs assessment. They wanted to assess women living in the area and use the information gathered to better focus the church's services to this population.

Congregants believed they needed to develop and test a data collection instrument to collect and analyze the gathered information. As opposed to a traditional research project completed by an external researcher, members of the church's Social Justice Task Force asked to be mutually involved in this systematic investigation because they wanted to develop their own responses for donors who were interested in validating how the church was using contributed funding.

After discussion, congregants and the faculty member determined that PAR was the best theoretical framework and methodology to use to collectively establish facts about the lived experiences of female residents in the neighborhood. PAR would involve community practitioners in the research process, from the initial design of the project to gathering and analyzing data to final conclusions and actions arising from the research (Creswell & Creswell, 2018; Whyte, 1991).

PAR considers the unthinkable as possible by attempting to conduct research "with" and not just "on" communities of interest. So, while its theoretical tenants were important for a project such as this case study, its research practice was integral to understanding what a community organization might "learn" by engaging with university students and faculty.

Implications for Theory and Practice – Community

The PAR project allowed for a concrete demonstration of McCarthy's (2004) tripartite model with the anticipated centering on the needs of the community rather than the participating instructor or students. Members of the Social Justice Task Force defined the problem; identified the theoretical framing they wanted to have used; obtained grant funding to provide interview participant incentives; recruited pilot participants; assisted with the development of the interview instrument; collected interview data; and subsequently learned how to code, trained others to code, and aided in the analysis of the interview data. They acted as mentors, subject-matter experts, and collaborative research team members for students and the instructor.

The overall project, utilizing the PAR approach, allowed for students, faculty, and community to engage in research, and learn from one another – a practice that is in alignment with applied nonprofit management education.

Human-Centered Design

Design thinking is a process that is increasingly being utilized in a range of disciplines and practices. Bevan et al. (p.138, 2007), positioned design thinking as:

> Design is not simply about the object or aesthetics but about a broader creative approach to defining the problem itself and then developing a process to solve it. … At a practical level, design offers a range of proven tools and techniques for transformation that connect organizations with their users, encourage collective participation and reveal insights in a variety of contexts.
>
> *Cottam & Leadbeater, 2004, p. 29*

Bevan et al. also developed their own four step design process:

> Reflection, analysis, diagnosis, and description; Imagination and visualization; Modeling, planning, and prototyping; Action and implementation.
>
> *Bevan et al., pp. 139–140, 2007*

Dr. Jennifer Madden utilizes design thinking fundamentals to create an approach for learning design (and ultimately ways to use it in teaching and practice in the nonprofit management arena). She focuses on, "…visualization and situational analysis, research, the use of a logic model, and tools for building effective collaborations." (Madden, p. 9, 2015)

Those features can be found in an exercise she developed for a course:

> During the fall 2020, during the ongoing covid19 pandemic, Dr. Madden designed a course capstone project that adhered to the principles of design thinking but maintained the safety necessary for students and others. The project involved the students in considering a "problem" that her institution, Carthage College, faced (along with all higher education): "City Challenge Brief – Challenge: Carthage College & COVID-19. Build a plan for stable enrollment for Carthage College given the COVID-19 pandemic."
>
> *Madden, 2020*

Students considered the problem, explored existing options, conducted research, developed, and refined prototypes, and pitched their solutions to a designated audience. Through this process, students, faculty, and "the organization" were all engaged in a layered process where each entity learned and shared with the other to produce an outcome that considered past strategies to build upon and develop new ones.

This example models a design thinking assignment that worked effectively in an applied fashion and was made adaptable to the current environment where in-person exchanges were not possible.

Dr. Madden's use of design principles in her work resulted in her using different tools to approach strategic planning. One of them, the "RTB – rose/thorn/bud" (positive/negative/opportunities) approach, allows for a different sort of engagement than the traditional SWOT analysis. It is a tool that she employed in a session about design approaches to strategic planning in the Axelson Center's BootCamp for New Nonprofit CEOs (Madden, Slides #33–35, Jan. 2021).

The exercise involves offering a common question to all participants. For example, "Consider Covid-19 and your organization" and apply the "RTB" approach. In other words, consider the positive, and negative impacts, as well as some opportunities that have resulted out of the Covid-19 crisis. It is a brainstorming exercise, carried out by each person, to consider these questions in relation to their respective organizations. In live classroom settings, each person utilizes sticky notes to jot their ideas. In the virtual setting, the "Mural" app is helpful, as it mimics the use of sticky notes. Once each person has developed concepts associated with "rose (positive)/ thorn (negative)/bud (opportunity)," the question is to look across those categories and search for themes. For example, an emerging theme might be "work from home." This theme was drawn from these comments: "deeper staff connection – need for community" and "greater flex on work/life balance" = "Rose"; "harder to connect with your team" and "harder to see programs in action/actual impact" = "Thorn"; "people who are there, are really there for you" and "develop policies and procedures re: work from home etc." = "Bud."

What does this have to do with human centered design? According to Dr. Madden, this "RTB" process is one that aligns with design thinking in that it, "…Moves beyond linear thinking, looks for connections, systems of overlapping spaces through inspiration, ideation, implementation" (Madden, PPT #10, Jan. 2021). In those ways, the human centered design process allows participants to draw upon their own experiences and perceptions as a starting point and encourages innovative thinking along the way.

Conclusion

The ability to build on a foundation of theory and the practical application, allow flexibility, and seek opportunities to "co-create" learning opportunities are features of applied approaches to nonprofit management education that are important to consider.

The NACC curricular guides (see Appendix) may be useful as a foundation, but then it is up to the individual faculty person or individual designing the program, as to what will work best, given the students targeted, the faculty desired, the ways in which "community" is considered, and the desired outcomes for the program. If the intent is to prepare students for service, or for research, or for high level leadership positions, or for policy positions – all those options should be taken into consideration. The traditional notion of faculty organizing programs around their areas of expertise will continue. However, we can enhance that with approaches that facilitate innovation through a recognition of the value of considering partnerships of all sorts with others outside of the usual ring of expertise within higher education – that is by considering the students, and the community as partners. Engaging in regular SWOT analyses, or in Dr. Madden's design version, the "RTB" approach (Madden, Jan. 2021), will remain useful tools to push the continual learning that is a desired trait of applied nonprofit management.

Overall, "applied" nonprofit management can be considered as an innovative dimension for nonprofit management education – a means to ensure connection with community, and learning that engages others as resources, including not only faculty, but students, organizations, and community, in building to consider a broad array of skills and experiences that will be helpful in preparing nonprofit managers and leaders for the future.

References

Ash, S. L., & Clayton, P. H. (2009). Generating, deepening, and documenting learning: The power of critical reflection in applied learning. *Journal of Applied Learning in Higher Education*, *1*(1), 25–48.

Axelson Center for Nonprofit Management. (c2006). *Hallmarks for Nonprofit Managerial Excellence*SM. www.northpark.edu/centers/axelson-center-nonprofit-management/about-us/hallmarks-of-nonprofit-managerial-excellence/

Bevan, H., Robert, G., Bate, P., Maher, L., & Wells, J. (2007). Using a design approach to assist large-scale organizational change. *The Journal of Applied Behavioral Science*, *43*(1), 135–152. https://doi.org/10.1177/0021886306297062

Bringle, R. G., & Hatcher, J. A. (1999). Reflection in service learning: Making meaning or experience. *Educational Horizons*, 77(4), 179–185.

Carpenter, H. L. (2014). A look at experiential education in nonprofit-focused graduate degree programs. *Journal of Nonprofit Education and Leadership*, *4*(2), 114–138.

Coule, T. M., Dodge, J., & Eikenberry, A. M. (2020). Toward a typology of critical nonprofit studies: A literature review. *Nonprofit and Voluntary Sector Quarterly*, 1–29. https://doi.org/10.1177/0899764020919807

Cottam, H., & Leadbeater, C. (2004). *RED Report 01. Health: Co-creating services*. London: Design Council.

Creswell, J. W., & Creswell, J. D. (2018). *Research design: Qualitative, quantitative and mixed methods approaches (5th ed.)*. Thousand Oaks, CA: Sage.

Creswell, J. W., Klassen, A. C., Plano Clark, V. L., & Clegg Smith, K. (2011). *Best practices for mixed methods research in the health sciences*. Bethesda, MD: National Institutes of Health. Commissioned by the Office of Behavioral and Social Sciences Research (OBSSR).

D5 Coalition (2015) "State of the Work: Stories from the Movement to Advance Diversity, Equity and Inclusion" (Fifth in an Annual Series). www.d5coalition.org/.

Dutt-Ballerstadt, R. and Bhattacharya, K. (May 17, 2021). Civility, free speech, and academic freedom in higher education: Faculty on the margins. New York, NY: Routledge (ebook).

Fals-Borda, O. (1996). *Research for social justice: Some North-South convergences.* Plenary address at the Southern Sociological Society Meeting, Atlanta, GA, April 8. http://comm-org.wisc.edu/si/falsborda.htm.

Fong, B. Y. (2020, November 18). Teaching Racial Justice Isn't Racial Justice. *New York Times.*

Hazelton, J. K., Eikenberry, A. M., Mirabella, R. M., & Sandberg, B. (2020, November 29). *Reframing Nonprofit Organizations: Democracy, Inclusion, and Social Change - Companion Instructor's Guide.* https://reframingnonprofits.wordpress.com/instructors-guide/

Katie, Byron (2012). The work of Byron Katie. Ojai, CA: Byron Katie International, Inc.

Kemmis, S., McTaggart, R., & Nixon, R. (2013). *The action research planner: Doing critical participatory action research.* New York, NY: Springer Science & Business Media.

Madden, J. R. (2015). Leveraging design: How the design process and a design framework strengthen nonprofit management pedagogy. *Journal of Nonprofit Education and Leadership, 5*(1), 6–11.

Madden, J. R. (2020). City Challenge Brief - Challenge: Carthage College & COVID-19. "Build a plan for stable enrollment for Carthage College given the COVID-19 pandemic". MB-DI Design Lab: Capstone 2020. Kenosha, WI: Carthage College.

Madden, J. R. (Jan. 2021). RTB analysis tool. Used in BootCamp for New Nonprofit CEOs. Axelson Center for Nonprofit Management, North Park University: Chicago. (Slides #33–35).

McCarthy, F. (2004). Service-learning as community engagement among colleges and universities in Asia. *Asia Pacific Journal of Teacher Education, 32*(2), 168–173.

Reason, P., & Rowan, J. (1981). *Human inquiry: A sourcebook of new paradigm research.* Hoboken, NJ: John Wiley & Sons.

Rogers, P. (Jan. 2002). "Operationalizing the Co-Production Model". Unpublished manuscript.

Rogers, P. (Oct. 25, 2016). "Human Centered Design & Diversity, Equity and Inclusion in the Nonprofit Sector". Unpublished manuscript.

Sandy, M., & Holland, B. A. (2006). Different worlds and common ground: Community partner perspectives on campus-community partnerships. *Michigan Journal of Community Service Learning, 13*(1), 30–43.

Senge, P. M., Scharmer, C. O., Jaworski, J., & Flowers, B. S. (2005). *Presence: An exploration of profound change in people, organizations, and society.* New York, NY: Doubleday.

Skilton-Sylvester, E., & Erwin, E. K. (2000). Creating reciprocal learning relationships across socially-constructed borders. *Michigan Journal of Community Service Learning,* 7(1), 65–75.

Skilton-Sylvester, S. (2001). *Higher education and public life: Restoring the bond.* Dayton, OH: Kettering Foundation.

Torres, J. (Ed.) (2000). *Benchmarks for campus/community partnerships.* Providence, RI: Campus Compact.

Voorberg, W. H., Bekkers, V. J. J. M., & Tummers, L. G. (2015). A systematic review of co-creation and co-production: Embarking on the social innovation journey, *Public Management Review, 17*(9), 1333–1357, DOI: 10.1080/14719037.2014.930505.

White, G. W., Suchowierska, M., & Campbell, M. (2004). Developing and systematically implementing participatory action research. *Archives of Physical Medicine and Rehabilitation*, *85*(S2), 3–12. https://doi.org/10.1016/j.apmr.2003.08.109.

Whyte, W. F. E. (1991). *Participatory action research*. Los Angeles, CA: Sage Publications, Inc.

Williams, D. E., (2020). *Double Pandemic and Strategies for Antiracism Remote Education*. Twin Cities, MN: College of Management, Metropolitan State University. MGMT360.

Stamborski, A., Zimmermann, N., Gregory, B. (2020). Scaffolded Antiracism Resources. https://bit.ly/3vlw73C.

14

A WEALTH OF OPTIONS

Making Sense of a Crowded Landscape

Michelle Wooddell

Background

The nonprofit sector in the United States has experienced tremendous growth over the past three decades, with the National Center for Charitable Statistics noting more than 1.5 million nonprofit organizations registered in the nation in 2018 (McKeever, 2018). This growth in nonprofit organizations has naturally resulted in an increasing number of nonprofit employees, to the point where the nonprofit workforce represented 10.2% of the US private sector employment in 2016 (BLS, 2018). But unlike other professions, the educational options for these workers have, until recently, been fairly limited. As late as 1990, the most comprehensive database of nonprofit management programs in the United States recorded only 17 programs offering graduate concentrations in the subject (O'Neill, 2007).

The establishment of the American Humanics organization (now the Nonprofit Leadership Alliance) in 1948 was one of the United States' first efforts to provide training for individuals working in social services, preparing professionals for careers in youth-serving organizations (Ashcraft, 2001). By partnering with colleges and universities, this organization was able to support the development of nonprofits by engaging primarily undergraduates in an understanding of work in this nascent sector, even if they were studying another major. Today, that same organization offers a certification process for nonprofit leaders that awards a Certified Nonprofit Credential (CNP) to individuals with a combination of experience and education in the sector.

In lieu of formal degree-granting programs in nonprofit management, membership-based organizations for nonprofit employees, board members, and volunteer leaders stepped in to fill the educational gap, helping their members develop the specialized skills necessary to move both their careers and their

DOI: 10.4324/9781003294061-15

organizations forward. The Association for Volunteer Administration (AVA), for example, was founded in 1961 and offered a Certified Volunteer Manager certification program for nonprofit managers. Although the organization disbanded in 2006, it and a successor organization (Association of Leaders in Volunteer Engagement), hosted annual conferences, offered training classes, and provided workshops for nonprofit professionals throughout the country. Likewise, the National Society for Fundraising Executives, now known as the Association of Fundraising Professionals, was formed in 1960 to provide similar opportunities for development professionals.

By the 1970s and 1980s, higher education had taken notice of the growing nonprofit sector and several universities began offering courses, certificates, and programs in nonprofit management (Rooney and Burlingame, 2020). In 1991, a group of representatives from these institutions formed what would become the Nonprofit Academic Centers Council (NACC), an international membership association for colleges and universities with programs or academic centers focused on nonprofit management and philanthropy. Today, the membership of NACC numbers approximately 60 and the number of institutions offering undergraduate and graduate degrees in these subjects has also grown substantially (NACC, 2021).

By the turn of the millennium, researchers had identified more than 90 graduate-level degree granting programs offering at least three or more courses in nonprofit management (Mirabella and Wish, 2000). That number grew to 426 by 2007 (Mirabella, 2007), an astonishing level of growth in just under a decade. Beyond these formal degree-granting programs, however, there was also substantial growth in nonprofit management education (NME) non-credit programs and continuing education programs offered at the university level; the most comprehensive database of NME in the country listed more than 150 opportunities in these areas at the end of 2020 (Seton Hall University, 2021a).

Understanding the "Customer"

At the same time that the nonprofit sector was experiencing exceptional growth, nonprofit organizations were also becoming more professionalized in their approach and orientation. This trendline is well documented (Hwang and Powell, 2009; Eikenberry and Kluver Drapal, 2004; Maier, et. al, 2016) and the implications for NME were enormous. The number of jobs in nonprofits was increasing and the skillsets required for success in those jobs was also becoming more prescribed.

There has been ample research demonstrating that, on average, nonprofit employees approach their work with a motivation that is more intrinsic than their counterparts in the public and for-profit sectors (Benz, 2005; Lyons, Duxbury and Higgins, 2006; Leete, 2006). However, researchers have noticed a disconnect between nonprofit employees' desire to establish a career that allows them to give back to their community and their knowledge of careers available in the nonprofit sector (Nelson, 2019). Others have noted that the next generation of millennial leaders is more sector-agnostic in terms of seeking careers that will meet their needs (Johnson and Ng, 2015; Ng and McGinnis Johnson, 2015).

As the nonprofit sector became more of an accepted and recognized career path, however, it was, and is, still filled with individuals who had never pursued formal education or training in any aspect of nonprofit management. A 2010 study (Suarez) of 200 nonprofit executives argued it was experience rather than formal education that had helped propel most of these executives into their positions. The study noted that there were many non-traditional paths to nonprofit leadership, including volunteer experience, personal knowledge of the mission, and technical skills in the nonprofit's main service area (zoologists leading nonprofit zoological societies, for example). Researcher Erin Nelson took this idea a step further when she used the term "The Accidental Nonprofiteer" to reflect the chance events and personal experiences, rather than formal education paths, that often lead people to find work in the sector (Nelson, 2019).

Research also showed that NME graduate students were pursuing their degrees with significant work experience already on their resumes. A 2002 study (Wilson and Larson) of more than 290 graduate students enrolled in nonprofit management programs showed that 95% of these students had work experience prior to enrolling in their program. Other studies showed similar results (Nelson, 2019; Suarez, 2010).

Clearly, nonprofit management graduate students were finding their way into programs after already experiencing the "real world" on some level, and educational institutions and nonprofit researchers began to explore the reasons that these students were seeking out a higher level of education. Human capital theory posits that, in essence, individuals will pursue a higher level of education if they are confident that their newly learned skills will translate into greater monetary rewards in the form of salary increases and promotions (Becker, 1964). Studies of nonprofit management students have supported this idea. A 2002 (Wilson and Larson) study found that "personal development" and "skill acquisition" were two of NME students' top reasons for enrolling in a graduate program. A more recent study found similar results, noting that increased sector knowledge and skill acquisition were the top reasons that alumni of nonprofit management programs had returned to school (Kuenzi, Stewart, and Walk, 2020). Another 2020 study showed some correlation between the skills gained through nonprofit management courses and the usefulness of those skills to jobs and careers (Blau, Hill, and Cannon, 2020).

Less research has been done on what drives individuals to enroll in nonprofit professional development programs outside of the traditional academic setting, or even through a university-based academic center that is non-degree granting. As noted above, many new nonprofit employees have no conception that they are joining "the nonprofit sector;" it isn't until they join their first nonprofit organization as a staff member that the concept of a larger sector may begin to take hold. However, the sheer breadth of these programs indicates that either employers or employees place some value on these programs as a mechanism for continuing their knowledge development. Whatever their reasons for pursuing additional NME and training, these students confront a myriad of choices that would have been unimaginable to nonprofit employees just a few decades earlier.

A Confusing Marketplace

Today, the educational and professional development options for nonprofit employees are seemingly endless, resulting in a dizzying array of options. In addition to the already-described growth in formal academic options in NME, there has been a proliferation of both private and nonprofit educational providers ready to train the current and next generation leaders of the sector. Add to that the more generic purveyors of management training, focused on topics like human resources and leadership that are generally more transferable across sectors, and the options become seemingly endless, setting up a situation where potential students, and their employers, have little to no real mechanism for judging the quality of the potential offerings.

Degree-granting programs based in institutions of higher education, of course, have built in credibility that can create confidence in the consumer. Wilson and Larson (2002) noted that nonprofit management students placed a high value on a university's reputation and specialization when evaluating educational offerings. The NACC has published a set of curricular guidelines to inform course development and program delivery at the undergraduate and graduate level (see Appendix). In 2018, NACC took that guidance a step further by launching a program to accredit stand-alone programs of nonprofit management at the graduate and undergraduate level (Hale, 2020), with the first programs becoming accredited a year later.

Much has been written about the fact that nonprofit management programs across the country are housed in numerous colleges on their respective campuses (Young, 1987; O'Neill, 2007; Mirabella, 2007), but much less has been written about the fact that some institutions are now competing within themselves for nonprofit students. The most comprehensive database of NME programs in the country listed 78 universities offering continuing education classes for nonprofit management (Seton Hall, 2021a). Of these, nearly one-half also offered degree-granting programs in nonprofit management (Seton Hall, 2021b).

A recent cursory examination of my own alma mater, New York University (NYU), offers a glimpse into this phenomenon. NYU's website and online catalog showed that the university offered the following options for anyone looking to further their nonprofit management knowledge: a 45-credit Master of Public Administration (MPA) with a concentration in public and nonprofit management; a 12-credit certificate in management for public and nonprofit organizations; a post-graduate diploma in project management for NGOs; stand-alone courses in fundraising that qualified as continuing education credits for Certified Fundraising

Executives; career advancement courses in nonprofit management that would qualify the student for a Professional Development Gold Standard Series Badge; and a series of half-day webinars in specialized topics in nonprofit management (nyu.edu, 2021). These programs were generally offered through two distinct schools – the School of Continuing and Professional Studies and the Wagner School of Public Service (nyu.edu, 2021). While this proliferation of offerings undoubtedly allows students multiple ways in which to expand their knowledge and skillsets, it certainly also has the potential to create confusion in the minds of consumers. That confusion almost certainly extends to employers who are trying to determine the practical significance of the education that employees might receive.

Furthermore, in institutions where a nonprofit or philanthropic academic center exists separately from the degree-granting academic department, the lines can blur even more, setting up an internal competition that has the potential to lead to more potential for confusion and conflict. Another example, this time from my own institution, should illustrate this point. Grand Valley State University, a public university located in western Michigan, currently offers a master's level degree in Philanthropy and Nonprofit Management, an MPA with a concentration in nonprofit management and a 15-credit graduate certificate in nonprofit leadership. However, across campus, the Johnson Center for Philanthropy, one of the nation's leading academic centers devoted to the study and practice of philanthropy, exists on its own, with few formal ties to the work of the academic unit. Among the Center's offerings are a variety of high-quality workshops, seminars, and courses targeted to professionals in the nonprofit field. The planned launch of a new College of Lifelong Learning in 2021 should further complicate the picture, with its new focus on providing opportunities for professional development and continuing education to working professionals in the region.

In summary, while debates about the proper "place" for graduate programs of nonprofit management have raged, the fact that those programs are now facing increased encroachment and competition from both external and internal entities has been somewhat overlooked. Digging deeper into this issue requires us to look closer at the types of educational opportunities that are being sought by students and offered by institutions.

For What Purpose?

In their seminal 1998 work, Wish and Mirabella outlined seven categories of nonprofit management courses that aligned with the training and development needs of nonprofit professionals (Wish and Mirabella, 1998). These seven categories collapsed into three broad areas (external relations, internal management, and boundary spanning) that they believed encompassed the needed skill sets of a successful nonprofit professional. A more recent inquiry seemed to confirm the prevalence of an NME doctrine, documenting a homogeneity among nonprofit management course offerings at the graduate level, particularly with respect to the core courses (Mirabella et al., 2019).

As previously noted, the NACC in its curricular guidelines for undergraduate and graduate NME students identified core content areas that are viewed as critical for students of nonprofit management and philanthropy. The most recent version of the guidelines lists 16 core areas for graduate students and 13 for undergraduate students (NACC, 2015). This comprehensive list provides an excellent roadmap for individual instructors and programs to follow when designing their degree-granting courses and the new accreditation standards for NME programs ask program directors to document how their programs address these core areas.

Despite the relative consistency we are now starting to see among many NME degree-granting programs in terms of curricular offerings, nonprofit academic centers, particularly those that are separated from their degree-granting counterparts at the same university, are not bound by such guidelines. In addition, most NME programs are not able to offer such a wide variety of courses as to meet all 16 of the NACC core areas. Thus, it falls to individual programs and centers to determine what is best for their students, faculty, and programs, creating a marketplace of uneven and different offerings.

That NME graduate programs exist to serve future nonprofit managers and leaders is probably self-evident; university education at its core is designed to help future professionals prepare for their careers. However, what is not as clear is the degree to which today's university-led NME should align with and serve *current* nonprofit practitioners. Research indicates that a significant percentage of NME graduate students are pursuing their studies while also working in the nonprofit sector (Wilson and Larson, 2002; Kuenzi, Stewart, and Walk, 2020). Those students are already actively pursuing their careers and, potentially, are in need of different skills and experiences than those students who have not yet begun their nonprofit careers. Is it preferable to serve both current and future nonprofit professionals utilizing the same courses and curriculum? Successful NME programs may be well served to survey their students in order to design programs that best meet the needs of their core audiences.

From a research perspective, collaboration between the academic researcher and the nonprofit professional has gained recognition and acceptance. The term "pracademic" has alternatively been used to define scholars who partner with professionals in their research projects or single individuals who straddle both the academic and professional landscapes (Powell et al., 2018).

Much less has been written about the challenges of aligning the needs of current nonprofit practitioners (and their employers) with the educational offerings available at universities. A recent survey (Nelson, 2019) of approximately 300 nonprofit employees showed that fewer than 1% of respondents had majored in nonprofit management in their undergraduate studies; reflecting that a significant number of nonprofit practitioners likely enter the field with little to no formal nonprofit education. At the graduate level, similar results have been seen. Suarez (2010) found that only 4 out of 194 nonprofit executives in his nationwide study reported having a graduate degree in nonprofit management, despite the fact that more than half of those surveyed possessed an advanced degree. Taking the research one step further, a survey of nearly 150 alumni from three NME graduate programs found that one of the main reasons that individuals chose to pursue their graduate degree was the specific content being offered by the program (Kuenzi, Stewart, and Walk, 2020).

Given this research, it seems clear that a large percentage of current nonprofit employees appear to have made it into the sector without the benefit of formal NME. Likewise, nonprofit employers, consultants, boards, and executive search firms who are looking to hire qualified candidates may also be unsure as to what credentials signal that a potential employee has received a quality education or training. But is an academically rigorous NME degree the right and logical next step for these individuals or would they, and by extension, the sector as a whole, be better off if they pursued more skills-based training opportunities? This, I believe, is one of the key questions that NME programs and academic centers must strive to answer over the next decade.

Prescriptions for the Future

Three decades ago, nonprofit practitioners who wanted to improve or upgrade their skills would likely have turned to the private sector for training classes, unless they happened to know about or live near one of the relatively few universities that offered courses in the subject. Today, current and future nonprofit practitioners have almost an embarrassment of riches in terms of educational options, even if the pathways by which they find out about these opportunities is somewhat tortured. Certainly, the different types, modalities, outcomes, and delivery methods of educational and professional development opportunities for current and future nonprofit practitioners is cause for celebration in many respects. What remains, however, is for the leaders of nonprofit management departments and academic centers to construct a framework for how the various opportunities available fit together and can best serve the goals and needs of the sector.

In 2005, Michael O'Neill, the founder of one of the nation's first NME programs, cautioned that NME in the United States needed to remain focused on the roles for which we were preparing students, letting students' current and future job responsibilities guide us as we shaped our programs (O'Neill, 2005). Now, 15 years later, it is somewhat difficult to see whether or not we have achieved that goal, or if that is even a goal still worth pursuing.

In response, I believe that today's nonprofit management educators and center directors need to take a step back and re-consider our core reasons for existing. Do we exist to infuse current and future nonprofit leaders with an understanding of the sector's origins and unique history, thus creating a professional workforce that is grounded in nonprofit and philanthropic theory? Or are we providing avenues to help nonprofit professionals sharpen and hone their skills in completing the tasks necessary for the success of their organizations? Put another way, does a professional fundraiser need a grounding in philanthropic theory in order to do their job well or would they (and their employers) be better off if they instead focusing on developing their grantwriting skills? If the answer is "we want to do both," ten it will be incumbent upon us to develop the systems and nomenclature that can help students and their potential employers differentiate between the types of offerings.

Some may argue that it is possible, in fact preferable, for us to do both. But in order for that successful merger to occur within one program or even one university, we must be increasingly deliberate about the subjects we teach, the students we recruit and the degrees, certificates and badges we offer to those students. Some of the key elements we should all consider include:

Determine a core audience and be prepared to fight to avoid mission drift. Just as we would teach our students to be on the lookout for mission drift in their own organizations, the leaders of academic centers and degree-granting NME programs need to be watchful over our own missions. If, for example, our academic unit is focused more on research and theory, perhaps the practical training programs and workshops for today's nonprofit leaders are best housed in an independent academic center or a department of lifelong learning.

Develop intentional pathways from K-12 education to successful careers in the nonprofit sector. Although not the focus of this chapter, there is evidence that entering college students have little to no experience with the idea of the nonprofit sector as a career choice (Altman, 2012; Brunt, et al, 2020). This fact, combined with the research that demonstrates that nonprofit employees often find multiple pathways into the sector that have nothing to do with formal nonprofit education at the university level, should help guide future collective action by NACC, NME educators and individual programs in this area. Promoting the sector as a place where individuals can grow and develop a successful career will be a critical first step in defining and explaining the specific value that a nonprofit management degree confers on the graduate.

Develop a set nomenclature for describing and defining NME offerings. NACC has provided baseline definitions for the credit requirements for NME degrees and certificates, but beyond that, there is little uniformity across and within programs. In addition, there is little standardization for terms (badges, for example) that are becoming more prevalent in conversations about NME. This might best be done in partnership with the membership-based organizations that represent current nonprofit employees. Who better to help educators craft a universal definition of the skills necessary for a fundraising badge or certificate than the Association of Fundraising Professionals?

Celebrate, respect, and promote the different offerings available to current and future nonprofit managers. Non-academic entities and schools of professional or continuing studies may be able to respond more quickly to ongoing changes in nonprofit management, as they are less encumbered by often unwieldy curriculum design and review processes. For example, the introduction of new accounting and financial reporting requirements for nonprofits in 2019 might best be covered in a targeted webinar or half-day course; as of this writing, many key nonprofit financial management texts that would be used in a degree-granting course (which are often years in the making) have yet to be updated to reflect these changes.

The discussion surrounding these and other related topics likely needs to happen at a broad level, with NACC and its member institutions leading the way. However, it will be important that we also develop pathways to bring practitioners and other nonprofit sector professionals into the conversation. Their insights could indeed prove invaluable in helping us understand the breadth of this issue.

Conclusion

In arguing that the nonprofit sector was indeed a profession that needed to take steps toward a formal accrediting process for its degree-granting higher education institutions, Evans and Kinoti (2017) wrote that the cost of leaving the vital work done by nonprofits to amateurs was too high for society to bear. Nonprofit management educators and their institutions, led by NACC, answered that call.

Now well past its infancy, NME in the United States has entered a new stage replete with the growing pains of adolescence. With an established set of curricular guidelines for undergraduate and graduate NME and a newly established accreditation process for stand-alone NME programs, it is now time for educators and center directors to move into a broader conversation about the various types of private, public, and university-led educational offerings available to future and current nonprofit employees. Only through a careful examination of the needs of our varied audiences can we hope to propel our programs and academic centers into a mature adulthood.

References

Altman, S., Carpenter, H., Dietrick, L., Strom, S.A., and VanHorn, T. (2012). Impact of the nonprofit leadership alliance, an undergraduate competency-based nonprofit program, on alumni career paths. Journal of nonprofit education and leadership, 2(3): 123–139.

Ashcraft, R. (2001). Where nonprofit management education meets the undergraduate experience: American humanics after 50 years. Public performance and management review, 25(1): 42–56.

Becker, G.S. (1964). *Human capital: A theoretical and empirical analysis.* New York and London: Columbia University Press.

Benz, M. (2005). Not for the profit, but for the satisfaction? Evidence on worker well-being in non-profit firms. *KYKLOS*, 58, 155–176. https://doi.org/10.1111/j.0023-5962.2005.00283.x

Blau, G., Hill, T.L., and Cannon, M. (2020). Exploring the relationship between nonprofit management education and career impact: Scale development and comparison. Journal of education for business, DOI: 10.1080/08832323.2020.1738990

Brunt, C., Dolch, N., Freeman, T., Mirabella, R., Weber, P., and Wooddell, M. (2020). Undergraduate nonprofit education: Between institutionalization and recruitment. Journal of nonprofit education and leadership, 10(1): 2–24.

Bureau of Labor Statistics (2016). U.S. Department of Labor, Nonprofits account for 12.3 million jobs, 10.2 percent of private sector employment, in 2016. The Economics Daily. www.bls.gov/opub/ted/2018/nonprofits-account-for-12-3-million-jobs-10-2-percent-of-private-sector-employment-in-2016.htm

Eikenberry, A.M. and Kluver Drapal, J. (2004). The marketization of the nonprofit sector: Civil society at risk? *Public administration review*, 64: 132–140.

Evans, C. and Kinoti, M.D. (2017). Are we there yet? Evaluating nonprofit management as a profession for program accreditation. *Journal of nonprofit education and leadership*, 7(1): 49–58.

Hale, M. (2020). Foreword. In Bezborouah, K. and Carpenter, H. (eds), *Teaching nonprofit management.* Cheltenham: Edward Elgar Publishing.

Hwang, H. and Powell, W.W. (2009). The rationalization of charity: The influences of professionalism in the sector. *Administrative science quarterly*, 54: 268–298.

Johnson, J.M. and Ng, E.S. (2015). Money talks or millennials walk the effect of compensation on nonprofit millennial workers sector-switching intentions. *Review of public personnel administration*, 36(3), 283–305.

Kuenzi, K., Stewart, A., and Walk, M. (2020). Nonprofit graduate education: Who gets the degree and why? *Journal of public affairs education*, 26(1): 11–30.

Leete, L. (2006). Work in the nonprofit sector. In W. Powell & R. Steinberg (Eds.), *The nonprofit sector: A research handbook* (2nd ed., pp. 159–179). New Haven, CT: Yale University Press.

Lyons, S.T., Duxbury, L.E., and Higgins, C.A. (2006). A comparison of the values and commitment of private sector, public sector, and parapublic sector employees. *Public administration review*, 66, 605–618. https://doi.org/10.1111/j.1540-6210.2006.00620.x

Maier, F., Meyer, M., and Steinbereithner, M. (2016). Nonprofit organizations becoming business-like: A systematic review. *Nonprofit and voluntary sector quarterly*, 45(1): 64–86.

McKeever, B.S. (2018). The nonprofit sector in brief 2018. Urban Institute. National Center for Charitable Statistics. Retrieved from https://nccs.urban.org/publication/non-profit-sector-brief2018#highlights

Mirabella, R.M. (2007). University-based educational programs in nonprofit management and philanthropic studies: A 10-year review and projections of future trends. *Nonprofit and voluntary sector quarterly*, 36(4), 11S–27S.

Mirabella, R., Hoffman, T., Teo, T.K., and McDonald, M. (2019). The evolution of nonprofit management and philanthropic studies in the United States: Are we now a disciplinary field? *Journal of nonprofit education and leadership*, 9(1): 63–84.

Mirabella, R. and Wish, N. (2000, July). Nonprofit management education: Summary of research on graduate degree programs. Paper presented at the meeting of the International Association for Third Sector Research, Dublin, Ireland.

NACC (2015). Curricular guidelines: Graduate and undergraduate study in nonprofit leadership, the nonprofit sector and philanthropy. Nonprofit Academic Centers Council.

NACC (2021). www.nonprofit-academic-centers-council.org/membership/nacc-members/ Retrieved on December 15, 2021.

Nelson, E. (2019). The accidental nonprofiteer. *Journal of nonprofit education and leadership*, 7(4): 287–305.

Ng, E.S. & McGinnis Johnson, J. (2015). Millennials: Who are they, how are they different, and why should we care. In R. Burke, C. Cooper, & A. Antoniou (Eds.), The multi-generational workforce: Challenges and opportunities for organisations (pp. 121–137). Cheltenham, UK: Edward Elgar Publishing Limited.

Nyu.edu (2021). Information was retrieved on January 3, 2021 at www.nyu.edu.

O'Neil, M. (2005). Developmental Contexts of Nonprofit Management Education. Nonprofit management & leadership, 16(1): 5–17.

O'Neill, M. (2007). The future of nonprofit management education. *Nonprofit and voluntary sector quarterly*, 36(4): 169S–176S.

Powell, E., Winfield, G., Schatteman, A.M., and Trusty, K. (2018). Collaboration between practitioners and academics: Defining the pracademic experience. *Journal of nonprofit education and leadership*, 8(1): 62–79.

Rooney, P. and Burlingame, D. (2020). Build it and they will come! Or built to last? Key challenges and insights into the sustainability of nonprofit and philanthropy programs and centers. *Journal of nonprofit education and leadership*, 10(4): 414–428.

Seton Hall University (2021a). Information retrieved on January 2, 2021 from: https://academic.shu.edu/npo/list.php?sort=state&type=ceu

Seton Hall University (2021b). Information retrieved on January 2, 2021 from: https://academic.shu.edu/npo/list.php?sort=degree&type=gconc

Suarez, D.F. (2010). Street credentials and management backgrounds: Careers of nonprofit executives in an evolving sector. *Nonprofit and voluntary sector quarterly*, 39(4): 696–716.

Wilson, M. and Larson, R.S. (2002). Nonprofit management students: Who they are and why they enroll. *Nonprofit and voluntary sector quarterly*, 31(2): 259–270.

Wish, N. and Mirabella, R. (1998). Curricular Variations in Nonprofit Management Graduate Programs. *Nonprofit management and leadership* 9(1): 99–109.

Young, D.R. (1987). Executive leadership in nonprofit organizations. In W. W. Powell (Ed.), *The nonprofit sector: A research handbook* (pp. 167–179). New Haven, CT: Yale University Press.

15

ENACTING NONPROFIT AND PHILANTHROPIC STUDIES

Academic Centers as Builders of Transdisciplinary Bridges

Robert F. Ashcraft

Introduction

When the history of nonprofit and philanthropic education is written, understanding the vital role played by Nonprofit Academic Centers is required. How courses, minors, majors, certificates, and degrees in the field were developed is illuminating. Such analysis reveals that nonprofit management and philanthropic studies is a story of disciplinary bridges built by academic innovators who engaged through the Nonprofit Academic Centers Council (NACC). The story reveals the value of transdisciplinary efforts to design, implement and sustain new fields of study. It also clarifies how education field building can occur in promising ways to inform higher education more broadly. Such insights are helpful as universities respond to forces questioning their continued relevancy, affordability, and sustainability.

Why does it matter how a field in higher education is conceptualized and enacted? If the story of NACC is understood through the metaphor of bridge-building, what bridges were built, by whom and for what purpose? What may be learned from the ways in which NACC fostered nonprofit education that can help inform others to successfully achieve desired results? How might academic leaders generally, and those who lead nonprofit academic centers and programs specifically, embrace transdisciplinary approaches to field building in response to societal pressures faced by higher education? These questions are best answered by first examining transdisciplinarity and its emergence within higher education.

DOI: 10.4324/9781003294061-16

A Framework for Transdisciplinarity in Higher Education

There are a variety of terms associated with how academics assemble themselves to enact research, teaching and service efforts. Terms such as "Disciplinarity," "Multidisciplinarity," and "Interdisciplinarity" are used, often interchangeably. As Evans (2014) argues, "…we administrators, faculty, and staff…use these terms rather loosely and too often without carefully considering their underlying meaning."

It is common to think of professors as part of academic disciplines. Universities have historically organized faculty through *disciplinary* "clusters" within departments, schools, and colleges. Initiatives that bring faculty from disciplines together around some research agenda or teaching/curricular goals are often explained as *multidisciplinary* or *interdisciplinary* efforts in nature. However, such terms are limiting when considering the way in which leaders of nonprofit academic centers developed the field of nonprofit management education and philanthropic studies. The emergence of *transdisciplinary* as a term that describes approaches to field building most accurately describes their story. First, though, it is important to examine what the aforementioned terms mean and what their relationships are to each other.

Disciplinarity – The idea of a discipline implies what Rigolot (2020) argues is "a specialization of knowledge within some sort of overriding unity of cognitive endeavor." He asserts the following characteristics of a discipline:

(1) some institutional manifestation in the form of subjects taught at universities or colleges, respective academic departments and professional associations connected to it;
(2) a particular object, or focus, for its research;
(3) a body of accumulated specialized knowledge specific to the discipline;
(4) theories that organize the specialist knowledge;
(5) specific terminologies; and
(6) specific research methods.

The actions of academics within traditional disciplinary structures in universities who work with others outside their discipline for some purpose are typically described in the following ways:

Multidisciplinarity – an approach that Petrie (1992) notes, occurs when

> a number of disciplines work together on a problem, an educational program, or a research study. The effect is additive rather than integrative. The project is usually short-lived, and there is seldom any long-term change in the ways in which the disciplinary participants in a multidisciplinary project view their own work.

Interdisciplinarity – an approach that implies more integration rather than just addition to the effort being undertaken. According to Petrie (1992),

> Interdisciplinary research or education typically refers to those situations in which the integration of the work goes beyond the mere concatenation of disciplinary contributions. Some key elements of disciplinarians' use of their concepts and tools change. There is a level of integration.

Over the past two decades innovative higher education models have emerged in response to societal pressures and demands. Thus, existing language is insufficient to describe promising practice to meet the challenges and opportunities associated with increased societal pressures on higher education. A relatively new term, transdisciplinarity, is offered here to describe ways in which academics enact fields to assure success of new models.

Transdisciplinarity – an approach that has been described by Russell, Wickson, and Carew (2008) as, "a practice that transgresses and transcends disciplinary boundaries, ... and seems to have the most potential to respond to new demands and imperatives." Characteristics include,

> a problem focus (research originates from and is contextualized in 'real-world' problems), evolving methodology (the research involves iterative, reflective processes that are responsive to the particular questions, settings, and research groupings) and collaboration (including collaboration between transdisciplinary researchers, disciplinary researchers and external actors with interests in the research).

Lang, Wiek, and Bergmann (2012) note that transdisciplinarity is, "increasingly mentioned as a promising way of producing knowledge and decision making." And, according to Scholz and Steiner (2015), such efforts are often characterized by the inclusion of non-academic stakeholders in the process of knowledge production.

When examining the story of nonprofit academic centers as bridge builders for conceptualizing, organizing, and advancing the field of nonprofit management education and philanthropic studies, it is *transdisciplinarity* that best explains 40 years of field building led by academic innovators.

A helpful visual model for understanding transdisciplinarity is offered by McGregor and Volckmann (2011; see Figure 15.1). They suggest conceiving and enacting research, knowledge generation, education, and outreach/service differently. Such approaches place a premium on:

- linking disciplines together along with community stakeholders;
- changing historic "town and gown" relationships to one of genuine university and community partnerships;

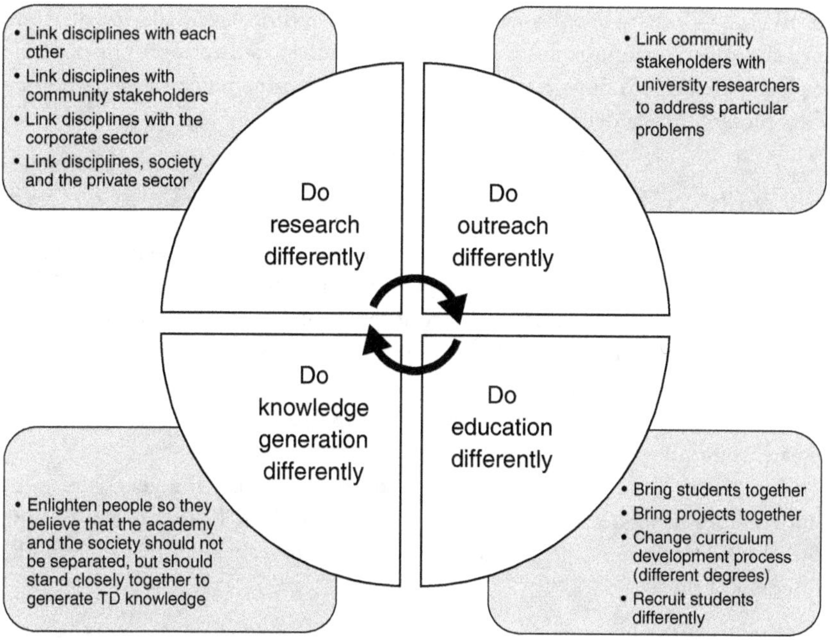

FIGURE 15.1 Transdisciplinary Synopsis
Source: McGregor and Volckmann, 2011

- advancing use-inspired research that is about problem solving based upon mutuality of goals; and
- reconceptualizing all facets of student engagement from recruitment to classroom pedagogy.

Transdisciplinarity is an appropriate lens by which to understand the story of field building through nonprofit academic centers. Yet it also holds promise for larger and more profound approaches to how colleges and universities can adapt to current forces they face which are challenging the very purpose and future of higher education. Thus, the example of NACC has far greater implications for informing who, how, and why stakeholders are brought together to assure long-term relevance, impact, and sustainability.

NACC – Transdisciplinarity in Action

The ways in which academics organized to advance the field of nonprofit and philanthropic studies speaks to the value of transdisciplinary approaches to field building. NACC's organizers likely never used the term *transdisciplinary (arity)* as they collaborated through NACC to build their field. Yet an analysis of who came together, how they worked together and what results occurred adds credence to the value of encouraging transdisciplinary approaches to such efforts. The resulting explosive growth of nonprofit management education and philanthropic studies is a testimony to the process.

A Brief History

Though a definitive, comprehensive, history of NACC has yet to been written, one of its founders, Dennis Young (2021), provides insights into the transdisciplinary nature of those who are credited with conceptualizing the field of nonprofit management education. He chronicles the rise of the nonprofit sector from colonial times to the present and how it was in the 1970s that, "scholars and policymakers began to conceive of nonprofits as a whole sector, deserving separate attention in research, education and public policy."

Young's historical essay is foundational to understanding the genesis of nonprofit studies in higher education generally and the NACC specifically. Among several inflection points, he acknowledges three significant ones that include the founding of the:

- Yale University Program on Nonprofit Organizations (PONPO) in 1978; the first academic center devoted to the study of the nonprofit sector
- Independent Sector (IS), founded in 1980; conceived as the voice of the nonprofit and philanthropic sector
- NACC founded in 1991.

As chronicled by Young and another of NACC's founders, Michael O'Neil, other efforts by individuals from the academic and practitioner communities also occurred during this era to foster the growth of nonprofit management education (Long and O'Neill 2010). The birth of Association for Research on Nonprofit Organizations and Voluntary Action (ARNOVA), founded in 1971 under its original name (Association of Voluntary Action Scholars), and the International Society of Third Sector Research (ISTR), founded in 1992, are two examples.

The critical role of the IS in fostering the development of research infrastructure of the field and the support of nonprofit academic centers cannot be overstated. Guided by the IS Research Committee (chartered originally in 1982), a 1991 report on "Academic Centers and Programs," notes a roster of 31 members with approximately half representing academics and half as practitioners (see Table 15.1).

Through IS, the committee members worked together to help define a field and to foster the growth of academic centers. Interestingly, academics represented a variety of disciplines including economics, history, social welfare, geography, public affairs and urban planning, psychology, and anthropology. Among practitioners were leaders of foundations (e.g., Ford Foundation, Charles Stewart

TABLE 15.1 Roster of 1991 Independent Sector's Research Committee

Chairperson
Stanley N. Katz
President
American Council of Learned Societies
New York, NY

Members
Gwendolyn Baker
Executive Director
YWCA of the USA
New York, NY

James Bausch
President
Save the Children Federation
Westport, CT

Thomas R. Buckman
President
The Foundation Center
New York, NY

Mary Ellen Capek
Executive Secretary
National Council for Research on Women
New York, NY

Geoffrey Carliner
Executive Director
National Bureau of Economic Research
Cambridge, MA

Emmett D. Carson
Assistant Program Officer
Ford Foundation
Street New York, NY

Charles T. Clotfelter
Director
Center for the Study of Philanthropy & Voluntarism
Duke University
Durham, NC

Carroll L. Estes
Director
Institute for Health and Aging
University of California at San Francisco
San Francisco, CA

Margaret Gates
National Executive Director
Girls Clubs of America, Inc.
New York, NY

Stephen Graubard
Editor
Daedalus
Cambridge, MA

Bradford Graubard
Director
Program on Nonprofit Organizations (PONPO)
Yale University
New Haven, CT

Judith M. Gueron
President
Manpower Demonstration Research Corp.
New York, NY

Dudley Hafner
Executive Vice President
American Heart Association
Dallas, TX

James Henry
President
Center for Public Resources
New York, NY 10017

Willard J. Hertz
Vice President
The Charles Mott Foundation
Flint, MI

Gerald Holton
Professor
Department of Physics
Harvard University
Cambridge, MA

Geneva Johnson
President
Family Service of America
Milwaukee, WI

(continued)

TABLE 15.1 Cont.

Barry Karl Professor of History University of Chicago Chicago, IL	Robert M. Rosenzweig President Association of American Universities Washington, DC
Reynold Levy President AT&T Foundation New York, NY 10022	Terry Saario President Northwest Area Foundation St. Paul, MN
Richard W. Lyman Director, Institute of International Studies Stanford University Stanford, CA	Paul G. Schervish Director Social Welfare Research Institute Boston College Chestnut Hill, MA
George Marcus Professor of Anthropology Rice University Houston, TX	Ervin Staub Professor of Psychology University of Massachusetts Amherst, MA
Kathleen McCarthy Director, Center for the Study of Philanthropy City University of New York New York, NY	Julian Wolpert Henry G. Bryant Professor of Geography Woodrow Wilson School Princeton University Princeton, NJ 98544
Michael O'Neill Director Institute for Nonprofit Organization Management University of San Francisco San Francisco, CA	Dennis R. Young Director Mandel Center for Non-Profit Organizations Case Western Reserve University Cleveland, OH 44122
Robert L. Payton Director, Center on Philanthropy Professor of Philanthropic Studies Indiana University Indianapolis, IN	

Mott Foundation, AT&T Foundation) and nonprofits (e.g., YWCA of the USA, Save the Children Federation, American Heart Association).

A subset of the larger IS's research committee met in 1991 on the occasion of the IS annual meeting in Atlanta to formalize the NACC idea. This was preceded by informal conversations beginning in 1986 by Dennis Young, Michael O'Neill, and others who engaged in IS Research Forums. Such gatherings provided opportunities for those engaged in the development of early centers and programs to converse and collaborate on scholarly matters including the challenges and opportunities of building and sustaining institutional support for a new field. There is a growing literature base that chronicles a history of the people, activities, events and outcomes associated with NACC, from ideation to enactment including Young (2021), Rooney & Burlingame (2020) Ashcraft (2015), Mendel (2015), and Larson and Barnes-Moorhead (2001).

In a seminal report authored by Crowder and Hodgkinson (1991) the authors note that the basic goal of IS's research program is, "to stimulate the development of an identifiable and growing research effort that produces the body of knowledge necessary to accurately define, describe, chart and understand the sector and the *ways it can be of greater service to society*."

The story of academics and practitioners working with IS to support the birth of NACC meets several criteria associated with transdisciplinarity. In particular,

- the problem focus *(e.g., the role of research to reveal how the nonprofit sector can be of greater service to society?)*;
- intentional collaboration (*the inclusion of non-academic stakeholders in the process*); and
- new knowledge production and decision making (*bolstering a new field in universities driven by use-inspired research and informed by practitioner perspectives*).

TABLE 15.2 Roster of Original Institutional Members of NACC

Boston College
Case Western Reserve University
City University of New York
Duke University
Indiana University-Purdue University at Indianapolis (IUPUI)
Johns Hopkins University
The London School of Economics and Political Administration
Northwestern University
National Center for Nonprofit Boards
New School for Social Research
New York University
Regis College
Seton Hall University
Texas Christian University
Tufts University
Union Institute
University of California-San Francisco
University of Missouri-Kansas City
University of Pennsylvania
University of San Francisco
University of St. Thomas
Virginia Polytechnic Institute and State University
Yale University

As Young (2021) notes, a goal of IS was to advance the infrastructure needed to support nonprofit sector research. Academic centers were seen as a way to accomplish the goal. The 1991 IS report highlights 26 programs/centers, "focusing on the study of philanthropy, voluntarism and not-for-profit activity," which was an increase from an original 19 centers highlighted in an earlier 1988 IS report. (Crowder and Hodgkinson, 1991).

With IS serving as fiscal agent, NACC was founded in 1991 and enjoyed a modest budget derived mostly from dues paid by its 25 founding institutional members (Rooney and Burlingame, 2020; see Table 15.2). Young (2021) notes how the early directors of academic centers valued the opportunity to converse with each other and sometimes commiserate over the reality of traditional university structures organized by discipline that had little room for boundary spanning to include nonprofit studies as an interdisciplinary, let alone transdisciplinary, endeavor. NACC's role in providing a means by which academic innovators could advance a common vision to build a field through research and education owes its beginnings to transdisciplinary leaders such as its founders, Dennis Young, Michael O'Neill, and others.

W.K. Kellogg Foundation – Accelerating Transdisciplinarity through Nonprofit Academic Centers

To understand fully the role of Nonprofit Academic Centers as builders of transdisciplinary bridges it is necessary to examine briefly the W. K. Kellogg Foundation's (WKKF) initiatives to bolster nonprofit management and philanthropic studies programs. Just as IS and the individuals who assembled to organize NACC must be acknowledged as crucial to the development of centers and programs of the field, so to must WKKF be examined for its role in accelerating the field's scale, reach, and impact.

The leadership of WKKF's Robert Long to the foundation's decade-long investments of over $15 million in the 1980's represented a profound inflection point in the history of the field. Through the foundation's *Academic Centers of Excellence grant strategy*, Robert Long recognized that, "even the most innovative and successful programs are at risk of failure if the organizations within which they operate are weak and unsustainable" (Larson and Barnes-Moorhead, 2001). WKKF investments to NACC affiliates such as the University of San Francisco, Case Western Reserve University, and Indiana University bolstered the field and were seen as models for other universities to follow in developing responses to educational needs of the nonprofit sector. WKKF placed a premium on investing in university programs that were prepared to meet the societal demands for more access and reach of nonprofit management education and philanthropic studies in direct response to community needs. Without using terms like *transdisciplinarity*, it was evident that WKKF sought funding partners that were not bound by traditional disciplinary structures within universities.

Though the primary goals for grants from WKKF initiatives were about strengthening and expanding the education field, Long's leadership also included support for the development of faculty from communities of color. With funding from WKKF, the NACC Faculty Fellowship Program was established in 2004. Its purpose was to honor the contributions of David Stevenson and William Diaz, two scholars in the fields of philanthropy and nonprofit management who both died in 2002. The multi-year Fellowship program was design to encourage the development of new research in the field of nonprofit and philanthropic studies. Such investments through NACC were demonstrations of confidence in the way in which the organization was able to foster boundary spanning approaches to the field.

Interestingly, at the same time as these efforts took place, the organization American Humanics (AH) was offering nonprofit management education to undergraduate students through a small network of colleges and universities. Founded in 1948, AH grew from its practitioner roots to develop partnerships with colleges and universities to offer curricular and co-curricular programming for students in the field [Ashcraft, 2001). Initially the focus was on preparing undergraduate students for careers in nonprofit youth and human service organizations. Despite a long history of education in the field, AH was largely disconnected from the conversations taking place at the time with IS involving the formation of NACC. However, during the period of 1994–2002 WKKF invested $2.5 million to expand the network of AH campus affiliates and from 2003–2012 invested another $5 million to fund senior internships that aligned with the foundation's larger capacity building strategy. As a result, AH became connected to NACC and other leading infrastructure and scholarly organizations such as IS and ARNOVA. AH was renamed the Nonprofit Leadership Alliance in 2011, and as the organization formalized its Certified Nonprofit Professional (CNP) credential, its connection to NACC and the nonprofit and philanthropic studies field more generally, was secure. Its mission, "to strengthen the social sector with a talented and prepared workforce" is guided by a competency-based framework (Nonprofit Leadership Alliance 2021). The results of AH being highly grounded in the field of practice are manifested in how it gives equal weight to practitioner perspectives and academic input into its competency-based form of education. Such an approach helps to inform today's transdisciplinary framework to field building given NLA's intersection with NACC in the nonprofit and philanthropic studies field.

In 1997 WKKF launched its "Building Bridges Between Practice and Knowledge in Nonprofit Management Education Initiative." Under Long's leadership the Building Bridges Initiative (BBI) had specific design imperatives built into its grantmaking philosophy that placed a premium on transdisciplinary approaches to field building. According to Heidrich and Long, BBI was about developing intentional bridges between academic programs and practitioners working in the field. Moreover, the initiative was about realizing better trained nonprofit leaders, and the need for racial and cultural diversity among those who

TABLE 15.3 Building Bridges Initiative – W. K. Kellogg Foundation Grant Recipients – 1997–2002

American Humanics
Arizona State University
California State University at Los Angeles
Case Western Reserve University
City University of New York
George Mason University
Georgetown University
Getulio Vargas Foundation (Brazil)
Harvard University
Indiana University
Johns Hopkins University
Nonprofit Services Consortium (St Louis, MO – USA)
Northwestern University
Portland State University
Southeast Center for Organizational Leadership (North Carolina)
State University of New York
The Learning Institute for Nonprofit Organizations (Wisconsin)
Universidad Bolivariana de Chile (Chile)
Universidad de los Andes (Colombia)
Universidad del Pacifico (Peru)
Universidad de San Andres Graduate Program in Nonprofit Organizations (Argentina)
Universidad Iberoamericana, Golfo Centro (Mexico)
Universidad Iberoamericana, Santa Fe (Mexico)
University of Pennsylvania
University of Sao Paulo (Brazil)
University of Texas at San Antonio
Western Michigan University
Yale University

lead and manage in the sector. In all, 20 projects were funded from $13.5 million in investments to advance the nonprofit management education and philanthropic studies field (Heidrich and Long 2002; Table 15.3).

In an evaluation report of the BBI Initiative, Larson and Barnes-Moorhead (2001) share insights as revealed in their report, "How Centers Work: Building and Sustaining Academic Nonprofit Centers." Based upon informant interviews of center director grantees, remarkable transdisciplinary approaches to the results being sought are revealed. Center directors challenge university structures, are hyper-focused on community needs and otherwise exhibit the characteristics associated with trandisciplinarity. The following examples of transdisciplinary thinking and actions were voiced by Center directors and are grouped by the outcomes sought:

Challenges to Traditional University Structures:

> "Centers need to be in the university, but not of the university. They need to talk academic language for sustainability while challenging academic assumptions."
>
> "Centers tend to be more task-focused and interdisciplinary than academic departments."
>
> "At this time, there is no one 'right' place for nonprofit centers within the university structure."

Inextricable Linkages to the Communities Served:

> "Centers tend to be boundary-spanning organizations that connect academic interests with external stakeholders."
>
> "Centers are flexible organizations that can change staffing and programs in response to societal demands for new knowledge."
>
> "A 'uniqueness' of nonprofit centers is that they expand their missions to meet societal demands and environmental opportunities, while keeping their core missions of focusing on the third sector."

Center Directors as Transdisciplinary Leaders

> "Nonprofit center directors often have experience working in the nonprofit, governmental or commercial sectors prior to their roles in academe. Thus, many center directors have experiences that traditional academics (may) lack." Such a background helps them, "…to empathize with practitioners and develop programs that are responsive to community concerns."
>
> "Nonprofit center directors are boundary spanners and must network and build relationships with key constituents – within and external to the university. These relationships contribute to both institutional and financial support."
>
> "Center directors are academic entrepreneurs – they are innovators, risk takers, and highly committed to the field."

A single study of nonprofit academic center directors during a time of large WKKF investments is but one way to understand the concept of transdisciplinarity. However, it is the larger body of effort and results that reveal a promising practice for decision making to advance field building in higher education. The ways in which NACC is organized, conducts its purpose, and produces results, therefore, add credence to the value of transdisciplinary approaches to nonprofit and philanthropic studies as a legitimate field of education.

The combination of Center directors (as academic entrepreneurs) and NACC (as an organizational structure) reveal the power of transdisciplinary approaches to accelerating the presence and scale of nonprofit and philanthropic studies in colleges and universities. Transdisciplinarity in action is evinced by NACC through outcomes associated with its field-building history. Examples include decisions made about membership criteria, leadership of curricular guidelines for the field, development of quality measures for centers and programs; the implementation of accreditation for the field; convening strategies; support for an academic-practitioner oriented journal; and, development of a student honor society. Each is described in more detail as follows:

Membership Criteria Decisions – NACC's membership has ebbed and flowed from its initial 25 institutional members in 1991 to its current total of 60 members in 2021. Membership is dominated by US-based institutions with a growing number representing centers/programs from outside the United States. As Rooney and Burlingame (2020) note, there have been enormous changes over the years in membership as some centers/programs thrived, some survived and other failed over the three decades since NACC's birth. Yet, evidence suggests that membership, despite how variable in any given year, is not defined by disciplinary boundaries. In fact, NACC's membership criteria make no mention of disciplines at all (NACC 2021a; Table 15.4). Thus, NACC's membership represents centers and programs housed in an array of institutional homes with a growing number that are free-standing from any specific department or school.

From Rooney and Burlingame's study (2020) they observe,

> Our interviews and case studies reinforced this heterogeneous dimension of the field and suggests that the best place to house philanthropy and

TABLE 15.4 NACC's Membership Criteria (2021)

To be eligible for general membership, the applicant must:

1. Operate within an accredited college or university. If the program or center is located internationally, accreditation will be appropriate to the home institution.
2. Have a primary focus on nonprofit, non-governmental sector management, or philanthropic studies (or related areas such as civil society, social economy, and social innovation).
3. Provide evidence of ongoing activity in at least two of the three programmatic areas – education, research, and community engagement – as defined below.
4. Demonstrate a substantial allocation of resources and programming to the programmatic area(s), including:
   a. designated faculty or staff position which has primary responsibility to direct programmatic activities. We recognize the title and exact scope and type of responsibilities may vary, and some responsibility can be shared among other faculty, staff, or students.
   b. Accountability to and association with the academic division of the school, college, or university (which can include continuing or professional education), rather than some other area, such as student affairs.
   c. Staff support for its activities. No minimum level of staffing is required.

nonprofit programs can, in fact, be anywhere. There is not a clear pattern about programs that failed or thrived and to which schools they were attached.

Leadership to Curricular Guidelines – Boundary Spanning Intentions – Perhaps no singular outcome of NACC's transdisciplinary efforts is more pronounced than its leadership in the development of curricular guidelines for the field (NACC 2015; see Appendix A). From years of earlier conversations among leaders of centers and programs, NACC began developing and disseminating curricular guidelines for graduate programs in 2001 and was helped in the effort through a grant from the David and Lucile Packard Foundation. The first-ever graduate guidelines were released in 2003. Responses from the field were such that is was apparent to leaders of NACC that ongoing attention to curricular guidelines was an imperative for the organization, including the development of guidelines for undergraduate programs in the field. In 2007 the second edition of the graduate guidelines and first edition of undergraduate guidelines were released. Yet another curricular revision was enacted with the release of the 2015 "NACC Curricular Guidelines for Graduate and Undergraduate Study in Nonprofit Leadership, the Nonprofit Sector and Philanthropy," representing the third revision of the graduate guidelines and the second revision of the undergraduate guidelines.

Details of the ways in which NACC organized the curricular guidelines efforts is evidence of transdisciplinary thinking and actions. The process by which the guidelines were developed and disseminated are well documented (NACC 2015). The inclusion of a wide array of academic and practitioner perspectives, representing diverse fields, disciplines and organizations, is a hallmark of the process. As a result, the guidelines have evolved over time. For example, the most recent guidelines, in comparison to earlier editions, represent more global perspectives and expanded content that includes philanthropic studies and social entrepreneurship/enterprise as curricular considerations.

Indicators of Quality Project – Standards Setting for Transdisciplinary Work

During the same era as the creation of curricular guidelines, and with the continued growth of centers and programs, NACC's leaders realized the importance of having quality measures in place. As part of the original Packard Foundation grant, the transdisciplinary approach to field building continued which resulted in the 2006 release of *"In Pursuit of Excellence: Indicators of Quality in Nonprofit Academic Centers."* Reasoning for developing quality measures was based on the following rationale (NACC 2006):

> As the field both matures and expands, nonprofit academic centers must ensure the quality and sustainability of their educational programs and

> activities. Recognizing that centers have distinct missions and programs, NACC is dedicated to strengthening these centers, however their missions are demonstrated, as one way to secure the long-term viability of non-profit and philanthropic education. Identifying benchmarks or indicators of quality of these enterprises is just one effort toward this commitment.

The Indicators of Quality project was designed to support the growing network of existing and emerging nonprofit academic centers. Its defined purpose was to serve:

- as a source of goals and/or objectives in center and program planning;
- as a source of measures that will demonstrate achievement and effectiveness;
- as a tool that both suggests and informs dialogue about partnerships and collaborations; and
- as a resource for academic departments and schools as they seek to create or strengthen centers within their own institution.

In keeping with NACC's transdisciplinary approach to field building, the quality measures project placed a priority on centers balancing activities in research, education, and service that reflect distinctive missions and purpose. No mention is made of prescribing a disciplinary home as a quality indicator. Measures of quality for the education mission of centers are focused on graduate level programs because the undergraduate curricular guidelines had yet to be developed. Quality measures across the research, teaching, and service missions place a premium on centers being responsive to community needs with emphasis on valuing community engagement strategies to realize goals. Such context provided a framework for supporting boundary-spanning thinking and action on the part of academics leading centers. Specific measures within the traditional research, teaching, and service paradigm of universities are detailed in ways that highly value use-inspired research, collaborative partnerships, and community engagement as markers of excellence. A context for measuring quality across research, education, and service is offered in the language used by NACC. Examples include:

- *Research* that is, "… relevant and responsive to current issues within the sector, within specific nonprofit organizations and within the larger community;"
- *Education* that is, "… (responsive) to current issues and needs of the field…," that "…ensures that both subject matter and pedagogy are responsive… to the diversity of the field… and the students;" with a focus on, "… student related outcomes…" including "… critical thinking and analytical skills," leading to, "… progress in their careers";
- Service that is, "…responsive to the needs of the targeted market," and, "… that provides opportunities for professional development and non-credit education."

Standards Setting through Accreditation – As an outgrowth of efforts stemming from the work on curricular guidelines, NACC's membership voted at its annual meeting in 2017 to develop and implement an accreditation process. Fox (2017) details NACC's intentions,

> to pursue the development of an accreditation process for its institutional members, all of whom provide graduate and/or undergraduate education with a focus on the nonprofit and philanthropic sectors. Why is this significant? As an academic discipline, the field of nonprofit studies only started to emerge about 35 years ago. This is in stark contrast to such established disciplines as the classic fields of liberal arts or sciences, which date back to our earliest universities. NACC's history of establishing published curricular guidelines, and now a move toward formal accreditation, is an important step in the ongoing maturing and professionalization of the sector.

Similar to the tone and content associated with NACC's institutional membership criteria, the principles guiding NACC's accreditation process, as detailed by NACC (2021b) are boundary-spanning. They accentuate the lack of disciplinary borders in universities where nonprofit and philanthropic studies centers and programs reside. A "nonprofit/philanthropy first philosophy" is prominent which speaks to the centrality of accredited programs having distinctive characteristics unbound from traditional disciplinary homes. According to NACC (2021c) a total of 11 programs representing 10 universities have been accredited since 2019 (see Table 15.5).

TABLE 15.5 NACC-accredited Programs since 2019

(All accredited in 2019 except where noted)	
Arizona State University	Bachelor of Science in Nonprofit Leadership & Management (2020)
	Master of Nonprofit Leadership and Management
Case Western Reserve University	Master of Nonprofit Organizations
Grand Valley State University	Master of Philanthropy and Nonprofit Leadership
Louisiana State University Shreveport	Master of Science in Nonprofit Administration
University of Oregon	Master of Nonprofit Management
Regis University	Master of Nonprofit Management
Seattle University	Master of Nonprofit Leadership
City, University of London	Charities Master Programme
University of San Diego	Master of Arts in Nonprofit Leadership and Management (2020)
University of San Francisco	Master of Nonprofit Administration
University of Wisconsin Milwaukee	Master of Science in Nonprofit Management and Leadership

Convening Strategies

NACC's role as a boundary-spanning convener was cemented in 2011 with the BenchMark 3.5 Conference on Nonprofit and Philanthropic Studies, held in San Diego, CA. This was the first large-scale conference of academics and practitioners whereby NACC was positioned as a national and global convening leader. The conference was built on the history of three decennial conferences of the field held in 1986, 1996, and 2006, each described as "benchmarks" for the field of nonprofit management education.

The 2006 Benchmark 3.0 Conference was organized by leaders from Arizona State University, and held in Tempe, AZ, USA. The two prior decennial conferences held in 1986 and 1996 were organized by leaders from the University of San Francisco. It was during the 2006 conference that attendees suggested not waiting ten more years for another "Benchmark" conference given the rapid growth of the field occurring each year. Thus, the 2011 conference was launched thanks to funding from a WKKF grant to Arizona State University that was then sub-granted as a "hand-off" investment to NACC. The idea was that field building through subsequent BenchMark type conferences was best led by NACC as a national/global infrastructure organization. NACC's leadership to this convening strategy was seen as complementary to the annual ARNOVA and bi-annual ISTR conferences. Since the 2011 conference, NACC has used its convening strategy to organize its bi-annual conferences.

A robust body of knowledge emerged from the decennial conferences leading up to and including the 2011 BenchMark 3.5 Conference. These sources are foundational to understanding NACC's subsequent leadership role in convening as detailed by O'Neill and Young (1988), O'Neill and Fletcher (1998), Ashcraft (2007), and Ashcraft & Stone (2012).

Boundary-Spanning Scholarship – *Journal of Nonprofit Education and Leadership (JNEL)*

The history of NACC's support of the *JNEL* is best understood as a boundary-spanning story among practitioners and academics. According to Western Kentucky University (WKU 2021) the Journal began in 1992 as a partnership between AH and the University of Northern Iowa (a campus affiliate of AH at the time). Known as the Journal for Leadership of Youth and Human Services the publication was released periodically until 1997. In June 2009, the AH board of directors voted to approve a formal partnership between AH and the WKU Research Foundation to create the *JNEL*. WKU was an affiliate of AH at that time.

WKU (2021) notes that the guiding philosophy for the journal idea was:

> … to incorporate the research talents of those working in academia along with the talents of nonprofit professionals working primarily in the field.

> While those in academia are more accustomed to submitting articles for potential publication, nonprofit practitioners are not, but each group has important information to share with each other and the profession. This new journal would allow for field practitioners to share best practices through a formal peer-reviewed format.

WKU (2021) also chronicles that JNEL was formally introduced at the Teaching Section Reception, sponsored by American Humanics, during 2009 at the ARNOVA Conference in Cleveland, Ohio. AH rebranded and was renamed the Nonprofit Leadership Alliance. The first issue of the *JNEL* was published in November 2010. In 2013 the publishing partnership between the Nonprofit Leadership Alliance and the WKU Research Foundation concluded. Since 2013, The WKU Research Foundation continues the operation of *JNEL* in partnership with Sagamore Publishing.

NACC formally endorses *JNEL* and the journal has become a significant distribution channel for its conference proceedings and research by scholars of the nonprofit and philanthropic studies field. Several dozen articles and special issues devoted to NACC-related topics, including conference proceedings, are a hallmark of the *JNEL* partnership (WKU, 2021).

Honoring Students of the Field through NACC's Nu Lambda Mu Honor Society – The international Nu Lambda Mu Nonprofit Honor Society was established in 2012 by NACC to recognize graduate students dedicated to the study of nonprofit management, philanthropy, and social entrepreneurship and enterprise. Its mission is to advance the study of nonprofit organizations and their function in society and to promote scholarly achievement among those who engage in these academic pursuits. In 2018, the NACC Board amended its guidelines to include a category for qualified undergraduate students.

Nu Lambda Mu seeks to recognize those who, as part of a degree or certificate program, have excelled in coursework and as leaders to others without regard for the disciplinary unit in which the respective program resides. By encouraging rigorous study in the field of public serving organizations, the Nu Lambda Mu Honor Society promotes the professionalization and ethical conduct of all who pursue careers of service. To date approximately 1,400 students from nearly 60 colleges and universities have been inducted into the Nu Lambda Mu Honor Society.

According to the Arizona State University Lodestar Center for Philanthropy and Nonprofit Innovation (2021) in the first year of its existence, Nu Lambda Mu introduced inductees from: Arizona State University, Baruch College, Bay Path College, DePaul University, Grand Valley State University, Indiana University-Bloomington, Indiana University, Purdue University-Indianapolis, North Park University, Regis University, Seattle University, Texas A&M University, University of Delaware, University of Missouri-St. Louis, University of Notre Dame, University of Oregon, University of San Francisco, University of Southern California, and University of Wisconsin-Milwaukee.

Implications for Higher Education

How the field of nonprofit and philanthropic studies was conceived, incubated, and is currently advanced by NACC may be an interesting story of field building without need for further analysis. However, NACC's story through a transdisciplinary lens holds potential for meaning to those more broadly engaged in leading institutions of higher education. Transdisciplinary design thinking and actions have the potential to successfully ameliorate the effect of forces currently disrupting higher education. As a result, such approaches may help academics in leadership roles to successfully meet institutional aspirations and goals within changing and challenging operating environments.

The effects of the 2020 pandemic have caused disruption to higher education. Yet, as noted by Chamorro-Premuzic & Frankiewicz (2019), Renn (2018), Lynch (2018), and Varvaloucas (2021) the trends of disruption preceded the pandemic and are profoundly affecting most colleges and universities. Such trends include, in part:

- declining enrollments in many universities;
- changing views on the return on investment value proposition of a college education;
- broken financial models threatening institutional sustainability;
- student debt that is rising;
- disconnect between higher education and skills for many jobs;
- declining state support of public universities; and
- innovation in learning modalities (e.g., virtual reality, MOOCs).

Of all the trends, Kak (2018) notes that innovation in learning modalities may result in traditional colleges and universities becoming obsolete. However, eliminating a larger threat to the relevancy and sustainability of colleges and universities is contingent upon their ability to adapt at scale to produce knowledge and solutions in response to societal needs. According to leading academic entrepreneur and president of Arizona State University (ASU), Michael Crow (2015) notes,

> Academic culture has not evolved sufficiently in its ability to mount adequate responses at scale and in real time to the progressively accelerating complexity that marks contemporary life.

To evolve higher education institutions, the traditional notion of discipline-based departmental structures is challenged. Crow (2010) observes,

> Rather than exploring new paradigms for inquiry, academic culture too often restricts its focus to existing organizational models. Perhaps the most obvious symptom of ossification is the perpetuation of the discipline based departmental structure that we now take for granted. Entrenchment in

disciplinary silos undermines our drive to develop formal languages comprehensible to practitioners of other disciplines.

As university leaders adapt their institutions to the changing operating environment, innovators like Crow are emerging. They are reimagining and reorganizing university structures through transdisciplinarity as an organizing principle. Crow is the architect of the "New American University" model that offers eight design aspirations that guide institutional objectives to advance excellence, access and social impact (Table 15.6). A growing literature base about the model includes two books by Crow and Dabars, "Designing the New American University" (2015) and The Fifth Wave: The Evolution of American Higher (2018).

Interestingly, as variations of the New American University model are being adopted, not only in the United States but globally, collaborations are developing across institutions to address societal issues. For example, the University Innovation Alliance, founded in 2014, is a national coalition of 11 leading public research universities committed to increasing the number and diversity of college graduates in the United States. It is through transdisciplinary design that the Alliance enacts its goals based upon the principles of collective impact that include, "establishing a common agenda, shared measurement system, mutually reinforcing activities, continuous communication and a backbone support organization." (Crow, 2015).

The New American University framework and the University Innovation Alliance are but two examples of recent innovations driven by transdisciplinarity that are promising to solve societal problems and to assure a relevant, responsive and sustainable ecosystem of colleges and universities. Lessons learned from the story of NACC, and the history of hundreds of transdisciplinary bridge builders who have shaped the field of nonprofit and philanthropic studies, serve as a prequel for innovative actions required from today's higher education leaders.

TABLE 15.6 Design Aspirations of the New American University Transdisciplinary Model

(Noted by Arizona State University (ASU)-specific context)

- Leverage Our Place (ASU embraces its cultural, socioeconomic and physical setting).
- Transform Society (ASU catalyzes social change by being connected to social needs).
- Value Entrepreneurship (ASU uses its knowledge and encourages innovation).
- Conduct Use-Inspired Research (ASU research has purpose and impact).
- Enable Student Success (ASU is committed to the success of each unique student).
- Fuse Intellectual Disciplines (ASU creates knowledge by transcending academic disciplines).
- Be Socially Embedded (ASU connects with communities through mutually beneficial partnerships).
- Engage Globally (ASU engages with people and issues locally, nationally and international).

Implications for Those Who Lead Nonprofit Academic Centers and Programs

Considering ways to enact transdisciplinary approaches to leading nonprofit academic centers and programs are directly informed by two primary streams of organizational design as revealed in this chapter. The first is to understand the chronology of NACC and its approach to defining and advancing the field(s) of nonprofit and philanthropic studies. From this vantage point, an emphasis on NACC's "Indicators of Quality" standards setting, offers insights for how to enact transdisciplinary approaches that realize successful outcomes for center and program leaders. The second is by considering the evolution of transdisciplinary efforts in higher education as realized by the design aspirations of the New American University model that places a premium on transdisciplinarity as an operating principle.

How might an educational innovator, informed by these two design streams, enact the organizational principles necessary to assure a relevant, impactful and sustainable nonprofit academic center and/or program? The answers are found in a fusion of the streams into a cohesive framework specific to the education, research, and engagement functions of centers and programs within the context of the institutional mission in which they operate.

Using both the NACC's Indicators of Quality frameworks and the Design Aspirations of the New American University Model offer an approach to realize the promise of transdisciplinarity for nonprofit academic centers and programs (Table 15.7).

Academic leaders who advance a NACC inspired center or program adhere to a number of common operating principles as informed by the "Indicators of Quality" framework and the new American University Model of transdisciplinarity. It is posited that as leaders of nonprofit academic centers and programs embrace the following eight NACC inspired principles (associated with the corresponding Design Imperative of the New American University in parentheses), they can achieve enduring relevancy, results, and sustainability.

The introduction of this framework for leaders of nonprofit academic centers and programs offers the overarching operating values emanating from the history of NACC and its transdisciplinary approach to field building, while being informed by the New American University model emerging in higher education. Within each of the design principles, it is acknowledged that additional consideration and inflection points are required to realize the full promise of an NACC-inspired center or program. NACC's "Indicators of Quality" foundational document provides additional insights to help those who operate nonprofit academic centers and programs in colleges and universities (NACC 2006).

Conclusion

The development of nonprofit and philanthropic education is an example of transdisciplinarity. NACC served a vital role as organizer of transdisciplinary leaders

TABLE 15.7 Design Features of NACC-inspired Centers or Programs

These principles affirm the following leadership intentions that:

- Focus on place-based strengths (Leverage our Place)
  - They embrace the cultural, socioeconomic and physical setting in which they exist; they respond to forces and trends in the nonprofit sector and higher education with resolve and in full alignment with their institution's particular mission and purpose.
- Transform communities with intention (Transform Society)
  - They value being connected to community needs by advancing solutions inspired by authentic stakeholder partnerships based upon mutual respect. They facilitate intersections between faculty and stakeholders to advance mutual interests.
- Embrace social innovation and enterprise (Value Entrepreneurship)
  - They are on the leading edge of boundary-spanning thinking and activities by putting knowledge to practice to encourage social value creation. They incubate ideas and test new approaches to the field of practice and scholarly pursuits.
- Conduct solutions-oriented research (Conduct Use-Inspired Research)
  - They promote research involving a community of scholars and pracademics that is relevant and responsive to current issues within the sector, within specific nonprofit organizations and within the larger community.
- Consider learners across a diverse spectrum (Enable Student Success)
  - They inspire and educate the full range of undergraduate, graduate, and professional development learners. Continuing education offerings are deemed essential in meeting learners' needs, complementary to academic degree offerings.
- Seek boundary spanning opportunities (Fuse Intellectual Disciplines)
  - They consider the value of engaging faculty and practitioners across disciplines and across sectors (nonprofit, government and business), affirming the value of scholarly inquiry to inform practice and practice to inform inquiry.
- Place a premium on collaboration and community partnerships (Be Socially Embedded)
  - They honor the value of practitioner engagement in activities and encourages applied research, technical assistance and/or management support to stakeholders while supporting research that builds theory and expands the knowledge base.
- Respond to the diversity of the nonprofit sector (Engage Globally)
  - They consider cross-border and cross-cultural engagement with stakeholders locally, nationally and internationally given increased globalization of issues that transcend single community locales and individual nonprofit types and forms.

and continues to support the field and its institutional members. Its members build bridges between theory and practice, between academics and practitioners, and between higher education and the communities in which they partner. The research, education, and service goals of nonprofit academic centers and programs illuminate transdisciplinary characteristics by enacting key design principles such as genuine community partnerships, use-inspired research, and student-centered education. Educational entrepreneurs who lead nonprofit academic centers and programs in the future will find that using NACC inspired principles to guide decision making is a way to assure relevance, results, and sustainability of their enterprise. Such boundary-spanning intentions fuse theory and practice in ways that produce mutually beneficial results for both society and universities. In doing so, nonprofit academic centers and programs are positioned well as essential enterprises to realize enduring results. Such transdisciplinary approaches may solve complex societal problems while assuring the relevance and sustainability of colleges and universities. As McCgregor and Volckmann (2011) remind us,

> These interconnected, complex problems cannot be solved by disciplines working along within the academy using independent, fragmented, disciplinary-focused knowledge. Their solutions cannot ignore the voices of the people or of merged perspectives. The university can no longer perceive itself as the last bastion of knowledge, especially because that knowledge tends to be siloed in individual disciplines (separate departments, library holdings, conferences, journals and professional associations).

References

Arizona State University Lodestar Center for Philanthropy and Nonprofit Innovation (2021). History of Nu Lambda Mu Honor Society. https://lodestar.asu.edu/content/nu-lambda-mu-honor-society-0.

Ashcraft, R. F., (2001). "Where Nonprofit Management Education Meets the Undergraduate Experience: American Humanics After 50 Years." Public Performance & Management Review, Sage Publications, Vol. 25, No. 1, 42–56.

Ashcraft, R. F. (Ed.) (2007). Benchmark 3: The Third Decennial Conference on Nonprofit and Philanthropic Studies. Nonprofit & Voluntary Sector Quarterly, Supplement vol. 36, no. 4, 55–105, December 2007. Association for Research on Nonprofit Organizations and Voluntary Action.

Ashcraft, R. F. & Stone, M. M. (Eds.) (2012). Special Issue: BenchMark 3.5 Conference on Nonprofit and Philanthropic Studies. Volume 23, Issue 1 Autumn (Fall) 2012, 5–11. Wiley Periodicals, Inc.

Ashcraft, R. F. (2015). The nonprofit academic centers council: Its past and future promises. Journal of Nonprofit Education and Leadership, 5(1), 2–5.

Chamorro-Premuzic, T. & Frankiewicz, B. (2019). 6 Reasons Why Higher Education Needs to Be Disrupted. November 19, 2019. Harvard Business Review. https://hbr.org/2019/11/6-reasons-why-higher-education-needs-to-be-disrupted

Crow, M.M. (2010). Viewpoint: Organizing Teaching and Research to Address the Grand Challenges of Sustainable Development. BioScience, July/August 20210, Vol. 60, No. 7, 488–489.

Crow, M. M. (2015, December 7). The Real Disruptive Force in Higher Education? Collaboration. https://president.asu.edu/read/the-real-disruptive-force-in-higher-education-collaboration

Crow, M.M. & Dabars, W. B. (2015). Designing the New American University. Baltimore, MD: Johns Hopkins University Press.

Crow, M.M. & Dabars, W. B. (2018). The Fifth Wave: The Evolution of American Higher Education. Baltimore, MD: Johns Hopkins University Press.

Crowder, Nancy L. and Virginia A. Hodgkinson. (1991). Academic Centers and Programs Focusing on the Study of Philanthropy, Voluntarism, and Not-for-Profit Activity: A Progress Report. Washington, D.C.: Independent Sector.

Evans, (2014, July 29). What is Transdisciplinarity? Purdue University Polytech Institute. https://polytechnic.purdue.edu/blog/what-transdisciplinarity

Fox, (2017, August 17). NACC Votes for Accreditation of Nonprofit and Philanthropic Academic Programs: An interview with the two co-chairs of the NACC Task Force on Accreditation: current NACC president Matthew Hale of Seton Hall University, and NACC president-elect Renee Irvin of the University of Oregon. Nonprofit Quarterly. https://nonprofitquarterly.org/nacc-votes-accreditation-program-academic-degrees-nonprofit-philanthropic-studies/

Heidrich, Katheryn W., and Robert F. Long. (2002). *The Story of the Building Bridges Initiative.* W.K. Kellogg Foundation. https://lodestar.asu.edu/sites/default/files/kellogg_building_bridges.pdf found on 2/28/2022

Kak, S. (2018, January 10). Will Traditional Colleges and Universities Become Obsolete? Smithsonian Magazine. https://smithsonianmag.com/innovation/will-traditional-colleges-universities-become-obsolete-180967788/

Lang DJ, Wiek A, Bergmann M et al. (2012) Transdisciplinary research in sustainability science: practice, principles, and challenges. Sustain Sci 7(1), 25–43

Larson, R. S., & Barnes-Moorhead, S. (2001). How academic centers work: Building and sustaining academic nonprofit centers. W.K. Kellogg Foundation. www.diffusionassociates.com/pdfs/centers.pdf

Long, R. F. (2010). Michael O'Neill – An interview with a father of nonprofit education and leadership. Journal of Nonprofit Education and Leadership, 1(1), 3–10.

Lynch, M. (2018, January 3). 5 Trends Disrupting Higher Education. The Edvocate. https://theedadvocate.org/5-trends-disrupting-higher-education/

McGregor, S. L.T., & Volckmann, R. (2011). Synopsis of Integral Leadership Review's Series on Transdisciplinarity in Higher Education. Transdisciplinarity in Higher Education, Part 7: Conclusion Integral Leadership Review, 11(7), http://integralleadershipreview.com/2630-transdisciplinarity-in-higher-education-part-7/

Mendel, S. C. (2015). Nonprofit first: The promise and potential of the Nonprofit Academic Centers Council. Journal of Nonprofit Education and Leadership, 5(1), 30–36.

NACC (2006). In pursuit of excellence: Indicators of quality in nonprofit academic centers. Nonprofit Academic Centers Council.

NACC (2015) Curricular Guidelines. Nonprofit Academic Centers Council.

NACC (2021a). Membership guidelines. Nonprofit Academic Centers Council. http://nonprofit-academic-centers-council.org/membership/membership-criteria-and-process/

NACC (2021b) Accreditation Guidelines. Nonprofit Academic Centers Council. http://nonprofit-academic-centers-council.org/accreditation/

NACC (2021c) Accredited programs since 2019. Nonprofit Academic Centers Council. http://nonprofit-academic-centers-council.org/accreditation/nacc-accredited-programs/

Nonprofit Leadership Alliance. (2021). https://nla1.org/

O'Neill, M., & Young, D. R. (Eds.). (1988). Educating managers of nonprofit organizations. Praeger.

O'Neill, M., & Fletcher, K. (Eds.). (1998). Nonprofit management education: U.S. and world perspectives. Praeger.

Petrie, Hugh G., Interdisciplinary Education: Are We Faced with Insurmountable Opportunities?, Review of Research in Education, Vol. 18 (1992), pp. 299–333, American Educational Research Association, Stable URL: http://jstor.org/stable/1167302.

Renn, A. (2018, May 29). 6 Forces Disrupting Higher Education. Urbanophile. https://urbanophile.com/2018/05/29/6-forces-disrupting-higher-education.

Rigolot, C. Transdisciplinarity as a discipline and a way of being: complementarities and creative tensions. Humanit Soc Sci Commun 7, 100 (2020). https://doi.org/10.1057/s41599-020-00598-5.

Rooney, P.M & Burlingame, D.F. (2020). Build It and They Will Come! Or, Built to Last? Key Challenges and Insights into the Sustainability of Nonprofit and Philanthropy Programs and Centers, Journal of Nonprofit Education and Leadership, 10(4), 414–428.

Russell, A. Wendy, Wickson, Fern, Carew, Anna L., Transdisciplinarity: Context, contradictions and capacity, Science Direct Futures 40(2008), 460–472, *Elsevier*, Stable URL: http://sciencedirect.com/science/article/pii/S0016328707001541.

Scholz RW, Steiner G (2015) The real type and ideal type of transdisciplinary processes: part II – what constraints and obstacles do we meet in practice? Sustain Sci 10(4), 653–671.

Varvaloucas, E. (2021, April 29). Brave New World: The Next Wave of Higher Education. The Progress Network. https://theprogressnetwork.org/disrupting-higher-ed/

Western Kentucky University (2021). History of the Journal of Nonprofit Education and Leadership. https://digitalcommons.wku.edu/jnel/history.html

Young, D. R. (2021, June). Once Upon a Time. NACC News. Nonprofit Academic Centers Council. Retrieved from http://nonprofit-academic-centers-council.org/news/

16

INTEGRATING NONPROFIT LEADERSHIP, SOCIAL INNOVATION, AND PHILANTHROPY EDUCATION ACROSS CAMPUS

Nathan Dietz, Katlin Gray, and Robert T. Grimm, Jr.

Introduction

While leaving a campus dining hall at the end of the night, a group of University of Maryland students noticed pounds of good food being thrown away. A lightbulb went off. They came up with an idea to collect and donate the leftover dining hall food to local food banks. Within a few years, the students transformed their original campus group into a multi-campus, student-run nonprofit organization that recovered thousands of pounds of uneaten food that would have otherwise been thrown away. Within 6 years, they operated on 229 campuses across the country and recovered more than two million pounds of food.

The ability of this multidisciplinary student group to become the country's largest student movement against food waste in America (the Food Recovery Network) evolved within a campus-wide social impact ecosystem. For decades, nonprofit education scholarship revolved around the question of whether there is an ideal place to focus its curriculum at a university (Mirabella & Wish, 2000). Would nonprofit academic programs and centers be better off if they anchored and focused their work through (e.g.) a school of Business, Public Administration, or Social Work? While that debate continues, it underscores that a campus-wide approach is atypical of how nonprofit academic centers and programs on nonprofits historically develop.

A recent series on "The Future of Social Impact Education in Business Schools and Beyond" in the *Stanford Social Innovation Review* argues that most universities approach social impact education quite narrowly. When a university social impact center breaks from this mold and tries to reach across campus, the efforts are characterized as "stretched thin." The series puts forward important questions for the future of nonprofit education: How can social impact education be opened to

DOI: 10.4324/9781003294061-17

a broader, more diverse population? How can we disrupt the traditional way social impact education is conducted?

Nonprofit education could be a part of the curriculum of every college, school, and major because people from engineers to teachers find themselves working for nonprofits and engaging with them to make an impact. The most recent data from the Higher Education Research Institute (HERI) suggest that student demand for social impact education has reached historical highs in the last decade. In 2019, 80% of first-year college students stated that helping others who are in difficulty is an "essential" or "important" objective, while 43.1% say the same about becoming a community leader (Stolzenberg et al., 2020). In this chapter, we look at what it takes to start and build a campus-wide educational effort focused on social impact, nonprofit leadership, and philanthropy. Through our experience building the University of Maryland's campus-wide efforts into the Do Good Institute and interviews with eight other universities leading campus-wide educational endeavors,[1] we identify key areas and lessons that could guide others who aspire to build a campus-wide program in the broad field of nonprofit and social impact education.

The key lessons in this chapter revolve around different stages. In the early years, it is important to exhibit an academic entrepreneur mindset. You often need to focus on building early success that hint at your potential impact and growth opportunities, begin to build relationships that break through traditional campus silos, hone your communications and educate the campus community and others about this field, and identify campus cultures, histories, or trends that could augment your efforts. As you pivot to developing a larger enterprise, campus-wide efforts need to identify and expand a value proposition that builds on your institution's incentive structures, engage students of all backgrounds, continue breaking through the usual campus silos through relationship building, and establish a long-term, sustainable approach.

Locating the Center Within the University

The positionality and location of nonprofit management education programs has been a longstanding debate among scholars, practitioners, and administrators alike.[2] Some programs are housed within particular schools or colleges – Public Administration, Public Policy, Business, Social Work – while others are situated in interdisciplinary or professional studies. The "best place" debate often focuses on the location and administration of credit-bearing degrees (Masters in Business Administration, Masters in Public Administration, Masters in Public Policy, Masters in Social Work) and certificates for executive, graduate, and undergraduate education.

Ultimately, nonprofit studies may require the administrative structure of an academic school or department to grant degrees and certificates. But what is missed in these discussions is the placement of the centers, offices, and initiatives that may not confer degrees yet still play a significant role in serving as champions, sponsors, and purveyors of nonprofit education. The focus areas of these types of centers may include social innovation, social impact, community service, civic engagement, philanthropy, and social entrepreneurship. Since these centers may not be degree-granting, their location can be flexible and varied – some are housed within schools or colleges, Student Life, the Provost or President's Office, or even act as stand-alone initiatives with multiple affiliations. Many of the centers included in this chapter are representative of this type of diversity in focus area and location.

A majority of the directors interviewed for this chapter discussed the ways in which center location ultimately affects exposure, management, clout, and campus-wide reception. Despite its status as a centralized entity within the (large, private) university's administrative structure, Director 1 described his center as the campus' "best-kept secret" because of its popularity with devoted supporters but general anonymity across the broader campus community. In some cases, centers are housed within academic units yet have campus-wide reach and expectations. As one example, the University of Maryland's Do Good Institute is situated within the School of Public Policy but serves as the university's wheelhouse for nonprofit leadership and management education. This location within the school, coupled with the campus-wide reach and influence of the Institute, has provided unique opportunities for the teaching and practice of social impact and social innovation both within and outside of the public policy discipline. Similarly, other directors were able to expand their center's presence and reach from within a single school.

The juxtaposition of centers functioning as campus-wide but administered as school-bound can present difficulties for management and expectations. Some interviewees discussed the challenges involved with managing an initiative that serves the broader university while still being responsible or beholden to the leadership, expectations, or operational structure of the school or college in which the center is headquartered. Director 2, from a large public university, described the tensions in being recruited to run a center struggling to launch from within a college of arts and sciences but whose funders had university-wide aspirations for the center's scope. Some centers have been purposely created by administrators or funders to have a university-wide presence. This type of stature, recognized and established by university leadership, affords a level of influence. Director 3, whose school was created by trustees to oversee civic engagement for the entire (large, private) university, discussed the advantages of having "a dean who is on the same footing with the other deans of the schools" (January 2021). Director 4, from a large, public university, explained how the motivation behind their office flowed directly from the university's original intent. Because social innovation had been part of "the core of the university from day one," Director 4's position was created by state funding to coordinate the work of every university entity that works in areas related to social innovation (January 2021). For the Do Good Institute, the campus-wide scope of its work and activities was endorsed and launched by the university president with its status as one of the few university institutes (In Maryland's academic terminology, there are many centers but few Institutes). In another case, a task force recommended the creation of a campus-wide center devoted to entrepreneurship. Despite its location outside of the business school of the large, private university, Director 5 still needed to overcome the association of the term "entrepreneurship" with the image of "avaricious Mark Zuckerbergs walking around" (January 2021). For some, these ideological, disciplinary boundaries were irrelevant. Director 6 discussed the benefits of being located at a large, public university where many of the units have been designed to be interdisciplinary: crossing school boundaries is easier since the silos had already been purposely broken down.

Regardless of positioning, these centers offer an important lesson that is discussed in the remaining sections of this chapter: campus-wide education for nonprofit education, social impact, and philanthropy can be successful in spite of (or perhaps due to) location. Aspiring campus-wide efforts will need to consider the opportunities and limitations different locations present. In some cases, decisions may be predetermined or guided by university leadership, donors, or external groups but it is our experience that the founders and leaders of these efforts can also influence placement.

Diversifying and Building Funding Sources

Reliable funding is one of the most important determinants of stability for any new initiative, especially in higher education.[3] In many instances (though not all), colleges and schools offering nonprofit education operate within institutions where tuition revenue is based directly or partially on enrollment numbers and program popularity within a specific academic unit. Similarly, most higher education revenue sources tend to be organized and siloed within a specific academic unit (such as a department, school, or college). This reality often creates disincentives to advancing nonprofit education across an entire campus or even outside one college due to concerns over competition or loss of revenue. In our interviews and our own experience, philanthropy often plays a starring role in breaking through such university silos and serving as a catalytic revenue source to enable campus-wide education. Philanthropic gifts can offer a level of independence that can help a nascent effort build early accomplishments and garner more support.

The scope and strategies of any educational effort will ultimately be influenced by the university's predetermined financial incentive structures. Several interviewees discussed important differences between whether a center is funded from a single administrative pot or has revenues flowing from a number of sources. For Director 2, the main challenge was "understanding how much independence you would have [and] how much gets carved out for various fees from the philanthropic contributions [and] getting clarity on that" (January 2021). Having a clear understanding of the expectations and disbursements surrounding funding is important for clarifying how much margin or sphere of influence a center may have. At many institutions, inter-school and inter-department conflict over tuition revenues led directors to pursue other sources of funding – especially earned income from providing services to clients or stakeholders. Director 3 described how grants and contracts, especially for research projects, ended up driving much of the center's work and its personnel's responsibilities. At other institutions, centers needed to overcome institutional resistance to receiving certain funding sources. Director 1, whose university has a significant endowment, discussed the stigma of receiving grants from national service programs. Some of the university's leaders felt that the university should not siphon these federal funds away from institutions with greater need.

Ultimately, funding sources and types will have reverberating implications on the center's decisions, activities, and reputation.

While many centers seek out earned revenue, philanthropic support from individuals and foundations were much more common. Although directors stressed observing the rules of the road (namely, as Director 2 put it, "you only go after prospects you're allowed to go after"), many attributed the success of their centers to the productive and supportive relationships they formed early on with their major donors. Philanthropy played a key role in providing over $100,000 annually for start-up efforts that ultimately became (six years later) the Do Good Institute. These operating dollars enabled us to launch experiential philanthropy courses with grants to local nonprofits, nonprofit management graduate courses, and subsidize a faculty appointment. Our first hands-on "Art and Science of Philanthropy" undergraduate courses culminated in a grant ceremony during the final exam. We recruited deans from across the campus, donors and prospective donors, foundation leaders, and other campus and external partners to attend. We recruited media including the Washington Post to profile it. The student work showcased during the event offered opportunities to further advance stewardship and partnership. After one ceremony, our Dean of Undergraduate Studies offered more than $50,000 a year to collaborate on the creation of a new living-learning program for first-year students focused on nonprofits and social change.

The strategic use of philanthropic resources to bolster more university support and flexibility is a theme in our interviews. Director 7, from a large, private university, arranged for a major gift to be paid out over 20 years. This placed pressure on the university's leadership to sustain the investment as a good-faith demonstration of the value of the center. Director 5 described how a mix of funding support from the university – annual funding, "straight out of the operating budget" and funding commitments from alumni – keeps the center from being "beholden to any individual school or any individual funding agency to do their bidding" (January 2021). Director 6 succinctly summarized the value (and costs) of diverse funding by saying, "There are ways that we can control our destiny that a fully state-funded unit never could. It allows us to be nimble" (January 2021).

Maximizing and leveraging initial philanthropic funding to build early successes can create pathways for campus-wide educational efforts to build long-standing and generative relationships. Ultimately, directors acknowledged the opportunities afforded by reducing dependency on select funding sources (particularly those from university administrators or tuition) and diversifying income from others (especially donors). Each funding source, depending on university and school policies, may have stipulations that can limit the growth of a campus-wide educational effort. In our experience, as was the case for many centers, philanthropic support provides the independence and flexibility that enables, not stifles, expansion across campus. We also want to emphasize that a significant million-dollar-plus gift is not required upfront: seed gifts used strategically can result in cascading outcomes and growth. Within a decade, seed gifts enabled us to raise other gifts that created four faculty endowments and multiple endowments for the Institute, which created an annual financial base of support for our campus-wide efforts. Keeping in mind both of these key lessons (diversification and startup funding) can ultimately lay the groundwork for creating a stable funding structure.

Garnering Support from University Leadership

Any successful academic enterprise needs to have support from the leadership of the school where the center is located and, ultimately, from university leadership if the goal is to operate campus-wide.[4] While building relationships and buy-in with philanthropic funders, a center's team can garner widespread support from the campus community by serving as an advocate and evangelist for a campus-wide effort.

Administrators of academic nonprofit education programs often find the need to educate institutional leaders (alongside students and faculty) about the value and function of the sector and their work. Director 2 recounted the trouble she faced in generating interest in a nonprofit minor: "They think it's going to lower their rankings because [the students are] going to get paid so little – that [the nonprofit sector] is where you go when you can't find a job anywhere else" (January 2021). She launched a successful marketing campaign involving an interactive, campus-wide scavenger hunt to debunk the myths of nonprofits. Working with advisors from each school, she was able to bolster the minor's enrollments by presenting it as a valuable supplement to departmental majors. Beyond educating the campus about the nonprofit sector, this effort raised the institute's profile and notoriety across the university. Other times, the center struggles to get leadership to recognize the value of their work. Director 3 reflected that his center (which is widely renowned for its research and thought leadership) was known on campus as "sort of a graft together of … a service center…and sticking it together with a think tank" (January 2021). As a result, the director faced initial skepticism from leaders of other schools and central administration around the quality of the center's academic contributions. Eventually, he was able to build a support network that included more than 100 faculty members across campus with allied interests. In both cases, these directors needed to make strategic maneuvers to establish a foundational, baseline understanding and buy-in "at home" before scaling and growing their work.

Leadership turnover is a reality in any large organization, and turnover at senior leadership levels can disrupt or accelerate the progress of campus-wide educational efforts. Conversely, the support of long-haulers at the institutional and school level can strengthen the center's efforts. Most of the directors underscored how leadership change played a role in the management of their centers and could introduce more instability. Director 7 discussed the challenges of introducing new campus leaders to the center's activities and institutional placement. She noted that new leaders sometimes "have a whole new view of what my job is," and may not understand the rationale behind long-standing institutional arrangements – for instance, that the center is located in the provost's office because the original funders expressed that preference (January 2021). Perhaps more rarely, the stable presence of a visionary and supportive leader can play a pivotal role in the center's potential success and growth. Director 6 credited the university's president with making entrepreneurship an institutional priority. This placed the center – a hub for projects involving the nonprofit sector and social innovation – in a place of prominence with the president and provost often pointing interested parties toward its expertise. Such support from the highest levels of leadership strengthens one's reputation without forcing the director to guard their turf: "And if you try to do that, first of all, it builds a silo that won't work, and secondly, suddenly all the opportunities you might have for collaboration, it becomes competition rather than collaboration" (January 2021). At the University of Maryland, the university's leadership as well as the trustees became valuable supporters. Over the last 10+ years, university leaders made regular appearances at major events and ensured campus-wide communications featured our efforts. Changes, transitions, and presence (or lack thereof) in university presidents, chancellors, provosts, deans, and others have the potential to impact the success of campus-wide efforts, no matter the size of the institution.

Here, the key lesson is that launching and sustaining a successful campus-wide educational effort without supportive university leadership can slow or hamper progress toward growing nonprofit education, social impact, and social innovation across a university. Aspiring center directors should be ready to educate, inform, and convince new and long-term university and school leaders of the center's value proposition – this will be critical in securing their endorsement, or, at the very least, acceptance. Still, university leadership alone may not guarantee success – some institutional cultures may resist a "top-down" approach of galvanizing or integrating nonprofit education across campus. Support from university and school leadership may be a supporting pillar, rather than a driving force for execution.

Fitting into the Culture of the University

Scaling nonprofit and social impact education campus-wide means breaking disciplinary boundaries that might otherwise keep these efforts stationary when headquartered in particular academic units. This level of expansion requires leaders of such efforts to identify, honor, and build on one's institutional history, culture, and trends in ways that may not have otherwise been required within the confines of a particular department. In many cases, this culture is aligned with an affinity or opposition with specific terminology, ideology, and values (such as the naming of or practice of particular pedagogies, approaches, and scholarship).

At a number of universities, commitment to community engagement has deep historical roots and is a fundamental element of the institution's mission and values.[5] This type of charge is often embedded into public, land-grant universities with expectations that research and teaching will also serve the public good (namely, extension work). At one major university, a commitment to social innovation dates back almost 200 years. While social innovation had been infused throughout the campus, it was heavily decentralized – "many flowers and very few gardens," in the evocative language of Director 4 (January 2021). In an effort to better coordinate and organize the existing work happening, the state government challenged the institution's tendency for decentralization by establishing a pan-campus center for social innovation.

Some directors of campus-wide initiatives described how they were able to change the university's culture through strategic communications – namely, purposeful language choices. Director 8, who works at a large, public state school, described the use of the term "public engagement" as a way to describe the role that community engagement plays in the university's mission. According to them, this change was mandated from the top levels of leadership: "Ultimately, the board of regents adopted the term, public engagement, as a formalized term to distinguish it from outreach, with clear focus on research, teaching, and outreach as embeddedness with communities across all parts of our mission" (January 2021). Director 8 went on to explain that the term signifies that public engagement "would be integrated, not be separate from research and teaching, but actually be a facilitator of strategy for achieving our research goals and our teaching goals." Director 5 noted that the term "entrepreneurship" invoked images of plutocrats with no social conscience:

> What I realized pretty quickly is that, if I wanted to get acceptance of this across the campus, I needed to create programs that were meaningful for the entire campus... It became obvious to me that I needed to tailor the program to meet the needs of the university, changing the terminology that we used.
>
> *January 2021*

Intentional and inclusive terminology can offer easier entry points for fields and disciplines that may otherwise have steered clear of a burgeoning campus-wide effort.

Another university center relies heavily on a set of public, published values and principles that guide the design and implementation of service programs. These values set the expectations for students, faculty, and community partners for engaging in service ethically and effectively. The center also uses the principles to design its evaluation strategy by collecting data (from both students and community partners) to determine the extent students fulfill these principles while performing service. In recent years, the university's commitment to engaged education and community-based learning translated into a recurring campus-wide assessment of all undergraduate education. According to Director 1, the assessment report's emphasis on this topic was a clear signal from university leadership that the center should expand and institutionalize its work around community service programs. Making explicit the beliefs and ideals of a campus-wide initiative can open opportunities to find common ground with the culture of the university and find shared values with potential partners.

New campus-wide initiatives should carefully consider the culture of the university – its historical formation, geographic location, student population, disciplinary reputation, and key activities – should inform how campus-wide educational efforts are presented and portrayed to the broader campus community. In our interviews, a key lesson was the importance of communications, language, and values. Even minute differences in language (such as moving away from entrepreneurship toward innovation or from nonprofit management to social impact) can drastically impact campus-wide reception. These changes in terminology can also more broadly appeal to a wider array of students who may not affiliate themselves with 'nonprofit studies' but do identify with terms and concepts that hail from the sector. Nonprofit education offers ripe multidisciplinary possibilities if presented with the campus culture and language in mind.

Breaking Down Silos

As our discussion on funding emphasized, administrative and financial structures of institutions can discourage, often even undermine, robust multi-disciplinary and interdisciplinary collaboration.[6] In order to operate campus-wide, a center will need to build effective and productive relationships both within and outside the university. Leaders will need to present a compelling value proposition that is attractive to potential campus partners: one that suggests collaboration across departments and disciplines can be mutually beneficial. Doing so will mean contending with systems that act as deterrents and maximizing those that act as catalysts.

For colleges and schools that rely on tuition as the primary source of revenue, any proposition that encourages students to venture outside of school boundaries is a direct hit to the bottom line. As Director 6 argues,

> What incentive is there for one college to, you know, cross list with another on site? I mean, it really disincentivizes collaboration. And it just does. And

> yet at a faculty level, people do good work…But you hit the administration level…the deans are fighting it out, absolutely.
>
> *January 2021*

Director 3 observed that other deans criticized his own center's financial arrangements with the provost's office since, "We don't get any tuition money. We are excused from paying most of the regular overhead that an entity would have to pay, which actually causes tension" (January 2021). Conversely, the fact that another center operates outside the colleges and schools in their institution means they are not viewed as a competitor for scarce resources. As Director 7 emphasized, "nobody would have worked with me" had they seen her center as competition (January 2021). It is critical for leaders with campus-wide aspirations to recognize and navigate their institution's financial incentive systems in ways that enhance the motivation to collaborate and reduce the hesitations of potential partners.

To grow nonprofit education across campus and disciplines, centers should consider how nonprofit and social impact education can manifest itself within a discipline, not just alongside. At the University of Maryland, one approach we took focused on honoring and amplifying the unique disciplinary expertise that each partner brought. We have worked to embed nonprofit education in such diverse academic disciplines as engineering and communications. The "Oral Communications: Principles and Practices" courses in the College of Arts and Humanities and the Gemstone living-learning program in Honors College provide two examples of this approach, which we discuss below.

The "Oral Communications: Principles and Practice" course is a General Education requirement at the University of Maryland. The partnership between the Institute and the Oral Communication Program began with gathering interested instructors in small faculty learning communities to discuss the ways in which social change and civic engagement were already manifesting in the communications field. This later evolved into piloting ten sections of the course with an experiential philanthropy exercise based around two existing, required assignments: an informative and persuasive presentation. Students selected a social issue about which to inform their classmates and then selected a nonprofit addressing that issue. In the persuasive speech, students had to convince their classmates that their section's philanthropic donation, underwritten by the Do Good Institute, should go to their chosen nonprofit. In this instance, the Institute did not direct students away or toward any particular school or college. Instead, we worked within existing curriculum requirements and with departments on where and how nonprofits, philanthropy, and social change were already distinct subfields within their disciplines and provided opportunities to strengthen and amplify those existing connections.

Similarly, Gemstone is University of Maryland's Honors College's only 4-year living-learning program. Under the guidance of faculty mentors and Gemstone staff, student teams design, direct and conduct significant research to explore the interdependence of science and technology with society. After engaging with the Institute through a two-year faculty fellows program, the Gemstone team revamped its curriculum to include social innovation and social impact into its first-year seminar. Now, conversations around research as "doing good" and social innovation are woven throughout the entire 4-year curriculum. In their junior year, students present their research progress during a junior colloquium. One criteria for learning assessments students must address is: "How is your research addressing an urgent societal issue?" Increasingly, students have demonstrated greater self-awareness of how research in biological sciences, engineering, technology, and more can be levers for social change. Recent projects range from reducing food waste through the development or improvement of food packaging techniques to the testing and development of an autonomous bicycle to assist in the redistribution of bicycles used in a bike sharing program.

When centers are located within a central administrative unit of the university, rather than a school, they may have even greater responsibility (and expectation) for coordinating activities and fostering collaboration. Director 1 used the term "de-centering the center" to describe the work involved in building collaborative networks across campus and throughout the community. One center, located within the provost's office, coordinates throughout a multi-campus university system. The center's director discussed work that takes place within individual neighborhoods ("engagement zones") and work to address a specific need ("issue area networks"). Often, the center's most pressing need is to collect information about activities within these zones and networks. Finding opportunities to build on the inherent collective knowledge and resources of the campus community often becomes an important step in building strong relationships and then partnerships.

Ultimately, a key lesson in breaking silos will be for campus-wide initiatives to identify and bolster the existing resources across the campus community. Trying to combat or disrupt the existing organizational structures of an institution will likely be fruitless. Indeed, leaders should acknowledge the realities and implications of the system they are in, but shift attention toward finding points of collaboration that can flourish and thrive. Doing so may mean searching for opportunities to share credit for the success of collaborative enterprises. In some cases, it may mean taking no explicit credit at all. In our experience, the most successful collaborations for breaking silos can involve co-creation, not co-opting; spotlighting, not self-centering.

Building University–Community Relationships

Experiential education, particularly service-learning, is a pedagogical approach that has garnered widespread support at universities across the United States. Research demonstrates that students participating in service-learning show gains in academic performance, civic engagement, and social skills (Celio, 2011). Of the eight universities whose center directors we interviewed for this chapter, six have acquired Elective Classifications for Community Engagement from the Carnegie Foundation. This classification signifies the institution's commitment to improving the educational effectiveness of the campus through the institutionalization of community engagement (Campus Compact, 2014). Community engagement initiatives – service-learning, community-based participatory research, pro bono consulting assistance, or collaborative partnerships – can be an effective way for nonprofit education to manifest itself within curricular and cocurricular settings across the campus.[7]

When done effectively, reciprocal and integrative service-learning opportunities can strengthen the relationship between an institution and its surrounding community while providing valuable experiences to students. Director 2 recounted that her center, with the assistance of an advisory board of allied faculty members, was able to create service-learning opportunities with local nonprofits. Over time, the local organizations benefited at least as much as the students from these arrangements:

> it really was maybe even a stronger value proposition for the nonprofit to be involved with our students than the students. I mean, it was win-win, but we just had this really strong emphasis on being a resource for these nonprofits, a true resource.
>
> *January 2021*

Director 1 described an innovative strategy that combined fundraising with community outreach. The center raised funds from local philanthropists to support dedicated service-learning projects for students with local organizations, which resulted in necessary funding for the service opportunities as well as increased community awareness of the center's programming. These types of hands-on experiences are particularly valuable for students in nonprofit studies but can also serve as entry-points for students outside of nonprofit studies. Active learning opportunities can attract students seeking to make an impact and apply their skills – students who did not intentionally seek out nonprofit education may still benefit from nonprofit education through campus-wide offerings.

Expectations from university leadership can subsequently influence how a campus-wide effort interacts with the community and thereby set the tone and tenor for any public engagement efforts. Director 8 explained how the motivations of the last three university presidents influenced this dynamic. The first president in the director's tenure was motivated by

> this notion of institutional transformation, that this is about building a different kind of university that's going to be engaged and addressing

> societal needs and not just doing work inwardly, you know, the ivory tower kind of thing, you know, shedding that whole image.

The second president placed more emphasis on publicizing the positive community contributions made by the university to "elevate the prestige and the look of the university." The third president is motivated primarily by the desire to provide meaningful experiences for students:

> And this current president is very keen on having our students succeed, about the diversity of our student body, giving students experiential learning opportunities that really engage them, build their sense of belonging. And so the engagement work is about how do we use engagement to help our students get connected to their communities.

These different goals – from serving the public, to promoting the institution's reputation, to engaging the student body – can drastically shift the tone and tenor of community engagement efforts and relationships.

Community engagement can offer a multitude of benefits for institutions and organizations. One that may be of particular interest to aspiring campus-wide centers is that it provides hand-on, experiential learning opportunities for students. These experiential learning opportunities can be a big attractor for students across disciplines and be an effective strategy for delivering nonprofit education outside the boundaries of a school or college. Leaders will need to be cognizant of the history and culture surrounding university-community relationships. In some cases, institution relationships are strong, reciprocal, and mutually beneficial – in others, town and gown divides persist. Any community engagement effort will need to be pursued with careful consideration of these dynamics. Director 3 summarized the main objective as:

> You have to figure out what your geographical community is, and then own it. Not own it, because it is not your community, but own it respectfully. Be clear about what your community is and match that to your institutional mission.
>
> *January 2021*

Attracting and Retaining Faculty Support

Building a successful campus-wide effort requires gathering widespread support from various stakeholders across and outside of the university. Earlier, we discussed the importance of relationships with philanthropic donors as well as university leaders and officials. Faculty of all backgrounds are another key constituency.[8] As with any stakeholder, it is important to consider the right incentives that will encourage interest and engagement with the initiative. Two areas worth considering for faculty engagement are including community engagement in the faculty review process, and using grants and other opportunities to support faculty research.

One challenge interviewees discussed is that many faculty are evaluated on three main functions: producing research, teaching classes, and providing service to the department. Unless initiatives are related to or support one of these three areas, faculty may be cautious about becoming involved. Director 8 discussed how his university made headway in allowing faculty members to discuss their public engagement work on progress reports reviewed during the promotion and tenure process. While public engagement doesn't receive the same weight as research, teaching, or service, it still counts:

> Every department needed to address the notion of public community engagement in their review of faculty. So it doesn't mean every faculty member has to do it. Or this work will be recognized and supported equally as it is in research and other kinds of. So it's basically an inducement and encouragement incentive for faculty to think about it. Those who do this work are not going to be held to a lower standard, for example, so it's not just about being seen as service, but when I fill out my faculty portfolio, the way it is, I have to list my grants. And then it says, did this have a public engagement component? And please describe.

In other cases, finding opportunities to provide benefits, resources, and status directly to the faculty member upfront can create buy-in. In the early days of the center led by Director 2, research grants were provided to affiliated faculty members. Some faculty members were disappointed when the grants were discontinued, but as the center grew, it was able to regain their support by offering new research and outreach opportunities (and later, by reinstating the research grants). As Director 7 observed, appealing to individual faculty members within a school which perceives the campus-wide center as a rival can help to neutralize opposition from the leaders of those schools. These strong partnerships can also open doors to broader collaboration after leadership changes within those schools.

Making a compelling value proposition for faculty means demonstrating how engagement with a campus-wide effort can directly support their particular interest and needs. As with many parts of the university landscape, this involves recognizing the incentive systems inherent to the university. These systems can run the risk of disincentivizing participation so leaders may need to find ways to use that system or find alternative points for engagement.

Engaging and Activating Students

One of the main objectives of any university is the education and development of its students. A campus-wide effort needs to have opportunities, whether inside or outside the classroom, to engage students.[9] Director 5 summarized his prioritization on educational outcomes by noting that

> we evaluate ourselves as teachers, not as incubators. Over the long haul, our goal is to positively impact the lives of as many of our students as possible. The president of the university and I agreed that our goal was not to create the next Tesla but to create more innovative students better prepared to go out in the world.
>
> *January 2021*

Centers for nonprofit education, social impact, and social innovation can attract and appeal to a diverse range of students when they focus across the campus. Centers can develop opportunities to provide depth for students already interested in the nonprofit field and offer experiences that might attract students not initially inclined toward nonprofit education.

Many interviewees noted that even when institutions support and prioritize a campus-wide effort's focus on public engagement, only particular subsets of students may take advantage of the available opportunities. Director 1, who leads a university-wide center, referred to three groups of students: "green light" students, who seemingly enrolled at the university because of the center's offerings; "yellow light" students, who need some encouragement to become active participants; and "red light" students, who have no time, energy, or apparent interest in active engagement. The director went on to describe a "networked approach" – which shows students the benefits of public service careers and provides service opportunities throughout and beyond their college careers – as the most effective method of moving students toward increased participation. The director noted that student demand for service experiences is triggered by the orientation message his center delivers to new students:

> You're going to have your eyes opened to a lot of problems throughout your college experience, and we want you to think about your college experience, not just as a ticket to better employment, but actually as how you're going to be making important contributions to society.

Directors talked about a number of reasons why some students are disengaged or uninterested in participating in civic life. Director 3 said of the "really engaged students" that "they do have a certain profile. They tend to be activists" (January 2021). The presence of these activist students, in the director's opinion, can depress participation among students right of center on the political spectrum. Director 8 pointed out that non-participating students tend to have excessive responsibilities, such as long commutes to campus, family obligations, or job responsibilities, that occupy the time they would have spent being actively engaged at school.

Where possible, several directors took steps to design opportunities for non-traditional undergraduate students to encourage broader participation across the campus community. Director 3 described how his center offers a number of service-learning opportunities for professional students from all disciplines. Director 1 pointed out that graduate students comprise a substantial portion of the student body: "So if we want to affect the culture of the institution, and we ignore [this much] of the student population, that's not going to do us much good" (January 2021). To meet this need, this center has developed ways to engage graduate students "as TAs or as teachers or where they're doing their research or teaching their courses in ways that are commensurate with community engaged scholarship practices and trends." Finding ways to make programs and experiences more accessible for non-traditional students – transfer, graduate, doctoral, or otherwise – can cast a wide net that translates into recruiting students who otherwise may not have known about or been engaged with nonprofit education.

At Maryland, we try to ensure students of any income background can participate in our programs by reducing the need to juggle their nonprofit interests with classes and jobs. As part of our Do Good Accelerator, students can advance a fundraising, advocacy, or other project for an existing nonprofit, build the capacity and impact of a nonprofit they created, or advance the social impact business they are building. Students spend a semester (or more) and/or the summer participating in mentoring and curriculum that supports their impact goals. Students are paid as part-time employees of the accelerator during the academic year and paid as full-time employees during the summer.

Students already interested in nonprofit studies and the nonprofit sector may flock to a campus-wide effort. In order for nonprofit education to be integrated into every college, school, and major, centers should consider how curricular and co-curricular opportunities can better meet the needs of a diversity of students with regard to political affiliation, degree program, and time availability.

Building a Cross-Campus Enterprise

A campus-wide approach offers the opportunity to encourage nonprofit education, social impact, and social innovation among the entire student body and across all academic disciplines. Such an initiative could offer students the opportunity to design their own social enterprises and to bring them to scale, even forming their own registered nonprofit or for-profit organizations. Experiential learning could be integrated into the curriculum of every part of the university, to offer hands-on opportunities for students to engage within their community. Faculty members could conduct policy-relevant research to better understand and support the nonprofit and social impact sector. All this work would be supported by the university's administration because the initiative supports the institution's primary mission and strengthens the connection between the university and the surrounding community.

To make this vision a reality, entrepreneurial center leaders should keep a few things in mind:

- Especially in the beginning, be intentional about the projects you take on, but stay nimble enough to contribute when the situation calls for it. A few quick wins will help others realize the value of collaborating with the center and will illustrate the center's current capacity and potential for future growth.
- Look for opportunities to build relationships that break through the barriers and campus silos that often work against a campus-wide mindset. Very often, academics in other disciplines and administrators lack basic knowledge about how the nonprofit sector works. With a creative and well-intentioned communications and relationship engagement effort, your center can educate and build campus community partners. Linking your center's activities and brand to the distinctive features of your university and its history will strengthen the bond between the center and the university's mission.
- Make sure that the center's value proposition feeds the incentives of its would-be allies and partners. University leaders (including leaders of other schools) benefit from mutually beneficial working relationships in which credit for successful collaboration is shared. Community organizations are focused on providing public goods or services, but will welcome the involvement of students who are capable self-starters and who are sensitive to community needs. Prospective faculty partners can work productively with the center as long as it helps them meet their basic needs: teaching, service and research, the three types of contributions for which they are evaluated.
- Work toward long-term financial and programmatic sustainability for the center's primary mission. Funding sources such as endowments are important, but stable funding can also result from institutional arrangements that steer revenues from other sources, such as earned income, donations, grants, contracts, and tuition.

Above all, as Director 4 observed, "If you are going to do pan-campus efforts, it has to be so others can fly high and reach their goals" (January 2021). The work that such an enterprise requires will eventually pay off for not only the center, but for the whole university community.

Notes

1 To preserve the anonymity of the interview subjects and their institutional locations, we will refer to interviewees by number ("Director X"). The first time an interviewee is quoted or cited, we will list the size and private/public status of the college or university where the center is located, using enrollment data for fall 2019 from College Navigator (National Center for Education Statistics, 2019). All eight of the institutions are "large" in size, according to the Carnegie Classifications for Size and Setting (Carnegie

Classifications of Institutions of Higher Education, n.d.), while four are public and four are private.

2 In addition to the Mirabella and Wish article cited above, please see Dobkin Hall, P., O'Neill, M., Vinokur-Kaplan, D., Young, D., & Lane, F. S. (2001). Where you stand depends on where you sit: The implications of organizational location for university-based programs in nonprofit management. *Public Performance & Management Review, 25*, 74–87; and Mirabella, R. Hoffman, T., & Teo, T. (2019). The evolution of nonprofit management and philanthropic studies in the United States: Are we now a disciplinary field? *Journal of Nonprofit Education and Leadership, 9*(1), 63–84.

3 Larson and Long (2000) identify stable funding, institutional fit, and community connection as the three main prerequisites for institutional stability for nonprofit management centers. Please see Larson, R. S., & Long, R. F. (2000). Academic centers: Moving beyond the periphery. *Journal of Higher Education Outreach and Engagement, 5*(2), 39–47; Wodarski, J. S. (1995). Guidelines for building research centers in schools of social work. *Research on Social Work Practice, 5*(3), 383–397; and Stahler, G. J., & Tash, W. R. (1994). Centers and institutes in the research university: issues, problems, and prospects. *The Journal of Higher Education, 65*(5), 540–554 for additional insights.

4 Several directors of philanthropic and nonprofit centers interviewed by Rooney and Burlingame (2020) discussed the challenges of securing support from university leaders without becoming too reliant on the support of a small number of people, who may leave or change positions. See Rooney, P. M., & Burlingame, D. F. (2020). Build It and They Will Come! Or, Built to Last? Key Challenges and Insights into the Sustainability of Nonprofit and Philanthropy Programs and Centers. *The Journal of Nonprofit Education and Leadership, 10*(4).

5 Larson and Long (2000) consider the link between the center's mission and the university's mission to be one of the two keys (along with faculty involvement) to establishing the academic credibility of a center on nonprofit studies. Mission orientation is still likely to be important for nonprofit centers, although Rooney and Burlingame (2020) note that academic credibility is no longer one of the primary objectives that center directors face, in part because of the growth and maturation of the field of nonprofit studies (p. 401).

6 The importance of collaboration with other units was a major topic in the 2000 panel discussion about organizational location (Dobkin Hall et al., 2001) cited above. One participant noted that "a quality nonprofit management program cannot really prepare its graduates if they do not gain the requisite knowledge and skills to perform in today's very sectorally intermingled environment" (p. 75), while another recommended a "troika" model, where "public sector, business, and nonprofit management are all given equal emphasis and where students can specialize in management in any one sector while also learning about the other sectors and how they all interact" (p. 79).

7 Rooney and Burlingame (2020) quote from the 2006 NACC document, "In Pursuit of Excellence," which lists several indicators of quality for academic centers of nonprofit and philanthropic studies. Among these indicators is that nonprofit centers should be considered "preferred providers" of information and service to the nonprofit sector, and that university leaders consider them to be "exemplary instruments for university engagement in the community" (p. 398).

8 Larson and Long (2000) argue that faculty support is one of the primary drivers of academic credibility for centers of nonprofit management. As centers grow, their goals may shift from attracting the support of affiliated or allied faculty members to obtaining their own faculty positions. Rooney and Burlingame (2020) note that conflicts over faculty

lines, in which university leaders take control of slots that were originally designated for philanthropic or nonprofit studies, were one of the main reasons why IUPUI's Center on Philanthropy decided to become a school.

9 As Weber and Brunt (2020) note, there is a large literature on teaching methodologies in nonprofit education. Many of these studies discuss experiential learning and service learning – and, particularly, student philanthropy. See Campbell, D. (2014). Practicing Philanthropy in American Higher Education: Cultivating Engaged Citizens and Nonprofit Sector Professionals. *Journal of Public Affairs Education, 20*(2), 217–231. doi: 10.1080/15236803.2014.12001783; Millisor, J., & Olberding, J. C. (2009). Student philanthropy in colleges and universities. *Academic Exchange Quarterly, 13*(4), 11–16; and McDonald, D., Miller, W., & McDougle, L. (2017).

Connecting Through Giving. Understanding the Effect of the Mayerson Student Philanthropy Project. *Journal of Nonprofit Education and Leadership*, 7(2), 110–122. doi: 10.18666/JNEL-2017-V7-I2-8177; all quoted in Weber, Peter C., and Carol Brunt (2020). Continuing to build knowledge: Undergraduate nonprofit programs in institutions of higher learning. *Journal of Public Affairs Education, 26*(3), 336–357.

References

Bara Stolzenberg, E., Aragon, M. C., Romo, E., Couch, V., McLennan, D., Eagan, M. K., & Kang, N. (2020). *The American Freshman: National Norms Fall 2019*. Los Angeles, CA: Higher Education Research Institute (HERI). Available at www.heri.ucla.edu/monographs/TheAmericanFreshman2019.pdf

Campbell, D. (2014). Practicing Philanthropy in American Higher Education: Cultivating Engaged Citizens and Nonprofit Sector Professionals. *Journal of Public Affairs Education, 20*(2), 217–231. doi: 10.1080/15236803.2014.12001783

Campus Compact. (2014) *Carnegie Community Engagement Classification*. https://compact.org/initiatives/engaged-campus-initiative/carnegie-community-engagement-classification/

Carnegie Classifications of Institutions of Higher Education. (n.d.) *Size & Setting*. https://carnegieclassifications.iu.edu/classification_descriptions/size_setting.php

Celio, Christine I., Joseph Durlak, and Allison Dymnicki. (2011). "A Meta-Analysis of the Impact of Service-Learning on Students." *Journal of Experiential Education, 34*(2), 164–81. https://doi.org/10.1177/105382591103400205.

Dobkin Hall, P., O'Neill, M., Vinokur-Kaplan, D., Young, D., & Lane, F. S. (2001). Where you stand depends on where you sit: The implications of organizational location for university-based programs in nonprofit management. *Public Performance & Management Review, 25*, 74–87. https://doi.org/10.1080/15309576.2001.11643646

Larson, R. S., & Long, R. F. (2000). Academic centers: Moving beyond the periphery. *Journal of Higher Education Outreach and Engagement, 5*(2), 39–47.

McDonald, D., Miller, W., & McDougle, L. (2017). Connecting Through Giving. Understanding the Effect of the Mayerson Student Philanthropy Project. *Journal of Nonprofit Education and Leadership*, 7(2), 110–122. doi: 10.18666/JNEL-2017-V7-I2-8177

Millisor, J., & Olberding, J. C. (2009). Student philanthropy in colleges and universities. *Academic Exchange Quarterly, 13*(4), 11–16

Mirabella, R., Hoffman, T., Teo, T., & McDonald, M. (2019). The evolution of nonprofit management and philanthropic studies in the United States: Are we now a disciplinary field. *Journal of Nonprofit Education and Leadership, 9*(1), 63–84.

Mirabella, R. M., & Wish, N. B. (2000). The "best place" debate: A comparison of graduate education programs for nonprofit managers. *Public Administration Review, 60*(3), 219–229. https://doi.org/10.1111/0033-3352.00082

National Center for Education Statistics. (2019) *College Navigator*. https://nces.ed.gov/collegenavigator/

Rooney, P. M., & Burlingame, D. F. (2020). Build It and They Will Come! Or, Built to Last? Key Challenges and Insights into the Sustainability of Nonprofit and Philanthropy Programs and Centers. *The Journal of Nonprofit Education and Leadership, 10*(4), 414–428.

Stahler, G. J., & Tash, W. R. (1994). Centers and institutes in the research university: issues, problems, and prospects. *The Journal of Higher Education, 65*(5), 540–554.

Stanford Social Innovation Review. (n.d.) *The Future of Social Impact Education in Business Schools and Beyond.* https://ssir.org/the_future_of_social_impact_education_in_business_schools_and_beyond

Weber, Peter C., and Carol Brunt (2020). Continuing to build knowledge: Undergraduate nonprofit programs in institutions of higher learning. *Journal of Public Affairs Education, 26*(3), 336–357. https://doi.org/10.1080/15236803.2019.1607804

Wodarski, J. S. (1995). Guidelines for building research centers in schools of social work. *Research on Social Work Practice, 5*(3), 383–397.

17

ASSESSING NONPROFIT ACADEMIC PROGRAMS

A More Inclusive Approach

Heather L. Carpenter

Introduction

Traditional assessment is defined as

> the ongoing process of establishing clear, measurable, expected outcomes of student learning; ensuring that students have sufficient opportunities to achieve those outcomes; systematically gathering, analyzing, and interpreting evidence to determine how well student learning matches expectations; and, using the resulting information to understand and improve student learning.
>
> *Suskie, 2009, p. 4*

Many books and articles are written about academic program assessment best practices. Over time, assessment has evolved into contemporary approaches and is more connected to student needs and integrated learning goals, curricular alignment, and the community (Suskie, 2009). Although helpful, traditional assessment methods tend to leave out key constituents and do not ask key questions as described by critical theorists.

Traditional assessment is used in nonprofit and philanthropic studies academic programs and these programs have grown exponentially over the last 30 years (Mirabella et al., 2019). They are housed in various schools and departments, such as public administration, business, social work, and liberal arts (Mirabella et al., 2019). Although assessment is used frequently across many universities and academic programs and is included in published articles in public administration, business, and social work (i.e., Braun, 2004; Kapucu, 2017), assessment in the context of nonprofit management education programs is still under development. Keeping critical perspectives in mind, this chapter provides recommendations and

DOI: 10.4324/9781003294061-18

concrete examples of how to create and manage more participatory and inclusive nonprofit academic program assessments at the certificate, undergraduate, or graduate levels and considerations for nonprofit and unique multidisciplinary learning goals philanthropic studies academic programs. The chapter also provides recommendations for overcoming faculty resistance to academic assessment and ends with a discussion and recommendations for the future of nonprofit academic assessment. Although this chapter includes critical perspectives, it also follows the normative assumption that student learning can be assessed and continuous program improvement can occur in nonprofit academic programs. This chapter does not attempt to argue whether or not one should do assessment or if one can assess student learning.

The Assessment Process Revisited

Before a nonprofit academic program director begins the assessment process, they should ask why they are assessing in the first place? There are many reasons to assess; however, the nonprofit and philanthropy program should be clear on why they, in particular, are conducting the assessment. Common reasons for assessment include external accountability requirements, improving student learning and satisfaction within the program, maintaining admissions standards, improving student recruitment, and enhancing faculty instruction (Rowntree, 1987; Lubinescu, Ratcliff, & Gaffney, 2001). Other reasons might be to create a participatory and community-focused program or to assess why and how the courses came about.

Part of understanding the purpose of assessment is familiarity with the various assessment requirements provided by the university for the academic review process, the requirements of regional accrediting bodies such as The Commission on Higher Education of the Middle States Association of Schools and Colleges (MSASC), the Commission on Colleges of the Southern Association of Colleges and Schools (SACS). Northwest Association of Schools and Colleges (NASC), The North Central Association of Colleges and Schools (NCACS), the New England Association of Schools and Colleges (NEASC), and the Western Association of Schools and Colleges (WASC); and knowledge of requirements of academic program accrediting bodies such as the Nonprofit Academic Centers Council (NACC), the Association to Advance Collegiate Schools of Business (AACSB), the Accreditation Council for Business Schools and Programs (ACBSP), the Network of Schools of Public Policy, Affairs, and Administration (NASPAA), and the Council for Social Work Education (CSWE). Although scholars argue the downsides to accreditation and assessment (i.e., Mirabella & Eikenberry, 2017; Powell, 2010), these accrediting bodies do exist and have requirements, therefore regulatory bodies need to be considered in the assessment process.

Whatever the reason assessment is to take place, the academic program director, administrator, or faculty member can begin with the traditional assessment process, which tends to follow similar requirements to the regional accrediting bodies and university program self-study requirements with (1) identifying the key stakeholders involved in the assessment process, (2) developing [or revising] program learning outcomes, (3) connecting program learning outcomes to course learning outcomes and assignments, and (4) determining the right internal and external assessments to measure learning outcomes. After they take these three assessment steps, they can complete the final step of (5) continuous program improvement.

The academic program director, administrator, or faculty member should also take into consideration the critical perspectives of assessment and how traditional assessment often excludes many stakeholders that nonprofit and philanthropic studies programs seek to include. Scholars argue that "performance measurement in nonprofit and voluntary organization studies is driven by a focus on summative outcomes and included increasingly by neoliberal business models" (Post & Dodge, 2019, p. 139). Nonprofit academic assessment is not immune to neoliberal business models either. In order to include a more inclusive assessment process, this chapter proposes a participatory evaluation approach along with traditional assessment steps in order to take into consideration why and how evaluation and assessment are conducted as well as the various participants involved in the process. Post and Dodge discuss four aspects of participatory evaluation that can also be considered in nonprofit academic program assessment.

1. Methodological tensions between engagement for social impact and performance excellence.
2. How is knowledge produced?
3. Who produces the knowledge?
4. Relevancy to the world of practice (Post & Dodge, 2019, p. 139).

In addition, the nonprofit academic assessment process should take into consideration social construction, whereas "recogniz(ing) the important of context perspectives and experiences and the development of authentic and relevant sources of knowledge production" (Blessett et al., 2016, p. 272). Moreover, scholars argue that one must understand the ecosystem in which one operates in order to create assessment measures (Ebrahim & Rangan, 2010).

Assessment Stakeholders

In order to create a more inclusive assessment process, it is important to identify the various stakeholders involved. The first and vital stakeholder is the student, who [should] benefit from the learning process. The second stakeholder is the faculty member who teaches in the program and who administers the course-level assessment. The third stakeholder is the academic program director, who is responsible for determining the program curriculum and who may or may not be teaching the courses and implementing the course-level assessments. The next stakeholder is the assessment coordinator, who may or may not be the academic program director. The assessment coordinator is responsible for implementing the program assessment and reporting back to the university assessment committee and the accrediting body if the program is accredited.

The next group of stakeholders is university administrators who are responsible for allocating resources to the academic program and who are responsible for collecting and reviewing program assessment data. The next groups are the accrediting bodies if the academic program is accredited, a program level accrediting body, and a regional accrediting body for the university. Another group of stakeholders is employers and the general public who hire program graduates and hire student interns. Each of these stakeholders' viewpoints must be considered and integrated throughout the assessment process.

The last most important group of stakeholders are the individuals who live in the communities served by the nonprofit organizations who will either benefit. At times, some of the stakeholders will have differing priorities and viewpoints about the assessment process. Assessment that is developed without considering these multiple stakeholder needs and wants has a chance of not being successful. Feit et al. explain,

> by incorporating a wider range of voices and perspectives in undergraduate and graduate nonprofit education, our nonprofit education programs will be better equipped to prepare students to fulfill the promise of the sector and meet the needs of a diverse world.
>
> *2017, p. 60*

Developing [or Revising] Program Learning Outcomes

Program directors must consider several things when developing program learning outcomes. First, they need to determine the overall purpose of developing learning outcomes. They also need to determine the process of developing the program learning outcomes, and last, they need to decide who will be involved in developing the outcomes.

Is the goal creating of the student learning outcomes to measure learning? Or perhaps to be accountable to an external accrediting body? Or for curriculum revision? Or make the program more inclusive and community centric? The purpose question is at the heart of creating program learning outcomes and is controversial because it infringes on the question of what should the students ultimately learn? Or reframed, what should be taught in the nonprofit and philanthropy academic programs (Hoefer, 2003)? It also impacts the view of the social construction of knowledge and asks the question, who creates knowledge?

Should the overall goal of the program learning outcomes to measure how students learn to think critically or learn to practice? Or perhaps both/and?

This debate and tension around teaching the students to learn how to do critical thinking or teaching students to succeed in their jobs are ever-present in the multidisciplinary field of nonprofit and philanthropic studies (i.e., Millesen, 2014; Burlingame, 2009).

The debate and tension of what the students should learn occur across many disciples in the academy. The liberal arts and traditional disciplines believe fields such as business, public administration, and social work are not teaching critical thinking or the liberal arts. However, business, public administration, and social work disciplines are newer; they argue they too teach critical thinking. There has also been a push to integrate the liberal arts into public administration and business (i.e., Braun, 2004). Nonprofit and philanthropic studies are not immune from these discussions and debates (i.e., Burlingame, 2009). Scholars argue that nonprofit and philanthropic studies program move to a more professional orientation is a result of standards imposed by accrediting bodies (Mirabella & Eikenberry, 2017).

Determining who will be involved in developing learning outcomes and how they will be developed should be integrated and discussed together. Although the learning outcomes development process can and should include multiple stakeholder perspectives over a year-long process, faculty involvement in developing program learning outcomes is also key and one of the main factors to getting faculty on board with the assessment process (Qvarnstrom, 2016). Another stakeholder group involved in developing program learning outcomes is an external program advisory board. For example, the nonprofit advisory board at the University of San Diego has subcommittees based on different programmatic aspects. One of those committees is the strategic planning and assessment committee, responsible for reviewing the program assessment results and providing recommendations for improvement.

Moreover, program directors can also conduct focus groups or surveys with students, nonprofit managers, community members, and alumni stakeholder groups to determine relevant skills, abilities, and other topics that should be covered in nonprofit academic programs (Larson, Wilson, & Chung, 2003). Once the who and how of creating program learning outcomes are determined, the program can develop the program learning outcomes.

Although one could potentially start from scratch in developing program learning outcomes, that is not typically recommended. It is recommended that six or less learning outcomes be created for each program (Suskie, 2009). In addition, various accrediting bodies provide some curriculum guidelines or competencies to help inform program learning outcome creation. For example, the Nonprofit Academic Centers Council created and subsequently updated the nonprofit academic curricular guidelines (2007, 2015; see Appendix A). The Nonprofit Leadership Alliance also developed a set of nonprofit leadership competencies that could inform program learning outcome development (Nonprofit Leadership Alliance, 2011). Experts recommend that "nonprofit management skill-based competencies would also be appropriate as learning outcomes for any nonprofit management education program" (Blankenberger & Cantrell-Bruce, 2016, p. 245).

To develop specific course-level outcomes, program directors can review nonprofit textbooks, which often provide learning outcomes. They can also explore nonprofit associations that cover in-depth course topics, such as the Association of Fundraising Professionals, BoardSource, Nonprofit Finance Fund, etc. Moreover, program directors can explore newer textbooks such as those that cover critical perspectives about nonprofit organizations and philanthropy (Eikenberry, Mirabella, & Sandberg, 2019) and various research studies about nonprofit competencies, needs of nonprofit managers, etc.

There are many different ways to create learning outcomes many which can be used, Ebrahim and Rangan provide an overview of the challenges and complexities of performance management in nonprofits and creating outcome measures (2010). Here we recommend Bloom's taxonomy as a useful tool to start from when creating learning outcomes from scratch (Anderson & Bloom, 2001). There are six levels, as shown in Figure 17.1.

The many benefits to using Bloom's Taxonomy in creating program learning outcomes include helping students and teachers understand the role of teaching, delivering appropriate instruction, and ensuring that assessments are aligned with learning outcomes (Anderson & Bloom, 2001). Program learning outcomes should be:

1. Meaningful – the question is one about which faculty want to know the answer.

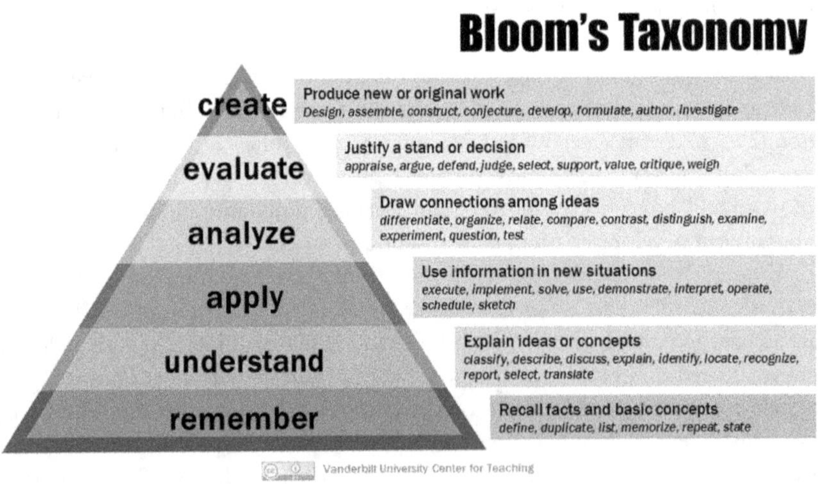

FIGURE 17.1 Blooms Taxonomy

Used with permission.

2. Relatable – the question is tied to course objectives, program goals, and campus-wide student learning outcomes.
3. Measurable – the question can be answered! Usually, that means specifying the question to an observable student performance.
4. Manageable – the process of collecting data is manageable. Complex assessment systems with multiple variables make for interesting research projects, but can be burdensome to faculty.
5. Actionable – the answers to the question provide faculty with information to make changes (Barrett, 2016, p. 12).

The first way is to structure learning outcomes to include a statement which should include:

> (a) some subject matter content and (b) a description of what is to be done with or to that content… [writing a statement] consisting of a noun or noun phrase – the subject matter content – and a verb or verb phrase – the cognitive process(es).
>
> *Krathwohl, 2002, p. 213*

An example program learning objective could be, *the student will understand the theories on nonprofit and philanthropic studies.*

The second way to structure the learning outcomes is to include a description of what is to be done (Krathwohl, 2002). For example, include the verb phrase first, then the noun and subject matter (see Table 17.1). Here is an example of an MA in Nonprofit Management degree revised program outcomes using Bloom's taxonomy informed by the NACC curricular guidelines.

A third way to develop learning objectives is to pay attention to Bloom's taxonomy levels, with the bottom level being *Remember* and the highest level being *Create*. The program [and course] learning outcomes can span across all six levels; however, some program directors choose to use the top three for graduate student program learning outcomes and the lower three for undergraduate program learning outcomes. Using the levels within Bloom's taxonomy is one way to

TABLE 17.1 Revised Program Goals MA in Nonprofit Management

1. Cultivate the skills and knowledge needed to succeed as leaders in nonprofit, philanthropic, social enterprise, and voluntary action.
2. Implement management processes, practices, forms, and structures in nonprofit, philanthropic, social enterprise, and voluntary action organizations.
3. Understand the theory, context of the nonprofit, philanthropic, social enterprise, and voluntary action sector from a global, national, local, and regional perspective.
4. Express critical thinking through strategic, ethical, socially responsible, well-reasoned action, and communication.

distinguish between undergraduate and graduate programs. For example, graduate programs often include higher-level program learning outcomes where students are expected to *synthesize theories on nonprofit and philanthropic studies*. Whereas, at the undergraduate level, which is less theory-heavy, students are expected to *remember theories on nonprofit and philanthropic studies*.

How the program director (along with all stakeholders) chooses to develop program-level learning outcomes, either the first, second, third way, or a combination of the ways described above; one must have strong knowledge and expertise in the multidisciplinary nature of nonprofit and philanthropic studies and the unique curriculum offered in these programs. Once program learning outcomes are created, they need to be connected to course-level learning outcomes and assignments.

Connecting Program Learning Outcomes to Course Learning Outcomes and Assignments

The main way to connect program learning outcomes to courses is through curricular mapping, which is determining how many hours the learning objective is being covered across the curriculum which is often done through determining the hours that the content is covered and the assignments that assess the curricular content. There are different views of assignments. In participatory evaluation, community organizations are involved and influence curricular content and student assignments that are connected to the real-world nonprofit experience. Assignments can include but are not limited to papers, service-learning projects, capstone paper, and simulations.

The article "Curricular Mapping Models and Other Processes that Might Work for Nonprofit and Philanthropy Accreditation" explains how the curricular mapping processes prescribed by accrediting bodies ACBSP, AACSB, NASPAA, and CSWE can be adapted for the nonprofit and philanthropy academic programs (Carpenter, 2017). This chapter expands upon the mapping article and provides nonprofit academic program curriculum mapping examples.[1]

AACSB recommends

> Programs develop their own "well-documented systematic process" for creating and maintaining learning goals that are appropriate for their degree... document how the curricula facilitate appropriate "student-faculty and student-student interaction"...and, demonstrate how the curricula and program design facilitate appropriate "time to degree" standardization across different credentials.
>
> *AACSB International, 2016b as cited by Carpenter, 2017, p. 113*

Therefore, AACSB provides flexibility for each program to define its own program learning outcomes and curriculum mapping process. NASPAA also provides flexibility beyond its universally required competencies for programs to develop their own specific competencies, program learning outcomes, and curriculum mapping process (Carpenter, 2017).

On the other hand, ACBSP is more prescriptive and recommends programs "explain the number of hours to earn course credits as well as ways in which the curriculum is delivered" (ACBSP, 2016b as cited by Carpenter, 2017, p. 114). ACBSP requires a program to demonstrate at least 30 hours of coverage of ACBSP Common Required Components.

"Nonprofit and philanthropy programs can use ACBSP's common professional component curriculum mapping process to demonstrate the 30 hours of NACC curricular guidelines across the nonprofit curriculum" (ACBSP, 2016b, as cited by Carpenter, 2017, p. 114). Nonprofit and philanthropy programs can create their own Common Professional Components that are most relevant to their curriculum. Table 17.2 shows an example of a MA in Philanthropy and Nonprofit Leadership program that mapped the number of hours each NACC curricular guideline covered in each course in the program.

This type of curriculum mapping could also be completed for an undergraduate, certificate, or specialization in nonprofit and philanthropic studies. Informed by the curricular mapping processes described above, NACC accreditation also includes its own curricular mapping process. It instructs stand-alone nonprofit and philanthropy programs going up for accreditation to demonstrate how a:

1. Program Meets a NACC Curricular Guideline at the Core or Mission Level
2. Program Meets a NACC Curricular Guideline at the Course Level
3. Program Meets a NACC Curricular Guideline at the Specific Course Assignment Level, or
4. Program Meets a NACC Curricular Guideline "Outside" the Classroom (NACC, 2021).

Faculty members and program directors typically perform curriculum mapping processes to ensure that program learning outcomes are integrated into courses throughout the program. For example, the program coordinator at Grand Valley State University used a similar method as described by Dunning (2014) when creating the Masters in Philanthropy in Nonprofit Leadership. He identified coverage of the NACC curricular guidelines in the curriculum, as shown in Figure 17.2; 0 = curricular guideline not covered or minimally covered, 1 = curricular guideline specifically covered but not emphasized, 3= curricular guideline emphasized and assessed.

Coverage Map

Once program outcomes are mapped to courses, assignment, and assessment metrics need to be connected. For example, a graduate-level nonprofit management

TABLE 17.2 Stand-Alone Nonprofit Degree Program with NACC Curricular Guidelines CPC Hour Coverage (EXAMPLE)

Core Courses	*1.0 Comparative*	*2.0 Scope and Significance*	*3.0 History and Theories*	*4.0 Values and Ethics*	*5.0 Governance and Leadership*	*6.0 Public Policy, Advocacy, and Social Change*	*7.0 Law*	*8.0 Economics*	*9.0 Finance*	*10.0 Fundraising*	*11.0 Financial Management*	*12.0 Leadership, Innovation*	*13.0 Human Resources*	*14.0 Marketing and Comm.*	*15.0 IT, Social Media and Data*	*16.0 Assessment and Evaluation*	*Total*
PA611 Research Methods															12	30	42
PA612 Human Resources in Organizations		3		9	6								48				66
PA614 Organizational Theory			15	6							9						30
PA660 Philanthropy and the Nonprofit Sector: History and Ethics	12	12	12	30													66
PA661 Nonprofit Management	6		6	10	3	3			3	3	3	3	3	3	3	3	52
PA662 Financial Management			3	3					15	18							39
PA667 Fund Development				3						42							45
PA669 Leadership Capstone	6	3	3	3	9							42					66
Totals	24	18	39	64	18	3	0	8	27	63	12	45	51	3	15	33	

PA COURSES

Rubric: **0** = not covered or minimally covered; **1** = specifically covered, but not emphasized or assessed; **2** = emphasized and assessed

0 Comparative Perspectives on the Nonprofit Sector, Voluntary Action and Philanthropy	520	535		611	612		614		619	640	641	643			660		661	662	663	664	665	670
1 The impact of global social, economic and political trends on the role and function of voluntary action, civil society, the nonprofit sector and philanthropy	0	0	0	0	0	0	0	0		0	0	0	0	0	2	2	0	0	1	1	1	2
2 How individual philanthropy, voluntary behavior and volunteerism is expressed in different cultural contexts	0	0	0	0	0	0	0	0		0	0	0	0	0	2	2	0	0	0	0	0	2
3 The structure and regulation of philanthropic and voluntary behavior within different	0	0	0	0	0	0	0	0		0	0	0	0	0	2	1	0	0	1	0	0	2
0 Scope and Significance of the Nonprofit Sector, Voluntary Action and Philanthropy	520	535		611	612		614		619	640	641	643			660		661	662	663	664	665	670
1 The role and function of philanthropic, nonprofit, voluntary and civil society organizations	0	0	0	0	0	0	0	0		0	0	0	0	0	2	2	0	0	1	0	2	2
2 The size, impact of, and trends in philanthropy, voluntarism and the nonprofit/nongovernmental sector	0	0	0	0	0	0	0	0		0	0	0	0	0	2	2	1	1	0	0	1	2
3 The diversity of types, forms and language that is used to describe voluntary action within society	0	0	0	0	0	0	0	0		0	0	0	0	0	2	2	0	1	0	0	1	2
4 The diversity of activity undertaken by nonprofit, voluntary and civil society organizations, including both charitable and mutual benefit organizations, as well as those formally and informally structured	0	0	0	0	0	0	0	0		0	0	0	0	0	2	1	0	1	0	0	1	2
5 The relationship and dynamics among and between the nonprofit, government and for-profit sectors	1	0	0	0	1	2	0	0		0	1	1	0	1	1	2	1	0	2	1	0	2
0 History and Theories of the Nonprofit Sector, Voluntary	520	535		611	612		614		619	640	641	643			660		661	662	663	664	665	670

FIGURE 17.2 Master of Philanthropy and Nonprofit Leadership, NACC Curriculum Guidelines

Source: Example provided by Salvatore Alaimo, Grand Valley State University.

course includes various assignments where a student demonstrates mastery of the course learning outcomes. One step further in the assessment process is to map the assessment metric(s) to assignments and course learning objectives. Assessments may include papers, projects, exams, and discussion posts; and, assessment metrics include rubrics and exam questions. A graduate-level Donor Motivations class mapping example is provided in Table 17.3.

The course learning outcomes, assignment, and assessment metrics mapping table should show:

1. program learning outcome(s) relevant to the course itself
2. the course learning outcomes
3. the assignments (data sources) and the assessment measure(s) or metric(s).

TABLE 17.3 Donor Motivations Program Learning Outcomes Mapped to Course-level Learning Outcomes, Assignments, and Assessment Metrics

Program Learning Outcome(s)	*Objective (Measurable Student Learning Outcome)*	*Data Source(s) aka Assessments*	*Assessment Metric(s)*
Demonstrate the knowledge and skills needed for effective ethical and legal philanthropy.	Understand the sociological and cultural influences on giving.	Sociological and cultural influences on giving paper. (Paper 1)	Rubric
Employ effective communications, technological, and interpersonal strategies to cultivate and steward relationships with donors through various philanthropic actions.	Analyze the types of information needed to identify prospective donors, including donor segmentation. Rate current and prospective donors on linkage, ability, and interest to prioritize and plan cultivation and solicitation. Establish a hypothetical plan of action for engagement, cultivation, solicitation, and stewardship.	Prospective donor acquisition, cultivation, and solicitation plan paper (Paper 2)	Rubric
Create persuasive written and oral arguments for support, evidenced by the ability to generate effective campaigns, plans, and proposals.	Prepare hypothetical donor-focused solicitation communications to facilitate informed gift decisions.	Donor solicitation paper (email, letter, phone script) (Paper 3)	Rubric

Note: This is not meant to be inclusive of an entire donor relations or philanthropy course. See Choi, K.J., & R. Mirabella (2019) "Mutuality, Equality and Participation: Practicing Critical Ethics in Philanthropy" on creating inclusive philanthropy.

TABLE 17.4 Stand-Alone Nonprofit Master's Degree Curriculum Mapping Example

Curricular Guideline	*Program Learning Outcome*	*Courses*	*Course Objectives*	*Course Units or Weeks Covered*	*Assignments*	*Assessment Metric(s)*
5.0 Nonprofit Governance and Leadership	5.1 Demonstrate role of nonprofit boards and executives in providing leadership at the organizational, community and societal levels through various structures and authority models	NPM-510	2,3,4	3	Final paper	Rubric
		NPM-520	1 1 2	1 1 1	Board Assessment Project*	Rubric
		NPM-510			Case Analysis of one theory of nonprofit governance	Case Rubric
	5.2 Understand theories of nonprofit boards and governance	NPM-520			Midterm Exam Question	Midterm Exam

More assessment metric examples are provided in *Nonprofit Education: Evaluating and Assessing the Skill Sets Our Student Learn* (Blankenberger & Cantrell-Bruce, 2016). The final step in connecting program learning outcomes to course learning outcomes, assignments, and assessments is to show where the program learning outcomes will be assessed throughout the program. CSWE recommends that "programs must show how competencies are integrated into program design, in the classroom, and in fieldwork" (CSWE, 2008 as cited by Carpenter, 2017, p. 116). Table 17.4 is an adaptation of CSWE's curriculum mapping process and shows how nonprofit Board Governance program learning outcomes are connected to specific courses and course learning objectives. The example also indicates when the learning objectives are covered within the course, assignments that assess the learning outcomes, and assessment metric(s).

Determining the Right Internal and External Assessments to Measure Learning Outcomes

The concrete examples provided help map the curriculum and connect program learning outcomes to course learning outcomes and assessment metric(s). However, there is also a debate and argument about choosing the right learning outcomes for assignments to measure learning outcomes. Some argue, how can one assess learning by an assignment or an exam (Qvarnstorm, 2016; Kramer, 2009)? Others might be overwhelmed by the amount of time and energy the curriculum mapping and assessment connecting process takes.

Traditional assessment practices recommend that both internal and external assessment metric(s) be included to measure program learning outcomes. In other words, the program learning outcomes should be tied to both internal course assessment metric(s) and external metric(s). For example, an internal course level metric could be a rubric attached to a course assignment in a capstone course. There should also be a discussion among faculty and the academic program director to ensure the program learning outcome is introduced and discussed in either a course or multiple courses throughout the program.

One to two internal metric(s) should be included for each program learning objective, for example, a final capstone paper that integrates all the program learning outcomes or a final portfolio such as the one used by the Master of Arts in Nonprofit Leadership at the University of San Diego (Donmoyer et al., 2012) is a recommended assessment metric. The program learning outcomes are introduced and emphasized throughout the program, and then students choose three major assignments for their portfolio to demonstrate their mastery of the program learning objectives. Then the portfolios are reviewed by an internal faculty member and several external advisory board members.

Another MA in Nonprofit Management's assessment practice uses the final capstone paper to assess the program learning outcomes. Again, program learning outcomes are introduced and emphasized throughout the program and then assessed in the final capstone paper's rubric. Other recommendations include using case studies and experiential projects to assess student learning (Cantrell-Bruce & Blankenberger, 2015). NASPAA provides a helpful process for mapping experiential education across the curriculum (Carpenter, 2017). Table 17.5 provides an example of a MA in Leadership and Management that mapped experiential education projects across the curriculum.

All examples of assessment metrics discussed thus far have been internal. An external metric is when students' performance are compared to students in other similar programs. Due to the diverse nature of nonprofit and philanthropic studies, this idea is quite controversial. However, as the field evolves, this idea should be discussed further. The external assessment metric can be part of an internal assessment. For example, with a simulation performed in a capstone class, student results can be compared with other programs and universities that have completed the same simulation in their capstone class.

External assessment can also be completed through an outbound exam or a third-party survey like ones administered through Peregrine Academic Services. These are multiple-choice exams on the various subject matter. There is much discussion over the challenges of assessing student learning with multiple-choice assessments; however, this should not be the only unit of measurement and should be combined with internal measurements. Unfortunately, outbound exam availability

TABLE 17.5 Experiential Education Mapped to MA in Nonprofit Leadership and Management Degree Program

Core Courses	*Experiential Learning*	*Fieldwork*	*Simulation*	*Practicum*	*Internship*	*Capstone*
LEAD 501	X		X			
LEAD 550						
LEAD 500	X					
LEAD 502						
LEAD 503	X					
LEAD 504			X			
LEAD 505						
LEAD 506						
LEAD 507	X					
LEAD 509						
LEAD 510						
LEAD 511	X					

TABLE 17.6 Internal and External Assessment Metric(s) and Program Assessment Results

MA in Nonprofit Management Learning Objectives	*Internal Assessment NPM690 Master's Project Rubric*	*Internal goal: 100% of students score over 84% on rubric component*	*Associated External Benchmark (subset of Common Professional Component Topics)*	*External goal: 50% of students achieve ≥ 90% average CPC*
Analyze the distinctive leadership and managerial challenges in the nonprofit sector.			Global dimensions	83% Met
3. a. Define leadership and ethics demands in nonprofits, including unique government relations.	Ethics Challenges	100% Met 100% Met	Business ethics Business leadership	83% Met 83% Met
3. b. Apply strategic analysis to nonprofit organizations	Strategic Comprehensive	100% Met 100% Met	Integration/ Strategic management	50% Met

in nonprofit management and philanthropy is minimal and contains some overlap with public administration and business elements. It is important to consider an external type assessment metric to compare student achievement of program learning outcomes to similar nonprofit and philanthropic studies programs.

Table 17.6 shows a snapshot of one MA in Nonprofit Management program assessment results that includes internal and external assessment metrics.

The internal assessment identifies the part of the internal assessment rubric [in this case, a capstone class rubric] used to assess the specific learning objective. It is recommended that department faculty develop these assessment rubrics (Blankenberger & Cantrell-Bruce, 2016). The assessment report's body includes the entire rubric and text explaining how many students took the assessment and what percentage met the assessment goals. In this case, 100% of the student met the internal assessment goals of scoring over 84% on the final project rubric components. The external assessment goals were met since 50% or more of the students achieved greater or equal to 90% of the average outbound exam scores [compared to other ACBSP programs]. The assessment committee then discussed the results and made a plan to introduce and emphasize strategy in earlier courses. In this case, the external benchmark topics are generic enough for the nonprofit students and the program learning outcomes; however, this isn't always the case with all the program learning objectives.

Another beneficial part of the assessment process is conducting a student exit survey. Much research shows that course evaluations are not a good measure of student satisfaction; however, exit surveys are helpful to see what students liked and disliked across the entire program. An exit survey or alumni surveys distributed across several nonprofit and philanthropic programs would also provide helpful external metric comparisons (e.g., Nonprofit Education Survey Project, 2021; Altman et al., 2012). For example, if technology and course frequency come up regularly on the student exit survey, the assessment committee could explore ways to improve these areas.

Some nonprofit and philanthropic academic programs also conduct satisfaction surveys of employers where students conduct applied projects (i.e., Donmoyer et al., 2012; Carpenter & Krist, 2011). Overall, the right internal and external assessment measures should measure the nonprofit and philanthropic academic program's unique learning outcomes and be meaningful to the stakeholders involved in the process.

All these assessment strategies are not meant to be mandates, however, provide insight into continuous program improvement. In addition, Ebrahim and Rangan (2010) discuss the complexities of developing nonprofit performance measures and nonprofit academic programs face similar challenges, therefore, nonprofit faculty, administrators must take into consideration assessment that is feasible for all stakeholders involved.

After a nonprofit academic program has undergone three years of program assessment, trends emerge. Program faculty, advisory board members, and the academic program director can meet to discuss those trends. If students do not meet the program learning outcomes, then program directors need to ask why and figure out ways to improve assignments, courses, and overall student satisfaction. For example, an assessment committee made up of diverse stakeholders such as faculty, advisory board members, and a student representative could meet monthly or quarterly to discuss assessment results and program improvement recommendations. The author participated in this type of committee during her doctoral studies, which provided a lasting positive impact of contributing to program improvement as a student.

Meta-assessment should also be explored, which means assessing the assessment process and seeing what works and what does not work with the assessment implementation. Often program learning outcomes need to evolve and change along with the curriculum.

Overcoming Faculty Resistance to Assessment

One of the biggest challenges of implementing academic program assessment is faculty resistance. There are many reasons why faculty members are resistant to assessment, with the number one reason being the time to implement the assessment. Other reasons include assessment stemming from corporate America, the lack of research on the effectiveness of assessment, the university culture for assessment, types of assessment measures being used, disconnect between assessment and actual student learning, or concern about being punished if students do not meet assessment standards (Powell, 2010; Kramer, 2009). Other faculty argue that one cannot assess learning with a multiple-choice test, assess quality, or quantify student learning.

Even with this resistance, it is still possible to develop, implement, and manage a robust assessment program for nonprofit and philanthropic academic programs. It may take a bit more time to develop the assessment program involving ALL stakeholders in the process and including faculty members as an integral part, but well worth it in the end!

Factors that influence reducing faculty resistance and increasing faculty satisfaction with the assessment are to:

a. Emphasize using student assessment for internal institutional academic improvement, establish institution-wide mechanisms – plans, policies, and administrative offices – to guide student assessment efforts, and monitor and report the various institutional benefits and impacts.
b. Emphasize more specific academic management activities such as task forces, faculty committees, forums, and seminars on student assessment, and give more attention to using student assessment for educational decisions and promoting faculty interest in teaching and instructional methods.
c. Educate faculty about and involve them with the external influences on student assessment (accreditation, state policy, etc.), provide them with professional development opportunities to learn about student assessment, and distributing evidence of the benefits of student assessment.
d. Promote the benefits of student assessment and use it for faculty reward and promotion decisions (Grunwald & Peterson, 2003, p. 203).

The Future of Nonprofit and Philanthropic Studies Assessment

The future of nonprofit academic program assessment can and should be participatory and mindful of the diverse needs and wants of multiple stakeholders and the academy's unconscious bias. It needs to take on a more global perspectives and be more inclusive of the community needs. The NACC curriculum guidelines are helpful, but they are also being updated to be more inclusive of diverse global stakeholders. Faculty are integral to the success of the assessment process, and getting them on board is key. However, an assessment process that is too detailed, not participatory, or covers too many learning outcomes and assessment points throughout the program isn't sustainable.

Nonprofit academic program directors should also consider developing and validating a standardized external assessment metric, such as an outbound exam. This outbound exam can be created involving multiple stakeholders similar to the inclusive assessment process described above. Programs can choose to opt in and participate in this external assessment, they can also choose which content areas of the outbound exam they want to administer to their students and then compare results to a national or international group of similar academic programs who have also self-selected into regional, national, or international comparisons.

In conclusion, the strongest academic program assessments involve multiple stakeholders to develop program learning outcomes. The assessment process also pays attention to accrediting bodies, Bloom's taxonomy, and connection to program course learning outcomes and assignments. Program assessments include both internal and external assessment metric(s). Assessment results are used to advocate for program resources, show coverage of nonprofit and philanthropic studies curriculum, and continuous improvement.

Note

1 All examples provided should not be used verbatim but be revised based on the unique curriculum of each nonprofit and philanthropic academic program.

References

Altman, S., Carpenter, H., Dietrick, L., Strom, S. A., & VanHorn, T. (2012). Impact of the nonprofit leadership alliance, an undergraduate competency-based nonprofit program, on alumni career paths. *Journal of Nonprofit Education and Leadership*, *2*(3), 123–139.

Anderson, L. W., & Bloom, B. S. (2001). *A taxonomy for learning, teaching, and assessing: A revision of Bloom's taxonomy of educational objectives*. London: Longman.

Barrett, S. (2016). Asking the right question, the key to good assessment. The Sixth Annual Assessment Conference of the Association for the Assessment of Learning in Higher Education (AALHE) "Assessing What We Value: A Focus on Student Learning." Milwaukee, WI.

Blankenberger, B., & Cantrell-Bruce, T. (2016). Nonprofit education: Evaluating and assessing the skill sets our students learn. *Journal of Nonprofit Education and Leadership, 6*(3), 243–253.

Blessett, B., Gaynor, T. S., Witt, M., & Alkadry, M. G. (2016). Counternarratives as critical perspectives in public administration curricula. *Administrative Theory & Praxis, 38*(4), 267–284.

Braun, Nora M. (2004) Critical thinking in the business curriculum. *Journal of Education for Business, 79*(4), 232–236.

Burlingame, D. F. (2009). Nonprofit and philanthropic studies education: The need to emphasize leadership and liberal arts. *Journal of Public Affairs Education, 15*(1), 59–67.

Cantrell-Bruce, T., & Blankenberger, B. (2015). Seeing clearly: Measuring skill sets that address the "blurred boundaries" of nonprofit Management Education. *Journal of Public Affairs Education, 21*(3), 367–380. https://doi.org/10.1080/15236803.2015.12002204

Carpenter, H. L. (2017). Curriculum mapping models and other processes that might work for nonprofit and philanthropy accreditation. *JNEL*, Special Issue I, 111–117.

Carpenter, H., & Krist, P. (2011). Practice makes perfect: A study of the impact and use of nonprofit masters students' applied projects on nonprofit organizations in the San Diego region. *Journal of Nonprofit Education and Leadership, 1*(2). http://digitalcommons.wku.edu/jnel/vol1/iss2/3

Choi, K. J., & Mirabella, R. (2019). Mutuality, equality and participation: Practicing Critical ethics in philanthropy in *Reframing nonprofit organizations: Democracy, inclusion and social change*. Angela M. Eikenberry, Roseanne M. Mirabella & Billie Sandberg Eds. 53–64. Irvine, CA: Melvin & Leigh.

Donmoyer, R., Libby, P., McDonald, M., & Deitrick, L. (2012). Bridging the theory–practice gap in a nonprofit and philanthropic studies master's degree program. *Nonprofit Management and Leadership, 23*(1), 93–104. https://doi.org/10.1002/nml.21055

Dunning, P. T. (2014). Developing a competency-based assessment approach for student learning. *Teaching Public Administration, 32*(1), 55–67. https://doi.org/10.1177/0144739414522480

Ebrahim, A., & Rangan, V. K. (2010). *The limits of nonprofit impact: A contingency framework for measuring social performance* (No. 10–099). Boston, MA: Harvard Business School.

Eikenberry, A., Mirabella, R., & Sandberg, B. (2019). *Reframing nonprofit organizations: Democracy, inclusion and social change*. Irvine, CA: Melvin & Leigh.

Feit, M. E., Blalock, A. E., & Nguyen, K. (2017). Making diversity matter in a nonprofit accreditation process: Critical race theory as a lens on the present and future of nonprofit education. *Journal of Nonprofit Education and Leadership*, Special Issue I, 59–68.

Grunwald, H., & Peterson, M. W. (2003). Factors that promote faculty involvement in and satisfaction with institutional and classroom student assessment. *Research in Higher Education, 44*(2), 173–204.

Hoefer, R. (2003). Administrative skills and degrees: The "Best Place" debate rages on. *Administration in Social Work, 27*(1), 25–46.

Kapucu, N. (2017). Competency-based curriculum mapping as a tool for continuous improvement for Master of Public Administration (MPA) programs. *International Journal of Public Administration, 40*(11), 968–978.

Kramer, P. I. (2009). The art of making assessment anti-venom: Injecting assessment in small doses to create a faculty culture of assessment. *Assessment Update, 21*(6), 8–10.

Krathwohl, D. R. (2002). A revision of Bloom's taxonomy: An overview. *Theory Into Practice, 41*(4), 212–218. https://doi.org/10.1207/s15430421tip4104_2

Larson, R. S., Wilson, M. I., & Chung, D. (2003). Curricular content for nonprofit management programs: The student perspective. *Journal of Public Affairs Education*, *9*(3), 169–180.

Lubinescu, E. S., Ratcliff, J. L., & Gaffney, M. A. (2001). Two continuums collide: Accreditation and assessment. *New Directions for Higher Education*, *2001*(113), 5–21.

Millesen, J. (2014). Thoughts on the relevance of nonprofit management curricula. *Nonprofit Quarterly*. Retrieved, February 10, 2022 from https://nonprofitquarterly.org/thoughts-on-the-relevance-of-nonprofit-management-curricula/

Mirabella, R., & Eikenberry, A. (2017). A critical perspective on nonprofit accreditation. *Journal of Nonprofit Education and Leadership*, Special Issue I, 24–31.

Mirabella, R., Hoffman, T., Teo, T. K., & McDonald, M. (2019). The evolution of nonprofit management and philanthropic studies in the United States: Are we now a disciplinary field? *Journal of Nonprofit Education & Leadership*, *9*(1), 63–84. https://doi.org/10.18666/JNEL-2019-V9-I1-9598

Nonprofit Academic Centers Council. (2007). Curricular guidelines for graduate study in nonprofit leadership, the nonprofit sector and philanthropy. Retrieved, February 16, 2022 from www.nonprofit-academic-centers-council.org/curricular-guidelines/

Nonprofit Academic Centers Council. (2015). Curricular guidelines for graduate study in nonprofit leadership, the nonprofit sector and philanthropy. Retrieved, Febrauary 16, 2022 from www.nonprofit-academic-centers-council.org/curricular-guidelines/

Nonprofit Education Survey Project. (n.d.). Home. Retrieved January 16, 2021, from https://nonprofiteducationsurvey.com/

Nonprofit Leadership Alliance. (2011). *The skills the nonprofit sector requires of its managers and leaders*. Kansas City, MO: Nonprofit Leadership Alliance.

Qvarnstrom, J. (2016). Faculty perspectives on program assessment. The Sixth Annual Assessment Conference of the Association for the Assessment of Learning in Higher Education (AALHE) "Assessing What We Value: A Focus on Student Learning." Milwaukee, WI.

Post, M., & Dodge, J. (2019). The Promise of Qualitative and Participatory Approaches to Performance Assessment: A Critical Perspective in Angela M. Eikenberry, Roseanne M. Mirabella & Billie Sandberg, Eds., *Reframing nonprofit organizations*, 138–151. Irvine, CA: Melvin & Leigh.

Powell, J. W. (2010). Outcomes assessment and other problems. *Journal of Academic Freedom*, *2*. Retrieved from: www.aaup.org/JAF2/outcomes-assessment-conceptual-and-other-problems#.YO3PIhNKj-Y

Rowntree, D. (1987). *Assessing students: How shall we know them?* Oxfordshire: Taylor & Francis.

Suskie, L. (2009). *Assessing student learning: A common sense guide*. 2nd ed. San Francisco: Jossey Bass.

18

THE NONPROFIT STUDIES FIELD AS A SOCIAL MOVEMENT

How Can We Strengthen It?

Renée Irvin

Background

Research on civil society blossomed in the 1980s with the emergence of research centers and scholars from multiple disciplines convening to study the growing nonprofit and voluntary sector. The professionalization of the third sector also prompted universities to offer coursework specifically addressing the unique professional skills needed to lead successful organizations. For example, Prof. Roseanne Mirabella's research on US universities offering nonprofit-specific coursework (2021) showed explosive growth throughout the 1990s and 2000s. Curricular guidelines issued by the Nonprofit Academic Centers Council (NACC 2019) provided a compass for emerging programs launching or expanding their curriculum (see Appendix A). Finally, full nonprofit degree programs at the undergraduate or graduate level can now undergo NACC's nonprofit studies-centered accreditation process (NACC 2021a, 2021b). Accreditation marks a watershed moment, as it provides an important quality audit and signaling process (Hale & Irvin, 2017) that marks the maturation of our niche in the professional world and in academia.

Just as it is impossible to know what the future holds, it is also folly to assume that the initial growth of the field will continue in the same pattern and with the same velocity. For example, the measurable shift to online nonprofit degree programs and the growth of undergraduate nonprofit studies marks a clear departure from the traditionally on-campus nonprofit graduate coursework of the 1990s and 2000s. It is advantageous from a programming standpoint to anticipate trends and be responsive to them. However, merely being ready for changes in our field is a fatalist approach. One can assume, in contrast, that readers of this chapter are interested in being actors in the broad movement in our field – that is, as we influence or even define the future of nonprofit and philanthropic studies.

DOI: 10.4324/9781003294061-19

The strategies introduced in this chapter range from lofty wishes to small, easy tasks. The suggestions are not comprehensive, and this chapter's intent to benefit the field will gain traction only if the suggestions spark additional ideas from others. Before turning to the perspective and recommended actions for each set of players in the social movement, it is helpful to outline some general conditions and trends that ultimately affect the focus and the tactics we use in field-building.

Conditions and Trends in the Field

Academic Tribalism

Given the territorial nature of academia and traditional reluctance of faculty members to venture outside disciplinary boundaries, nonprofit studies field-building relies on our leading associations like International Society for Third Sector Research (ISTR), Association for Research on Nonprofit Organizations and Voluntary Action (ARNOVA), NACC, European Research Network on Philanthropy and others to launch and guide initiatives to unify our voice and strengthen our academic presence. The guiding hand of an association to bring disparate academic groups together is vital. Nevertheless, the boundary-spanning activities of the associations must compete with the atomizing forces of academia.

Doctoral students learn methodologies that are specific to their academic fields and study a narrow range of topics in order to best master the research and literature of that field. Even if their research centers on the nonprofit sector, it is often conducted solely through the academic lens and favored methodologies of their doctoral training. Is it no wonder that nonprofit-centered academic programs, wherever their academic home, have curricula that is usually dominated by the methodologies, research, and theory base of that home discipline (Mirabella & Wish 2000)?

Though nonprofit researchers may congregate in subtopic groups (economics and finance, critical theory, philanthropy, governance, and so on), the fact that multidisciplinary associations have thrived across decades, welcoming a variety of academic tribes to the nonprofit conference podium, is reassurance that some cross-disciplinary tolerance exists in our field, and with the encouragement of the associations, may continue to exist.

Student Demand and Competition for Students

The explosive growth of the nonprofit sector across the world in the past four decades fueled a demand by organizations for well-trained professionals and a desire by prospective students for professional degrees that prepared them for nonprofit careers. Our prospective students want to make positive steps toward solving problems and they see our programs as the vehicle for learning those skills and obtaining the necessary credential for their career trajectory (Burlingame & Hammack 2004; Stewart, Walk, & Kuenzi 2020).

It does not take academia long to recognize a potential new source of graduate tuition. Universities responded with quick adaptations of existing allied degree programs in business, public administration, social work, and other fields (Mirabella 2021). That is, students interested in nonprofit and philanthropic organizations now had nonprofit certificates and specializations to entice them to enroll in Master of Business Administration (MBA), Master of Public Administration (MPA), Master of Social Work (MSW), and other degrees. This curricular response, of course, expanded in scope to full nonprofit-specific masters, undergraduate, and now PhD programs.

Competition for graduate students is national and international in scope: the prospective student self-selects into the nonprofit field first, and then researches which graduate programs best fit their nonprofit goals. Undergraduate demand for nonprofit curricula and competition for students is different from graduate student demand. In the US, the high school senior quite often chooses the university first, and then only gradually "finds" nonprofit coursework well into their undergraduate studies on that campus. Thus, in the US higher education environment, competition for undergraduate majors is more likely to occur on campus, in contrast to the national and international competition of incoming graduate students. Faculty members who are interested in launching a nonprofit undergraduate program may face resistance from colleagues across campus, as the launching of an attractive undergraduate degree might be viewed as a zero-sum game and any increase in nonprofit undergraduate majors implies a decrease in other majors. If upper-level administrators are convinced that a new nonprofit undergraduate program can attract a new, additional source of students, however, they are likely to be allies in assisting a new nonprofit program to overcome resistance from existing academic departments on campus.

Student Demographic Change

Each country can easily see how enrollment is likely to trend on the horizon for in-country student numbers by examining birth rates over time. For example, the (US) National Center for Health Statistics (2020), reporting natality data, suggests that student demographics have fluctuated considerably over the past century, with US birth rates falling far below the peak of 1957 births until a half century later. In the US, one of the low points in births (1997; 3.9 million births) suggests a low census of 24-year-old graduate students in 2021, rising modestly to an expected local peak of 24-year-old graduate students in 2033. Restrictive immigration policies may further tighten enrollment in Europe and the US, yet these policies imply growth of nonprofit programs elsewhere to meet in-country demand.

Cultural Change

Millennial and Generation Z generations show deep dissatisfaction with global trends, from climate change (Pew Research Center 2021) to ongoing racial (Winograd & Hais 2011) and economic inequality. Some are gravitating away from democracy (Bennett Institute for Public Policy 2020), while others turn to public service careers to drive change. The nonprofit sector, including both downstream service provision and upstream policy advocacy, provides a clear career pathway for young people seeking to promote and implement solutions to problems increasingly seen as imminent crises (Case Foundation 2019). Thus, our programs stand to benefit from a generational surge of interest in advocacy, systems change, and public service.

Affordability

Accessibility of post-secondary education is threatened by several factors: Tuition – in Europe and the US, in particular – has risen dramatically faster than the inflation rate (OECD 2012). Undergraduate students have taken on significantly more debt to finance their bachelor's degrees, making graduate school a riskier financial gamble (Bhutta et al. 2020). Increasing income and wealth disparity may further reduce the number of middle-class students who will pursue post-secondary degrees. Finally, the shock to university enrollment from the Covid-19 pandemic may persist, as the "lost" freshmen of 2020 may never opt to enter college.

Undergraduate and Graduate Program Prominence

Due to the strong desire by parents to enable their children to obtain a college education, and considering the declining affordability of graduate degree programs as noted above, it is sensible to assume that undergraduate enrollment will be more resilient than graduate enrollment over the next decade or two, and undergraduate nonprofit-specific degree programs will expand significantly (see Weber & Brunt (2020), who show prevalence of undergraduate nonprofit programming in US universities). Okada (2021) demonstrated that nonprofit studies has grown first and predominately at the undergraduate level in Japan. If one posits that enrollment in a major is reflective of the sector size in an economy, these nonprofit-specific undergraduate programs are not likely to be more than 20% of the size of traditional undergraduate degrees in business administration. At the graduate level, however, a university's nonprofit-specific degree program could in theory rival the size of a traditional MSW or MBA degree program if it develops a strong reputation and consistently attracts students from outside its region. Stewart, Walk, & Kuenzi (2020) found that the reputation of the school or college where a nonprofit graduate program is located is viewed as more important than the reputation of the university itself.

Online Versus Campus-based Delivery

In the decade prior to the Covid-19 pandemic, robust online student enrollment grew to eclipse on-campus enrollment at the universities that offered both options (Carmichael et al. 2021). Of course, the pandemic accelerated that shift to include all programs, at least temporarily. The momentous shift to online delivery is too recent to provide meaningful data for the field regarding total enrollment effects of online delivery, leadership training outcomes for our students, and educational outcomes affecting career trajectory. The outlook appears almost certain that on-campus graduate nonprofit programs will be soon (if not already) in the minority in terms of both student enrollment and eventually in numbers of programs offered worldwide. Of course, "online" describes a variety of delivery modalities (hybrid, synchronous/asynchronous, etc.; see Carmichael et al 2021), and the decades ahead may reveal a dominant online curricular model that most schools adopt.

Undergraduate nonprofit programs, though still growing, may take longer to convert to the online format. An on-campus college experience is a rite of passage eagerly anticipated by teenagers, and the social amenities of university life may never be replicated well in an online format. Older students attending college, however, are gravitating toward an online format that accommodates the constraints of family and work obligations.

Higher Education Disruption

The shift toward online education (Kim & Maloney 2020) and the declining affordability of higher education are factors in the difficulties that higher education currently faces. In the US, disinvestment by government in public higher education has occurred at two points – in declining state revenue allocated to public universities, and also via reduced federal grants to students attending college (Zhao 2019). Online growth has led to sharply divergent enrollment patterns: Lederman (2019) describes the rise of newcomer mega-universities like Western Governors University and Southern New Hampshire University, both with enrollment of over 100,000 students in 2018, as students shifted away from traditional private and public universities. American Association of University Professionals (2021) describes the decades-long decline in tenure-track and tenured faculty on US campuses to a low of 37% of total faculty in 2019. In addition, institutional debt at US colleges and universities increased sharply over the 2009–2019 decade, eclipsing per-student revenue growth by over 40%.

Given the fundamental fiscal challenges in higher education underway, new or expanding academic programs are unlikely to attract resources unless firm proof of student demand exists. Where enrollment is weak, difficult budgetary decisions can result in the elimination of an academic program with dispatch.

Prominence and Reputation of the Nonprofit Sector as a Career

Decades ago, the concept of a career in the nonprofit sector (or even the existence of a "nonprofit sector" – see McDougle 2014) was largely unknown. People who became nonprofit sector leaders, development directors, foundation program officers, and so on, describe having "fallen into" their profession. Now, however, in many countries with large third sectors, university students can easily envision themselves pursuing careers in the arts, environmental protection, humanitarian services, and so on. Nonprofit brands have substantial prominence (Kylander & Stone 2012).

Public Awareness of Nonprofit-Specific Curricula and Degree Programs

Despite the increase in public recognition of the nonprofit sector's existence, awareness of a dedicated curricula that serves the profession is at best minimal. At the very least, some nonprofit employers intentionally seek graduates of our programs; well-prepared employees who show deep understanding of the constraints, opportunities, and implementation complexities of the nonprofit work setting.

However, few if any high school students list "nonprofit leadership" among the top five majors they would like to pursue in their upcoming university studies. Once on campus, they do not see the nonprofit curriculum, hidden as it is under the umbrella of more prominent majors (business, education) or predominately graduate programs (policy, public administration). University enrollment managers, normally focused on the undergraduate market, are unaware of nonprofit coursework that may be predominately pitched to graduate students. In sum, university recruitment practices, focused on the undergraduate audience, may not cover the nonprofit curriculum, which means a critical marketing touchpoint with the broader public is not engaged. Aside from the perceptive nonprofit executive seeking well-trained new talent for a position opening, there is no growing *public* awareness of the nonprofit curricula offered by hundreds of universities spanning the globe.

Perspectives and Strategies for Growth

What Can Associations Do?

Associations such as ISTR and ARNOVA provide excellent convening opportunities for scholars to learn from one another with respect to research and teaching the curriculum. NACC provides an additional venue for collaborative research and learning about administration of nonprofit programs. External advocacy on behalf of our field has been pursued by these organizations and others, as they respond to country-specific nonprofit-sector regulations and other points of concern. However, their collaborative effort and voice could be utilized more to build the nonprofit academic field.

Specifically, NACC and other convening associations could pursue strategies that promote public awareness of our academic field. The atomized nature of graduate nonprofit degree programs is illustrated by the 11 accredited nonprofit masters programs with a total of nine different titles such as Master of Nonprofit Organizations, Master of Nonprofit Management, Master of Nonprofit Leadership and so on (NACC 2021a, 2021b). This Wild West labeling inhibits public name recognition and suggests a need for association-level coordination or encouragement to coalesce around a common degree name.

Convening organizations can also collaborate to design and promote a ranking system that accounts for the independent existence of nonprofit-centered degree programs. In the US, only the nonprofit programs that are specializations (not full degrees) within an MBA or MPA are included in US News & World Report's published rankings. Our associations could use awards more strategically: Association awards are largely focused on research, but our associations currently do not give out prominent awards for teaching or programmatic excellence. Awards could also focus externally on nonprofit organization or foundation excellence. Whether honoring a university program or a nonprofit organization itself, an annual award can be a relatively inexpensive way of drawing media attention to the awarding organization and thus to our academic field.

Another idea for promoting nonprofit studies is to award electronic badges to graduates of our programs. Badges are emerging in fields such as computer science and engineering to provide credentialing of a skill that a student has gained. NACC has begun awarding badges to graduates of university nonprofit programs, but it is too early to tell if graduates will adopt them in large numbers, or even if badges become a prominent job market signaling tool.

What Can Universities Do?

In addition to ensuring that our future curriculum is relevant and useful to third sector organizations, universities will be grappling with demographic shifts in student populations, changes in higher education technology and delivery, and declining revenue (in many countries). Our programs in social theory, nonprofit management, philanthropy, and social enterprise must respond to these shifts nimbly and appropriately. To be blunt, the program must attract students continuously through economic booms and recessions alike.

Universities can assist the student recruitment process by recognizing that recruitment for nonprofit-focused students should be tribal. That is, students interested in careers in the nonprofit sector are looking for nonprofit-specific curriculum. Traditional university admissions and enrollment professionals, adept at stressing high-profile degree programs (business, journalism, political science, etc.), may be oblivious to the potential interest of prospective students in newer nonprofit-specific degrees and certificates. Universities also have a habit of burying nonprofit programs under layers of programmatic jurisdictions. University of Oregon is an example of this: the nonprofit programs (PhD specialization, full master's degree, graduate certificate, and undergraduate minor) are within the School of Planning, Public Policy & Management, which is under the academic umbrella of the College of Design – providing prospective students with zero indication that the university has any nonprofit curriculum. One obvious solution is to place the program under the dedicated label of a School, Department, or Center with an identifying keyword (nonprofit, etc.) in the title.

Program Perspectives and Strategies

Each individual program must be more than the product of one or two professors' entrepreneurial zeal. If a founding professor retires, other faculty should be present to carry the program forth. Nonprofit programs must market themselves on campus to increase their visibility to students, and to enable administrators to see that nonprofit programs are economically sound. That is, upper-level administrators may not even be aware that the university's students are enrolling in nonprofit-specific courses in large numbers. Obviously, programs must also market themselves to prospective students via close connections with regional nonprofit organizations. Fortunately, ample material exists in stories of successful recent alumni to formulate attractive stories for marketing to prospective students. What program faculty and administrators lack is the time to push those stories outward to an external audience.

Drawing from the suggestions for associations above, another strategy to enhance programmatic visibility is to give out an annual award to an organization (grant maker or nonprofit) in the program's home state or region. The award could highlight exemplary nonprofit activity in the community, but would have the secondary effect of drawing attention to the program itself on a regular basis.

Faculty Perspectives and Strategies

Faculty members' engagement with local nonprofit organizations is a powerful way to sustain and enhance the flow of prospective students into the program if it is performed with care. Faculty can also point out to current students the value to their career from promoting their degree program. Public awareness of the field is squarely in the hands of its students and alumni: their numbers provide the leverage needed to break through the chatter and register in the public memory bank.

Current Student and Alumni Perspectives and Strategies

With solid professional training and depth of understanding about civil society organizations, our graduates are highly sought-after for leadership positions. To promote broader public understanding of the value of the nonprofit-specific curriculum, students and graduates of our programs would do themselves as well as our field a favor by listing certain courses that they have taken on their resume and social media profiles. Doing so highlights the attractive skillsets that our graduates bring to a nonprofit organization or foundation. Graduates could also link their credentials (Master of Social Enterprise, Master of Nonprofit Management,, etc.) with a hyperlink to the degree program on their employer's website listing of staff members. Finally, NACC is currently developing an e-credential badge for graduates of nonprofit programs, as noted above.

Current students should be aware that the reputation of their degree program follows them throughout their degree. If their university's nonprofit program gains prominence as a highly respected degree program in our field, this good reputation reflects back on them for the rest of their careers. Although prospective employers focus their attention on the last degree that the graduate accomplished, students tend to emotionally imprint on their undergraduate degree program, not their graduate professional degree program. Since much of the curricular focus in our field is still at the graduate level, alumni loyalty is somewhat more difficult to motivate. Queensland University of Technology's outreach to their Centre for Philanthropy and Nonprofit Studies alumni provides an exemplar, with frequent professional engagement points throughout the year.

In addition, however, it is up to current students and alumni themselves to take the initiative to promote their degree alma mater and the field's development in general. Faculty should challenge alumni to show their alma mater some affection with thoughtful social media call-outs. Current students can also pursue deliberate strategies to enhance the name recognition of their degree program as they connect with nonprofit organizations during their studies, as noted above. In essence, students must realize that they are the core constituency of nonprofit studies as a social movement. Students' engagement with the external world outside of campus is a critical component for dramatically widening the knowledge and strengthening the depth of public understanding of their degree.

The Narrative Approach

A unifying narrative could be promoted widely, involving the participation of association, student, alumni, and faculty participants in building the field. For example, what phrases currently come to mind, with respect to nonprofit-centric university programs – "service," or "make a difference"? Casey (2018) describes a narrative of the nonprofit sector as a low-wage, almost pathetic place, disparaged in recent movies and television shows. The best way to combat a negative narrative is to replace it with something more memorable and compelling (Lakoff 2014). Students are more likely to respond to a message that emphasizes nonprofit studies' solutions to problems: Note the contrast with other academic fields that merely examine societal and environmental problems. "Make the change," for example, might appeal to a generation of university students who are unhappy with current affairs, plus the phrase provides a subtle competitive nudge to consider a nonprofit-relevant major.

Conclusion

If we conceptualize our field as a social movement, the scope of "activism" widens, and we can also consider not only the role of associations, but also actions by universities, individual faculty members, alumni, and current students as they all can assist in building the field. This exploratory chapter discussed current and anticipated challenges to our programs, including rising tuition burdens, the public's lack of familiarity with our field, and other concerns. Suggestions for enhancing the resilience of our field include actions as disparate as renaming our degree programs and getting alumni to strategically promote their academic accomplishment. There is a role for everyone in this movement.

References

American Association of University Professionals (AAUP) (2021). The Annual Report on the Economic Status of the Profession, 2020–2021. www.aaup.org/reports-publications/aaup-policies-reports/standing-committee/econ-status, accessed July 30, 2021.

Bennett Institute for Public Policy, University of Cambridge (2020). Faith in Democracy: Millennials Are the Most Disillusioned Generation "In Living Memory." www.bennettinstitute.cam.ac.uk/news/faith-democracy-millennials-are-most-disillusioned, accessed July 8, 2021.

Bhutta, Neil, et al. (2020). Changes in U.S. Family Finances from 2016 to 2019: Evidence from the Survey of Consumer Finances. *Federal Reserve Bulletin* Vol. 106(5). www.federalreserve.govpublications/files/scf20.pdf, accessed July 8, 2021.

Burlingame, Dwight and David C. Hammack, Editors (2004). *Education for a Civil Society: A Summary of the 2004 Conference*. Indianapolis, IN: Center on Philanthropy at Indiana University.

Carmichael, Calum, Allison Body, Craig Furneaux, Mark Hager, Patrick Rooney, and Renee Irvin, (2021). Within and Across Borders: Designing and Delivering Online Graduate Philanthropy Programs on a National or International Basis. Roundtable session, ISTR Annual Conference July 14, 2021, convened online. https://istr2021.us2.pathable.com/meetings/virtual/yyxWSABAwwJ4GYDkv, accessed July 10, 2021.

Case Foundation (2019). The Millennial Impact Report: 10 Years Looking Back. www.themillennialimpact.com/latest-research, accessed July 8, 2021.

Casey, John (2018). Is Millennial Mocking of Nonprofits Disruptive (And is it Useful in the Classroom)? Network of Schools of Public Affairs and Administration Annual Conference, Atlanta, GA. https://sites.google.com/site/johncaseypublications/community-sector, accessed January 28, 2021.

Hale, Matthew and Renee A. Irvin (2017) A Position Paper on Accreditation on Nonprofit/Philanthropy University Curricula. *Journal of Nonprofit Education and Leadership* 7(Special Issue 1), 126–137.

Kim, Joshua and Edward Maloney (2020). Learning Innovation and the Future of Higher Education. Baltimore, MD: Johns Hopkins University Press.

Kylander, Nathalie and Christopher Stone (2012). The Role of Brand in the Nonprofit Sector. *Stanford Social Innovation Review*. https://ssir.org/articles/entry/the_role_of_brand_in_the_nonprofit_sector#, accessed July 30, 2021.

Lakoff, George (2014). The All New Don't Think of An Elephant! White River Junction, VT: Chelsea Green Publishing

Lederman, Doug (2019). The Biggest Movers Online. Inside Higher Ed, December 17, 2019. www.insidehighered.com/digital-learning/article/2019/12/17/colleges-and-universities-most-online-students-2018, accessed August 3, 2021.

McDougle, Lindsey (2014). Understanding Public Awareness of Nonprofit Organizations: Exploring the Awareness-Confidence Relationship. *International Journal of Nonprofit and Voluntary Sector Marketing* 19(3), 187–199

Mirabella, Roseanne (2021). Nonprofit Management Education. http://academic.shu.edu/npo/, accessed January 28, 2021.

Mirabella, Roseanne and Naomi Bailin Wish (2000). The "Best Place" Debate: A Comparison of Graduate Education Programs for Nonprofit Managers. *Public Administration Review* 60(3), 219–229.

National Center for Health Statistics (2020). Natality Trends in the United States, 1909–2018. www.cdc.gov/nchs/data-visualization/natality-trends/index.htm, accessed June 16, 2020.

Nonprofit Academic Centers Council (2019). Curricular Guidelines. www.nonprofit-academic-centers-council.org/curricular-guidelines/, accessed January 28, 2021.

Nonprofit Academic Centers Council (2021a). Accreditation Guidelines. www.nonprofit-academic-centers-council.org/accreditation/, accessed January 28, 2021.

Nonprofit Academic Centers Council (2021b). List of Accredited Programs. www.nonprofit-academic-centers-council.org/accreditation/, accessed January 30, 2021.

OECD (2012). Education Indicators in Focus: How Are Countries around the World Supporting Students in Higher Education? www.oecd.org/education/skills-beyond-school/49729932.pdf, accessed July 8, 2021.

Okada, Aya (2021). Panelist for: *Nonprofit Education Research Summit: Discussing and Comparing Eastern and Western Nonprofit Higher Education Programs*. International Society for Third Sector Research pre-conference summit, July 12, 2021, convened online. https://istr2021.us2.pathable.com/meetings/virtual/piwBB4AT6Y3T5nDaJ, accessed July 30, 2021.

Pew Research Center (2021). Gen Z, Millennials Stand Out for Climate Change Activism, Social Media Engagement with Issue. www.pewresearch.org/science/2021/05/26/gen-z-millennials-stand-out-for-climate-change-activism-social-media-engagement-with-issue/, accessed July 8, 2021.

Stewart, Amanda, Marlene Walk, and Kerry Kuenzi (2020). Competencies and Reputation: What Appeals to Nonprofit Graduate Alumni? *Journal of Public Affairs Education* 27(1), 16–33.

Weber, Peter C. and Carol Brunt (2020). Continuing to Build Knowledge: Undergraduate Nonprofit Programs in Institutions of Higher Learning. *Journal of Public Affairs Education* 26(3), 336–357.

Winograd, Morley and Michael D. Hais (2011). Millennial Momentum: How a New Generation is Remaking America. New Brunswick, NJ: Rutgers University Press.

Zhao, Bao (2019). Consequences of State Disinvestment in Public Higher Education: Lessons for the New England States. Federal Reserve Bank of Boston New England Public Policy Center Research Reports 19-1. www.bostonfed.org/publications/new-england-public-policy-center-research-report/2019/consequences-of-state-disinvestment-in-public-higher-education.aspx, accessed August 3, 2021.

APPENDIX

NACC Graduate Curricular Guidelines

1.0 Comparative Global Perspectives on the Nonprofit Sector, Voluntary Action, and Philanthropy

- 1.1 Relationship of global social, economic, and political trends on the role, function, and impact of voluntary action, civil society, the nonprofit sector, and philanthropy.
- 1.2 Theoretical frameworks for societal value and socioeconomic dynamics in philanthropy and volunteering in a global context.
- 1.3 How individual philanthropy, voluntary action, and volunteerism is expressed in different cultural and global contexts.
- 1.4 Structure and regulation of philanthropic and voluntary behavior within different political contexts, including formal, informal, and alternative associational forms.
- 1.5 Role of various religious and cultural traditions in shaping philanthropy and voluntary behavior.

2.0 Scope and Significance of the Nonprofit Sector, Voluntary Action, and Philanthropy

- 2.1 Evolving role and function of philanthropic, nonprofit, voluntary, and civil society organizations in relation to other sectors including the emergence of new forms of social enterprise.
- 2.2 Size, impact of, and global/cultural contextual influences on philanthropy, voluntarism, and the nonprofit/nongovernmental sector.
- 2.3 Diversity of types, forms, and language that is used to describe voluntary action within society.
- 2.4 Diversity of activity undertaken by nonprofit, voluntary, and civil society organizations, including both charitable and mutual benefit organizations, as well as those formally and informally structured.

- 2.5 Relationship and dynamics among and between the nonprofit, government, and for-profit sectors including public private partnerships and hybrid forms of structure to achieve social purpose.
- 2.6 Comparative global trends distinguishing civic engagement and voluntary action from nonprofit direct service providers and other nonprofit/nongovernmental forms.

3.0 History and Theories of the Nonprofit Sector, Voluntary Action, and Philanthropy

- 3.1 History and development of philanthropy, voluntarism, voluntary action, and the nonprofit sector within particular contexts and how this experience compares and contrasts to the development of comparable sectors in various parts of the world.
- 3.2 Civil society, social movements, and related concepts that are important to understanding philanthropic behavior and voluntary action.
- 3.3 Theoretical explanations for the nonprofit sector, philanthropy, and social entrepreneurship including (but not necessarily limited to) political, economic, religious, and socio-cultural perspectives.

4.0 Ethics and Values

- 4.1 Values embodied in philanthropy and voluntary action, such as, trust, stewardship, service, voluntarism, civic engagement, shared common good, freedom of association, and social justice.
- 4.2 Foundations and theories of ethics as a discipline and as applied in order to make ethical decisions including, but not limited to an understanding of measuring impact for social mission outcomes as an indicator of trustworthiness, transparency, and competence.
- 4.3 Issues arising out of the various dimensions of inclusion and diversity, income inequality, and their implications for mission achievement.
- 4.4 Trends associated with social responsibility, sustainability, and global citizenship within cross-cultural and global contexts.
- 4.5 Standards and codes of conduct that are appropriate to paid and unpaid staff working in philanthropy and the nonprofit sector.

5.0 Nonprofit Governance and Leadership

- 5.1 Role of nonprofit boards and executives in providing leadership at the organizational, community, and societal levels through various structures and authority models.
- 5.2 Theories of nonprofit boards and governance.
- 5.3 History and function of nonprofit governing boards and how these roles and functions compare to governing boards in the public and for-profit sectors.
- 5.4 Distinctive roles and responsibilities between nonprofit boards and nonprofit executives and the role of boards and the executive team

in stewarding and achieving the mission and vision of nonprofit organizations.

5.5 Role, function, and structure of boards that serve to advance networks of nonprofits and through multi-sector partnerships to achieve a mission.

5.6 Process of board development as a tool to not only create effective governing boards but also to ensure a successful board-executive relationship, succession planning, and board renewal.

5.7 Role of structures and policies in effective governance.

6.0 Public Policy, Advocacy, and Social Change

6.1 Various roles of nonprofit organizations and voluntary action in effecting social change, including but not limited to, influencing the public policy process in local, national, and international contexts.

6.2 Public policies of significance specific to the nonprofit sector and their past, current, and potential impact on the sector, nonprofit organizations, and philanthropic behaviors.

6.3 How individuals as well as nonprofit organizations can shape public policy through strategies such as community organizing, association and movement building, public education, policy research, lobbying, and litigation.

6.4 Role of board members, staff, and volunteers as agents of and for social change, grounded in particular mission-driven effort.

6.5 Framework and guidelines for lobbying, as allowable, within different types of nonprofits as delineated across local, national, and international contexts.

7.0 Nonprofit Law

7.1 Legal frameworks within which nonprofit organizations and philanthropy operate and are regulated across jurisdictions.

7.2 Legal rights and obligations of directors, trustees, officers, and members of nonprofit and voluntary organizations.

7.3 Legal and tax implications related to charitable giving, advocacy, lobbying, political, and commercial activities of tax-exempt nonprofit organizations.

7.4 Legal implications for nonprofit operations including, but not limited to risk management, financial reporting, and board level fiduciary roles.

7.5 Oversight responsibilities of national and sub-national regulatory bodies.

8.0 Nonprofit Economics

8.1 Economic theory as it applies to the nonprofit sector and as understood in multi-sector economies.

8.2 Impact of market dynamics on the sector as a whole, within nonprofit sub-sectors and between and among the public, for-profit, and nonprofit sectors.

8.3 Economic impact of the nonprofit sector.

8.4 Managerial economics for effective social enterprise and nonprofit management including the use of economic tools such as cost-benefit analysis and social impact measurement.

9.0 Nonprofit Finance

9.1 Theory and practice of nonprofit finance, including knowledge of concepts such as liquidity, solvency, and cash flow strategies and the various types of revenues pursued by nonprofit organizations, the strategic choices, and issues associated with each type of revenue, and the methods used to generate these revenues.

9.2 Relationship between and among earned income, government funding, and philanthropic gifts and grants as sources of revenue, and how each can influence fulfillment of an organization's mission.

9.3 History and function of philanthropic gifts and grants as distinctive dimensions of the nonprofit sector.

9.4 Emergence, growth, and implications of government funding as a significant source of sector revenue.

9.5 History, expansion, and implications of earned income as a significant source of nonprofit sector revenue.

9.6 Recent and emerging trends in sources of sector revenue, e.g., micro-enterprise, social enterprise and entrepreneurship, use of capital markets, and a critical examination of their use as a means for mission achievement.

10.0 Fundraising and Resource Development

10.1 Various forms and structures in and through which organized fundraising and resource development occurs within philanthropy.

10.2 Components and elements that are part of a comprehensive fund development process.

10.3 Ethical processes and practices of different fundraising strategies to be considered such as annual fund, planned and major giving, foundation and corporate fundraising, and special events.

10.4 Understanding of generational and cultural differences in giving and implications for fundraising.

10.5 Trends in fundraising approaches such as the role of on-line giving, the use of social media, and crowdsourcing strategies.

11.0 Nonprofit Financial Management and Accountability

11.1 Role and function of financial literacy, transparency, and stewardship in the effective oversight and management of nonprofit organizational resources.

11.2 Application of accounting principles and concepts including financial and managerial accounting systems (including fund accounting) in nonprofit organizations.

11.3 Analysis and use of accounting information in financial statements and other reports to stakeholders as needed for responsible stewardship, including an understanding of social accounting.

11.4 Financial management, including financial planning and budget development and controls, management of cash flows, short- and long-term financing, investment strategies, and grants, contracts, and endowment management policies and practices Graduate Curricular Guidelines.

11.5 Use of financial information as related to such operational considerations as marketing, pricing, cost structure, and sustainability when considering new ventures, mergers, and other strategies.

11.6 Understanding financial decision making that includes, but is not limited to, portfolio and grants (from government and non-government sources) management systems, operations, reporting, and oversight.

11.7 Role of external agencies related to financial scrutiny of nonprofits and implications for transparency and accountability.

12.0 Assessment, Evaluation, and Decision-Making Methods

12.1 Methods that managers use to evaluate performance and social impact at both organizational and programmatic levels.

12.2 Methods and modes of assessment and evaluation to develop a nonprofit's culture that embraces continuous improvement strategies.

12.3 Decision-making models and methods and how to apply them to nonprofit organizational settings.

12.4 Use and application of both quantitative and qualitative data in measuring social impact and in improving the effectiveness of nonprofit organizations.

12.5 Role of information and the use of technology in the pursuit of a nonprofit organization's mission.

13.0 Professional and Career Development

13.1 Role of field experiences and experiential learning that are grounded in and linked to curricular goals and projected outcomes.

13.2 Role of professional associations and mentoring in professional development.

13.3 Ways that various professionals contribute to and are engaged with philanthropic and nonprofit sectors.

13.4 Opportunities for service and volunteerism that exist in the community.

13.5 Standards and context of professionalism, e.g., conduct and speech appropriate to the respective profession.

14.0 Nonprofit Marketing and Communications

14.1 Marketing theory, principles, and techniques, in general, and as applied in a philanthropic and nonprofit environment, including the dynamics and principles of the marketing "mission" in a nonprofit context.

14.2 Specific application of marketing theories to the development of financial and non-financial sources of support, e.g., fundraising, social marketing, and entrepreneurial ventures.

14.3 Link between marketing theories and concepts and their use in nonprofit organizations, e.g., strategies in organizational communication and public relations.

14.4 Stakeholder theory and its effective use and function in the nonprofit context and in relation to marketing theory.

14.5 Interrelationship between services marketing and donor marketing and resultant uses of social media and other means for advancing communications and public relations to internal and external stakeholders.

15.0 Information Technology, Social Media, and Data Management

15.1 Roles of information technology, social media, and "big data" in advancing the causes of civil society.

15.2 Appropriate and ethical use and application of information technology, social media, and data in order to increase productivity and effectiveness in the pursuit of a nonprofit organization's mission.

15.3 Types, sources, and location of information that are useful to the effective operation of nonprofit organizations.

15.4 How various technologies can be used to assess nonprofit performance and effectiveness.

15.5 Trends in technology use including innovations that affect nonprofits being able to meet their mission and within the context of privacy and security concerns.

16.0 Assessment, Evaluation, and Decision-Making Methods

16.1 Methods and modes to evaluate performance and effectiveness at both organizational and programmatic levels.

16.2 Decision-making models and methods and how to apply them in nonprofit organizational settings.

16.3 Use and application of both quantitative and qualitative data for purposes of leading and managing nonprofit organizations, the nonprofit sector, and the larger society through mixed method approaches.

16.4 Trends in social impact measurement within the context of evidence-based practice approaches including logical models and theories of change.

NACC Undergraduate Curricular Guidelines

1.0 Comparative Perspectives on Civil Society, Voluntary Action, and Philanthropy

1.1 Structure – both formal and informal, individual, and collective – of civil society and philanthropy across cultures and global contexts.

1.2 How individual philanthropy, voluntary behavior, and volunteerism is expressed in different cultural and global contexts.
1.3 Role of civil society, voluntary action, and nonprofit/nongovernmental organizations in social movements and social change.
1.4 Role of various religious traditions in shaping civil society and philanthropy.

2.0 Foundations of Civil Society, Voluntary Action, and Philanthropy

2.1 History, role and functions of civil society and voluntary action organizations (nonprofit, nongovernmental, voluntary) across time and place.
2.2 Size, impact and trends in philanthropy, nongovernmental organizations, and associational development in a global context.
2.3 Diversity of forms of philanthropic action and the diversity of fields of activity.
2.4 Relationship and dynamics among the governmental, nonprofit, for-profit, and household sectors and evolving forms of social sector forms.
2.5 History and role of social entrepreneurs and innovators in contributing to societal advancement.
2.6 Various theoretical explanations for the nonprofit/voluntary sector such as economic, political, sociological, and anthropological.

3.0 Ethics and Values

3.1 Values embodied in philanthropy and voluntary action, such as trust, stewardship, service, freedom of association, and their implications for societal advancement.
3.2 Foundations and theories of ethics as a discipline and as applied in order to make ethical decisions.
3.3 Standards and codes of conduct that are appropriate to professionals and volunteers working in philanthropy and the nonprofit sector.
3.4 How values and ethics are identified and advanced that affect strategic decisions of a nonprofit in meeting its mission.

4.0 Public Policy, Law, Advocacy, and Social Change

4.1 Key public policies and their past, current, and potential impact on the nonprofit sector, nonprofit organizations, and philanthropic behaviors.
4.2 Legal frameworks under which nonprofit organizations and social enterprises operate and are regulated.
4.3 Legal and tax implications related to various kinds of nonprofit activity, including but not limited to charitable giving, advocacy, lobbying, and any commercial activities of tax-exempt nonprofit organizations.
4.4 Roles of individuals and nonprofit organizations in effecting social change, social movements, and influencing the public policy process.

4.5 How individuals and nonprofit organizations shape public policy through strategies, including but not limited to public education, policy research, community organizing, lobbying, and litigation.

5.0 Nonprofit Governance and Leadership

5.1 Role of nonprofit boards and executives in providing leadership at the organizational, community, and societal levels.

5.2 Role of nonprofit boards and executives in providing leadership at the organizational, community, and societal levels.

5.3 Role of boards and executives of some nonprofits as agent(s) of and for social change and social justice at both the organizational and societal levels.

6.0 Community Service and Civic Engagement

6.1 Value of community service and civic engagement in the development of civil society.

6.2 Direct exposure to nonprofit organizations through internships, service learning, community service, and/or experiential learning.

7.0 Leading and Managing Organizations

7.1 Organizational theories and behavior as they apply in nonprofit and voluntary organizations including issues of work design and implications of operational policies and practices.

7.2 Theories of leadership and leadership styles.

7.3 Role of strategic management and organizational planning, including an understanding of ways to identify, assess, and formulate appropriate strategies.

7.4 Role of networks, partnerships and collaborative activity among and between nonprofits, government, and for-profit entities in achieving organizational missions.

7.5 Steps and processes involved in establishing a nonprofit organization, a social enterprise, and other entrepreneurial forms of organization.

7.6 Role of social entrepreneurs and social innovation and their implications for nonprofit leadership and management.

7.7 How trends in nonprofit accountability expectations shape the strategic management of nonprofits.

8.0 Nonprofit Finance and Fundraising

8.1 Various sources of revenues in nonprofit organizations, the strategic choices, and issues associated with each type of revenue, and the methods used to generate these revenues.

8.2 Relationship between and among philanthropic gifts and grants, earned income, and government funding and how these influence fulfillment of an organization's mission within the context of stewardship and ethical practices.

8.3 Fundraising and resource development process including, in part, commonly used fundraising strategies, such as annual appeals, special events, non-cash contributions, major gifts, capital campaigns, and planned giving.

8.4 Trends in the evolving use of technology in nonprofit finance and fundraising.

8.5 Evolving trends related to social enterprise, micro-enterprise, and social entrepreneurship, and their implications for societal advancement, organizational performance, and mission attainment.

9.0 Financial Management

9.1 Application of accounting principles and concepts including financial and managerial accounting systems (including fund accounting) in nonprofit organizations.

9.2 Financial management including financial planning and budgeting, management of cash flows, short- and long-term financing, and endowment management policies and practices.

9.3 Ethical considerations of financial management such as transparency, honesty, and accountability to advance trust among stakeholders.

10.0 Managing Staff and Volunteers

10.1 How human resource processes and practices in both formal and informal nonprofit organizations are different from the experience in public and for-profit organizations.

10.2 Principles of strategic human resources management and their use in a nonprofit context and implications for recruitment, supervision, motivation, engagement, retention, and development of paid and unpaid staff.

10.3 Strategies for advancing teamwork and group dynamics and their implications for organizational performance and mission attainment.

10.4 Dimensions of individual and organizational diversity within the nonprofit sector and their implications for effective human resource management.

10.5 Role, value, and dynamics of volunteerism in carrying out the work and fulfilling the missions of nonprofit organizations.

11.0 Nonprofit Marketing

11.1 Marketing principles and techniques and their application in philanthropic and nonprofit settings, including the dynamics and principles of marketing the "mission" in a nonprofit context.

11.2 Link between marketing theories and concepts and their use in nonprofit organizations.

11.3 Use of social marketing as a tool for mission attainment of a nonprofit.

11.4 How technology is used to advance the marketing and communication strategies of a nonprofit.

12.0 Assessment, Evaluation, and Decision-Making Methods

12.1 Methods that managers use to evaluate performance and social impact at both organizational and programmatic levels.

12.2 Methods and modes of assessment and evaluation to develop a nonprofit's culture that embraces continuous improvement strategies.

12.3 Decision-making models and methods and how to apply them in nonprofit organizational settings.

12.4 Use and application of both quantitative and qualitative data in measuring social impact and in improving the effectiveness of nonprofit organizations.

12.5 Role of information and the use of technology in the pursuit of a nonprofit organization's mission.

13.0 Professional and Career Development

13.1 Role of field experiences and experiential learning that are grounded in and linked to curricular goals and projected outcomes.

13.2 Role of professional associations and mentoring in professional development.

13.3 Ways that various professionals contribute to and are engaged with philanthropic and nonprofit sectors.

13.4 Opportunities for service and volunteerism that exist in the community.

13.5 Standards and context of professionalism, e.g., conduct and speech appropriate to the (respective) profession.

INDEX

Notes: Tables, figures and boxes are indicated by an italic *t*, *f* or *b* following the page number.

For Product Safety Concerns and Information please contact our EU representative GPSR@taylorandfrancis.com
Taylor & Francis Verlag GmbH, Kaufingerstraße 24, 80331 München, Germany

www.ingramcontent.com/pod-product-compliance
Lightning Source LLC
LaVergne TN
LVHW052033200926
848481LV00005B/1668

* 9 7 8 1 0 3 2 2 7 7 8 0 6 *